E X   L I B R I S

CLEO REED

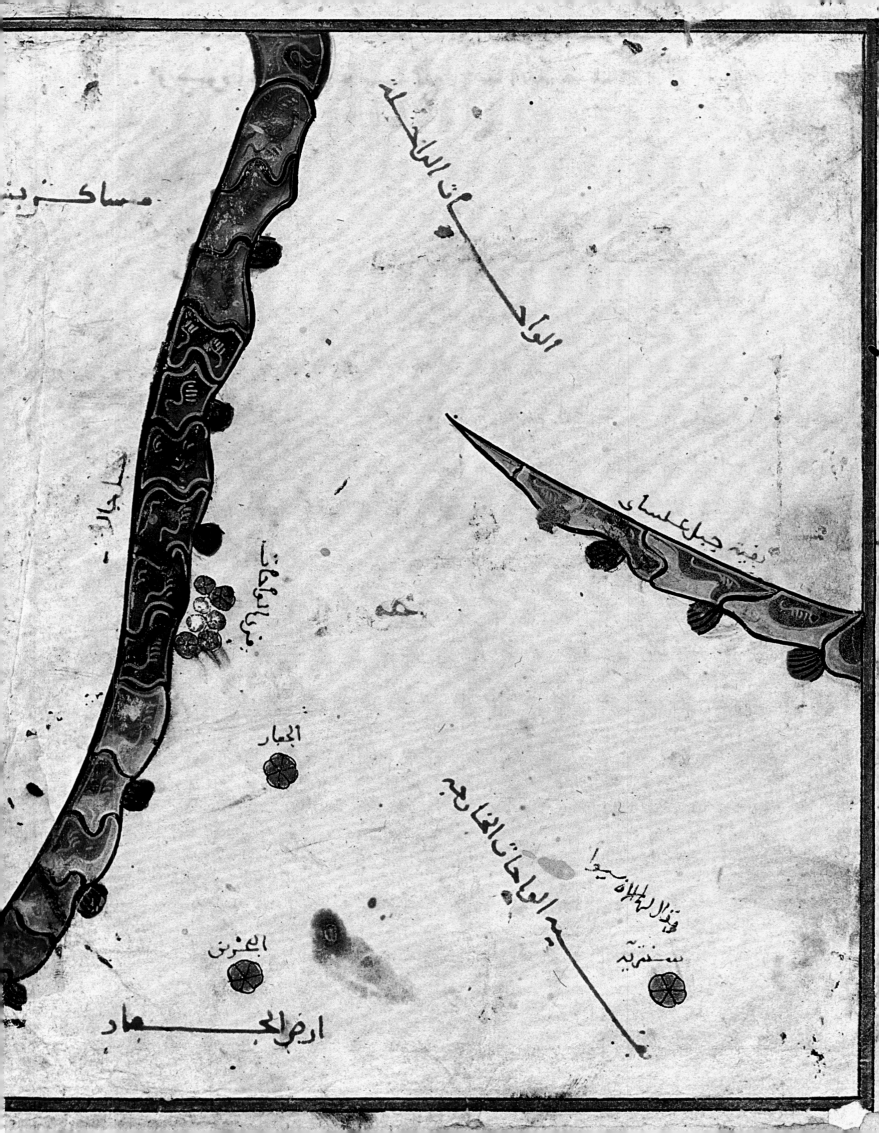

Africa Aeterna

Conceived and produced by Georges and Rosamond Bernier

Africa Aeterna

The pictorial chronicle
of a continent
Text by Paul Marc Henry

Translated by Joel Carmichael

Contents

Africa Aeterna

Introduction

In 1960 Africa, least-known of all the continents, became a full-fledged member of the world community. More than twenty African nations, no more than a dream only a few years before, achieved their sovereignty, and for the first time in its history Africa as a continent moved onto the stage of world affairs in an independent role.

To countless observers this dramatic change of status came like a bolt from the blue. Africa and its numerous peoples, a plaything of external forces for so many centuries, were regarded as permanently condemned to passivity by the inherent nature of their geographical and historical position. Only a short while ago the idea of African initiative or creativity would have been more or less politely sneered at.

It is true that the rapidity of the African transformation has been bewildering. Only a century ago, in 1860, a historian of Africa (d'Avezac) could write that Africa did "not belong to the history of the development of human civilization... It is fond of its own isolation and ignorance and makes itself hostile and inhospitable to others."

Such, in fact, was the view of Africa that prevailed during the centuries it was veiled from outsiders—indeed from itself—by an almost total ignorance.

Yet it has taken only a hundred years since the first massive contact with Europe for the Black Continent to recover itself and set out, precipitately, on the path to the reconstitution of its identity, an identity that until very recently would have seemed almost entirely obliterated by the overwhelming physical and spiritual ascendancy of European governments and, above all, of European culture. The institutions, customs, ways of life, indeed the actual personalities of the African peoples seemed extirpated by the loss of the continent's millennial isolation.

We now see how delusive this view of African inferiority was. It has become obvious that throughout the century it spent familiarizing itself—the hard way!—with European culture Africa was quietly husbanding its forces, preparing to make a mighty leap into the light of day after tearing off its various colonial masks. If the African personality, or personalities that have emerged are still wearing masks, at least they are their own masks.

Now, with the colonial century of African history definitely over with, it has become clear that, like other continents, Africa too was always a subject as well as an object of world history. The fact that the well-springs of its inner life were unknown to our first informants, the Greeks, and barely suspected by the Muslim and later the European travellers who succeeded them, can no longer obscure the richness and vitality of indigenous African life, even though it has been lived out in an arena that was not open to our public.

What is baffling about African history, if it is viewed as an ensemble, is that our knowledge of it is derived almost entirely from the periphery of the continent. Only a few limited areas, favoured by climate, played an active role in the cultural and commercial exchanges that contained the seeds of universality. It was primarily, for instance, the Nile Valley, near the junction of Asia and Africa, that gave rise to the

Independent Africa emerges

Page 12
The Nile. Herodotus, the Greek historian, already placed the origin of the peoples and cultures of Africa in the valley of this river; it is the hinge between Africa and Asia. With the Niger, it is one of the few rivers giving access to the African interior. Due to the regular rhythm of irrigating floods, agriculture has been possible along its banks since earliest Egyptian history, attracting populations of varied origins. The Nile also provided a "marine façade" to the African continent, linking it with the Mediterranean. This encouraged commercial exchanges, particularly for Egypt, and contacts with Mediterranean civilization.

13

ancient culture of Egypt and served as seed-bed for the elements of civilization that were ultimately to permeate the body of the continent.

Geography has laid a heavy mortgage on the development of African culture. It is only in our own era that technology has been able to relieve it to any extent, and to lay down the preconditions for an ultimate African unity. Vast regions of Africa were bound to be isolated by the mere physical nature of the continent. There are only two African rivers that can be navigated uninterruptedly from the coast for any appreciable distance into the interior. There are mountains, plateaus and deserts everywhere, making commerce if not downright impossible at any rate expensive and dangerous. The coastal plains are narrow, hemmed in by impressive escarpments, and they are generally unhealthy.

Until our own day Africa was inherently untameable: with no natural communications, it was crippled by its own vastness, by the monotony of the desert wastes or the density of the tropical jungle. Africa was bound to remain a mere word, based on no physical unity whatever and hence with no possibility of any serious cultural interaction. Throughout a large part of its expanse, moreover, the climate saps the energies even of the native inhabitants. Nor are the water resources and the arable soils evenly distributed: indeed, the Black Continent itself, the home of the numerous Negro peoples, is a creation of the greatest desert in the world, the Sahara, which separates the North Africa of the white man from the Sudan—the "Blackland" of the Negro peoples.

It is this basic fragmentation of the African continent within itself, as well as its thoroughgoing isolation from the rest of the world, that has made it difficult to envision the logic of any comprehensive history of Africa as a whole. Its scattered populations seem to have lived in more or less insulated spheres, highly compartmentalized and at best with only superficial mutual contacts.

There are, of course, a few exceptions. For many centuries there have been commercial and cultural links between the great river-empires of the Niger and the kingdoms of northern Africa, as well as between the dynasties of the lower Nile and the heart of Nubia. The eastern coast of Africa has always been a part of the vast network of navigation, trade and culture represented by the Indian Ocean, where the Chinese, Indian and Semitic worlds have impinged on each other for millennia.

But these are no more than exceptions. External isolation and internal fragmentation constitute the overriding features of African history as a whole; thus the essential difficulty in any assessment of African history is in the reconciliation of our own view of world-history—founded on the notion of the gradual formation of a universal society— with what should be more properly regarded as the ethno-history of scattered clusters of peoples whose differences overwhelmingly overshadow their unity.

This difficulty is put in relief by the duality of our sources. On the one hand we have a certain amount of written history, which with an accepted system of chronological references covers relatively well the portions of the continent penetrated by the outside world: the Nile valley, the Red Sea, the coastal regions of northern, eastern, and western Africa, and the Niger valley, connected with the trans-Saharan trade. Until as late as the sixteenth century Europe had to rely for its knowledge of these parts of Africa on Herodotus, the Roman historians, and the accounts of various Muslim travellers. In the more modern period these were succeeded by Portuguese navigators and a great many other Europeans, who, while contributing substantially to our knowledge of the areas they penetrated, did so, unfortunately, with a contempt for the "natives" that was bound to warp their view of what they were looking at.

Nowadays, however, the recently developed sciences of archeology, anthropology, and linguistics have lessened our dependence on merely written accounts. We can

Erosion in the Ruanda region, part of the high plateau of equatorial Africa.

Page 16
Dunes of the Sahara, photographed in Libya about 100 miles south of
Tripoli near the town of Sebha.

correct the artificial perspective of individual historians through material evidence and the systematic collection of orally transmitted traditions.

The African world is revealing itself through itself. It is coming into its own not via the biased, inadequate and superficial accounts of individuals remote from what they were describing, but through the more impersonal study of artifacts and institutions. It is in just those regions that have until recently been dismissed, solely on the basis of external sources, as presenting cultural voids and a pre-historic chaos, that we have come to perceive the growing complexity of the great events and the mutual influences in the past lives of the numerous societies now lumped together as "African." A growing army of specialists and experts in various disciplines is now able to detect a lively interaction between many groups and cultures hitherto regarded as quite unrelated.

The rediscovery of Africa, in short, has been proceeding apace, and, in the mirror of this rediscovery, Africa too has been able to find itself.

It may be too soon to assess the relative importance in African history of the external as against the internal factors, but there is already enough evidence to prove the obvious —that Africa, like Asia, Europe and America, has had its conquerors and its conquered, its invaders and invaded, its colonizers and its colonized, its master-races and its slaves. The immemorial cleavage between the desert and cultivated land, a commonplace of Asian history, is still unresolved in many parts of Africa too; it has conditioned the culture of many an African people.

Like many others, the African peoples too have resisted with great liveliness, either by peaceful or by warlike means, the spread of the great religious and political ideas with which they have come in contact. Such ideas were often no more than imperialist devices, and very rarely represented a disinterested attempt to involve the Africans in a universal civilization. A fundamental effect of the immense potency of these ideas was the stimulus they gave the awakening, in our own day, of a national and even a continental feeling of identity. Thus, while the resistance to the universal ideas coming from abroad has been in one sense unsuccessful because of the inevitable isolation, ignorance and backwardness of so many African peoples, it has in another sense been so vigorous that the impetus to unity of these same peoples has been all the more dynamic.

Entering so late into the world arena Africa is in a position to benefit from modern technology relatively more than any other continent. Physical isolation, the hazards of health and climate, disease and poverty, can all be overcome within a foreseeable future. Its natural resources, hidden or unsuspected, may be detected and exploited, and the magic work of science, inestimable everywhere, may play all the greater role in the future destinies of Africa just because it has come from so far behind.

Africa has entered a revolutionary period of its history, at the precise moment when its own leadership, matured, however unwillingly, in the school of a Western tradition, is meeting halfway the emissaries from the world outside, themselves chastened by recent experience into a positive respect for all human values, including those of Africa. This novel attitude of respect for Africa has been a long time coming, but it is now here, and here to stay.

The general history of Africa contemplated in this book will underline the chief stages in the progressive assimilation of the continent into universal history. We shall try to link together the internal history of Africa, as ascertained by archeology, anthropology and linguistics, with the history of the past century of European colonization, undeniably a decisive factor in the sum total of African history.

The contemporary character of the only recently ended total occupation of Africa by Europe will, to be sure, make it difficult for African and non-African alike to assess all its consequences. At one time European colonizers and invaders assumed the total responsibility, after all, of moulding several generations of Africans. Emotions are apt

Rediscovery of Africa through modern techniques

Page 18
The savannah begins in equatorial Africa. The road crossing Libya runs through desert which suddenly disappears, to be replaced by grassy savannah. Here there are mimosas and gum-trees; leopards, antelopes and gazelles, and birds: buzzards, bustards and partridges.

to be stirred by the re-thinking of a past so recent, and drenched so tragically in violence, blood, and humiliation. For that matter the work of reconciliation and mutual understanding has barely begun. The wounds are still open: they are all deep, and many of them are festering. Africa is still in immediate contact even today, indeed more so than for some time, with all the manifold effects of violence. Who can tell, at this time, whether both Europe and Africa will consent to keep their skeletons locked up in the cupboard of history?

Meanwhile we regard it as our task to trace the outline of an evolution that may conceivably lead in the direction of universal society, in which Africa, after so many millennia of misunderstanding and oppression, will ultimately merge with the main stream of human progress.

Africa is now largely free of non-African domination; its leaders have all fought for the international recognition of the African personality. It must be admitted that they have won. Africa's cultural contribution to the common treasure of mankind is now acknowledged on all sides. Even African history, long thought of as a parochial phenomenon, is now conceded by European and American scholars, in agreement with African politicians, to be of universal significance.

If we allow some seven thousand years as the span of human history (as distinct from pre-history) it must be admitted that the African peoples have successfully withstood their historical ordeal.

And they are now bringing to the general revolution our whole planet is involved in that amazing vitality that has enabled them to surmount the countless challenges, both of physical nature and human cruelty, that have beset them down to the present.

Africa and the Ancient World

Major events

and personalities in other parts of the world

3rd Millennium B.C. - 5th century A.D.

B. C.

3rd-2nd Millennium	Minoan civilization in Crete
15th cent.	Palace of King Minos in Cnossos (Crete)
13th-12th cent.	The Trojan War
11th cent.	Homer
About 960-935	Reign of Solomon Construction of the temple of Jerusalem
8th (715?)	Foundation of Rome by Romulus
490	Victory of the Athenians over the Persians at Marathon
472	Death of Pythagoras
479	Death of Confucius
494-429	Pericles in Athens
447-432	Building of the Parthenon
390-389	Capture of Rome by the Gauls
347	Death of Plato
356-323	Alexander the Great
51	Caesar conquers Gaul
19	Death of Virgil

A. D.

71	Jerusalem captured by the Romans
79	Destruction of Herculanum and Pompei
161-180	Marcus Aurelius
276	The Great Invasions. Franks, Burgundians and Vandals in Gaul
306-337	Reign of Constantine. Christianity becomes the official religion of the Empire
331	Constantine makes Byzantium the capital of the Empire under the name of Constantinople
410	Rome captured by the Visigoths
475	Fall of the Roman Empire in the West

Chapter I
Egypt, First Nation in Africa

The first civilization produced by Africa is probably also the oldest civilization in the history of mankind. In the famous phrase of Herodotus, Egypt is the "gift of the Nile," a majestic river whose riches, in the form of fertilizing silt brought up all the way from the heart of the African continent, have been an inexhaustible source of life since time immemorial. In Egypt we perceive a cradle of culture based on the discipline of sedentary life, the specialization of functions, and a well-defined system of military and social security, all embedded in a coherent intellectual and spiritual universe.

The Nile civilization

Egypt connects the Mediterranean with the Red Sea. Thus it was able to establish a line of communication with the great tropical oceans and the other centers of sedentary civilization that were emerging along the banks of the Euphrates, the Indus and the Yellow River. Thanks to the Nile, it also brought the interior of the continent, hostile to human settlement, into intimate contact with the world of the sea. Ideas and products —the vital elements of civilization—could be exchanged via the two-way channel of a great river.

The seasonal floods of the Nile guaranteed an agricultural abundance, and as far back as the Fifth Millennium B.C. its banks were settled by a constantly growing population. Near the mouth of the Nile itself this population seems to have been closely related to the Hamitic and Semitic races as we still know them; further south, in the Middle and Upper Nile, it graded into the great Negro tribes that still hold sway there and whose first migrations through the African continent go dimly back to immemorial antiquity.

Egypt both benefited by and suffered from its strategic location at the cross-roads of the world. Straddling the Red Sea and the Mediterranean, it became an integral part of an ever-widening system of international exchange. This naturally entailed the ready acceptance of foreign influences; the full rewards of commerce could only be reaped in conditions of racial tolerance and religious freedom. At the same time Egypt's proximity to the continental masses of Asia and Africa made it highly vulnerable to the military onslaughts of the barbarians; its ruling class established a strict hierarchy of authority and imposed a heavy military burden on the populace.

There is some difference of opinion as to the earliest origins of national organization in the Nile Valley. Some historians would like to "give Egypt back to Africa and to re-examine its history, starting from the South, and not from the North or the North-west" (Cornevin). Others make a point of the Semitic connections of the first kingdom, which was established in the Delta during the Fourth Millennium B.C., and refer to the differences between the urbanized, commercial northern civilizations and the feudal, land-bound empires of Upper Egypt (Pirenne).

But there is no need to involve ourselves in the disputes of scholars. Let us accept, as a working hypothesis, the likelihood of an expansion southward and a counter-expansion northward. Influences flowed in both directions. Letopolis, the trading city, and Heliopolis, the Holy City, sent out advance parties that met the emissaries of the Upper Nile kingdoms at the level of the First Cataract of the Nile. Here gold, ivory, and ostrich feathers from the south were exchanged for manufactures from the north. And it was along this frontier, or rather channel of civilization and commerce, that cities were built, like Tynis, Abydos, Coptos, Ombos, and Nekhen, whose wealth was to serve as the groundwork of a more sophisticated political system.

Thus, during the Third Millennium, two great poles of cultural concentration were established—the Red Crown in the north and the White Crown in the south. These, while rooted in quite different concepts of economic and political power, were indissolubly linked together by the facts of geography. A southern king, Menes, was the first to bring together the whole of Egypt under one rule, while the holy city of Heliopolis enveloped the south with its religious ideas.

*Expansion
to the east and south
brings new contacts*

Having achieved union, Egypt was obliged to turn east or south in order to expand commercially. The Mediterranean shore of Asia was settled by various Semitic peoples, of which the Phœnicians, speaking a language very close to Hebrew, were the boldest and most inventive. Their cooperation in the trade routes of the Red Sea gave the Egyptians access to the expanding civilizations of India and China, and further south to the trading posts of East Africa. The great desert of the Sahara, lying immediately west of Egypt, constituted a formidable barrier, though the mysterious civilizations that somehow flourished there seem to have exchanged both goods and ideas with Egypt at the very dawn of history.

Turning southward, upstream into the valley of the Nile, Egypt showed a remarkable faculty of assimilation. The settled populations whose lives were equally dependent on the great river saw no difficulty in accepting a civilization developed by worldlier minds disciplined by the same natural world order. They were fully integrated in the Egyptian system, and thus ceased being enemies. Some, indeed, created new dynasties that aspired and for that matter succeeded to supreme power.

Like other river civilizations Egypt was an island continuously buffeted by surging tides. History was a constant shuttling back and forth between defeat and victory, offensives against invaders from steppe, desert and mountains, and abrupt retreats. The conquered finally assimilated their conquerors, though at a tremendous cost in human suffering and material destruction. These man-made calamities had the matter-of-fact rhythm of a natural cycle.

Sedentary empires had many interests in common. The prosperity and peace of one ensured the prosperity and peace of the other. Nevertheless, when the riches of the Euphrates were harnessed to the aggressive designs of a tyrannical regime the Nile valley found itself in mortal peril. Any imbalance between the two great centers of power, the Nile and the Euphrates valleys, would naturally involve shifts in the alliances with the various people wedged in between them—the Phoenicians of Byblos and Tyre, the Sabeans of Arabia Felix, the Aegeans of the Western Mediterranean.

The equilibrium between these two great centers, fragile enough to begin with, was practically shattered by the great Aryan invasion of the Second Millennium. A new world erupted into being. The Hittites conquered the Anatolian plateau; the Achaeans made their way to the shores of the Mediterranean from the hinterland of the Hellenic peninsula; the Medes and Persians settled on the Iranian plateau and soon smashed the Babylonian Empire's control over its own eastern frontiers. The new "barbaric" peoples, tough and warlike, proved more than a match for the wealthy, cultivated, civilized world. The Babylonian Empire, itself a victim, could no longer stave off the great invasions from the northeast.

Exposed in its turn to these turbulent movements of peoples, Egypt was at the same time going through one crisis after another, brought about by the conflict between the traditional religious and military castes and the sophisticated cosmopolitans on the

Page 25
The pyramid and sphinx of
Chefren, at Gizeh; 4th dynasty
(about 2500 B.C.). This period
was the height of the Ancient
Empire. Menes had unified the
Red Crown of the north
and the White Crown of the south,
bringing together the whole
of Egypt under one rule.

Page 26

Colossal figures of Ramses II at the Nubian temple of Abu-Simbel (about 1250 B.C.). Ramses II achieved temporary peace with the war-like Hittites after the battle of Qadesh in Syria (1278). The Hittites, who conquered the Anatolian plains, had made frequent raids on the Egyptians, bringing on a long period of war. Finally Ramses married Nefertari, daughter of the Hittite king. She too has her temple ar Abu-Simbel. World-wide concern over Abu-Simbel was aroused when it became known that the temples would be completely submerded by the backed up waters of the new Aswan dam. After international consultations, a system was adopted that literally lifts up the site beyond danger.

coast. When foreign invasion finally struck Egypt directly its native dynasty was to lose its sovereignty for a century.

The invaders who undid Egypt for so long were known as the Hyksos. They surged in from the Anatolian plateau through Syria, and by 1710 B.C. were in control of the Nile valley, where they set up a new foreign dynasty. The legitimate Egyptian kings, based in Thebes, kept up some form of national resistance at the extreme south of the country, though there they were uncomfortably close to the Biblical land of Cush (now Ethiopia). The legitimate dynasty finally repulsed the Asian invaders, and by the beginning of the 16th Century B.C. the so-called New Kingdom was born in the travail of a national victory.

Egypt soon found itself at the peak of its power and glory. Under the Pharaoh Thutmose III its population probably reached 10 million. Egyptian businessmen were in full control of the continental and maritime routes leading to central as well as monsoon Asia. Babylon, Egypt's natural rival, had become no more than a satellite of the Aryan military empire that had been established on the Iranian and Anatolian plateaus. The Hyksos had been thrust back to and contained within the Mythanian state on the upper reaches of the Tigris and Euphrates Rivers.

For a time all seemed well. Political order and material prosperity created a background for the refinement of religious ideas, and Amenophis IV (self-styled Akhenaton) in his capital at El Amarna, could feel justified in proclaiming that the divine order of things had been transplanted to earth. The god Aten was symbolized by the solar disc, the dispenser to all mankind of life and justice.

But Egypt could not elude the countless hazards and contingencies of a world in evolution. The Euphrates Valley was dominated once again by a militaristic people, this time the Assyrians. The Hittites who had conquered the Anatolian plateau now swept toward the plains of Syria. Between them these two aggressive peoples divided up the state of Mythania.

Internally, meanwhile, Egypt was completely enfeebled by what we would call today an ideological split. Akhenaton's monotheism had aroused the hostility of the clergy at a moment when the masses of the people were growing restive. The world ruled over by the Rameses Pharaohs had become dangerous and unstable, and Egyptian power degenerated to the point where Rameses II, after a long drawn-out, exhausting, and indecisive struggle against the Hittites had to accept a compromise settlement with them in 1278 B.C.

The Egyptian Empire was in a state of siege; to face the deadly threat of Assyrian hegemony Egypt was forced to turn itself into a military power.

Beyond the Egyptian Delta there lay a potent magnet—the vast expanses of Africa. The invaders of Europe, who had come to the shores of the Hellenic peninsula through the back door, kept pushing still further south. The Cretans and the Achaeans, themselves the vanguard of the Aryan invasion, were now pushed further southward by waves of still more recent invaders from the depths of Asia. They settled on the shores of Africa, at the very gates of Egypt. Centuries later the Greek poet Pindar was to describe the gift made to Cyrene of "ancient Libya, which will receive the illustrious nymph in her golden palace and present her a fertile land, rich with all fruits and abundant with wild life, to be made subject to the law."

Egypt, perhaps the first nation in history and in any case the first nation in Africa, was now surrounded by rivals and enemies: the Philistines had infiltrated from Syria, the Achaeans and the Aegeans were established in Lybia. There was also an enemy within—the Hebrew tribes settled in the Delta since the Hyksos invasion. Their loyalty to the Egyptian state must have been, to say the least, questionable, and during the 13th Century the Pharaohs decided to deport them *en masse* beyond the Sinai Peninsula.

The Hebrew view of all this is given, of course, in the Old Testament, which abounds in expressions of resentment at the power and prestige of the Empire. From the Hebrew point of view Egypt was undone by the wrath of Jehovah: water became blood, frogs rained down, vermin multiplied, cattle perished, men were covered with sores, crops were destroyed by hail and locusts, the land was covered with darkness, the firstborn died of a mysterious disease. The Hebrews longed for Egypt to be wiped off the face of the earth: "when this is accomplished not even a dog will move its tongue."

The Delta swarmed with foreigners, Phœnicians from Byblos and Tyre and Libyans from Cyrenaica. Foreign dynasties took power in various cities, attempting to base their power on shifting compromises between the various military, commercial and religious pressure groups. The prosperous Kingdom of Bubastis was really nothing more than an ally of the organization of Phœnician cities that now exercised a commercial and financial control beyond the shores of the eastern Mediterranean, as far as the great trade routes of the east and west.

The valley of the Upper Nile, on the other hand, was just as sheltered from foreign influence as it had been a thousand years before. There the traditional ruling castes —religious and military—were able to organize against the secessionist influence of the north a resistance that was backed by the landowners and a docile peasantry. But this resistance had to be paid for to a certain extent by an increasing rigidity of thought: conservatives were profoundly hostile to any attempts at enlightened reform, such as that undertaken by King Bocchoris in the 18th Century B.C. Egypt seems to have been pinched between two pernicious influences—the overwhelming military pressure of Assyria and the corrosive effects of its cosmopolitan commercialism.

For a short while a coalition of southern soldiers led by a Libyan, Shabaka, with the support of Nubian mercenaries, managed to establish a military regime that unified the Southern Crown and the Northern Crown (717-701 B.C.). But Shabaka overreached himself by challenging the immense power of Assyria and supporting Nineveh's enemies in Jerusalem and Sidon. He was utterly defeated: King Esarhaddon brought his armies to the heart of Egypt, and in 661 B.C. Thebes fell. For the first time in 4,000 years the traditional core of Egyptian religious and political power was under a foreign yoke. The southern (Cushite) dynasty was thrust back beyond the great cataracts; it settled in Napata in Nubia (now the Sudan) where it was to eke out a precarious existence for several centuries. It now fell to the northern dynasties to sustain the national character of Egypt within a new empire that for a brief spell encompassed the complex of power, civilization and commerce between the Tigris and the Nile.

But pressure from one barbarian people or another proved relentless. The great Assyrian Empire itself began to sag under the blows of nomads from central and eastern Asia—the Scythians and the Sarmatians. The Hellenic civilization that lay just outside the orbit of Assyrian power emerged as an independent center of trade and culture. In the Egyptian Delta itself the kings of Saïs encouraged the settlement of Greek colonists, a fateful step that ultimately led to the integration of the whole land of Egypt into the Greek world that was being born.

Under the umbrella of what remained of Assyrian power, the new Egyptian rulers coöperated with the Phœnician cities in trade and exploration. A canal was begun, to connect the Red Sea with the Mediterranean; Phœnician expeditions like the first circumnavigation of Africa were financed by Egyptians. The Phœnician navigators are said to have gone through the Red Sea and come back through the Pillars of Hercules (the Straits of Gibraltar). On their way southwest they saw the sun rising on their left, from which Herodotus was to conclude that Africa is surrounded by water. The Saite dynasty, while keeping a close watch on its rivals in Nubia, staked the fate of the nation on the economic subjugation of the Phœnicians and on the mastery of the seas and what that involved, including the growing religious, linguistic, and philosophical influence of the Greek city-states that were now in the ascendancy.

After Nineveh had fallen and Assarbanipal, cursed by the Hebrew prophets, committed suicide in 612 B.C. under the assault of the Medes, it became clear that Egyptian independence could only be guaranteed if the Greek world and its natural heir, the Roman Empire, remained free. The Semitic empire of the Assyrians, expiring, gave rise to a final wave of conquest, represented by the short-lived villainy of Nebuchadnezzar, who reached the frontier of Egypt in the 6th Century. From then on both the Nile Delta and the Greek cities were threatened by the Euro-Asian invasions of the Scythians and the Medes, heirs of Babylonian and Chaldean power.

The strength of the Achaemenian Empire, which inherited from Babylon and Nineveh a fundamental distrust of an independent Egypt, was based on the martial race of the Iranian plateau. It was to make Egypt a Persian satrapy when Cambyses, son of Cyrus the Great of Persia, moved south, defeated the Egyptian army at the mouth of the Nile, and took Memphis, the center of Saite power.

It was not until an alliance was formed with the Greeks that Egypt was to recover a measure of its past freedom, but this could only be done at the price of losing almost its entire spiritual heritage, and adopting the language and customs of the Hellenistic world.

Meanwhile, however, Egypt benefited from the powerful and efficient administration of Cambyses's successor, Darius, who finished the canal linking the Mediterranean to the Red Sea that had been started a century before by the Pharaoh Narchao.

At the dawn of the Hellenic-Roman era Egypt had already spanned four millennia of history, during which it had played the role both of defender of Mediterranean freedom and, in relation to Africa, of an outpost of the universal civilization in the making. Even to the Greeks Egypt seemed "the mother of arts, arms and laws." The Greek historians regarded Egyptian history as the umbilical cord connecting Mediterranean civilization with the origin of time. Egypt, which had traded by land and sea with mysterious peoples beyond the limits of the known world, was also the source of all geographical knowledge, of the African continent, and of the world.

Greek view of Egyptian history

The Egyptian people, patient and disciplined, had been harnessed to vast enterprises, and throughout a difficult and violent history had displayed constant docility and forbearance. And although the urban centers of the country were to lose their native stamp and become thoroughly Hellenized, foreign domination somehow struck no roots elsewhere. The sophisticated world of the eastern Mediterranean never extended beyond the coastal fringe. The peasant, whose life is as cyclical as that of the land he tills and the river he venerates, remained the primary source of Egyptian wealth. The great masses of the peasantry clung jealously to their national character and to their language, even though their rulers adapted themselves to the prevailing cultural climate.

A new phase of Egyptian history was to unfold after the Persian occupation. A new city, Alexandria, became the capital of a Hellenized Egypt, and this focus of cosmopolitanism remained the gate that opened on to the African world. It was left to the Roman Empire, with its celebrated and successful formula of centralizing the administration of distinct national units, to bring within its vast fold the known lands of Africa.

Chapter 2

A Continent at Stake in the Mediterranean

The successive invasions of the martial peoples from Central Asia not only stimulated the resistance of Egypt as an African power, they also modified the outlook of the Mediterranean population itself and gave rise, as we have seen, to colonizing movements that were simultaneously racial, religious and commercial, and that were directed toward the supposedly empty territories of the African continent.

The Phœnicians, the Greeks and then the peoples of the Italian peninsula took turns in incorporating Africa, or what they knew of it, in their geopolitical calculations. By virtue of its very geography the Mediterranean coast of Africa was bound to play a role in the Middle Eastern and South European conflicts. This relationship was unmistakable more than five centuries before the modern era and has continued uninterrupted down to our own day.

The Greek world of the fifth century B.C. had the same interest as Egypt in defending African soil both against the military and political domination radiating from the plateaus of Central Asia and Asia Minor and against the commercial control of its approaches by the Phœnicians and their colonies. For that matter there was a constant risk that the two forces would join hands. The Greek victory at Marathon in 490 put a decisive stop to the expansion of Darius, the Persian heir of Assyrian imperialism.

Efforts to throw off Persian domination 6th/4th cent. B.C.

Egypt was subjugated by Persia; it had been a satrapy (together with the neighbouring Greek colonies of Cyrene and Barca) ever since the sixth century. It was in the resistance of the Greeks that it found the political inspiration and the military and financial aid it needed for its own resistance. From 525 to 332, when it was absorbed into the Empire of the Macedonian, Alexander the Great, the history of Egypt may be summed up as a series of constantly renewed efforts to free itself from the Persian imperial power that had turned it into a satellite and forced it to deliver grain, soldiers, and sailors.

On its western border the colony of Cyrene, which had been founded by the Greeks in the sixth century, played an important role as a foreign enclave on African soil, an enclave that could establish itself and grow only at the expense of the indigenous peoples. These peoples were described by Herodotus on the basis of reports coming from the Greek colony: they were nomadic tribes constantly engaged in crossing the Libyan desert, where they kept colliding with other African peoples, the "Ethiopian troglodytes" (probably the present-day Tubus). In these expeditions of theirs the nomads made use of chariots drawn by horses, not by camels, which were not to come through Egypt from Asia until several centuries later.

On the other side of the Triton Lake (the great Tunisian *shotts*) the inhabitants were peasants who were breaking ground in a region that was still quite wild and rich in animal life—antelope, buffalo, hyenas, and porcupine. At the farthermost point of the western Mediterranean, a thriving Phœnician colony, Carthage, founded in the seventh century, had become a financial center that followed its own policy of commercial and maritime expansion.

All colonial powers follow the same rules, which are rooted in the very nature of things. The Cyrenians did the same. This is how Aristotle describes their attempt to solve the problem created by the co-existence of a foreign ruling people and the local populations: "Increase the number of tribes and groups, wipe out as far as possible the former characteristics of the various nationalities, and absorb special religious observances into the general cult. In a word, do everything to secure a general fusion and to destroy the power of the old customs."

It did not take long for Cyrene to become a microcosm of the eastern Mediterranean world, which before the emergence of the Roman Empire was remarkably complex. Even the Greek elements in it were of quite diverse origin. The Dorians, who were Aryans, and the Ionians, who were Greeks proper, imposed their contradictory temperaments on a political system that alternated between aristocracy and democracy. The city and the plantations surrounding it gave contemporaries the impression of wealth and power. Grain, rice, grapes, olives, wax, honey, cattle and horses were abundantly present. The products of mysterious empires located south of the great desert came to its market-place via the chain of oases. It was a city of intellectuals, mathematicians and philosophers, and of athletes who were often included in the Olympic honour lists. The Cyrenian school lived by a doctrine of pleasure and a sort of cheerful scepticism; it was favoured by fortunate historical and geographical circumstances that were, however, rather tenuous. As a matter of fact the nomad world remained encamped at the gates of this commercial city and on the border of the territories being exploited by a technique based on discipline and method. The nomads were incapable of destroying Cyrene, but at least they could refuse to be submerged in its civilization; they could profit by its internal divisions and external difficulties and thus play the role of a perpetual threat.

The fate of Cyrene was soon to be mingled with that of Hellenized Egypt, whose capital took the name of Alexander the Great in the fourth century. After Alexander became King of Egypt in 332, and had a temple erected to himself in Memphis, the ancient religious capital, the Hammon oracle, located in an oasis of western Egypt, announced to Alexander that he was going to become ruler of the earth. While crossing the desert Alexander met some emissaries from Cyrene who brought him, among other things, a gift of three hundred chargers and five chariots of great beauty. Thus Cyrene turned its back on the western Mediterranean and, like Egypt, looked toward Asia. But it could not fail to realize that beyond "a plain of solid sand, with neither river nor mountain to mark out the boundaries," the colony of Carthage, founded some four centuries before as a simple Phoenician trading-post, had become an implacable rival.

Carthage, which maintained close ties of all sorts with the cities of Phoenicia, the source of its population, its religion, and its commercial and maritime ambitions, was pursuing a deliberate policy of westward expansion. It fought Cyrene in order to put a stop to any western expansion on the part of Greek merchants who were progressively absorbing the trading-posts of the Libyan coast.

Carthage and Western expansion 7th/3rd cent. B.C.

Its frontier was finally laid down roughly at the eastern limit of present-day Tripolitania (after the celebrated sacrifice of the Philene brothers, who accepted burial alive at the very spot where they met the Cyrenian emissaries). Thereupon Carthage flung itself into an imperialist campaign that extended throughout the coasts of Spain and to the great islands that cover the approaches of Italy (that is, Sicily and Sardinia), and went as far up as the southern approaches to the world of the Celts and Gauls (Phocia).

Carthage—"New City"—was the starting-point of one of the teams of Phoenician vessels that from the beginning of the First Millennium sailed to the very limits of the known world without instruments by stages never extending beyond forty or fifty nautical miles. It was thus in its way a foreshadowing, in its civilization and politics, of the European trading-centers that twenty centuries later were to be studded over the eastern and western coasts of the African continent.

Good trade depends on good politics: treaties of mutual understanding had to be arranged, and a protectorate had to be established, if possible, over the neighbouring indigenous populations who could not be disregarded. These native peoples represented at best unstable and corruptible allies, as they had been for Cyrene; they turned hostile at the first sign of weakness, and were always ready to go over to the enemy. When they supplied mercenaries for the armies of the hated ruler there was always a risk of a general insurrection. The Revolt of the Mercenaries under the reign of Magon, in the fourth century B.C., was an event that was to find frequent echoes in the history of North Africa.

Carthaginian exploration and exploitation

It may be asked how it was that Carthage, whose geopolitical hold on African soil was so frail, was able to embark on such an ambitious policy. From the fifth century on, indeed, Carthage set itself a series of irreconcilable goals. It attempted to dominate Mediterranean Europe and to control the commercial routes, both by land and by sea, from Phoenician Asia to the Gates of Hercules. In daring explorations it flung back the boundaries of the known world, encroaching on the Greek world and colliding with the burgeoning power of Rome. And it could obtain the financial and military means for its imperialism only by expelling the native peoples from their best lands and by imposing on them extravagant levies of men and goods.

The fleets of Carthage crossed the Straits of Gibraltar, reached the Atlantic side of Morocco, and may have established a station on the Mauritanian coast and at the mouth of the Senegal River. They isolated the Sicilian colonies and disembarked on the mother island itself, in this way provoking a counter-offensive of Greek armies on African soil. When Agathocles, a Greek general from Syracuse, launched his troops on African soil he made himself the theoretician of the strategy of the indirect approach that Africa was to pay for so dearly so often afterwards. "Outside the besieged country the enemy can be conquered by his own forces and by his rebellious allies, who, weary of a lengthy bondage, will receive the foreign liberators with joy... Africa itself will become an enemy far more redoubtable for Carthage than Sicily. Everything will band together against the city, which has hardly any prop but its name. Thus we shall draw from this enemy country the forces we lack."

Yet the Greeks lacked the means to pursue with enough energy and consistency the policy of mobilizing Africa against its colonizers. It was Rome that was to do this, at the price of a titanic struggle with alternating defeats and victories that have remained celebrated, and in which it very nearly lost its independence itself.

Luxury and navigation

At the pinnacle of its economic and intellectual prestige and on the eve of the Punic Wars, Carthage in the third century presented an unalloyed picture of prosperity. According to Diodorus of Sicily, "the country was covered with gardens and plantations, and cut across by canals to irrigate them. Magnificent country houses revealed the wealth of their owners. The soil was planted with grapevines, olive-trees, and fruit-trees." Under the command of generals of eastern origin the Carthaginian armies took in Berbers, Iberians, and Gauls. Its navigators were the most skillful and the most daring of the age.

During the course of the three Punic Wars waged against the power of Rome, the battlefield shifted from Sicily (abandoned by Pyrrhus of Epirus in the third century) to continental Italy, via the Iberian peninsula, and finally settled on African soil, where Carthage was to perish because of the coalition between its African and Roman enemies.

The disaster of Cannae put the Romans at the absolute nadir of their fortunes. Hannibal was practically the master of continental Italy when the Roman Senate placed the destinies of the Eternal City in the hands of Scipio. The latter, like Agathocles, realized that Africa had to be roused against its rulers. The battle of Zama saw a decisive confrontation between the Carthaginian armies, made up of Iberian, Gallic, and Berber contingents, and the Roman legions with the support of the supplements provided by the tribes of the interior, irreconcilable enemies of the wealthy foreign merchants and haughty soldiers who governed Carthage.

It was, as a matter of fact, the Numidians, an African people mobilized and armed by Rome who, in carrying on their own war under Massinissa (193-152) against the foreign city, laid the ground for its irretrievable collapse. After five centuries of imperialism Carthage finally found itself alone to face the double threat of the Africans, inspired by a xenophobic fury, and of the Romans intent on laying their rival low once and for all.

In spite of last-minute Carthaginian concessions on the political and military plane, Rome made its decision—Carthage was to be destroyed and its soil cursed. Its heroic resistance, under Hasdrubal, foreshadowed that of Constantinople against the Turks and of Mexico against the Conquistadors. Contemporary accounts make much of horrifying scenes of destruction (146 A.D.) that were, alas! to be repeated so often on the soil of Africa and elsewhere.

Carthage's real weakness lay in its persistent inability to establish itself in a firm way on a continent where in the last analysis it was never considered anything but an occupying power. The revolts of mercenaries that were such a commonplace in its history demonstrate the fragility of the relations it kept up with the natives of the neighbouring regions; they indicate the fundamental vice of a recruiting system that depended on foreign contingents. The great nomadic tribes that roved about the deserts south of the city (Garamantes) or the high plateaus in the west (Getules) represented a merely episodic danger. On the other hand, the Berbers of the mountains of Kabylia and the Aures, like the tribes of the coastal plains that were in constant touch with it, were a permanent seed-bed of agitation that constituted a threat to any political and commercial institution imposed by foreign powers. These latter were able to seek a temporary alliance, offer them asylum, and sponsor their reigning dynasties, but they could not conquer the ordinary people, who had a natural tendency to regard their own leaders, if they became too intimate with the occupiers, as partisans of a compromise that was impossible between fundamentally alien civilizations.

The Romans had thought they could exploit North African nationalism for their own purposes against haughty Carthage; they were to learn this lesson of history in their own good time.

After the defeat of Carthage the Roman Republic seemed to be weighed down by its conquest. Not only did it have to take the place of the ruined power in the zones it dominated directly around the cities it controlled, but it also had to keep the extremely dangerous promises it had made to its Numidian allies of the moment. Thus it had to pursue a policy of direct rule and at the same time, at its borders, a policy of protectorates and alliances with the tribal chieftains whose people were kinfolk of those suffering from the dominion it had acquired by force.

The peoples of the Italian peninsula, led and organized by Rome, benefited in their Mediterranean policy—which included North Africa—from the political and military credit won by the heroic resistance of Greece to the Asian imperialist powers. The triumphant counter-offensive of Alexander's Macedonians, following the patriotic upsurge of the league of Greek cities, supported by the Egyptians and the Greeks of Africa, made much of Asia understand the consequences of resisting superior military power and superior technique. Shielded in this way against the various Asian despots, the Romans were able first to find their own equilibrium and then start off in their turn on the conquest of the known world. In three centuries they broke the Phœnician power in Sicily, ruled the Greek world, reduced a Hellenized Egypt to the level of an ally, defended the world of trade and exchange against the barbarians of northern and eastern Europe, inherited the existing commercial channels with opulent monsoon Asia, and fended off the hostile peoples of an Africa that was still unknown and fundamentally alien.

Rome as an African power

As an African power Rome had to cope with four secondary military and political power centers: the Berber kingdoms of North Africa—a new Roman colony on African soil that was soon thriving; the New Carthage; Cyrenaica, heir of ancient Cyrene; and finally Egypt, an African power that was now Hellenized and orientalized.

In the two latter it was only a question of resolving some subsidiary questions, where the allegiance of the local factions, with respect to those of the imperial city, played a role that was greater than the national reactions of the masses. The recognition of the Berber kingdoms as political entities, on the other hand—an alliance with which might be desirable—progressively led the power emanating from Rome to associate itself with the fortunes of local dynasties, while these resisted the Romans the more the better they knew them.

The cultural and military integration turned Jugurtha, for instance, the grandson of the great Massinissa, into the very picture of a turncoat. He had behaved extremely well as a member of the Roman general staff responsible for the pacification of North Africa, and even though in Rome itself he had done some direct financing of political factions, that did not prevent the Senate from giving him authority against the foreign barbarians. In addition to this ambivalent nationalism of his, Jugurtha benefited from his family alliances (including the King of Mauritania, Bocchus, who controlled the region of present-day Oran and eastern Morocco). When the Roman

Stele found at Carthage. Roman
art, 2nd cent. A.D. One
represents a Berber
(undoubtedly taken as a slave),
the other a Negro woman.

Pages 38-39
Amphitheater at Leptis Magna,
Libya, on the Tripolitanian
coast, 62 miles east of Tripoli.
This splendid cluster of
columns by the sea was built
under Augustus during
the early years of the Ist century
A.D. A century later
a native son, Septimus Severus,
was proclaimed emperor.
He undertook a vast construction
program—a port basin,
a forum circled by a three-sided
portico, a street lined with
250 columns, a basilica, many
fountains and an Arch
of Septimus Severus to commemorate his victory over
the Parthians in 204 A.D.
The remains of these
achievements make Leptis Magna
a magnificent sight today.

army, led by Marius and made up of plebeians who fancied that they were establishing social justice, made war on Jugurtha, it was not a renegate ally it was attacking but an assimilated Roman who had become a nationalist leader in order to favour the big landowners.

As a matter of fact the Roman factions made use of the African enemy for their own purposes, thus giving him indirectly the power to use the domestic politics of the city for the purpose of blackmail. One day this was to lead to its ruin.

Julius Caesar, who won his battle against Pompey (assassinated in Egypt in 48 B.C.) on the African continent, was plainly aware of the geopolitical link between Egypt and the independant Berber kingdom. The Ptolemaic dynasty represented by Cleopatra was a financial and military debtor of Rome; this was paradoxical, since Egypt actually controlled the trade with the east that was the real source of Mediterranean wealth. Caesar had himself acknowledged as a son of Amon, thus establishing himself squarely as a legitimate descendant of Alexander and the Hellenized dynasties that had integrated Egypt in the Mediterranean world.

Julius Caesar and Cleopatra, 47 B.C.

In North Africa Caesar took up again the policy of Scipio Africanus against Carthage by exploiting, this time, the Berber factions against King Juba, who had become a friend of Pompey. Thus the conflicts of North Africa were transferred to Roman soil, just as those of Rome had been to African soil. Juba and Cato, Roman-Berber partners, were driven to suicide in the city of Utica, which had taken Carthage's place for a time as a meeting-place between Rome and the African powers.

Juba and Cato symbolize in their own way that alliance which has always been pursued, and often attained, between Europeans and Africans who imagined themselves able to fuse in a struggle against a common enemy interests that were otherwise naturally opposed. But the divisions on both sides remained too strong: two negatives do not make a positive.

Nevertheless it remained a fact that the Moors of western North Africa as well as the Numidians of eastern North Africa proved to be adversaries or allies of importance. Their military value could hardly be gainsaid: at that time their cavalry was first in the world in its swiftness and vigour.

Moreover, North Africa played an essential role by virtue of the natural wealth of its coastal plains; this made possible abundant harvests of cereals, wine and oil wherever the military administration could defend the farmers against the depredations of the nomads and against social upheavals.

The creation of the Empire by Caesar Augustus in 27 B.C. enabled a more stable system of alliances to be organized with the new King of Numidia, Juba II, whose lands stretched from the frontier of Africa Nova (those of the old Carthage that were directly administered by Rome) to Tangitanian Mauritania.

Egypt lost its royal house and its independence after the catastrophe at Actium in 31, in the course of which Antony, Octavian's rival, and a successor to Caesar both as King of Egypt and as Cleopatra's lover, played for and lost the primacy of the Orient in the new Mediterranean Empire being formed. The Egypt of the Pharaohs became wholly Roman. Rome dominated Alexandria completely while graciously inclining its head to its intellectual and philosophic prestige.

Emperor Augustus busied himself in restoring peace and stability in Africa. He had decided to reconstruct Carthage as a Roman city capable of competing with the two great metropolises. The Romans placed their armies without reserve at the disposition of the allied dynasties that were defending themselves against the incursions of the great nomadic Berber tribes. With the aid of his Italian ally, Juba II led the Numidian kingdom to its zenith. The Berber king had a statue in Athens; he was granted the citizenship of the city of Cadiz and took as his second wife the widow of Herod's son;

Page 40
Aerial view of the ruins of Timgad, Algeria, at the foot of the Aurès mountains. It is one of the most complete existing examples of an ancient town and a model of Roman city planning with its regular checkerboard plan of 144 identical units. Left center, the theatre, 161-169 A.D. with room for about 4000 spectators. Next to it, the Forum. Timgad grew over five centuries: founded by Emperor Trajan in 100 A.D. as fort and market place, it acquired a library, 14 baths, many temples and later, under the Christians, churches.

he even became a distinguished historian of Arabia and Assyria. Yet this Romanized sovereign never succeeded in having Roman civilization accepted by his own people.

When Tacfarinas, a mercenary in the Roman army, then a deserter and the chieftain of a band, federated the areas of agitation and discontent at the frontiers of Nubia, he ringed Roman Africa round with a circle of hostile tribes. The Roman army was compelled to face up to the classical dilemma: Should the rebellion be tracked down to its sources, and thus an expensive and endless war be undertaken, or should it be negotiated with, thus dealing a fatal blow to the political prestige of the imperial power?

That power could not, in fact, use as an effective prop more then two categories of allies, outside those territories where it exercised sovereignty directly: the kings or princelings of native origin (who were grudged neither titles, nor favours, nor flattering family alliances) and the professional career soldiers recruited locally, who could swiftly climb up through the hierarchy of the ruler's legions by benefiting from the imperial army's great reservoir of prestige and power.

Tiberius's Rome had to devote an important fraction of its forces to the protection of its African province by expelling the rebels as far as the Libyan desert and the Aurès mountains. Tacfarinas was killed in 24 B.C. His death was followed by the surrender, somewhat provisional, of the Garamantes.

By the very logic of its triumph the Empire was tempted to push back the limits of its effective rule as far as possible toward the west and the south. The political organization of Roman North Africa was a combination, often modified, of provinces administered directly and of more or less autonomous protectorates, in which the common denominator was represented by the undisputed control of the legions. These were rather few in number, recruited in quite different ways, and progressively extended to populations that had to be organized and defended while in the service of the Empire.

From the second century A.D. on, in fact, the Roman army in Africa was an African army. Its elite troops were given privileged treatment. Their encampments, situated at the advanced posts of a frontier that kept being pushed forward, often represented the chief element in the prosperous cities that served as a magnet for peoples who wanted to take advantage of active commerce under efficient protection. Some of them, especially toward the south, were springboards for a real movement of colonization by soldier-workers who were ready to curb the harrying of the nomads by force of arms.

The North African zone that was directly under the various Roman agencies had been stretched progressively from a coastal strip in Libya, from one half of present-day Tunisia, and from the Algerian plains near the coast to the region of Tangiers, the region of the Scyrtes (present-day Tripolitania) and the Tunisian *shotts*, reaching as far as the border of the region of the oases at the foot of the Saharan Atlas and the southern flank of the coastal Atlas ranges, without, however, effectively controlling the mountainous islets of the Aurès.

Through their police actions and reconnaissance, the Roman armies attained a remarkable level of geographical information. The Egyptian geographer, Claudius Ptolemy, had a precise idea of "the division of the central Sudan (in the heart of Africa) into two great interior basins, remaining unaware only of the maritime outlet of the Niger, which was not discovered until the nineteenth century... He laid down the elements of an African geography that was only surpassed by the efforts of the scientific civilization of the nineteenth century" (André Berthelot).

The armies of Rome crossed the Atlas under General Suetonius Paulinus in the first century. General Balbus, pursuing the Garamantes until beyond the present-day city of Gadmes, got as far as the oases located on the road to Fezzan. It was even said that one of his lieutenants, Meternus, discovered, four month's march south of the capital, a great river pouring into a lake where rhinoceroses were to be seen (Lake Chad). In

Egypt the Roman armies occupied the out-posts that had already been organized by the Egyptians on the Upper Nile. Their advance guards settled themselves in the Nubian cities of Napata and of Meroe, which were commercial centers between Egypt and Ethiopia, and interior way-stations on the route of the Red Sea and Arabia Felix, into which the Roman legions failed to make their way.

In this way, by maintaining a vigilant guard at frontiers that often coincided with those of the known world, the representatives of Imperial Rome were obliged to confront on African soil all the inevitable disorders created by racial and religious differences, and by the economic inequalities between the big landowners and rural labour.

It was only the firm hand of a uniform administration based on written laws that was capable of keeping within the same sphere peoples that were so diverse and urban centers that were so different, from cosmopolitan Alexandria to Berber Caesarea, from Roman Leptis to Phoenician Carthage. The non-African peoples, of Greek and oriental origin, established over the entire length of the coast lively and tempestuous communities with no real loyalty toward Imperial Rome. Italy itself, which had progressively lost its peasant base, was economically dependent on the agricultural surpluses of the African granaries, including grain and oil, that were the basis of a monopoly that was highly profitable for the ruling classes of Rome. Corruption became the rule. The legions rose up often against a capital governed by luxury, debauchery, and political ineptitude.

Foreign groups carried over their implacable struggle against Rome onto African soil. The Jews, who loved neither Greeks nor Romans, were suspected of a lack of loyalty toward Rome. From the reign of Caligula to that of Vespasian anti-Semitic riots in Alexandria and Cyrene kept multiplying. Religiously and racially motivated intrigues kept churning up the penniless proletariat of the big cities. Emperor Trajan, who waged war along the eastern frontiers of the Empire in order to eliminate the threat hanging over its commercial land-routes, had good reason to believe that treachery was at play there. The historians of the time make much of some very impressive figures to point up the importance of the uprising and its repression. Dion Cassius says that 220,000 people were supposed to have died in Cyrenaica and 240,000 in Egypt and Cyprus. The lovely city of Alexandria escaped total destruction by a hair's breadth, after ferocious battles in which Jews and Greeks massacred each other.

Foreign agitation against Rome

Yet these repressions of foreign agitation in the cities did not undermine the equilibrium of the Empire. This did not hold for the constant agitations of the Berbers along the borders. These had joined the ranks of the enemies of the Empire, and were no longer simple nomads capable of making only occasional trouble for the established cities and the cultivated zones around them. The commanders of the frontier regions became dukes as well as pro-consuls. They did not hesitate to fling the weight of their sword into the balance of power that was being upset by the domestic agitation within the Empire and by the joint pressure of its external enemies.

The displacement of the geopolitical center of gravity of this vast ensemble of unified rule toward the western Mediterranean and the African coast is graphically illustrated from the second century on by the advent to the throne of Africans like Septimus Severus, born at Leptis Magna and made emperor in 173 A.D., of Macrinus the Kabyle, who succeeded Caracalla in 217, by the three Gordians who followed each other from 229 to 237, and by agitators like Sabinanus and Selsus, short-lived despots who perished by the sword. They were all directly engaged in the fundamental problem of the security of the frontiers, while all the time the weight of the imperial administration grew heavier and heavier on the peoples directly under it.

In the course of the third century the advance elements of the Teutonic invasions, which had begun crossing all frontiers in Europe more and more easily, added to the general confusion. The Franks crossed the Gates of Hercules from Hispania to Tangitanian Mauritania in their first invasion, in the reign of Gallien, and complicated a local situation that revolved around a general revolt of the Berber tribes. In these disorders, as well as in the succession of natural calamities such as the plague, earthquakes, tidal waves, and locusts, eloquent spokesmen of nascent Christianity saw the signs of the approaching end of the abominated anti-Christ—Imperial Rome.

Christian propaganda: an expression of discontent

The periods of relative quiet between the various insurrections provoked by the border elements, by the urban proletariat of the cities and by the peasants, or by armed factions, became shorter and shorter. In the fourth century the struggle between Alexander and Maxentius for the control of the empire led to the destruction of Constantine and the burning of Carthage. The religious quarrels caused by the lightning development of Christian propaganda were very often the expression of a deep discontent that sought in the Kingdom of God a recompense for the shortcomings of human society. When Emperor Constantine reorganized the whole of his African holdings in 326, he had to purge the army, fortify the coastal cities, and the villages and farms of the interior. In 364 Leptis Magna, capital of Tripolitania, was laid siege to by the big Berber nomadic tribes, which were now mounted on camels. A few years later North Africa started an uprising under the leadership of Firmus; Emperor Theodosius paid with his life for leading the Roman armies as far as the high plateaus and borders of Algeria in order to force the rebel chief first to capitulate, then to commit suicide.

At the end of the fourth century the Roman Empire had suffered at least as many decisive defeats in Africa as in Europe and the East. Indeed, its own division was reflected on the African continent since the Eastern Empire, with its capital at Constantinople, included Egypt, which itself was divided into six provinces (including Cyrenaica, Marmarica, and Egypt proper). The Western Empire, for its part, controlled Tangitanian Mauritania (Tangiers), which was attached to Spain, and Roman Africa, which was attached to Italy. Roman Africa was subdivided into "Africa" proper (Carthage), Numidia, and Byzacene (from Constantine to the south of Tunisia), Sitifian Mauritania (Lesser Kabylia), Caesarian Mauritania (province of Algiers and Cherchell) and finally Tripolitania (Leptis Magna). (See map on page 332.)

All these territories were under the heavy hand of a civil and military administration —pro-consuls, deputies, officers in charge of supplies and patrimonial estates, great infantry and cavalry chiefs, military commanders of the frontier regions, counts, dukes and district provost marshals. Crushing taxes in silver and in kind were levied in order to sustain this imposing, expensive, and tyrannical apparatus. Agriculture, which was deprived of its normal return by the organization of the large estates, had to find a remedy for its decreasing productivity by extending its area. The lands grazed over by the nomads were hastily and badly put under cultivation. According to Tertullian, "the world is becoming better cultivated and richer from day to day...houses everywhere, people everywhere, communities everywhere, life everywhere. What better evidence is there of the increase in the growth of the human race?...The same complaint is voiced by every mouth: nature is going to fail us" (Julian).

It is best summed up by saying that within the technology available at the period the strain imposed on the native population by its foreign rulers had become too intense. Africa neither could nor would serve for long as a basis for a Roman imperialism that was threatened on other fronts and that was finally to demonstrate its inability to withstand the dual peril created by the conjunction of domestic agitation and external pressures.

Chapter 4
The Destruction of Roman Africa

For the Empire the part of Africa it dominated was no more than one theater of operations among others. The legions, still called Roman, which had generally become units made up of soldiers recruited in the very regions they were supposed to defend, tended more and more to regard their own theaters of operations against various barbarian worlds as separated from one another, each one in its own local political framework. Nevertheless the unity of the Roman world remained an essential principle, even if it seemed broken up into two distinct entities. Language, architecture, principles of government, and a refusal to surrender that resisted every movement questioning Roman civilization itself and the prestige of the imperial city—all helped strengthen the bonds that in spite of everything retained a certain effectiveness.

The contemporary awareness of the profound danger to which the Empire remained exposed, that of an invasion by barbarians from Asia and Africa, was translated into a reaction of obduracy against every doctrine and movement that seemed to bring into question the foundations of the imperial power.

Fear of invading barbarians increases Roman intransigeance

The barbarians from the north and from Asia were far more then rebels: they were enemies pure and simple and treated as such. In the same way, the Berbers of the North African mountains and steppelands were contained and watched because they were able to recognize a superior military force. In contrast the religious movements that denied the value of the Roman Empire as a divine institution personified by an emperor were attacking the very foundations of power. In the third century Tertullian, Christian Bishop of New Carthage, defied the decree of Septimus Severus, who in 180 had ordered the death penalty for all those who refused to swear by the person of the emperor.

Tertullian was actually the first theoretician of the "fifth column" enemies. "We are here only as of yesterday, and we will fill everything you have—your cities, your fortified places, your colonies, your villages, your assemblies, your camps, your tribunals, your decuries, the palace, the senate, the forum. We leave you only your temples." Another Carthaginian, St. Cyprian, who became bishop of the African metropolis in 248, openly attacked the official cult in a treatise entitled "On the Vanity of Idols". He was beheaded ten years later, under Emperor Decius, after having been accused of sacrilege, conspiracy, and defiance of the Roman gods and the sanctity of the laws. Hundreds of his fellow-Christians were burnt alive. The Roman power, harassed by the unflagging Christian attacks, had to confront at the same time the growing divisions between the populations of the cities and their mutual animosities. Christians and Jews had become mortal enemies. At the very core of the Christian doctrine there was a proliferation of sects —Donatists, Manicheans, Pelagians, and Arians, who could not agree about the nature of God, or the divinity of Christ, or the nature of man, or, naturally, about the organization of the state.

Philosophic currents of oriental origin agitated all levels of the society, while the higher functionaries of the Empire in Africa made a show of zeal and staked their careers on their attitude toward the rebellion, either masked or open. The more or less spontaneous concessions of Emperor Constantine in the first half of the fourth century merely reflected the tardy recognition by the central power of the revolutionary significance of the mass agitation, which was scarcely veiled by the religious pretexts used so widely.

The official recognition by the state of the Catholic Church as an official institution meant that the Empire was paralleled by a new hierarchy, which had disciplined and organized the Christian faith. But it did not mean the integration within the Empire of the discontented masses, who were really reaching out via Christianity toward the destruction of the established social order. The uprising of fanatical peasants, the Circumcellions, who laid Roman Africa waste in the fourth century, was in the service of a particular schism, Donatism. But in fact the revolutionary forces represented "barbarian" Africa while the official Donatists represented "civilized" Africa. The principal accusation leveled against the official Catholic Church by the schismatics was precisely that it had compromised with the Roman enemy, that it had, in sum, abandoned the holy cause of the resistance. "In Donatism there is something that is typical of Africa in general. It was the spirit of independence with respect to the emperor and the hatred of Unity, whether of the temporal unity of the Empire or the religious unity of the Church... In Donatism what was at issue was not at all, as it was in most heresies, the independence of the human spirit, but the independence of Africa" (Saint-Marc Girardin).

Conflict between official Catholic Church and Donatism

Thus we are very far here, in the world of political reality, from the image that has been projected so often of a Roman Africa that had become Christian and by its political weight had contributed to the Christianization of the entire Empire. On the contrary, it seems that the revolutionary movements in the big cities and in the countryside around them persisted and made use of all the doctrines that tended to break the unity of the Empire on the political plane and even, when the Empire became Christian, on the religious plane.

Teutons invade Africa 429 A.D.

In 410 the Roman power had suffered an irreparable defeat when it was sacked by its own mercenaries, at this time Teutons, and when other Teutons invaded Africa in 429, after having overwhelmed the Iberian peninsula, they found the terrain quite ready for a relatively easy conquest. Their appearance triggered a coalition between all the enemies of Rome on African territory: the Berbers of the Moroccan and Algerian mountains, the untamed peasants who were ravaging the countryside, the followers and the clergy of the persecuted schismatic churches, in a word all the natives, Romanized or not, who were hailing with delight what they thought was the end of all government, all drudgery, and all taxes.

It was, in fact, the end of a world.

The only African who attempted to reconcile, within one coherent philosophical edifice, a respect for imperial grandeur, the unity of the Catholic Church and its orthodoxy, together with an awareness of the profound originality of the Berber people he came from, made no mistake about this. St. Augustine lauded his contemporaries' spirit of resistance to the enemies of their cities, the barbarians, just as he did the spirit of resistance to the enemy of their life, the sins of spirit and body.

Augustine wrote and spoke under the influence of the deep impression produced in the imperial world by the victorious irruption into the Eternal City of its former mercenaries. Every year of his ministry as Bishop of Hippo was marked by new calamities. He indignantly refuted the argument put forth by the believers in the ancient imperial cults, according to which it was the expansion of Christianity that was the chief cause of imperial decadence. He witnessed the ruin of the countless churches of Africa of which only Carthage, Hippo, and Syria had been preserved (from the Vandals) "by the special protection of God". He died of anguish and exhaustion (in 430) in Hippo, which was besieged by the Vandals and whose walls were surrounded by mounds of corpses of prisoners whom they had just butchered.

Aerial view of El Djem in Tunisia, between Sousse and Sfax, showing the largest African amphitheater still preserved (450 by 402 feet) with three rows of sixty columns. El Djem was founded by Caesar and developed as an "oil capital" (Italy depended on oil and grain from its African colonies). Its prosperity continued under Hadrian (117-138 A.D.) and the Gordian dynasty. It was an important crossroads communicating with the coastal ports.

The victory of this people, the Vandals, who were just as alien to Africa as they were to the Latinized world, and who were followers of Arianism, consummated for the first time in almost ten centuries the political rupture between northern Africa and Mediterranean Europe. The latter now had as its principal base Constantinople, capital of the Eastern Empire, while the Western Empire, with its capital in Ravenna, was practically dominated by the Teutonic tribes whose allegiance to the established power was purely nominal.

The victorious Vandals; Rome sacked 455 A.D.

Valentinian, emperor of the West, bowed to the accomplished fact. He made Genseric, King of the Vandals, the sovereign of the proconsular province and of the neighbouring regions in Numidia, as far as Hippo. For the inhabitants of these provinces, as well as for those who were still under Roman authority in other parts of Africa, social and economic conditions scarcely changed. Once again the riches of North Africa were in the service of a foreign imperialism, which meant forced labour, requisitions and taxes. Once again it served as a point of departure for new expeditions against Italy. Just like Hannibal, Genseric, no longer faced by men of the stamp of Scipio Africanus, wanted to seize Rome. He entered Rome 2 June 455, on the summons, it was said, of Empress Eudoxia. He was received at the gates of the Eternal City by the Catholic clergy led by the Bishop of Rome, who were submitting to the Teutonic heretics.

For fourteen days and fourteen nights the city was handed over to the Teutonic and African military, who were avenging five centuries of exploitation and arrogance. All the riches of Rome, including the sacred ornaments of the Temple of Jerusalem, were removed to African soil. The King of the Vandals made a general round-up of society women, including the empress herself and her daughters, one of whom was to marry a son of Genseric. As for the booty, it was shared out among the warriors according to the rules common to both Teutons and Berbers.

The Gothic empire of North Africa, at the height of its power in the second half of the fifth century, extended from Tangitanian Mauritania as far as Tripolitania. The Western Empire was destroyed by another barbarian general in September 476. The Vandal fleet, without a rival ever since the destruction while at anchor of what was left of the imperial fleet in 468, ravaged the coasts of Italy, conquered Sardinia and Sicily, and pushed out salients as far as Greece and Asia Minor. Genseric died in 477, undisputed sovereign of the western Mediterranean.

Nevertheless this victory was merely apparent. The Vandals, like the Carthaginians and the Romans, were the natural enemies of the Berbers, who resumed their pressure on the frontiers of a kingdom that was too spread out and too poorly defended by the degenerate descendants of the great Teutonic tribe. The Vandal armies, like the Roman armies they had conquered, remained powerless in the face of an enemy who could always find an impregnable refuge in its mountains and deserts. Genseric's successors were reduced to demanding the support of the fleet and armies of Byzantium to help them in their internal conflicts. The vestiges of Roman civilization that were maintained in coastal cities that had become so many besieged fortresses, were to go on progressively degenerating, ultimately to disappear in a final civil war on African soil between the Hellenic and the Teutonic heirs of ancient Rome.

For its part Byzantium never abandoned the dogma of imperial unity. The surrenders of territory to the various Teutonic tribes that had been agreed to by the Western Emperor were regarded as null and void. The barbarian kings were considered to be no more than temporary occupants.

Thus, in the eyes of Emperor Justinian, the reconquest of the Gothic Empire of North Africa was merely one aspect of a general plan. Universal law as conceived by an Emperor who had codified it in a deathless juridical monument, could not tolerate

Page 48
Sculpture from an Algerian Christian sarcophagus. (Louvre Museum, Paris). Christianity was established early in Africa where it was viewed with hostility by the Roman authorities; they feared it would undermine their imperial power.

the existence on Roman lands of racial and tribal law. The Byzantine fleet that set sail in June 533 was commanded by the toughest warrior of Byzantium, Belisarius, whose orders covered contingents of Egyptians, Sicilians, Macedonians, and even Huns from Central Asia now installed in Bulgaria and Hungary. The Vandal chief Gelimer was definitively beaten on 15 December 533; he had to solicit temporary refuge among his former enemies, the Berbers of Kabylia. He ended his days as a prisoner of Byzantium on a lovely estate in Asia Minor.

For a brief moment one might have thought the imperial authority restored in all its ancient splendour. Africa was once again divided into three consular provinces: Carthage, Byzacene and Tripolitania (that is, present-day Tunisia and Tripolitania), and four presidios: Numidia, Mauritania I, Mauritania II, and finally Sardinia, which had been wrested from the Vandals. Force of circumstance kept the administration essentially military. The Berbers continued to agitate, and for more than a half-century all the Byzantine installations on the coast of North Africa were constantly on the defensive. In addition, the African front was of only secondary importance for Byzantium, which had to defend itself against the constant attacks from Persia and to contain new Slav invasions within the Balkan peninsula.

In spite of a series of exceptional men—Justinian, Maurice, and Heraclius—the Empire was incapable of restoring Africa to the equilibrium it had lost ever since the fourth century. The coating of Hellenistic influence and of what was left of Latin influence, began to show cracks where the provinces were not settled by either Greeks or Romans. In the most Hellenized part of Africa, that is, Egypt and its neighbour Cyrene, the indigenous populations kept reaffirming their own linguistic and political individuality more and more. Just as had happened in North Africa with the Donatist church, the Monophysite heresy served as a convenient pretext for a resurgence of the Egyptian nationalism that had been submerged for a long time by the Greco-Roman rulers. The foreign elements gave the natives an impression of weakness because of their constant fallings out.

The Empire was, in fact, no longer anything more than an enfeebled federation where the forces of separatism were clearly dislodging the forces of unity. Ancient Roman Africa no longer had any cohesiveness of its own. The Vandal invasion had dealt it an almost mortal blow. The Arab invasions were to give it the coup de grâce.

As for Byzantium, it was destined to survive as a Christian power in the midst of Islam only by abandoning to their fate the African Christian communities, which, divided and impotent, had lost all feeling of belonging to a universal society.

Islam: a New Dimension of Africa

Major events
and personalities in other parts of the world
6ᵗʰ century A.D. - 1800

571-632	Mahomet
618	T'ang dynasty in China
635-640	Asia Minor conquered by the Arabs
697	Foundation of Venice
711	The Arabs in Spain
768-814	Charlemagne. The Western Empire
831-878	The Arabs in Sicily
870	Persia breaks away from Arabs' control
?	The Inca Empire
962	Otto I. The Holy Empire Byzantium christianizes Russia
1054	The Great Schism between Rome and Byzantium
1066	The Normans invade England
1095	The First Crusade
1125	The Republic of Florence
1147	The Second Crusade
1150	University of Paris established
1167	University of Oxford established
1147-1190	The Aztecs invade Mexico
1189	The Third Crusade
1189-1199	Richard the Lionhearted
1193	India conquered by the Muslims
1154-1226	Gengis Khan. The Mongols in China, Persia and Russia
1204	The Fourth Crusade. Capture of Constantinople
1215	Magna Carta in England
1217	The Fifth Crusade
1228	The Sixth Crusade
1240	The Guelphs and the Ghibellines struggle for power in Italy
1226-1270	King Louis IX of France "St. Louis"
1226-1274	Saint Thomas Aquinas
1214-1294	Roger Bacon
1274	The Mongols invade Japan
1271-1295	Voyages of Marco Polo
1305	Rival Popes in Avignon and Rome
1320	Dante Alighieri — The Divine Comedy

1325	The Aztecs found Tenochtitlan (Mexico City)
1341	Beginning of the Hundred Years War
1396	The Ming Dynasty begins in China
1333-1405	Tamerlane
1412-1431	Joan of Arc
1436	Gutenberg invents printing
1453	Constantinople falls to the Turks. End of the Byzantine Empire
1453	The English driven from France (end of the Hundred Years War)
1461-1483	Louis XI - French unity
1492	Moors driven from Granada—Spanish unity
1492	Discovery of America by Christopher Columbus. The first watch is made in Nuremberg, Germany
1498	Vasco de Gama to the Indies
1511	"In Praise of Folly" by the Dutch humanist Erasmus
1514	The Portuguese in China
1483-1546	Martin Luther
1520-1521	Magellan sails around the world
1473-1543	Copernicus—the earth moves around the sun!
1509-1547	Henry VIII
1519-1531	Pizarro and Cortés in Central and South America
1533	England breaks away from the Church of Rome
1534	Ignatius of Loyola founds the Society of Jesus
1542	Portuguese navigators land in Japan
1509-1563	John Calvin
1563	First newspaper in Venice
1562-1592	Religious Wars in France
1571	Battle of Lepanto—decisive naval victory over Turks
1533-1592	Michel de Montaigne
1558-1603	Queen Elizabeth of England
1588	The Spanish Armada
1589-1610	Henri IV

1547-1616	Cervantes
1564-1616	Shakespeare
1585-1642	Cardinal de Richelieu—French dominance in Europe
1618-1648	Thirty Years War
1628	Harvey discovers the circulatory system
1596-1650	Descartes - *Cogito ergo sum*
1599-1658	Oliver Cromwell
1644	China conquered by the Manchurians
1623-1662	Blaise Pascal
1608-1674	John Milton
1643-1715	Louis XIV
1649	Execution of Charles I of England
1606-1669	Rembrandt
1663	Spinoza starts work on his "Ethica" which will be published in 1677 after his death
1674	Nieuw Amsterdam becomes British and is renamed New York
1682	Accession of Peter the Great of Russia
1683	The last Turkish attack on Vienna defeated by John III of Poland
1687	Newton discovers the laws of gravity
1700	Foundation of the Kingdom of Prussia
1646-1716	Leibnitz
1762	Accession of Catherine the Great of Russia
1763	The Treaty of Paris ends the Seven Years War: Canada ceded to Britain
1768-1771	First voyage of Captain Cook
1776	Declaration of Independence
1694-1778	Voltaire
1781	"The Critique of Pure Reason", by Emmanuel Kant
1789	The French Revolution
1756-1791	Mozart
1793	Louis XVI beheaded
1733-1794	C.F. Wolff, beginning of embryology
1743-1794	Lavoisier, beginning of modern chemistry
1732-1799	George Washington

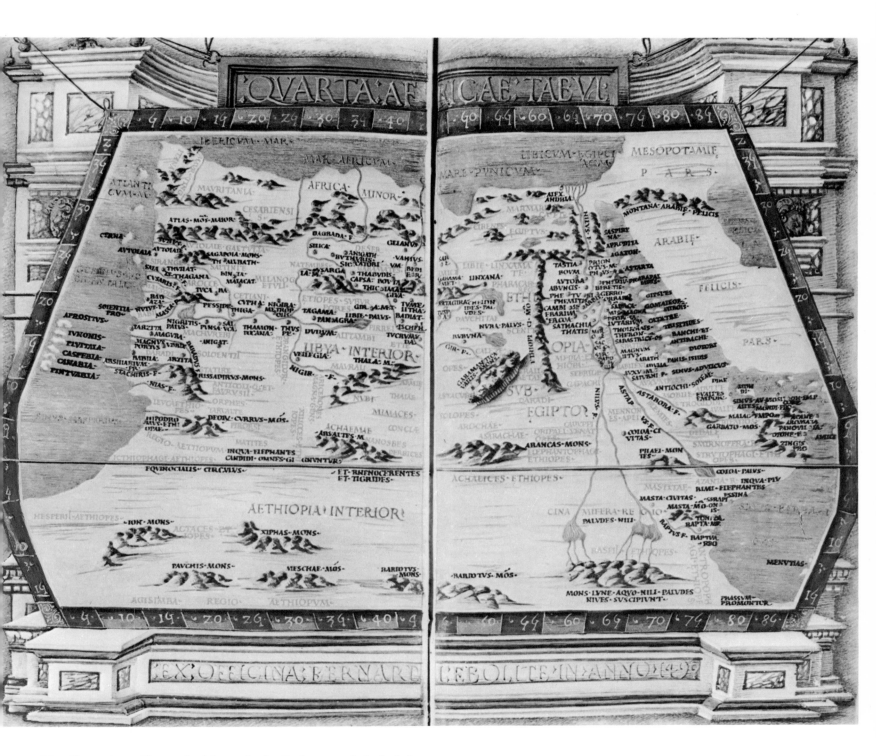

Map illustrating a Geography Manuscript by Ptolemy, made in Italy in 1491. The trapeze-like shape given to Africa by Ptolemy was gradually modified as navigators defined a more precise description of the coastline, as of the beginning of the 16th century.

The Ibn Touloun mosque, one of Cairo's finest monuments, built in 879. After Egypt's Byzantine rulers had been expelled from the African soil by the Arabs (Treaty of Alexandria, 641), Egypt became an Arab province. Ibn Touloun, son of an Abasside high official, became himself military commander and financial administrator of the province. Under his leadership Egypt grew to be extremely prosperous, achieving an almost independent status although still theoretically subject to the Abasside caliphate of Bagdad.

In Asia Minor, despite the desperate efforts of Emperor Heraclius, the Roman Eastern Empire had failed to succeed again in confronting the Persian armies and the new Arab armies. The decisive battle of the Yarmak (in the north of present-day Syria) in August 636, had opened the eastern gate of Africa to the new conquerors, who doubtless had never even expected such lightning conquest.

When the armies of nascent Islam (some 4,000 horsemen) crossed the Sinai peninsula in 640 after a series of brilliant victories that had integrated Syria, Palestine and Iraq into the new order brought forth by the Arabian desert, they were to find before them a whole world in a very ferment of evolution. On the delta and along the coast the urban populations, under the imposing edifice of the Byzantine administration, dissimulated rather poorly the deep-rooted hatreds between the indigenous community (Monophysite Copts) and the immigrant elements (Melchite Greeks and Jews). In the interior of the country the peasantry, crushed by taxes, regarded the Byzantine administration as an alien body. Even before, during the brief Persian occupation by the Sassanids (616-628) the inhabitants had openly expressed their relief at the departure —unfortunately only temporary—of the Byzantines. In the arrival of the Arabian horsemen the contemporaries saw a divine revenge for "the wickedness, the cruelty, the fury and the rapacity of the Romans." It was only fortified cities like the African Babylon and Alexandria that offered a serious resistance to the invaders.

Byzantium was completely expelled from African soil after the Treaty of Alexandria in November 641. It was an authentic capitulation, due to the Byzantine prelate Cyrus, who combined the functions of Patriarch of Alexandria and head of the civil administration. The Byzantine armies evacuated Alexandria on 17 September 642, after the capitulation of African Babylon in September 641. After a futile landing of the Byzantine fleet (645-646), the largest Afro-Hellenic city in the oriental world broke its last links with the Roman civilization it had done so much to spread. The splendour of the Egyptian metropolis stunned the Arab military chieftains, accustomed to the austerity of their native deserts. The city had 4,000 palaces, 4,000 public baths, and 400 theatres. The astonishment of the invaders at so much luxury recalls that of the Vandals when they occupied St. Augustine's Carthage.

Byzantium expelled from Africa by Arab invasion 641-42

It seems clear that the conquerors made no attempt to assimilate the country, either religiously or politically. They simply substituted themselves for the Byzantine power, collecting the same taxes while adding others, and made use of the same functionaries. Indeed, they committed themselves to respect religious liberty, and even to protect Upper Egypt against Nubian invasions.

In order to maintain their moral and religious integrity the Arabs settled outside the existing cities. It was because of this that at the gates of African Babylon (formerly Memphis), the Arab commander-in-chief, Amr Ibn al-As, built the first mosque on Egyptian soil, at Fustat, later to become Cairo. There seems no reason to believe the tradition that would make these first conquerors responsible for the sack of the famous library of Alexandria: apparently that had been destroyed several centuries before. By the end of a half-century the armed vanguard of the new faith had extended its dominion throughout Tripolitania to what remained of Byzantine North Africa. This advance proved to be more difficult than might have been thought. The distances were formidable, and the coastal cities were used to defending themselves. As far as they were concerned the Arab armies arriving by the desert were no more than nomads of a new type, and in any case enemies.

Though Byzacene was reached by 647, after the occupation of Cyrenaica, the Arab armies still had further efforts to make; they had to found the city of Qairowan, on the borders of Roman Africa, as a base of operation in North Africa, in order finally to eliminate the Byzantine garrisons in 698. Meanwhile the Berbers showed just as much hostility to the new masters as to the old; the brilliant chief of the Arab armies, Uqbah Ibn Nafi, was killed in an ambush at the edge of the Sahara, south of present-day Biskra.

The spread of Islam
711-15

The Arabs realized they had to seek an alliance with the Berber chiefs, and not their enmity. They succeeded in this and it was, in fact, Islamized Berber armies that crossed the Straits of Gibraltar in 711, crushing the armies of the Visigoth Christian kingdom in the battle of Wadi Bakkah, where King Roderick was killed. Gibraltar, the mountain fortress that seemed to protect the gates of Spain against the African promontory of Tangiers opposite retains the name of its Muslim conqueror (Jebel Tariq). In less than four years the whole of Spain was conquered. The Arab generalissimo of the Berber armies, Abd al-Aziz, brought considerable booty back to Damascus, at that time under Khalid ibn al-Walid, who had become the undisputed sovereign of an empire stretching from Persia and Arabia through all North Africa and Iberia as far as the gates of the Frankish and Visigoth kingdoms of ancient Gaul.

The Christian world, which remained divided between Rome and Byzantium on the religious plane, and split up on the political plane by the numerous kingdoms that had succeeded to the universal Empire of the Romans, found itself in contact on every front with the powerful armies that grouped together martially vigorous peoples under the banner of the Prophet. For more than a millennium the geopolitical conception of every European state with any claim whatever to Mediterranean or African interests was dominated by the existence of this "barrier of Islam," which was fortified almost to the point of invincibility by the countries of North Africa until the technological revolution of the twentieth century.

It seemed as though Islam, unlike Rome and even Christianity, had succeeded in arousing in the peoples of North Africa latent forces of expansion whose consequences Europe was to combat both at sea and on land for a very long time. Black Africa, south of the great desert, also suffered its effects, since the Islamized Berbers made their way overland as far as the great rivers of the Senegal and the Niger. In fact, from the beginning of the eighth century on the world of Islam controlled the great land routes that linked the Orient with Africa via Egypt and the lands of the Blacks with the lands of the Whites via the Sahara. The Arab-Berber rulers had also ensured themselves a solid position in the Iberian peninsula, the western entryway into the African continent. It is true that they suffered a checkmate at Poitiers in 732 in the face of the united Frankish armies, where, as certain historians maintain, they retired voluntarily since their chiefs were divided on the prudence of advancing so far from their initial bases.

The purely military occupation of the Muslims was succeeded by a regime where the masses, progressively converted to the new religion, tended to assimilate their invaders. The Arab Empire, in short, evolved along lines comparable with those of the Roman Empire, that is, toward a federation in which ethnic differences were very often reaffirmed through religious heresies and military intrigues. It brought together elements of very diverse origins and very different levels of civilization. Nomadic and sedentary Berbers, Arabs from eastern cities in Mesopotamia and coastal cities of the eastern Mediterranean, Bedouins from the desert who were compatriots of the Prophet, descendants of the Romanized Christians of the ancient Byzantine cities, Iberians and Visigoths from the Iberian peninsula, and, very soon, nomads of the highlands of Central Asia and Asia Minor—all made up an authentic universe that found its only principle of unity "in military glory, the classicism of the language (that of the Quran and of the great masters) and the wholeheartedness of the affirmation of God." (Berque).

At first it was the Berbers of central North Africa who affirmed their political autonomy through the Kharijite movement, a scarcely veiled transmutation of native nationalism. Kingdoms were set up in the desert zones along the borders of present-day Tunisia, in the Aurès mountains, the traditional stronghold of all rebellions, and in eastern Morocco. Their organization was based on a theocratic principle: the Imam, the representative of God's will on earth, was also a civil ruler. It was also the Berbers who, under Idris, a religious chief descended from Ali and Fatimah, created a kingdom in the fertile region whose capital under the Roman Empire had been Volubilis, a great administrative and military way-station of the Roman legions on the way to Tangis (Tangiers) and Tangitanian Mauritania. Moulay Idris was built in an eagle's nest at the gates of the Roman ruins. The city of Fez was founded by his son in 790.

Just as in the great days of the Roman Empire, North Africa maintained fruitful contacts with the Orient, so much more evolved and the authentic depository of fundamental knowledge bequeathed by Greco-Roman civilization. The Orientals, who often provided the governor generals of the great provinces, brought to Africa their pomp, their architecture and their cast of mind. The brilliant Umayyad civilization shed its light as far as the depths of Iberia, which for four centuries had endured the yoke of the Teutonic invaders. Techniques of irrigation, the cultivation of the arable slopes by the terrace system, new plants and refined techniques of craftsmanship were brought to peoples that had practically forgotten Roman civilization and retained no more than the memory of its rapacity.

Though the diverse native states that were set up and knocked down in North Africa rejected, on the whole, the political domination of the Orient they revolted against at frequent intervals, they kept up cultural and religious ties and benefited by a genuine material renaissance. The standard of living and the public order of the Berber cities, down to the eleventh century, did not lag in any way behind those of the cities of Egypt, Syria, and Iraq. At the end of the eighth century the Emperor of the Franks, seeking the alliance of the Muslim Empire against his Visigoth rivals, did not hesitate to send ambassadors as far as Baghdad, where the Caliph Harun al-Rashid was the ruler of the Islamic world, and even as far as the new capital of Muslim Africa, Abbasiyyah (south of Qairowan), on the pretext of reclaiming the relics of St. Cyprian.

Benefits of Oriental civilization brought to North Africa

In fact the natural richness of the coastal plain of North Africa and the favourable situation of its ports with respect to trade with southern Europe, had permitted the resurrection of a new kingdom on the territories of ancient Byzantium. The Aghlabid dynasty, just like its Roman and Carthaginian predecessors, made its fortune on the maritime traffic that passed through the Straits of Sicily, and grew bold enough to conquer the great Italian island, where for two centuries Muslim civilization was to restore the prosperity lost ever since the Vandal invasions. And just like them, too, it was threatened by the constant disorders on its eastern borders due to the untamable resistance of the mountain Berbers and the propensity of the coastal Berbers to embrace any cause that allowed them to flaunt their dissidence.

It was among these latter that the real or pretended descendants of the Fatimids, followers of the Shi'ite heresy born along the banks of the Euphrates, found first refuge and soon military support. In one century the North African armies destroyed the

Aghlabid kingdom, after having subjugated western North Africa, crushed a Berber uprising in the south, and finally conquered Egypt in 969, after a bitter struggle. The new city of Cairo was founded with the name of its first caliph, Muizz. The Fatimids made themselves the restorers of Islamic purity; they imposed a quasi-puritan discipline while systematically discriminating against Jews and Christians, still numerous in the delta. Like all dynasties, the Fatimids were soon to lose their initial vigour as well as their puritanism. Elements from the north were to put an end to the reign of the North Africans, thus demonstrating a law that was to be expressed four centuries later by Ibn Khaldun, the philosopher of Muslim history, that is, that military virtues born in poverty and maintained in austerity are dissipated through contact with urban civilization.

The Fatimid Caliphate
late 10th cent.

By a curious reversion it was the Fatimid caliphate that, in order to get rid of the Bedouin tribes threatening the Egyptian delta, sent them to pillage the opulent settlements of what had become a rebellious protectorate, divided between the Zirid dynasty in Tunisia and the Hammadid dynasty in Algeria. Once again the nomad tribes deliberately destroyed the order and prosperity so painfully restored by the sedentary dynasties after the Vandal catastrophe and the Byzantine re-conquest.

The real Arabization of North Africa is traced back to the Hilal invasion. Dialects from the Arabian peninsula forced the Berber dialects back into the hinterland and also destroyed the cultural unity of the North African cities of the coast and Middle East, the advanced points of the most evolved Muslim civilization.

At a moment when the sedentary kingdoms were thus shaken up by eastern invasions of a Bedouin and Arab character, they were also being threatened by other nomad tribes, who belonged to the old native stock of North Africa. The heart of Berberdom reaffirmed its vitality and originality in a new manifestation of the almost irresistible power born of an alliance of faith, poverty and physical courage.

The Almoravids were originally great nomads roving about the deserts of present-day Mauritania and thus in control of the communications between North Africa and the world of the Negroes living along the great rivers on the border of the Sahara. In less than fifty years an obscure clan (the Lamtuna), inspired by a mania for religious purity, progressively assembled the tribes of the strip northwest of the Sahara, occupied Marrakesh in 1062, seized Fez in 1070, Tangiers in 1078, arrived at the gates of Algiers in 1080, landed on the coast of Spain in 1086 and finally took all Muslim Spain under the reign of the great Yusuf at the beginning of the twelfth century. Neither the Arab kingdoms in the hands of the enfeebled descendants of the great Umayyads, nor the Spanish principalities (the leader of one of which, el Cid Campeador, did not hesitate to enter into agreements with local Muslim chieftains) were able to withstand the rough soldiers of Africa.

The Berbers restored the Islamic empire, occupied the Balearics and reorganized Morocco. Thanks to the severity of these monk-soldiers the religion of the Prophet returned to its origins. Architecture in the Syrian taste, with its subtle lines, was succeeded by the purity and austerity of Moroccan architecture, whose vestiges in present-day Spain are the best testimonial to Muslim grandeur.

The Almoravid empire was to be destroyed in its turn by a new flaring up of religious fanaticism, in which other Berbers, the Almohads, mountaineers from the Moroccan south, inspired like their predecessors by a religious message that had originated in the Orient, turned against it the arms of purity and military valour. They criticized it for a rigid formalism that could not conceal the spiritual emptiness and the decadence due to material prosperity. The power of the Almoravids lasted almost a century, as did that of the Almohads, who attained their zenith at the end of the twelfth century. The Almohad dynasty was to perish beneath the blows of still another Berber tribe of the Zenata group, which left the south of Morocco and made its way progressively

Interior of the Grand Mosque at Kairouan. The town of Kairouan (called El Garouan by its Arab founders) was established in 670 at the limits of Roman Africa. Its purpose was to assert Arab domination over the Byzantine garrisons which still held out in North Africa some fifty years after the Muslim victory at Alexandria. The mosque was to be enlarged several times, reaching its final form by 836 under the Aghlabid emirs who ruled this region (now Tunisia) for the caliphate of Bagdad.

northwards. In 1275 it died out in the heart of the Atlas where it had been born. A century later Ibn Khaldun, meditating on the dynastic changes and on the periodic destruction at almost regular intervals of certain groups that at first are martially vigorous and are then weakened by other groups undergoing the same evolution in their turn, thought he could extract from this certain historical laws. In his *Prolegomena* he laid down the foundations of a real sociology of history. Like St. Augustine he lived in a universe "that was changing in nature in order to undergo a new creation". In the fermenting Muslim civilization of Spain, located at the cross-roads of oriental, African and occidental influences and steeped in Jewish thought, it was the whole conception of the world as a phenomenon in constant evolution and of the relationship of men to the state that was the object of his critical examination.

Ibn Khaldun maintained that civilization is the result of the gathering of men in societies subject to the disciplines of settled life, and that it thrives in temperate zones. He observed that it was constantly being menaced by the less civilized peoples, who find in their very poverty the vigour needed for the most extended conquests. The nomads, among whom he includes the Berbers of the south, the Zenata of western Mauritania, and the "Arabs" (that is, the Hilali Bedouins), are regarded by the inhabitants of the cities as "wild beasts, untamable and rapacious." There can be a transition from the nomadic way of life to the sedentary way of life, but in an inevitable cycle the inhabitants of the plains end up by founding cities, taking on luxurious habits there, forgetting all discipline and finally becoming the handpicked victims of the peoples that have remained in the solitude of the desert. For that matter the purity of the race is bound up with this solitude. The sedentary peoples, on the contrary, tend to ally themselves in marriage with neighbouring tribes, to weaken their family ties and even to lose their national spirit. Ibn Khaldun saw with melancholy that "the civilization of the sedentary life is the culminating point in the existence of a people. It is also the sign heralding its decadence and the end-term beyond which there is no further progress". Such are the disabused reflections of a man who knew North Africa, Spain and Egypt, had made the pilgrimage to Mecca and had even been prisoner of Tamerlane, the chief of one of those nomad tribes that Khaldun had emphasized would be necessarily victorious in the war against the debilitated civilizations.

In the course of the thirteenth century, in fact, Arab-Berber Islam of North Africa was to feel the initial effects of the European reaction to Islam, a world that was tumultuous and agitated by contradictory currents, where vigourous military dynasties kept replacing each other at the gates of Spain and Italy and stepping into the shoes of those considered debilitated by the luxury and by the proliferating contacts with the powers of the West.

In the eastern Mediterranean the Crusaders had gone back along the route followed by Byzantium in the sixth century. What was at stake now was the liberation of the Holy Land occupied by the Infidels and the leading back under the spiritual authority of New Rome, first of all, the lands subject to the yoke of Islam, then eventually those under the rule of schismatic orthodoxy. In this great enterprise the new Kingdoms of France, Germany and England, and other principalities of western Europe saw a goal that was capable of calming local disputes while satisfying the commands of a lively faith defended by a Church whose universal mission did not raise, at that time, the slightest doubt.

The Italian republics, whose prosperity was then based on their active participation in the maritime trade between Orient and Occident, took into account the new political situation opened up by the prospect of succeeding to what remained of the Byzantine Empire. It was not long before North Africa figured in the calculations of the western powers. In the Iberian peninsula the Castilians and the Portuguese regarded their struggle against

Page 60
Pages from a 14th century manuscript recounting the Crusades: "The tale of Godefroy de Bouillon and of Saladin and of all the other kings who crossed the seas up to St. Louis who was there recently" (Paris, Bibliothèque Nationale). Among the events illustrated is the Crusader army capturing Damietta (Lower Egypt) from the Saracens in 1248, under the leadership of King Louis IX of France. In spite of this victory, the expedition was later routed in the Nile delta by the better equipped, better organized enemy.

the Muslim enemy as a part in the crusade. The "Reconquista" was only one part of the operations of the Christian counter-offensive and of the Muslim resistance that unfolded simultaneously in the eastern and in the western Mediterranean.

On the whole the European armies, while not marking any decisive successes, kept on growing stronger, while the Berber and Arab armies grew weaker. In the western Mediterranean a complex situation emerged. Like the Muslims, the Christians failed in their attempt to unite. On the African side, the crude fanaticism of the Berber nomads failed to effect a genuine consolidation of the Islamic conquests away from African soil. On the Christian side, political opportunism prevailed. Strange alliances took place between "believers and unbelievers". Trade, in fact, was coming into its own again. It actively resumed between North Africa and Spain, and in the interior of the latter between the Muslim kingdoms of the south and the Christian kingdoms of the north. In spite of the dangers of the sea routes, Italian, Catalan, Greek and Marseillais vessels set sail for the ports of Africa. It was the same in the eastern Mediterranean, where the Italians did not have the smallest desire to lose the immense profits they were drawing from their relations with Islam and via Islam with Asia.

It was the French armies that distinguished themselves in the attempts, as brilliant as they were futile, to cut the communications of the Muslim world between the east and the west. The army commanded by St. Louis suffered a total rout in 1248, in the Nile delta, in the face of the Saracen armies that were well organized and better equipped than the western armies, and even had a new weapon, the Greek fire, the secret of which had come to the Muslims from the Byzantines. St. Louis was to perish on African soil, in Tunisia, in 1270, after another defeat.

North Africa began to take on a more stable political form. The concept of "Morocco" crystallized progressively to include the Berber mountains, the tribes that had come up from the south, and the mixed populations strung out along the coast from former Tangis as far as the new ports of the Atlantic. Central Berbery consolidated its relative independence around the kingdom of Tlemcen, which, after having been one of the last bastions of the Almohad dynasty, was painfully fighting for its life against its western neighbours and the powerful Tunisian dynasty of the Haffisids. This last, whose power extended from the borders of Tripolitania to Algiers, was recognized as a great power by both Occident and Orient. Its ruler, El-Mustansir, received embassies from distant Scandinavia as well as from the rulers of Central Africa. It was he with whom Saint Louis had been trying in vain to grapple.

The Merinid dynasty of Morocco (which founded the new city of Fez in 1271, to commemorate a victory over the Spaniards), as well as the Haffisid dynasty in Tunisia, represented political and military successes that could be favourably compared with those of the European states of the same period. Like them these dynasties were to know numerous political crises arising in their case out of the failure to achieve equilibrium between Berber and Arabized elements, inhabitants of the countryside and town-dwellers, nomads and sedentary people, religious fanatics and philosophical sceptics. In Spain the dissensions between Arab and Berber leaders accelerated the dwindling away of a power that had only been sustained by successive injections of African vigour.

Fortune turned against the Muslims from the fourteenth century on; the Iberian peninsula was wholly lost in 1492. From then on it was the Portuguese, the Castilians, and the Catalans who carried the war over to African territory. Arab and Berber Islam was on the defensive everywhere at the very moment that Turkish Islam launched its own offensive against eastern Europe. The Muslims of Spain and the refugee Jews in North Africa took with them the keys to their houses in Cordoba and Granada; for centuries they were to intensify the fears and the desire for isolation of a world threatened by a Europe frankly turned aggressive.

Trade relations between Muslim North Africa and Christian countries

Chapter 6
The Red Sea, Eastern Key to Africa

The Christian powers of the West, throughout the Middle Ages down to the Renaissance, and even beyond, regarded Islam as an insurmountable barrier to the free circulation of ideas and goods. This was in fact more a matter of political propaganda than a historical reality. Throughout this period there was constant circulation of people, ideas, and merchandise, with all the attendant cultural and commercial advantages. The very fact that the new religion permitted the co-existence of an immense variety of different peoples in one vast unit of civilization helped to carry on and in some cases to improve the flow between Asia and Africa, to say nothing of western Europe. The African resistance to Islam, or to its orthodox version, was rooted in a refusal of local peoples to dissolve their own identity in a world that seemed borderless. In this respect the eastern coast of Africa played a decisive geopolitical role.

We have already observed in this book that the historic achievement of ancient Egypt was dependent on the combination of the patient toil of the sedentary peoples of the Nile valley and the lively trade carried on via the Mediterranean ports between Asia and the eastern Mediterranean and ultimately as far as the western Mediterranean. The products of India and China, of the Indian Archipelago and the Persian Gulf destined for Europe were naturally transported by the sea routes that went from the Asian ports as far as the eastern coast of Africa and from there up the Red Sea, to be discharged in the Egyptian warehouses on the African and Mediterranean coasts. We know that the prosperity of the cities and civilizations of the Nile and of the eastern shores of Egypt was always closely linked to this commerce.

Prosperity of the Nile civilization linked to trade via Mediterranean ports

Even at its zenith, and even aided by foreign arms, Egypt never exercised a military control over the peoples along the middle reaches of the Nile, or over those of the Ethiopian plateau. On the other hand, state-supported maritime and commercial relations with the lands of Punt (i.e., Yemen and its hinterland) have remained active down to the modern age. At the crossroads of the Nile water-routes and the routes leading to the ports opening on the Red Sea, a culture can be discerned today that could accept the consequences of a profound philosophical skepticism.

The city of Meroe probably belonged to a sort of Hanseatic League of the Near East, where material opulence made possible a higher level of culture. From before the Christian era the inhabitants of Meroe derived the maximum profit from their geographical location at this crossroads. Ethnically they were probably Nubians, that is, the Sudanese of today. Culturally they were part of the Egyptian world, though jealous of their own autonomy. For that matter the trade in goods from the Far East was not the sole source of their wealth. From the other side of the Red Sea the Sabean Kingdoms which had been able to apply the most advanced contemporary irrigation techniques to the cultivation of a highly inaccessible mountain range, as well as of the semi-desert adjacent plains, badly needed this chain of cosmopolitan peoples, which provided a meeting-place for all races, all products, and all ideas.

Commercial cities and sedentary kingdoms both had to face the same dangers. They were the outposts of a civilization based on agriculture and trade, and in constant opposition to the nomadic and barbarian peoples. The advanced civilization of Arabia Felix seems to have culminated in the normal phenomenon of overpopulation, in a stream of emigration that moved down towards the plains of the littoral and up the slopes of the Ethiopian mountain range. The result was a true movement of colonization leading to the cultivation of the highlands that had hitherto served only as a transit area for the local Hamitic peoples.

Thus, from the very dawn of history, trade and migration between Asia and the eastern part of Africa constituted the two factors that in combination with the influence of Egypt progressively moulded the profile of "Nubian" and Ethiopian Africa.

Even more than ancient Meroe, which was Egyptian in its trade and customs, the city of Axum at its peak illustrates the syncretist character of African civilization enriched by commercial and cultural contacts. The influence of the Semitic peoples (i.e., those originating in Arabia) can be found there in its architecture and laws. Greek, then Jewish influences predominated. It has been thought that these were sufficient, before the emergence of Mahomet, to convert the tribes of the great desert.

In many respects Axum played in the Red Sea the role of Carthage in the western Mediterranean. Like Carthage, and without the catastrophe of the Punic Wars, Axum was able to adapt itself to the situations resulting from the immense shifts in the power relations between the Hellenic world, the Roman world, and the various Asian imperialisms. This people of merchants and warriors could not remain isolated with respect to the great religious movements that affected the eastern Mediterranean. It was via Axum that Christianity established itself in Abyssinia, just as it was via Carthage that it penetrated into the mountains of Berbery. Just as Carthage was to perish because of the rupture of its intricate bonds with the empires of Rome and Byzantium, so Axum, whose very existence depended on the world of exchange, was not to survive the great Islamic upheaval that replaced the old commercial routes with new ones. The fall of Byzantium tolled the knell of the two great merchant cities, which in all probability had had a common origin in the depths of Semitic Arabia Felix.

The zenith of the Christian city of Axum was signalized by the conquest of the Judaized Kingdom of the Himyars, who at that time were in occupation of the Yemenite uplands. This was in 524, at a moment when the social and religious ferment among the peoples of Arabia was preparing them for the great revolution of Islam. A century later, Monophysite Christianity, which as we have seen was no more than a translation on a religious plane of the reactions of Egyptian nationalism against Byzantium, accepted as liberators the Muslim conquerors who condemned the churches of the Upper Nile to asphyxiation while ruining Axum altogether. While the Nubian kingdoms of Nobotia, Makoria, and Alotia were to go on eking out a precarious existence, only to disappear progressively in the anonymity of Islam, Monophysitism was to find its true haven in the natural fortress of the Ethiopian mountains, where the sedentary populations who had originated in Yemen were to welcome it as a rallying cry against all the nomads besieging their verdant fortress.

In the conflict between the great powers of the epoch, that is, Byzantium and Persia, the peoples caught between them could only suffer. Monophysite Christianity lacked the power to mobilize them. It was the moment for a popular religion propagated at the point of the sword.

Cut off from its sources of philosophic renovation, with no historic virtue other than the defense of a few specific ethnic groups, the Christianity of eastern Africa gained in depth what it lost in extent. It became the affirmation of a specific national character much more than of an allegiance to a universal idea. It was a factor of material defense more than of spiritual conquest.

Page 65
Emperor Constantine, from a 15th century Ethiopian manuscript: a book of Psalms with texts commemorating the saints (Paris, Bibliothèque Nationale). Such books, with naive images of saints and scenes from the Bible, were very frequent in Ethiopia. Favorite figures were Solomon— according to legend, his son by the Queen of Sheba founded the Ethiopian dynasty—and Constantine.

The presence of these points of support surviving in a world dominated by Islam from the seventh century on was to play a decisive role in the idea formed by western Christianity of a grand strategy with respect to the hated enemy of the true faith.

The Papacy attempted to conceive on a world scale of a counter-offensive whose direct effect in North Africa and the eastern Mediterranean we have already seen. We have also seen that the Western offensive, which kept growing in force and boldness, was reacted to by the resurgence of most martial (and least civilized) races, that is, the Berbers of the eastern frontiers of the great desert and the Turks of central Asia, who became the defenders of the decadent Arab empire of the Near East.

The Christian world had good reasons for thinking that beyond the Islamic barrier there were Christian communities that asked nothing better than to extend a helping hand in an attack on the common enemy's rear. Travellers from Egypt, the merchants of the Near East who were already familiar with the Nestorians of Iraq, made a point of the existence of a Christian kingdom in the heart of Africa, and of others in India and on the borders of China. Marco Polo went off to search for Prester John over the Asian land routes, though it was not for another two centuries that Portuguese navigators were able to land reinforcements on the coasts of the Red Sea to aid the Emperor of Ethiopia defend himself against Muslim invaders.

The opposition between Islam and Christendom in eastern Africa did not have the same character of a struggle between two radically hostile worlds as it seemed to have in the Mediterranean. It was, as we have seen, more historic and in certain respects more ethnic and quasi-tribal than philosophical. The relations between Arabia, once it became Islamic, and the Semitic peoples that had become Christian and were in control of the approaches to the Ethiopian plateau, were numerous and complex.

At the beginning of his mission Mahomet felt closer to the Christian monotheists he knew than to his compatriots who had remained idol-worshippers and refused to follow him. The first sovereigns of Ethiopia (the Solomonids, the Lions of Judah who claimed to belong to the tribes of Israel) did not deny their support to a movement that at that time seemed to be no more than a new sect scarcely deviating from the Christian faith. It was, rather, the movements of the nomad tribes, also from Arabia, that give us one of the keys to the progressive isolation of the Ethiopian people, an isolation that was to make it so conscious of its historic vocation as defender of Christianity against Islam in this part of the world.

During the obscure history of the Ethiopian nation that had emerged out of the civilization of Axum, the Monophysite Coptic Church of Egypt served as a rallying point and also a bridge to the Holy Land, where the church of Egypt had secured a number of special privileges.

Limited at first to the region of the Tigré, the dynasty's power was extended toward the coast and went up toward the highlands. Unfortunately, the pushing back of the nomads did not break the commercial isolation the new empire found itself in, since the Red Sea routes were controlled by Arab navigators. This confirmed the impression of encirclement, which for more than ten centuries the Emperors made vain attempts to break through.

In this way Islam, a close cousin at first of Monophysite Christianity, became a double enemy of the nascent Ethiopian nation. By its control of the land and sea routes it reduced it to calamitous isolation. By the Islamization of the nomad tribes that constantly kept trying to penetrate the natural fortress of the Ethiopian highlands, it represented a seditious movement that aimed at nothing less than the destruction of the nation.

Egypt was the lung Ethiopia breathed by; at the interior of the empire it was the bosom of the church that kept the national virtues warm. Little by little the coasts of

Page 66
Painting from St. George's church at Godfour, Ethiopia. Like the manuscripts, the very numerous church paintings in Ethiopia have a naive character that hardly changed over the course of centuries.

the Red Sea and the free access via the Nile to the delta defined themselves as the two chief poles of Ethiopian policy, which in other respects tried to control the totality of the highlands by converting, forcibly or peaceably, the pagan peoples already there.

In the fifteenth century, at the dawn, that is, of the great revolutions in navigation that were to enable Europe to outflank the northern gates of Africa, Ethiopia was already capable of threatening the Turkish masters of the delta with a deflection of the course of the Nile if they did not ensure the religious liberty of their subjects, while at the same time it confined the sultanates of Adal to the coasts of the Red Sea. An alliance with Ethiopia was eagerly sought by the Christians of the West.

Navigation and trade

Thus this movement of colonization was stabilized, creating a new and irreversible factor in the evolution of the eastern part of the African continent. This did not have a direct effect on the lucrative trade that since time immemorial had linked the West and East via the Red Sea. All it did was to limit its civilizing effects in the interior of the continent. Africa continued to export gold, ivory, slaves, ostrich plumes and even good-quality iron forged in eastern and central Africa. Pearls, porcelains, fabrics, and cereals came from the east. Europe was the goal of spices and of the luxury products of Asian craftsmanship. South of the Red Sea and beyond Cape Guardafui a multitude of African ports helped, through all sorts of exchanges, to create a new unit of civilization of an Arab and Islamic stamp. It compared favourably with a Mediterranean African world that had never been able to recover its standard of living.

Arab and Indian navigators served as intermediaries between India, the Indian Archipelago, China, and the way-stations of the African continent. They piloted extremely well-made ships, knew about the stars, used magnetic needles, and ventured on the high seas. Thanks to them trading centres of exchange and civilization sprang up progressively all along the maritime façades of the Red Sea and the Indian Ocean. The African world, via its eastern shores, benefited in this way from currents of civilization that were borne by the sea and by the favourable alternation of the prevailing winds, and that linked up the sedentary civilizations of the Far East with that which had come down from the Nile delta and was trying to extend itself toward the heart of a somewhat inaccessible continent.

At this great moment in history, when an equilibrium existed between the empires of Asia and their African relay points, the sea routes were combined with the land routes to amplify the approaches to the continent. The religion and architecture of the trading cities, many of which have disappeared or are in ruins today, expressed at that time a civilization dominated by exchange, and by the acceptance of the cultural and racial differences that are an indispensable prerequisite for it.

Page 69
Benin bronze, 17th century, representing the "Oba" (king) and his assistants (British Museum, London). The king wears coral necklaces around his neck and up to his jaws.
Assistants and pages hold royal insignia. These metal plaques, cast by the lost wax process, decorated the sides and square pillars of the Royal Palace. Europe only got to know this highly evolved art when the British punitive expedition of 1897 brought back over 2000 pieces. These bronzes give a lively idea of Benin etiquette, costume and ceremony.

Vegetation of Guinea, engraving from "Petits Voyages" published by
Théodore de Bry at Frankfort in 1603. The text accompanying this plate
enumerates the plants shown including, in the center—an ear of corn.
De Bry, born in Liège but established in Frankfort, published illustrated
travel books with editions in Latin, German and French.

If eastern Africa looked toward Asia to which it was linked by sea routes, western Africa was to depend on land routes until the decisive moment in its history, which was to be marked by the opening up of the ocean routes. In other words, western Africa turned its back on the sea and looked northwards, toward North Africa, or eastwards, across the heart of the continent as far as the valley of the Nile and along the river toward the Red Sea.

We have already seen that the most advanced patrols of the Roman armies had not been able to cross the Sahara, except possibly for a few scattered raids. The remarkable phenomenon of Islam as a civilization that took in the Asian and African commercial routes and integrated, in the bosom of a universal civilization, both sedentary and nomadic elements, was necessarily going to affect the most advanced civilizations of Africa south of the Sahara.

From the eighth century on detachments of Muslim armies would cross the Sahara by leaving South Morocco; they reached the Niger River, where the Kingdom of Ghana controlled the routes used for gold and salt, the essential elements of African trade. It is likely that Ghana itself was born when the Berber nomads who used their camels as "ships of the desert", organised zones of exchange and of agricultural production that were inhabited by Negroes in the immediate proximity of the great rivers of western Africa. The capital of the Kingdom is generally thought to have been in the south of present-day Mauritania. The abundance of precious metals and the skilful organization of the trading cities, which may be compared with the Red Sea ports as long as it is agreed that the Sahara is a difficult sea to cross, have always struck travellers, whose accounts have helped create the flattering, if somewhat mistaken reputation of the land of the Blacks as a great source of gold. The Arabs and Berbers have given a name to this frontier region that is the precise translation into Arabic of "Ethiopia" of the Greeks —Balad al-Sudan, i.e., the Country of the Blacks. They tended to think that the great river, which seemed to follow an east-west course, was a branch of the Nile, which disappeared underground and came out again to form a lake (the Chad). This hypothesis concerning the origin of the frontier river that marked the boundary of the Sahara was to haunt the imagination of East and West until the nineteenth century.

As far as the rapidly islamized white Berbers were concerned, it was first of all a question of having access, directly or indirectly, to the sources of the wealth of the country of the Blacks, that is, to the gold mines, and of levying tribute on the lucrative trade between the north and south and east and west of the regions bordering the great desert.

It was along the frontiers of this world that the Almoravids found the wellsprings of their national vigour, whose effects were to be felt at the very gates of the western world. They had powerful racial, religious, and material motives for embarking on the conquest of the opulent African cities. From the dawn of the eleventh century on, the Kingdom of Ghana was attacked by Berber converts to Islam, and in 1076 it became

*The Kingdom of Ghana
8th cent.*

Muslim. It is not certain that this material and spiritual conquest brought the Almoravid empire the gold and men it needed to maintain its power. In fact, the other black kingdoms bordering on Ghana and acknowledging its ascendancy, adapted themselves to the new situation. They gradually accepted Islam without at the same time restoring, in favour of their new rulers from the north, the highly brittle commercial relations in which religious and traditional elements played a role that was at least as important as mercantile considerations.

Negro civilization, basically peasant, played a role at the frontiers of Islam that was comparable to that of the civilization of the Nile. It was a source of material wealth and an element that led to settlement. The symbiosis between the Berber and the Negro peoples made progressive headway, based more on the complementary interests of the two races, one of great travellers and messengers of a quasi-universal civilization, the other of farmers enriched by the gold trade, than on a common religion.

The Mali Empire
New dynasties settled in the Niger valley and ruled over various Mandingo peoples. Mali is the best known of these political entities, whose territorial frontiers were not always clearly marked but which corresponded to a network of allegiances revolving around an undisputed power centre. Born in the thirteenth century, it reached its zenith in the fourteenth, to perish at last under the blows of the Moroccan army in the sixteenth. We know its splendours through the Muslim historians, who pay homage to its prosperity and efficiency. It was a Muslim empire; its rulers made the pilgrimage to Mecca and so knew of the great continental and maritime routes where Whites and Blacks fused together in one great stream of a common civilization. (See map on page 332.)

Sundiata, the first great Mandingo ruler, in bringing the Sudanese territories together under a common regime, foreshadowed the achievement of the great European and Asiatic unifiers. One of his successors, the great Kankan-Musa, was a genuine African Charlemagne. In the south of his Empire, the countries of the "desert of natural gold," inhabited by "wild pagans" came under his rule. In the north, the white Berbers who three centuries before had threatened the Negroes with complete domination, had to pay him tribute and acknowledge his laws. The "Lemtuna," the enfeebled descendants of the great Almoravids, were also subdued.

When Kankan-Musa made the pilgrimage to Mecca "he left his country with a hundred loads of gold, which he handed out in the course of his pilgrimage, either among the tribes whose paths he crossed from his country to Cairo, or in Cairo itself, or between Cairo and the noble Hijaz, coming and going". He poured the torrents of his generosity over Cairo. He spread so much gold around that the merchants "lowered the rate and depreciated its price". Muslim scholars noted with respect that his kingdom was "about a year" long. Others give it as "four months in length and the same in breadth". (Allah al-Ohmari).

The government of such an empire was based on oral instructions, in the preparation of which the reports of the king's personal lieutenants played a great role. The sovereign was surrounded by Qadis (doctors of the law) and secretaries. Court protocol was rigid. Everything was done to exalt the majesty of the throne. The empire was in constant warfare with the pagan Negroes, whom it showed the critical condescension that civilized people imagine they ought to display toward primitives.

Further to the east of the Mandingo kingdom, whose decadence was to be accentuated in the course of the fifteenth century, another empire of the Niger, the Sonrhai Empire, initially its vassal, was to become its peer and then burst into a brilliant radiance of its own. The Sonrhai at the beginning flattered themselves that they were the defenders of traditional Africa against Islam, which they considered alien, and against its allies and emissaries, the Berbers of the Saharan territories and the Islamized Mandingos. Starting out from Gao in 1469, Soni-Ali took possession of Timbuktu and fought against the

Peuhls (originally probably an eastern people) and the Mossis of the south. It was the Sonrhai Empire that the Moroccan armies were to collide with in their attempt to conquer the countries of the Sudan, even though these had accepted Islam at the beginning of the sixteenth century.

One city, located at the gates of the desert and at the entry to the countries of the great river, has become the symbol of this brillant episode of African history. Timbuktu, probably founded by the Berber Tuaregs, conquered by the Mali rulers then by the Sonrhais, became, in the eyes of the outside world, the glamorous metropolis of the mysterious Negro Empire. In the fifteenth century there were a great many judges, doctors and priests in the city, "all well appointed by the king." Leo Africanus tells us "that many manuscript books coming from Berber Kingdoms are sold there. More profit is made from their sale than from any other merchandise. A little further to the east bread and meat in great abundance are found, as well as vegetables of all kinds. Goods from Europe and from Berbery, such as fabrics, arms, garments, and drugs are paid for at very high prices". Such accounts made their way to Europe and gave rise to the myth of African wealth.

Timbuktu

East of the Kingdom of Gao, other Negro peoples had organized themselves into hierarchical kingdoms that were effective both politically and militarily. The Hausa peoples, who on the level of their ruling class probably realized an effective symbiosis between the Islamized Berbers' influences and Negro-African traditions, had thrust back toward the south the tribes that had remained pagan, or subjugated them in the thirteenth century. Contacts with the civilizations of the north via the caravan routes brought Arab and European weapons of war (such as coats of mail) into the very heart of the continent. Kano became a real commercial and political capital of the various Hausa states, which did not, of course, fail to stimulate the appetite for conquest of their Sonrhai neighbours. The eastern neighbours of the Hausa Kingdoms dominated the region of the Chad, and thus found themselves at the mouth of the great trading route that since time immemorial had linked central Africa to the region of Tripoli on the Mediterranean coast via the oases of Fezzan. Tradition ascribes the settlement of this region to Berber conquerors. Recent discoveries indicate that there was also a mingling of cultures and of ruling classes between a Negro people that was already quite advanced, the Saos, and the whites who had come from the north. In the thirteenth century this led to the creation of a powerful state, the Kanem-Bornu, which controlled the important cross-roads of the east-west routes in the south of the Sahara and of the north-south routes too. This state extended from north of Fezzan westwards as far as the Hausa country, which it dominated from time to time, and eastwards as far as another grouping, that of the Waddai, which itself was in contact with the intermediate valley of the Nile via the Darfur. This time Islamization came from the eastern and Egyptian coasts of Africa. Arab influences proper were more directly visible in the habits and language of these peoples in the intermediate zones between these areas.

Thus, in less than five centuries, Islam encircled the great desert with an uninterrupted belt of white and black kingdoms that accepted the discipline they had in common. The great movements of peoples and of civilization that agitated northern Africa from the beginnings of history were transmitted by gradually attenuated waves as far as the border zones of Black Africa. Those borders had been gradually pushed back southwards by the pastoral peoples, generally of Hamitic origin, that were mixed with Negro elements in variable proportions, though some of them preserved an original way of life by adapting themselves to the austere milieu of the great desert. These movements, which have left traces in the chronicles of antiquity, and especially in the Saharan archaic remains, ended up by linking together the historic destiny of the southern borders of the Sahara and that of the northern regions.

The belt of Islamic Kingdoms

*Mythic origins
of the black race*

In the fourteenth century the Muslim historians used to say that Islam came from the "Libyan" races and moved toward the "black" races. The religious and hence cultural assimilation of the non-Arabic-speaking peoples had long since been in full tide: Islam, both a monotheism and a social order, was creeping southward then as it is today. The "black" races at the frontier of the known world stimulated the curiosity and imagination of the Arabs, just as they had that of the Greeks and Romans. The natural obstacles that had been so formidable a barrier to the interior for the Romans made penetration of the continent almost as difficult and adventurous for the Muslims too. In this way the myth of a separate act of creation for the white and the black race was perpetuated for more than a millennium.

Oddly enough, many Asian and African legends agree in assigning the black race a chronological priority: the cradle of mankind is often situated at the foot of the Mountains of the Moon in Central East Africa. According to tradition, the blacks were masters of the whites in the beginning, but the latter multiplied gradually, shook off the yoke of their black masters, and from slaves turned into slave-holders. Soon the black race in its turn was forced to wear the shackles of white tyranny.

The enlightened Hellenistic world had also reverently inherited from the Egyptian priests the age-old tradition of a vanished continent—Atlantis. Vestiges of this lost world were thought by the Greeks to be jealously guarded within the bosom of Africa. From this point of view the Negro Africans became the defenders of buried secrets; it was only natural for them to resist any commercial or religious attempt to integrate them into a world with its centre in Europe or Asia.

The German ethnologist, Frobenius, traces this spirit of resistance to a last-ditch defensive action of the lost continent: "In this part of the world, Africa, we find civilizations still alive whereas in our world we are limited to the excavation of unrelated and misunderstood bits and pieces. There, they live and they speak. Not only do they speak with the mouth, they speak also with the soul as living beings. They speak to all those who have a soul and are not stultified by their own intelligence and the technique of cleverness." Thus pagan Africa was assigned the role of a guardian of cultures, fusing together harmoniously coherent cosmogonies and cultural techniques rooted in a fundamental balance between vulnerable man and hostile nature. This approach has proved highly fruitful: it has enabled many students to rediscover phenomena of civilization systematically ignored by Christian and Muslim missionaries.

The diverse Negro populations were to find themselves the victims rather than the agents of the great currents of conquest and trade that penetrated the heart of the continent along the natural overland routes leading from the north. They lacked the will, or perhaps the opportunity, to link their own history to a universally understood chronology, which in any case would have been quite alien to them. But this did not prevent them from having a keen sense of ageless continuity, doubtless the antithesis of our own view of history as meaningful change. Though the remote ancestors of the

Funeral of a Guinea king, from volume 6 of Théodore de Bry's "Petits Voyages", 1603. So that the king will still find his entourage around him after death, his family and servants are killed and their heads set around the place prepared for the corpse.

tribe or clan were lost in the obscurity of time and mythical lineage, tradition insisted on keeping a precise genealogy of all tribal chiefs.

The secrets of national identity were handed down uninterruptedly through well-regulated ceremonials generation by generation. On the highest level of mystical phantasy the nation was conceived of as part of a total universe, in which living beings were merely the visible portion and where the dead played as active a role as the living, both interacting in a drama that must be made intelligible to the members of the clan. Wars and conquests were celebrated by poets, who were literally the public archivists of the community. Each group was persuaded that it belonged to a self-contained world, and elaborated for itself a coherent explanation of the universe on the basis of its immediate experience, indifferent to comparison and challenge.

These fragile and technically backward systems of thought were the products of a closed world; understandably, they proved incapable of resisting the brutal assault on their integrity by armed emissaries of a universalizing, monotheistic message powered by a far more elaborate technology.

In this respect Muslim propagandists and their Christian successors have something in common: from the very outset they denied in principle the cultural values inherent in the traditional African systems. This fundamental rejection was unfortunately bound to affect, for more than half a millennium of our own era, the attitude of all those who came to Africa for either material or spiritual conquest. This general attitude was quite independent of whether the newcomers arrived by land or by sea. It is only in our own day that a new philosophical view, based on a respect for the intrinsic values of diverse human civilizations, has enabled us to rediscover, under the conquerors' veneer, the bright and motley colours of the authentic Negro civilizations.

African values denied by Muslims, then Christians

For both Muslims and Christians—especially Muslims—the problem was not one of skin colour, but of culture. We have already commented on the war waged by the Emperors of Mali against the pagans on their southern border on the pretext that the latter indulged in such abominations as cannibalism. During the fourteenth century of our era trade relations between the Negro populations and the representatives of the so-called civilized world were just what they had been in the time of the Phoenician traders. Products were exchanged in a no-man's land by a process of silent bargaining, keenly supervised by both parties from a distance, that was by no means conducive to cultural intimacy.

The alternative was conquest, a natural temptation for great kingdoms, established along fertile rivers, that were in need of slave labour. The slaves could come only from the non-Muslim areas; thus the Hausa kingdom of the northern valley of the Niger and the Bornu kingdom of Chad, for instance, naturally tended to expand into the "pagan" regions, or to push the non-Muslim populations off the fertile land into the least accessible parts of the country. The Muslim Nubians, the natural successors of the Egyptian southern kingdoms, were in permanent conflict with the Negro tribes of the upper Nile, who to this day have rejected Islam.

Hindsight tells that the Muslim historians, in their chronicles of the victorious southward march of Berbers, Arabs and Nubians, gave a very fragmentary and distorted idea of a world, complex and many-sided, on which modern science is only now beginning to shed a somewhat uncertain light.

Let us recall, first, that Africa south of the Sahara has always been sparsely populated. In the nature of things centers of political power are established at the most favourable spots for trade or defence or both. Those peoples that willingly or forcibly accept a common allegiance regroup themselves around these centers, very often separated from one another by immense distances who make for a peaceful co-existence. The peace is broken when groups are forced to move by the pressure of natural

Page 76
Treasure of the Ashanti king, Kofo Kakari, 17th century. The Ashanti, who lived in what is now Ghana, were skilled in casting objects out of pure gold or using thin sheets for ornamentation. What is probably a funerary mask, the weapons and jewellery, are part of the precious objects brought back to Britain by Field Marshal Wolseley after his African expedition of 1874. (Wallace Collection, London.)

77

catastrophes: epidemics, the exhaustion of the natural resources, or invasion. Thus even the remotest and most obscure tribes are subject directly to the pressure of such calamities, which are altogether beyond their intellectual grasp, to say nothing of their technical ability. Most external factors are naturally hostile; it is in its manpower and its productivity that the group generally suffers from the impact of external influences.

On the other hand, there is a contrary effect, too: certain peoples, especially those that happen to come in direct contact with the alien element, seem to derive some initial political benefit from the influx of currency and weapons created by a superior technology. Most of the kingdoms that have somehow survived the currents and crosscurrents of conquest and resistance affecting the Negro Africans have all been marked by organizational efficiency and the possession of an advanced military system. It is this system that makes the principal difference between the warlike tribes and those that have clung to traditional agriculture.

Even before the arrival of the Europeans, Negro Africans showed great capacity for organization: the Mossis, the Yorubas, the Ashantis, the Dogons, the Dahomians, and the Benin Kingdoms in West Africa; the Bamilekes, the Bakangos, the Balubas, the Baluandas, the Azandes in Central Africa, and many others constituted so many political power centers, of which African history is bound to take full cognizance. Every one of these, at a given stage of history, has played an important role in the resistance of African Negroes to foreign invasions. Hamites and Semites from North Africa and the Middle East, Portuguese, English and French from Europe have had to reckon with them on their march to African dominion. For some kingdoms, like those of the West Coast of the western Congo, the testimony of foreign traders and travellers can give us something to correlate the traditional native chronicles with and thus help us arrive at an approximate chronology. For others, in East and Central Africa, the vagueness of our sources makes it difficult to see clearly what such political entities as the Monomotapa empire—the terror of the Portuguese—might have been. It was perhaps nothing more than a loose confederacy of tribes based on shifting alliances.

Organizational ability of Negro Africans

The Negro African peoples have ultimately appeared in history as we know it only insofar as they succeeded in organizing themselves to face the challenge of a superior technology. The better means of transport and the more powerful weapons at the disposal of the invaders have been instrumental either in the physical elimination of whole peoples and tribes or in their cultural absorption by the conqueror. This is just as true of Africa as it is of other continents. Some peoples, on the other hand, simply gave up their land and took refuge in natural fortresses, to remain isolated there until a new technology broke through to them; in Africa this is a very recent phenomenon. They were "rediscovered" as political entities, and confronted with the opportunity of accepting—or again refusing—integration in the political and economic framework.

This may explain how the progressive introduction of the African continent, including its most inaccessible parts, into an international system of exchange helped, initially, to "fossilize" whole populations, and then at a second stage made them reappear on the stage of history in a startling reversal of roles.

In this way the conflict and competition between the peoples of Africa have been intensified and accelerated by the armed penetration of Christianity and Islam, the two great monotheisms born in the Middle East, together with the economic, political and military systems that seem to have been their bulwark and their corollary. In the final analysis pagan Africa was bound to suffer before it could benefit from its forced entry into universal civilization.

And it was during the fifteenth century that the Arabs, masters of the overland routes, were succeeded by the Portuguese navigators, who were destined to seal the fate of the African continent by flinging open its ocean gates.

Chapter 9
The Oceanic Gates of Africa

Like Rome, Islam stopped at the borders of the Negro world, whose richness, wealth and variety it suspected without having any direct access to it. For western Africa its advance was overland, for eastern Africa by sea. The Muslim navigators who had demonstrated their brilliance in the development of trading relations with the Africa facing the Indian Ocean showed themselves to be remarkably faint-hearted, as explorers of the Atlantic routes. The reason for this is that the system of winds favoured sea voyages that could be accomplished by relatively small ships in the first zone while when combined with adverse currents it was eminently unfavourable to any navigation beyond the Moroccan coast toward the Gulf of Guinea. Departure was possible, but it seemed impossible to come back. Down to the middle of the fifteenth century the Portuguese believed in the menace of "unbelievable heat" and of "a raging sea". It was also thought that intense darkness prevailed beyond the tropics. Galleys that made about 15½ miles a day and stopped at nightfall were able to free themselves from the contraint of the prevailing winds. But on the other hand they were victims of the rigours of the climate, of the treacherous coastal currents, of the presence of shoals and of the difficulty of water supply, increased by the existence of hostile nomadic tribes.

Why the Atlantic routes had remained unexplored

From the twelfth century on, navigation by sail was to benefit from decisive technical improvements, such as the invention of the rudder that replaced the steering oar, the adoption of an efficient system of sails that divided up the effective sail surface fore and aft of the ship, and finally the use of the compass and the astrolabe, combined with the staggering advances in map-making. On this last point it was the Portuguese who put to profitable use the intensive labor of the Catalans and the Italians and themselves gave technique a decisive impetus by the manufacture of the "portolanos".

At the beginning of the fifteenth century Portuguese vessels could navigate in the open sea, make use of contrary winds and take the ship's bearings at any time. Man had freed himself from the tyranny of clinging to offshore sailing and of navigation by the eye. It has been estimated that from the thirteenth to the fifteenth century the distance covered by one day's sailing went from 46 miles to more than 124. A barrier had been crossed—a new world lay open to the pioneers of the high seas.

It was no accident that the European peoples of the Iberian peninsula were the first to utilize these new techniques for a policy of expansion. The co-existence of the Christians and the Muslims, their close dynastic and commercial ties with Italy, itself an intermediate world between the western and the eastern Mediterranean, and finally, and perhaps above all, the activity of Jews who were simultaneously Hispanicized and Arabized, enabled Portugal and then Spain to express in concrete achievements the creative fermentation of a world bursting with vitality. The Jews, who were numerous in Portugal and in both parts of Spain, had had access to Greco-Roman culture via the Muslims. Often occupying the highest diplomatic position, in the service of the Cross as well as of the Crescent, the Jews played the role of intermediaries and interpreters. Thanks to them the Kingdoms of Portugal, Castile, and Aragon had multiple sources of information at their disposal the moment their ruling classes were able to free themselves of the immediate exigencies of the *Reconquista*. The Portuguese carried the war against Islam over to the coasts of Morocco and settled in Ceuta in 1415, turning it into a quasi-permanent base for intervention by land. The Western navigators, who from the fourteenth century on were decisively superior to the Muslims on the Atlantic coast, made regular voyages along the coasts of Morocco; they reached the Canaries in 1341 and "discovered" Madeira and the Azores in the same era. The Castilians and the Normans occupied the Canaries in 1405; the Portuguese got to Madeira in 1425; Cape Juby was weathered in 1405 and Bogeador in 1434.

Early in the fifteenth century the discovery of the antipodes and of a possible southern access to the Christian kingdoms whose existence was suspected in the "Indies" (that is, beyond the Muslim barrier) had become a very real issue.

It was in Lagos, on the southern coast of Portugal, that the Prince Henry, son of King John I, conqueror of Ceuta, set up the first international center of oceanic studies. The prince brought together the greatest scientists and cartographers of his time as well as the best sailors. He paid huge sums to all those—humble fishermen of the Moroccan coasts, Catalan and Italian merchants, Jewish or Christian philosophers, prisoners and hostages brought back by his sailors—who could help elucidate the image he had little by little shaped in his mind of a world still unknown and that his country ought to play a decisive role in. The discovery of the Oceanic routes, like the conquest of outer space in our own day, was an enterprise that demanded a firm and enlightened command and a programme supported by financial and administrative means with some guarantee of continuity. The "dark seas" were fraught with dangers and with terrors. The very existence of the world of the antipodes was questioned by the scholastics who, because of splendid reasons extracted from texts, demonstrated that the southern hemisphere was an inaccessible ocean. The Muslims knew Ptolemy better than the Westerners, who had to rediscover the accuracy of certain of his theories in the school of experience, and not as a result of philosophical hair-splitting.

It was in fact in 1441 that the Portuguese reached Cape Blanc and after a short landing brought back hostages and gold. It was finally proven that, contrary to the hypotheses of the theologians and their theories about the "vacuum of the antipodes", the tropics were not impassable; natives sound in mind and body and with no singularities other than their color, lived there quite normally without walking on their heads. In chronicles such as those of Cadamosto, a Venetian gentleman, the Europeans rediscovered that the Moors had lucrative trade relations with the Timbuktu Empire exchanging horses for slaves and gold. Which, of course, the Muslims were already quite familiar with. The Senegal was soon reached, and seemed to the Portuguese to be a new world on verdant shores embracing prosperous villages. The gold route seemed to have been discovered. When, in 1481, King John II mounted the throne the Portuguese crown found itself directly interested in the improvement of a trade whose pioneers were gradually advancing as far as the Gulf of Guinea.

Consequently the Europeans set up their first permanent establishment south of the tropics at a point they called "El Mina", in a region that was to keep its name down to our own day as the Gold Coast. The inhabitants gave a decent welcome to these white navigators, whom they regarded as simple merchants, even though they showed some reticence with respect to their plans for a permanent Portuguese fort.

In 1486 St. George de Mina officially became a Portuguese and Catholic municipality, thus signalizing the first territorial expression of European claims to the control of the Gulf of Guinea. Other forts were built all along the coast. One of them was to go on existing to our own day as an enclave of Portuguese sovereignty in an African republic—St. João Baptista de Ajuda ("taken back" by the Dahomey Republic in 1961).

In 1484 Diego Cao rounded Cape St. Catherine and reached the mouth of the Congo. He took back four "ambassadors" to Lisbon, leaving four of his compatriots there instead. For the first time the idea of "Christianizing" the African kingdoms sprang up in Europe. The Portuguese were obsessed by the geopolitical necessity of establishing land or sea ties with the Christian kingdoms located beyond the Islamic world. By the time they reached the Gulf of Benin they had heard with a quiver of hope some talk of a spiritual leader whose authorization was necessary for the legitimization of the local chieftains. (Perhaps Oni of Ifé, the spiritual guide of the Yoruba Kingdom, whose ethnic and historic significance has been emphasized by Frobenius.)

After the return of Diego Cao together with his would-be converts, John II decided to explore simultaneously the ocean route toward the south and the land and sea route toward the east, in order to find Prester John, Emperor of Ethiopia, whose resistance to the Islamic conquest had carried his name beyond the gates of Egypt. It had in fact become urgent for the western world to free itself from the perpetual blackmail Islam was exercising over Christendom through effective control over the commercial land and sea routes linking Asia and Europe. The Arab danger, already greatly attenuated by the Christian counter-offensive in the Iberian peninsula and by the Crusades, had been succeeded by the still greater danger embodied in the Turkish conquests.

The thrust toward Ethiopia and Prester John

Constantinople, the last vestige of the Byzantine Empire, fell in 1453. The Turks were already in control of Egypt. Europe had to confront a seemingly invincible combination of a powerful army and an excellent fleet, whose crews were recruited among the descendants of the Greek, Phoenician and Egyptian sailors who had dominated the Mediterranean for millennia through their boldness and navigational skill. The attempts of the western kingdoms to convert the Mongol peoples encamped at the gates of eastern Europe in the thirteenth century had foundered, as had the first attempts to evangelize the Chinese Empire. Europe had been profoundly disappointed by this setback, for which the only parallel may be found in our own day in the reactions of the Atlantic world when Red China refused to become an associate.

Bartholomew Diaz, at the head of a small squadron, sailed boldly beyond the farthermost western cape of the African continent in 1486, and touched briefly on the African coast of the Indian Ocean after having unknowingly rounded the southern cape of the African continent, which he baptized successively "Cape of Storms" and "Cape of Good Hope." At the same moment, Pedro de Covilham followed the classic land route all along the northern coasts of Africa as far as the Sinai Peninsula; he went as far as the trading-posts of India aboard Arab vessels. He came back via Cairo, and went to Ethiopia, where he became the emperor's favourite. He communicated the secrets of the classic Indies route to the Lisbon court at the very moment it was learned that this same route could be crossed by the south once the African continent had been rounded. A new expedition headed by Vasco da Gama left Lisbon on 8 July 1497, rounded the Cape of Good Hope, passed by Sofala, and cast anchor on 1 March 1498 off the Island of Mozambique, then the most important southern base for Arab trade in the Indian Ocean.

The emissaries of the two hostile civilizations had met. The Arab merchants had expected to see some Turks—that is, Muslims from the eastern Mediterranean—instead they had come upon "infidels". The riches of the world around the Indian Ocean had a mesmeric effect on the Christians. The cities of the coast, rich and well built, and their inhabitants were in sharp contrast with the desolate regions inhabited by pastoral tribes (the Hottentots) with whom they had established some meager relations during the course of dangerous stops. A breach had been opened: all western Europe was to pass through it in order to subjugate the Kingdoms of India and the Indian Archipelago, before coming to grief before the Japanese and Chinese fortresses. For the Muslims as well as for the Hindu world, Vasco da Gama's expedition suddenly revealed the military power and wealth of the western world, which did not hesitate to force open the southern gates of a commercial and maritime empire it considered inviolable.

This epic drama, highlighted by glamorous names like Vasco da Gama, Cabral, Almeida, and Albuquerque, inspired contemporary poets, who saw the great importance of this discovery of new worlds in Africa and Asia, and marks the exceptional character of this century of renaissance. Camoëns, the greatest Portuguese lyric poet, was a child of this century. A soldier in North Africa, navigator and warrior in India, corsair in the Red Sea and finally a notary in Macao, he did not go back to his homeland until after a long sojourn in Mozambique, the meeting-place of east and west. He found Portugal struck down by the Black Plague, with its prosperity already suffering from the counter-blows struck in the savage competition with the other European powers, whose appetites were now aroused. It was by singing of the feats of his great navigators that Camoëns tried to lift up the courage of his compatriots.

In a celebrated dialogue the poet brought to life the decisive interview between the earthy Portuguese navigators and the refined Muslim merchants who knew they belonged to a universal civilization whose law was Islam: "We are the Portuguese of the West. We seek the lands of the East. We have sailed the seas that go from the North Pole to the South Pole, crossed Africa in all its length and come to know many lands and many skies. We are the subjects of a mighty king on whose orders we have sailed into the unknown in quest of the eastern lands where the Indus flows." The Muslims reply: "We too are strangers here, and have nothing in common with the natives. They are pagans, and without civilization. We are faithful Muslims, believers in the True Faith like the rest of the world. This little isle we live on is called Mozambique. It is a way-station for all navigators all along the coast of Kilwa, from Mombasa to Sofala." (Lusiad, Canto I.)

Camoëns knew that the rest of Europe did not care to accompany the Portuguese in their new crusade against the infidel; it amounted to entering the world of Islam by the service door. For him the Germans were betraying their duty as Europeans because they opposed the Pope, the English because they were anti-Catholic, the French because they were trying to dominate Italy and Spain, and because they had shown themselves to be unworthy sons of Charlemagne and St. Louis, and Italy, finally, because of its dissension, its indolence, its wealth and its vices. The Turkish infidels were winning one victory after another while the Western Christians were "tearing themselves to bits in civil strife". Even the gleam of African gold failed to unite them. The Christian peoples of Greece, Thrace, Armenia and Georgia had been enslaved by the Turks, while the Christians of the west were using superior weapons to destroy themselves instead of turning them against a common enemy. "Only the little country of Portugal does not lack those who will do and dare everything for Christianity. In Africa it already controls the coastal bases, as it does in Asia; it is tilling the fields of the New World."

A grandiose misconception   Thus a grandiose misconception led an heroic though small people to embark on an enterprise that was inspiring, yet clearly beyond its powers. It had simultaneously to colonize the vast territories of Brazil (discovered by Cabral en route to Africa), defend the commercial monopoly of the Indies route that had been wrested from the Arabs and Indians against its Dutch, English and French competitors, and finally stabilize the African way-stations by entering into contact with the neighbouring peoples through negotiation, trade, or force. In many respects Portugal was carrying on for its own ends the policy of Carthage, but on a scale still more vast. A nation of navigators, merchants and soldiers was attempting to arouse and exploit many slumbering worlds, whose nightmares were to haunt it for five centuries.

Chapter 10
A New World for Portugal

It was with a good conscience that the Portuguese embarked on the conquest of the world in general and of Africa in particular. The Pope had given them a right of eminent domain to all the lands they discovered. On 8 January 1455, in a bull addressed to King Alfonso V, Pope Nicholas V granted him the right "to invade, conquer, attack, vanquish and subjugate all the Saracens or Pagans or other enemies of Christ wherever they may be found, also their kingdoms, duchies, principalities, domains or any other property, real or movable, possessed by them. They may also reduce to perpetual slavery their persons, domains, and possessions". Nothing could be more explicit: there was a general obligation to bring the Muslims back to the Catholic faith by force or by persuasion, and to bring the pagans to the Gospel.

Now, the Portuguese lacked the material means indispensable for any possible conquest, which for that matter they did not seem to be aiming at. In this respect the remarkable epic of the Portuguese in Africa was profoundly different from the ferocious conquest accomplished with such slim means by the Spanish conquistadors in Mexico and the high Andes. On the coast of the Gulf of Guinea they found various peoples who, while aware of the advantages of trading with the foreigners, were rightly mistrustful of anything that looked like a permanent settlement. The coastal peoples (probably the vanguard of migrations from the north and the northeast) were in close touch with the peoples of the interior. Their participation in the new commerce fortified the local chieftains and in general accelerated the settlement of the new groups that came down the coast and the immediately adjacent plains. The European forts (like the one at Mina) were in fact enclaves around which there gradually grew up communities whose members learned the language of the natives for the sake of trading with them. They depended entirely on the good will of the Africans, who were, after all, quite indifferent to the nationality of the occupiers as well as to the character of their internecine disputes.

Farther south, the Portuguese navigators thought for a short while that they had succeeded in producing a sort of miracle when their missionaries, without a shot being fired, opened up the Kingdom of the Congo discovered by Diego Cao in 1485. Frobenius echoes the Portuguese chroniclers when he speaks of the magnificence of the former rulers of the Congo: "Magnificent carved ivories, splendid fabrics like silk and velvet, and the complex organization of the state". If one believes him "this admirable Congo of old" asked for nothing better than an alliance with the West.

It is true that the "Manicongo", the African chieftain who controlled the region now divided between the Republic of the Congo and Angola, was remarkably receptive. Under the influence of four of his compatriots who had returned from a more or less voluntary trip to Lisbon and who dressed like Portuguese, spoke their language, shared their faith and were unflaggingly eloquent in praise of Portugal, the King demanded to be baptized, and took the name of John I. A contemporary hailed this decisive event in these terms: "In the most remote spots on earth and among the most barbarous

83

peoples, where we might well have thought that the word of the Apostles had not made its way, today there can be seen (in São Salvador) in a cathedral altars covered with offerings and sacrifices addressed to God Himself in the name of Jesus Christ His Son and Our Redeemer... A king who is barbarian by blood and Catholic by faith, ruling over a kingdom as great as the Congo and a great people, believes in Jesus Christ, adores Him, and recognizes Him".

A premature African policy

King Manuel of Portugal realized that there was a miraculous opportunity here of ensuring the collaboration of an African and a European kingdom on the basis of a common faith. In broad strokes he outlined a theory of cultural and religious assimilation with all due respect for local custom. In a proclamation that some find prophetic —the "Regimento"—he laid down a doctrine that was, unfortunately, well ahead of his time. In point of fact Portuguese influence turned out to remain superficial. Missionaries, men and women, lived in material conditions that were precarious. What was still more serious, at a time when they were supposed to protect the inhabitants of the kingdom against all their enemies they had to withstand the pressure of their own countrymen who, settled on the island of São Tomé, a natural way-station for the South American route, demanded their quota of slaves in order to ensure the exploitation of the virgin territories of the Amazonian continent. In less than a century the city of São Salvador, the capital of the kingdom of the Congo, which had become an archbishopric, was no more than a dying city from which the last Europeans were soon to vanish. In fact the hour had not yet come for Europe to grapple seriously with the problems of transforming Africa. Portugal, which actually was no better or worse than the other European kingdoms of the fifteenth and sixteenth centuries, lacked both the means and the sustained effort indispensable for such an enterprise.

On the other side of the Cape of Good Hope the situation was rather different. Trading-posts existed there in the form of prosperous cities inhabited by Arab merchants who did not hesitate to marry the local women and were quite free of any proselytizing zeal. In 1505, when the Portuguese built the fortress of Sofala on the outskirts of the Arab city of the same name, they intended to ensure control over one of the most ancient commercial routes of the world; it led from the coast to the wealthy kingdoms of the interior over pathways that were practically secret. At all times, in fact, gold, iron (of exceptional quality), copper, ivory, ostrich plumes and, finally, slaves, were the commodities of exchange, exported in return for fabrics, pearls, porcelains, and arms from the great eastern empires that came aboard Arab and Indian vessels. This lasting commerce, reduced by both sides equally to the most utilitarian purposes, was based on a fragile equilibrium made up of unwritten conventions, marked by guile and violence and at the mercy of the internal agitation provoked by local chiefs seeking their own advantage in this fruitful exchange.

The legendary Empire of Monomotapa was, in fact, a federation of kingdoms (mostly in the area of the present-day Rhodesias) that were themselves in commercial relations by the land-routes with the Kingdoms of the Congo and of Angola. The legend, so widespread, of the cities of gold (the Zimbabwes) inevitably turned the heads of the Portuguese conquerors while at the same time the Moroccan armies could not resist the temptation to break the control of the Sudanese empires over the gold routes of western Africa. Less than three quarters of a century after their entry into the Arab commercial world the Portuguese, scarcely settled on the coast, decided to destroy the Monomotapa Empire. On 23 January 1569 an assembly of ecclesiastics took as pretext the assassination of a Portuguese missionary in order to authorize a war against the peoples who opposed the propagation of the true faith. The King of Portugal was authorized to "build fortresses and send armed men into the ten kingdoms and domains of the Monomotapa... If the Kaffirs and other peoples in the conquered countries do not

Page 85

Above: An engraving of Azimour, on the Atlantic coast of Morocco about 50 miles southwest of Casablanca, one of the first Portuguese settlements in North Africa. From a volume published in 1572: "Civitates Orbis Terrarum" by G. Braun. Below: a photograph of Azimour today showing a bridge built by the Portuguese in the foreground, and ramparts. After the Portuguese carried the war against Islam to the Moroccan coast, settling Ceuta in 1415, they gradually extended their hold to other coastal forts, all points of departure for commercial routes. Many of these towns still have ramparts, cisterns, bastions and the ruins of churches built by the Portuguese.

Pages 86-87

The capture of Arzila by Alfonso V of Portugal in 1471: a tapestry, part of a series woven at Tournai in 1480 after cartoons by the celebrated Portuguese artist Nuño Gonçalves, to commemorate the Portuguese victories at Arzila and Tangiers.

AZAAMVRVM.   Templum D. Virginis   Eremitar. habitatio.

Castrum

ESCOSIA

Irlanda

ingalaterra

FLÃDE

framça

itali

a

bordes

Liscaia

secilia

As Ilhas terceiras

Portugal

Castella

tunis

As canareas

Seuta

ouraons

Mõ

te os claros

Ilhas do cabo Rde

Africa

Serra lioa

mina

Reino
beni

wish to allow the entry of the said ministers, or to permit them to teach the Gospel with all the precautions indicated, or oppose violence to the hospitality and to the trade that are the common right of men, the captains and the vessels of the King will very rightly take all measures of defense with all necessary moderation." The King was also enjoined "to abrogate the tyrannical laws" and pernicious rites.

The Portuguese expeditionary corps that landed on the African coast opposite the Island of Mozambique found its work cut out for it. The country was teeming with wild animals, including hippopotami, lions, crocodiles, rhinoceroses, elephants and buffalo, as well as snakes and huge lizards. The soldiers were decimated by disease and lost their way along paths that proved to be blind alleys. It took them five years to reach the approaches of the Rhodesian plateau, where they soon realized the illusory character of their plan for an effective military conquest. The Portuguese finally had to be satisfied with a few points of support in the Zambezi valley (Tété and Séna) without developing the slightest political or religious sphere of influence. Not only did the Monomotapa display remarkable military prowess, but they showed above all an unflagging devotion to their customs, which were founded on a coherent system of relations between the individual and the universe, both visible and invisible. It was nature itself, indeed, that proved to be the best defender of these sealed off kingdoms that were determined to keep the secret of their treasures.

In the last analysis the military means at the disposal of the western powers proved to be just as inadequate as their political and religious means. Nevertheless the prospects opened up by the destruction of the Muslim maritime empire in the Indian Ocean were dizzying. The navigators who without firing a shot inherited practically all the Muslim maritime and commercial bases along the coast of eastern Africa, made their way up to Mombasa at the beginning of the sixteenth century and occupied Zaida at the gates of the Red Sea. Here they came into contact with another branch of the Muslim world, this one in the process of dynamic expansion—the Ottoman Empire, which, threatening the heart of Europe and controlling the Mediterranean, could not put up with an attack from the south.

The Christian Kingdom of Ethiopia had appealed to the countries of the West for an alliance against the threats of the Muslim sultanates of the coast. The court of Lisbon had been in contact with that of Queen Helen of Ethiopia at the end of the fifteenth century, but the first Portuguese embassy did not manage to get to the court of her successor, Emperor Lebna Dengel, until 1520. Once the country of Prester John was discovered it lost something of its mystery, but to make up for that it became one of the elements of Portuguese grand strategy against the eastern empires. When the Ethiopians were defeated by armies from Somaliland and Eritrea in 1529, and when the Muslims got as far as the fortress of the Tigré, where they were joined by Nubian contingents, the cause of Christian Ethiopia seemed doomed. Though the Portuguese rescue expedition, 400 strong, got to the Ethiopian plateau in 1541, and in 1542 the Somali invaders were beaten back, the Portuguese soon had to confront a Turkish army made up of Arabs, Turks, and Albanians; their arms too had come from Europe, and had been provided by Genoans who attached a rather limited importance to the idea of any European geopolitical strategy. The head of the Portuguese expeditionary corps, Cristovão da Gama, was imprisoned and beheaded, but the battle nevertheless gave the Ethiopians time to catch their breath, repulse the Somalis and finally turn to confront still another invasion, this time of a people neither Christian nor Muslim that had probably come from the Arabian steppes—the Gallas.

Thus, as far as Africa was concerned, the sixteenth century was the century of the Portuguese. In the wake of their brilliant discoveries the African was integrated into the world of that time. Conflicts that had arisen elsewhere were projected into Africa,

Alliance with Ethiopia
1520

Page 88
16th century map showing the Portuguese forts on the west coast of Africa. At the bottom, São Jorge da Mina, on the Gulf of Guinea, first permanent European establishment south of the tropics, founded in 1486. Prince Henry the Navigator spent lavishly to push discovery of the sea routes around Africa.

where they simply exacerbated the local disputes. Portuguese vessels were able to go around the whole continent as far as the Red Sea and drop anchor in Portuguese ports. The control of the coastal way-stations remained, to be sure, highly precarious, since neither in North Africa, nor in the Congo, nor on the coasts of the Indian Ocean could their initial successes be turned into an effective territorial control, of which Portuguese power was militarily and politically incapable.

Impact of the Portuguese on Africa

The great Portuguese enterprise was to leave profound traces. Indeed, in its architecture, its languages, and its agriculture, Africa still shows the effects of the vigorous effort of this small country, which through the skill of its navigators succeeded in overcoming the isolation of the continent. For almost three centuries the other countries of the West, which were seeking to seize control of the maritime routes in Africa as they were in Asia and America too, were to imitate the Portuguese pioneers in making their way along the shores of the African continent and trafficking in the most easily exportable wealth—gold and people. France, Spain, the Netherlands, England, and after them the Scandinavian countries, actually followed the Portuguese very quickly in the trade in manpower, which at that time was needed for economic reasons.

We already know that the Catholic Church thought it a shrewd stroke in the struggle against the infidels (whether positive infidels like the Muslims or negative like the pagans) to "reduce to perpetual slavery their persons, domains, and possessions." Africa was a victim made to order for this idea, since the coastal principalities that the navigators entered into contact with seemed entirely willing to deliver slaves, and since the Arab navigators on the eastern coast had long been engaged in the "shameful traffic" between Africa and Arabia.

For that matter the men of the Renaissance saw nothing shocking in the enslavement, as a result of war or trade, of human beings who were then assigned to the most menial tasks. In addition, the Muslim and Christian worlds agreed in denying any civilized dignity to the Negro societies. Like Leo Africanus they thought "the countries of the Negroes are all inhabited by men who live like beasts, without a king, without a ruler, without a republic, without a government, without customs. They scarcely know how to plant seeds. They are dressed in sheepskin. None of them has a woman who is really his own." For the Islamized rulers, accordingly, as well as for the European merchants who came in contact with the coastal kingdoms in the Gulf of Guinea, the Africans were the object of a legitimate traffic.

The opening up of the virgin territories of the American continent, in the sixteenth and seventeenth centuries, created a gigantic demand. The missionaries sent to the New World, dismayed by the destruction and subjugation of the great Indian empires, cried out for the importation of Negroes to prevent the total disappearance of the American Indian population. It was wholly natural for the Portuguese of the Guinea coast, of the Island of São Tomè and of the way-stations of Angola, as well as for the Spaniards of Fernando Po, to be the first to go in for the transport of slaves across the Atlantic. The English shipped out their first load in 1562; the Dutch began in 1595. In the seventeenth century, the French, after settling in the Antilles, also became active competitors.

In less than a century the western powers transferred economic and strategic conflicts to African soil. The coastal states, which were the natural intermediaries between the European points of support and the countries of the interior, whose routes were often under the control of militarily well organized native states, found themselves involved in these disputes. In a fatal cycle the goods that were imported in exchange for the delivery of slaves and gold, that is, arms and alcohol, hastened the deterioration of relations among the Africans themselves.

Those regions that had received arms from the West and from the Muslim East gradually organized themselves around military oligarchies that managed to impose an unscrupulous rule over the sedentary groups. A merchant class of go-betweens appeared at the side of the warlords and proved receptive to the attraction of western civilization in its most materialistic forms. In spite of themselves the Negro peoples were drawn into the grandiose exploitation of the New World, while in Africa itself whole peoples rose up against the deep-rooted injustice they suffered from, very often at the hands of, their racial kin, for the profit of inscrupulous merchants from east and west.

A civilization that had been at least peaceful, if not brilliant, had given way to a merciless competition. Its surest victims were the inhabitants of the regions south of the extreme point of Islamic penetration from North Africa and the Nile, west of the zones controlled by the Arabs of the Indian Ocean, and finally north and east of the coastal regions where the European trading-posts had grown up.

Disruptive influence of exploitation

It has been estimated that in two centuries Africa lost millions of people in the slave trade. It is difficult to arrive at a proper evaluation of the cumulative effects of this loss of energy and of its moral and cultural consequences. These were heightened by the cyclical effects of the great endemic diseases, the food famines due to the growing insecurity, and finally the basic poverty of the soil that was difficult to cultivate and that tended to lose its fertile components because of the severity of the climate.

Up to the great philosophical reaction of the eighteenth century Europe itself had lost all critical sense concerning an enterprise it derived a certain profit from. Commercial companies were set up whose sole object was for all practical purposes the transport of slaves; they benefited by official charters. The highest civil and military dignitaries of the European kingdoms had a financial interest in them. These companies even engaged in military operations against their competitors, thus creating a state of permanent conflict and insecurity in which the weaker countries like Portugal, Spain and Holland gradually exhausted themselves. The permanent settlements on the coasts of Africa, which had to reduce their local expenditures to a minimum, had no other purpose than to realize a maximum of profit by any means whatsoever. The conditions of the transport and sale of masses of men, women and children, torn away from their homelands, were marked by a radical brutality rarely tempered by charity.

The relations between Europe and Africa were to suffer down to our own day from the consequences of a postulate that was never frankly expressed but only too often was unconsciously taken for granted by Europeans and Orientals—that of the "non-humanity" of the African.

While the Western Europeans, at the dawn of the sixteenth century, saw opening up before their eyes the great oceanic routes, they were being menaced on sea and land by the staggering expansion of the Ottoman Turks.

Expansion of Turkish power

Indeed, it had needed no more than a few decades after the fall of Constantinople for the Turks to take charge of the destinies of the Islamic world, which seemed to have been radically enfeebled by the attacks of Spain and Portugal as well as by its own internal decadence. Constantinople quickly became once again a centre of power and commerce comparable to what it had been in the glorious days of Byzantium. This time the empire was benefitting from a relative peace on its eastern borders, since Persia, ravaged by successive invasions from Central Asia, had ceased to be a great power. The Ottoman Empire found the source of its military vigour in the virile population of Anatolia, and of its naval power in the Greek and oriental crews descended from Hellenic and Phoenician ancestors. The system of selection of the ruling castes, however odd it may appear to the eyes of the West, opened the highest positions to brilliant individuals without consideration of race or even of religion, provided loyalty to the state was unquestioned. The rewards were the counterpart of the dangers; assassination tempered nepotism. The only criterion was success or failure.

This formidable political power organized the peoples of eastern Europe south of Russia, those of the Near East and soon those of North Africa. Charles V, himself the ruler of a world where the sun never set, was attacked at the very gates of his capital. Italy, Austria, and Russia were on the defensive. In Europe, commercial powers like Venice, or political and military powers like France, sought the aid of the Ottoman Sultan in the struggle against their own European rivals.

The Ottomans tried to expand southwards beyond the Euphrates toward the Nile delta. Like their Hittite and Byzantine predecessors, they collided with the Syrian advance posts of the Mamluks, who ruled Egypt. These Mamluks had turned into a military aristocracy quite out of touch with the local population. Leo Africanus defined them in this way: "The Mamluks were Christians captured as small children by the Tatars in the province of Circassia on the Black Sea. From there they were sold in the city called El-Kafa (today Feodosia). From there they were brought to Cairo where they were bought by the Sudan (Sultan). The latter made them renounce their baptism at once and handed them over to professors of Arabic and Turkish and to military instructors. They were gradually promoted in rank and dignity and sometimes attained supreme power".

In its *esprit de corps* and in the very reason for its existence, that is, pure power, the Mamluk caste was reminiscent of the Janissary corps that in Istanbul and later in Algiers was also to make law, nominating and deposing at will sultans and beys. But the Mamluks were a century behind in military technique. They had never gone beyond the Greek fire, which had done wonders before the armies of St. Louis but did not have the slightest effect on Ottoman artillery, serviced by technicians from Venice

Page 93
The west coast of Africa, according to an atlas drawn by Guillaume Le Testu in 1556. Le Testu, a captain and pilot, made several expeditions to the New World with Drake; he published a "Universal Cosmography according to ancient and modern navigators" consisting of 50 plates which included the map shown here. The work of Mercator and his pupils considerably advanced the art of map-making in the second half of the 16th century.

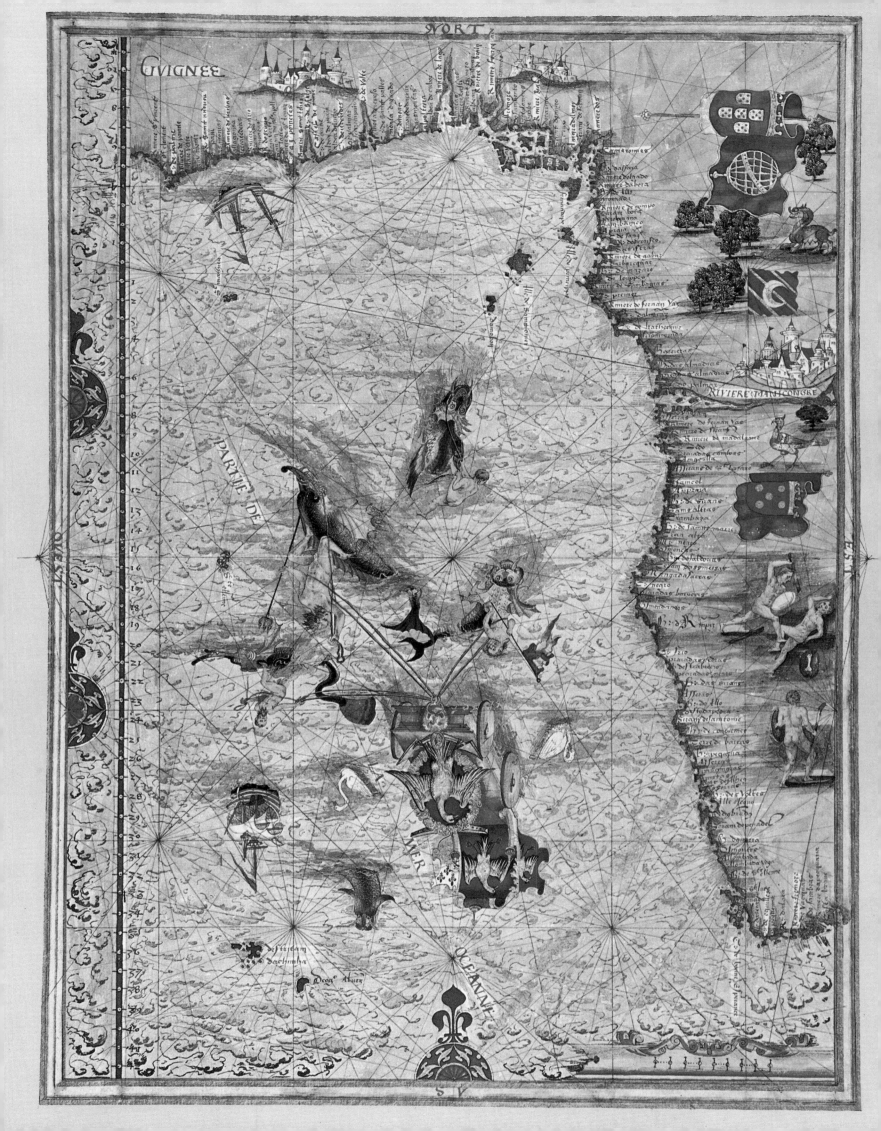

Page 95
More fanciful illustrations from Théodore de Bry's "Petits Voyages",
(1599, vol. 2: 1 and 2) Unknown animals. 3) The King of the Congo,
converted by the Portuguese, orders idols to be burnt. 4) Ways of travel-
ling. Horses are unknown, the caption reads, and the oxen too large to be
harnessed, so men are used. 5) The King of the Congo, converted to
christianity, asks for missionaries for his people. The Portuguese immediately answer the request, adding ornaments, holy pictures, crucifixes, etc.
6) From vol. 6 of the "Petits Voyages": How the inhabitants of Guinea
hunt and catch wild animals in traps.

"Bravery of the Monomotapa women", an 18th century engraving.
The Monomatapa Empire, on the east coast, was a federation of kingdoms
occupying roughly what is now Rhodesia. The Portuguese decided to
destroy it in 1569, ostensibly as a heathen city, in reality for its riches-gold,
iron, copper, ivory, slaves. They found the defenders fanatically brave
and after five years they had only established a few beachheads. Many
legends sprang up about this mysterious region with its "towns of gold"
and its "amazons" who fought along with their men.

Another engraving from Théodore de Bry's "Petits Voyages" 1599,
vol. 2. Here the Dutch disembark near the mouth of the Gabon river.
The King and his wife are on the left. The natives receive the strangers
"some with joy, others with hostility". The Dutch had arrived in Africa
four years before this engraving was made, immediately starting to trade,
most of all in slaves.

and western Europe. In 1517 Egypt was subjugated (after the Mamluk defeat at Damascus in September of the preceding year). What was left of the Abbasid Caliphate was transferred to Istanbul. In August 1517 the keys to the Kaaba in Mecca were given to Emperor Selim, who now ensured the symbolic control over the holy places of Islam.

The Ottoman Empire became also the holder of the keys to the Red Sea, which meant the Sinai Peninsula and the Nile Valley. It took in the revenues derived from the control of the great commercial routes that linked Europe to the Euphrates, Arabia, and beyond, to India and China.

In their descent southwards the Ottoman armies came up against the Portuguese, who, after having destroyed the Arab-Hindu trade in the Indian Ocean had crossed the Straits of Bab el-Mandeb and settled in Massawa. The Turkish government could now transport the reinforcements it needed in order to re-establish the threatened prestige of the Muslim sultanates of the Somali coast.

The Portuguese were expelled from Massawa in 1557, after the Turks had taken Suwakkim. A desperate effort had to be made by the Emperor of Ethiopia in 1589 to defeat the Muslim coalition armed by the Turks and aided by the Genoese. This new threat helped accentuate the isolation of the Ethiopian Christians. The attempt of the Church of Rome, conducted by the Jesuits from 1625 to 1634, to bring the schismatic kingdom back into the bosom of the Catholic world was to peter out ingloriously. Indeed, Amhara sovereigns were even to make common cause with the Turkish pashas of Suwakkim and Massawa in prohibiting the entry of any Catholic priest in the region. Shielded by the Ottoman Empire, Ethiopian nationalism demonstrated its political agility as well as its unconquerable attachment to its own religious individuality and its independence. For two centuries the country was immersed in domestic quarrels complicated by the attempts at invasion of barbarian peoples—the Gallas and the Somalis. The pro-western chapter of the Kingdom of Prester John was closed.

The Ottoman thrust had put a dead stop to the brilliant Portuguese attempt to round the Islamic barrier via the south. It had effects on the geopolitical situation of North Africa that were just as far-reaching, directly through the effective control of the principal ports of Tunisia and Algeria, and indirectly by reinforcing the isolation of the Moroccan regime. Morocco, in fact, now had to defend itself against the incursions of the Turkish-Algerian armies at its eastern frontier at the very moment it had to confront numerous renewed attacks on the part of its Portuguese and Spanish enemies.

Notwithstanding, the Turkish power soon appeared to be the sole guarantor of North African independence against the European itch for conquest. Italy and Spain realized that the new Ottoman power was raising once again the whole question of the security of the western Mediterranean. At the beginning of the sixteenth century this seemed to them to represent the culmination of a military and religious counter-offensive that was already many centuries old. Without the intervention of the Turks and thanks to the Portuguese occupation of all the ports on the Atlantic coast of Morocco as well as to the tempting nearness of the Mediterranean coasts of North Africa, the struggle between the Cross and the Crescent might well have been continued on the very soil of Africa.

The Spaniards knew that the Moors who had come from Cordoba and Granada and were exiled in North Africa, as well as the Jews expelled by the implacable fanaticism of the Catholic rulers, were seed-beds of resistance and possibly of revenge in the cities of North Africa. In Spain itself the subjugated Muslims, who had been guaranteed liberty of conscience, revolted en masse in 1500 against their northern rulers. Under the leadership of Cardinal Ximenes the Spanish Catholics accepted the idea of a new Holy War that was supposed to destroy the Moorish peril at the very sources of its power and of its potential renewal. Spanish armies landed at several points on the coast. Mers-el-Kabir was conquered in 1505, Oran in 1509, Bougie and Tripoli in 1510. From 1511 to 1522 Spain seemed to be the undisputed ruler of North Africa. Military success seemed so easy that Ximenes thought of seizing Egypt itself, then the Holy Land. But it is significant that the only Spanish defeat was inflicted (in 1511) by a Turkish garrison on the island of Djerba, an outpost of the Barbery "pirates" whose exploits were soon to reverse the situation completely.

These latter were really Greeks, originally from the island of Mytilene who had been converted to Islam, and were a sort of Janissary corps of the sea. Aruj and his brother Khair-ed-Din displayed exceptional ability as generals. Intermittent allies of certain Italian principalities, and even of the King of France, who was also threatened by the Spanish expansion, they threw themselves into a series of onslaughts on the Algerian ports, which were badly defended by inadequate Spanish garrisons. Installed in Djidjelli, the Barbarossa brothers (a European nickname) were soon reinforced by Turkish detachments. The Spaniards were forced to abandon Algiers in 1516; and the Algerian collaborators of Spain were also expelled from there. Aruj himself, however, was defeated by the Arab-Spanish armies at Tlemcen, and killed during the retreat in 1518.

Khair-ed-Din at Algiers
1516-1546

Algiers became a base of land and sea operations under the energetic leadership of Khair-ed-Din. It was a city organized for defence as well as for attack; peopled by extremely diverse elements, in the nature of things it had to maintain satisfactory and neighbourly relations with the Kabyle tribes of the interior. Its remarkable military and civil organization, under the authority of a Turkish garrison that played a role similar to that of the Egyptian Mamelukes, made it a permanent danger to the security of the European sea routes in the Mediterranean.

Emperor Charles V resumed as an interest of his own, with all the powerful means of the Teutonic Holy Roman Empire, the improvized advances of the soldier-cardinal Ximenes. The Spanish fleet landed near Tunis on 14 July 1535 in order to avenge a defeat at the hands of Khair ed-Din the preceding year. In 1541 a very substantial expedition made an attempt to seize Algiers, but it was undone in a complete rout. This may have been responsible for the elimination of Spanish influence from North Africa and the repulsion of the Moroccans, who had profited by the Algerian disturbance and advanced as far as Tlemcen and Oran.

Meanwhile Istanbul was perfectly well aware that in North Africa, in a different form, the same global conflict was going on that had opposed the Ottoman Empire to that of Charles V. From having been a Greek pirate Khair-ed-Din became a grand admiral of the fleet, and as such he coordinated the grand strategy of total warfare against the Christian empire.

The Spaniards vainly attempted to take advantage of the disorders on the eastern frontiers of Morocco in order to harass Algiers. They also tried to reoccupy the island of Djerba, where after a brief occupation, they met with another setback. It was only after the naval defeat suffered by the Turks at Lepanto that Don Juan of Austria could reoccupy Tunis, and then only for a year (1573). In fact the ambitious Spanish policy of conquering North Africa was a fiasco. Philip II had to acknowledge this when he signed a truce with the Sultan in 1581. Three years before, the King of Portugal, Dom Sebastian, had been killed on Moroccan soil at the head of the finest Portuguese armies in the course of the battle of the Three Kings. His defeat marked the end of Portuguese ambitions in North Africa and for more than a century the surrender of the independence of the Portuguese crown, which was linked to the crown of Spain.

Thus the Ottoman power played a decisive role in eliminating the European threat from the coasts of North Africa and of Egypt. Without exercising authority directly, and

Left: The Barbarossa brothers,
engraving from the work of
Father Dan: "History of Barbary
and its pirates", published in
Amsterdam in 1684.
Barbarossa was the name given
by Europeans to two pirates
of Greek origin, converted to
Islam. Their exploits finally ended
in driving the Spaniards
from the North African coast.
Below: Capture of Tunis by
Charles V in 1535 according to
a 16th century engraving.
The town had fallen to Barbarossa
and the Turks the year
before. After their victory, the
Spaniards remained until 1573.

"Mission of Monsieur Pidou de St. Olon to Marrakesh". France sought
an alliance with the Moroccan ruler Moulay Ismail against Spain and
in 1693 sent Pidou de St. Olon to negotiate a commercial treaty. The
negotiations were not successful. Next year St. Olon wrote an account
of his mission and voyage: "Present state of the Moroccan Empire".

Algiers at the end of the 16th century. After the defeat of Charles V in 1541, Algiers became an Ottoman base for land and sea operations against the Christian empire. The capture of boats and slaves in the Mediterranean continued during the entire 17th century.

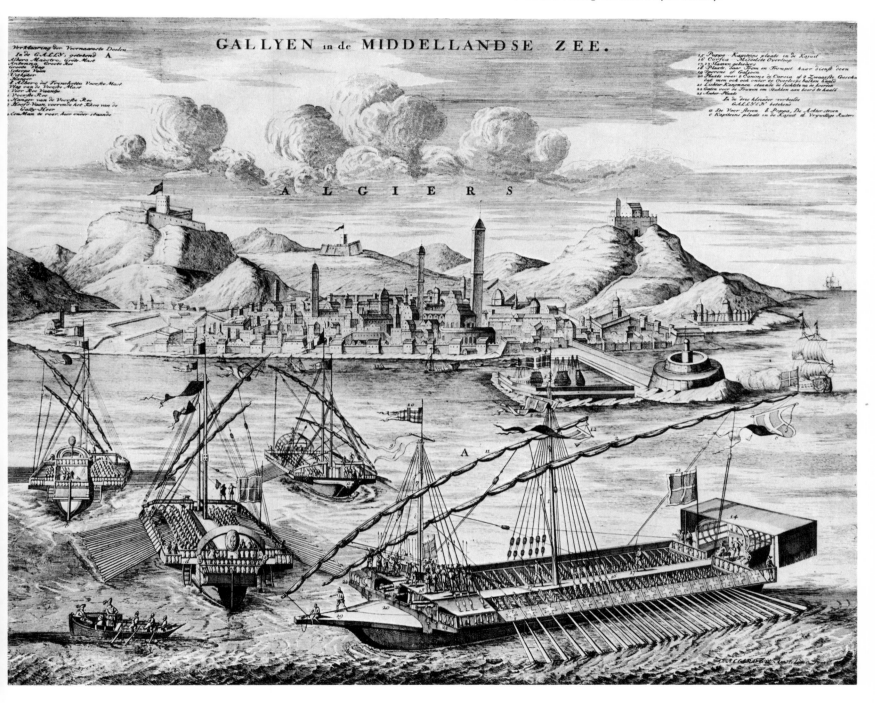

GALLYEN in de MIDDELLANDSE ZEE.

A L G I E R S

Fortress village of Amerdoul high in the East Atlas mountains with communal houses of individual dwellings within barricades. Such citadels protected populations and food stocks. They were built and rebuilt over the centuries and used until the pacification which took place at the beginning of the last century.

Page 102
Dutch expedition and bombardment of Tunis, from Father Dan's book, "History of Barbary" (see page 107). Tunis was taken by Khair-ed-Din (Barbarossa) in 1533 to be passed back and forth several times between Ottoman and Christian hands: the Turks finally reconquered it in 1574 eliminating Europe from North Africa.

The arrival of the Moroccan ambassador Abd-el-Mathi in Vienna in 1783. Though a system of international agreements, by the late 18th century the Cherifian empire had established an international status, even recognized by a fledgling power: the United States.

Page 104
Ruins of Moulay Ismail's palace at Meknes. This powerful Moroccan monarch (1672-1727) ruled an army of mercenaries and made Meknes, the royal city, into an "African Versailles". He used his 25,000 Christian slaves to build palaces, mosques, pools, orchards and fortified gardens. One of the captives was the Sieur Mouëtte (see page 112), a Frenchman who worked on these grandiose schemes and later wrote his memoirs. Shown here are ruins of what are said to have been the stables, large enough for 12,000 horses. More probably they were store-rooms.

The Pyramids of Egypt; engraving from "True Description of the
African countries" by O. Dapper published in Amsterdam in 1668.
Dapper was a Dutch doctor who wrote descriptions of Asia, Assyria,
Palestine and America—all from travellers' accounts; he never went
to any of these places himself. His books were highly successful.

while contenting itself with rather theoretical bonds of allegiance, it was to maintain the Mediterranean equilibrium for more than two centuries, until the era when it grew enfeebled and then vanished in its turn as a result of blows inflicted on it by enemies at home and abroad.

Morocco benefited most directly from the retreat of the Christian powers. When Portugal perished as a North African power together with its King on the field of Tamista in August 1578, modern Morocco was given the groundwork of its present unity. Until then, indeed, the division of Morocco between the principalities of Fez and Marrakesh, the frequent intervention of foreigners in local dynastic squabbles, and the authentic political osmosis that had persisted so long between the Iberian peninsula and the northern sections of the country, had been just so many factors contributing to confusion and separatism.

Moulay Ahmad Mansur, who had been proclaimed sultan on the field of battle, was the real architect of the Moroccan institution of the Makhzen, which has existed down to our own day. He founded the Saadi dynasty, which in spite of frequent crises had turned Morocco into a brilliant and respected state by the beginning of the seventeenth century. Its wealth was based on excellent agricultural productivity, a liberal policy with respect to the foreign merchants settled in the ports of the Atlantic coast, and finally the control of the Sahara routes leading up to the very sources of the opulent Negro empires on the Niger River.(See map on page 332.)

The Saadi dynasty: Moulay Ahmad Mansur

In fact the Moroccan armies, led by the Spanish renegade Jouder, crossed the Sahara, with immense hardship, and occupied Gao and Timbuktu in 1590. The Sonrhai Empire was conquered even though it had been recently converted to Islam. The Moroccans installed a sort of military aristocracy that reigned despotically for almost two centuries. Substantial amounts of gold were confiscated from the wealthy merchants of the African cities whose prosperity and level of civilization have already been described. In the end the clearest result of these incursions was the destruction of a thriving commerce, rooted in the mutual respect of the two parties for each other's independence. The Moroccan tyranny struck a fatal blow at Sudanese Africa, which buried itself in isolation and decadence at about the same time the Kingdom of Abyssinia was doing the same thing and for comparable reasons. Africa of the rivers became an area for exploitation and the recruitment of civil and military manpower for the Moroccan Empire just as coastal Africa was to become one for the Europeans.

Morocco was at its zenith under the Alawite dynasty, which mounted the throne in 1666. Like the Deys of Algiers, the Mamelukes of Egypt, and the Janissaries of Istanbul, Emperor Moulay Ismail based his authority on the use of a military force that was wholly devoted to the interests of power and because of its origins was quite distinct from the native population.

The imperial guard was, in fact, an army of African mercenaries, some from the Sudan (Abid), others from the oases in the extreme south of Morocco (Harratines). Moulay Ismail had his mercenaries take their oath of loyalty on a book written by one of the commentators on the Quran, Sidi Boccari, from which the name of "Alboccari" was given to his personal guard. Having complete control of the situation at home (after numerous civil wars whose cruelty was heavily emphasized by the chroniclers of the period), Moulay Ismail attacked the last of the European enclaves, including Tangiers, where the English had been settled since the marriage of an English king to a Portuguese princess. Tangiers was evacuated in 1684, but the Moroccan ruler was to lose out at Ceuta and to be beaten by the Algerians in his efforts to go beyond Tazza.

France, which was always eager to outflank the Spanish forces and to establish itself in the western Mediterranean, sought an alliance with Moulay Ismail as more than a century before, in the days of Soliman the Magnificent, it had sought one with Khair ed-Din. The Moroccan ambassador at Versailles, Admiral Ben Aissa, conveyed a request by the Moroccan emperor for the hand of the Princess de Conti, the natural daughter of Louis XIV and Mademoiselle de la Vallière. A little later these verses were to be composed on this request:

> Your beauty, great princess,
> Carries its enrapturing features
> unto the most savage places;
>
> Africa capitulates to you
> And the conquests of your eyes
> Go farther than those of Hercules.

The request was considered "unsuitable to the religion, to the piety of the King, and to the difference of customs and habits of the two nations", and the quasi-matrimonial rapprochement came to nothing. In our day there are at Meknes the imposing ruins of an African Versailles built by Christian slaves, which, in common with its model, was an edifice whose extravagance and grandeur made one forget the miseries of its builders.

The brutal firmness of Moulay Ismail kept tribal agitation in check. His successors, lacking the same energy, had to contend with a resurgence of Berber unruliness and above all with the political pretensions of the Negro Moroccan guard, which had become a state within the state. Nevertheless the Moroccan empire did not cease expanding its international trade, especially with England and France. It benefited from the activities of its Jewish population, descendants of the refugees from Spain, which kept in touch with all the great markets of western Europe. British merchants set themselves up in Tangiers, while the French preferred Salé. As for the Portuguese, they lost Mazagan, their last territorial enclave on the Moroccan coast, in 1769. Sultan Sidi Muhammad (1757-1790) gave the Alawite monarchy a new lustre just before the crises of the nineteenth century descended on it.

There is no question but that the existence of prosperous Morocco carrying on lucrative relations with the Christian powers of the west was due to the Mediterranean equilibrium sustained by Ottoman diplomacy and arms. In a letter from Moulay Ismail to Louis XIV, the Emperor of Morocco expressed the interest he had in "the Ottoman house because of our holy law, which it is defending against its enemies, because it holds in its power Egypt and the city that is so holy (Mecca) and is respected by everyone who calls himself Moor and acknowledges one all-powerful God." At that time the common enemy was Austria. In return for the French alliance the Christian slaves were to be bought back; the alliance was crowned in 1777 by a peace treaty between Louis XVI and the Emperor Sidi Muhammad, which finally established a system of legal protection for persons and goods in both countries.

Alliance with France
1777

Through a series of international treaties the Moroccan empire established an international status for itself that was universally acknowledged (by the United States, too, a newly fledged power) from the end of the eighteenth century on.

During this same period the relations of Algiers and Europe were far less happy. Indeed, the struggle between the sea powers, the acts of piracy that accompanied it, including the use by both sides of prisoners as galley-slaves subject to very degrading conditions, reciprocally embittered the relations between Algiers, considered to be a haven for Barbary pirates, and France, the dominant power in the western Mediterranean. France organized several punitive expeditions against the city of Algiers, of which the most important were led by Duquesne in 1682 and Tourville in 1687. The hunt for pirates was a European sport throughout the eighteenth century. In 1775 the Spaniards even repeated the grand attempt at conquest made by Ximenes, as a result of which an army of 30,000 men, equipped with first-rate artillery and led by O'Reilly, was completely crushed by an Algerian army three times as large in which Arabs, Turks and Berbers fought side by side.

In the meantime Egypt, while accepting Ottoman suzerainty, fell once again under the control of the Mamluks. The army, defeated for a short time, had kept intact its personal ties and its *esprit de corps*. After resuming power in 1666, its sole policy had been to milk the country, whose misery in the eighteenth century made a strong impression on all travellers.

Thus, during the two centuries of relative Ottoman predominance, western North Africa as a whole made incontestable progress. But in the background lay two questions that were to haunt the minds of European statesmen from the end of the eighteenth century on—the Algerian question and the Egyptian question.

Two problems: Algeria, Egypt

In both cases a foreign military caste controlled all contact between the outside world and the population of the interior, which was kept down to a level of subsistence in which any conceivable progress was blocked by a deliberate policy of economic and social stagnation.

Such a situation must be assessed in the light of the fact that pre-industrial Europe was scarcely in a position to contribute any elements of transformation itself. Ottoman dominion, both direct and indirect, must be credited with the great religious liberalism of a world that based its principle of unity on the awareness of belonging to a unit of civilization vast enough to tolerate the existence of foreign minorities. These were to play an essential role in contemporary history.

Meanwhile the countries of North Africa that were most directly exposed to the European counter-offensive kept intact not only their identity but their latent forces of resistance.

While the Ottoman Empire was putting an end, directly or indirectly, to the dreams of Iberian hegemony over the North African coast, Portugal was exhausting itself in its efforts to dominate the hinterland of southern Africa. We have seen the fiasco resulting from the expedition launched against the Monomotapa. The Bantu tribes from the north took advantage of the political imbalances brought about by the Portuguese intervention to begin a great movement southwards that was not to come to an end until three centuries later, on the battlefields of Blood River. The Portuguese garrisons of the coast, such as that of Sofala, eked out a precarious existence while following the path marked out by their Arab predecessors intermarrying with the local population.

Their difficulties were due to natural conditions and to the poor communications with the metropolis. It was heightened by the hostility of the population and by the weakness of a commercial monopoly that produced every sort of abuse. It was what disqualified the Portuguese from creating any genuine permanent settlements.

By contrast, their British and Dutch competitors, especially the latter, were able to seize all the advantages inherent in the creation of a base at the end of the known world, at the very place where the waters of the Atlantic mingle with those of the Indian Ocean and where Africa seems to give way to the way-stations leading toward Asia.

Emergence of the Dutch;
Capetown founded
1652

The first Dutch squadron rounded the Cape of Good Hope and sailed for Java in 1595. Dutch merchants, industrious and austere, benefited from the political errors committed by the Spanish monarchy, which from the end of the sixteenth century after the disaster suffered by the Portuguese armies on African soil, found itself responsible for the immense empire the Portuguese explorers had bequeathed it. Amsterdam became the haven of enlightened minds and of skillful bankers. The Netherlands inherited indirectly, as far as Atlantic and Asian trade was concerned, an entire network of intelligence talents, and contacts; it became a worthy successor to the commercial empire of Venice, which had dominated the Mediterranean routes for almost five centuries.

The Dutch surgeon Van Riebeck, after a trip to the East Indies, turned in a report on it to the Amsterdam Chamber of Commerce in 1648 (the year the Treaty of Westphalia put an end to the Thirty Year's War in Europe). Basing himself on the experience of some shipwrecked men from Haarlem, who had been able to live for almost a year in a country with a reputation for hostility, he demonstrated that permanent colonization was possible as well as necessary in the interests of Dutch navigation and commerce.

Capetown was founded in 1652 and governed by Van Riebeck with firmness for ten years. He made treaties with the Hottentot herdsmen, who ceded the Cape Peninsula to the new arrivals, some say by a regular treaty, others say by force. The new colony was organized according to the strict laws of the Dutch East Indies, with the capital in Batavia, which delegated powers to a "Commandant".

In the eyes of the West India Company the principal task of the new colony was the supplying of fresh victuals, vegetables, meat, and drinking water to the crews of its fleet, which lay over at the Cape after the long trip and which soon had to set sail again. In

1657 the colonists were authorized to settle under the protection of the company on the rich land bordering the original community. The tribes roving about the interior were divided into Bushmen—primitive peoples who had not gone beyond stone age techniques—and Hottentots, who understood metallurgy, had relatively good weapons and whose husbandry was perfectly well adapted to the natural conditions. The natives lacked both the material power and the social organization that might have enabled them to resist the effects of physical contact and of commerce with the new colonists, who for their part considered them "stinking, lazy beasts."

But the first German and Dutch landowners needed manpower. Since the raw natives proved hostile or useless, servants from Asia and Africa, who were in fact slaves, had to be imported. The colonists were even too few in number, which is why the Company was favourable in 1686 to the request presented by the Huguenots, expelled from France after the revocation of the Edict of Nantes the year before, who wanted to settle in the new African colony. Two hundred people from France, men, women and children, were transported at the Company's expense to the distant settlement. The heads of families had accepted draconian conditions. The religious question, to be sure, was not raised, but on the other hand they had to resign themselves to abandoning the French language for their children, who had to be educated in the schools of the rigid Dutch community. In one generation this convention was to end in the total fusion of the new arrivals with the initial group. To be sure, the newcomers introduced new crops like the grapevine; socially and intellectually, they raised the general level of the European population. From the middle of the eighteenth century on, the population of the Cape displayed well defined characteristics that distinguished it from its Dutch, Teutonic and French ingredients. A new nation was putting forth its roots in the African soil. Its political and social ideas were strongly marked by the distance, at that time very considerable, that separated it from the sources of its culture and by its co-existence with African tribes that were, on the contrary, very close indeed.

French Huguenots join the Dutch

For almost two centuries the new colony was confined within a limited space. A hundred and fifty years after the first settlement it numbered scarcely 20,000 inhabitants, of whom more than half were non-Europeans of menial status. This relative stagnation accorded with the policy of the Company, which had no desire to meet the expense of any military adventures or expansive explorations in the north. Yet the Dutch, like the Portuguese in Sofala, heard of the Bantu peoples, whose great migrations were underway at the time. A mythical city—Vigiti Magna, capital of gold and copper—was the goal of Simon van der Stel, who went to look for it in 1685 at the head of an expedition that included "57 Europeans, a prince of Macassar and their black servants." It took more than two months to cover a distance that was not more than 75 miles as the crow flies from the Fort of Good Hope.

In 1761 a new convoy (this time made up of 17 Europeans and 70 Hottentot half-breeds) followed the same route, going over the Copper Mountains and reaching Namaqualand west of the great Kalahari desert. It was at this time that the European reconnoitring parties met the scouts of the Bantu peoples that had just crossed the Gonubie River in their descent toward the south. The Orange River, near its mouth, was not reached until 1760, and was not crossed in its upper reaches until 1799.

This frontier, which was slowly pushed northwards, played a decisive role in the formation of the national character. The farmers of the rich valleys of the Cape peninsula implanted on the soil of Africa the Dutch, Teutonic and French way of life in their customs, architecture and sedentary habits. Further to the north, on the lands suitable for stock-breeding, the Europeans who had thrust back the Hottentots tended to take over certain of their habits, which indeed corresponded to the laws of the environment. The stock-breeders, coarse hunters and fighters, soon developed a view of the world quite different from that of their cousins who had remained farmers or winegrowers. The European outposts, on the borders of the tribal lands and exposed to the murderous raids of hostile peoples, played a cardinal role in the formation of the national mentality in Africa, as they did in America. The white man had a natural tendency to curb without mercy the incursions of the Bushmen, who were great cattle-thieves, and to thrust back the Hottentot clans who occupied the best pasture-lands.

Bantu "Kaffirs"

This naturally led to the creation of the equivalent of "commando" groups, which were first organized in the form of light units for reconnoitring and protection. They collided with the vanguard elements of the Bantu migration in 1799, near the Fish River. These were the "Kaffirs" the Portuguese had known of since their expedition toward the heart of the Monomotapa. They were Africans with a highly developed sense of the relations between men and land. Their practices of rotating cultivation and of mixed farming were to give their European rivals the mistaken impression empty and ownerless land was available, when these in fact formed part of a complex system. The occupation of these lands by European settlers was bound to be a source of conflict.

Furthermore, the Bantus were militarily organized, with excellent arms. From the second half of the eighteenth century on, the north-east frontier (the Zuurveld) was a danger zone. The European colonists often started hostilities themselves. They lived in constant fear of a Bushmen or Kaffir raid that would destroy their stock and harvests and massacre their families. They often preferred forestalling this, by acting in advance, to inspire in their African neighbours a fear they thought salutary.

The officials of the company, however, who lived in the sheltered hierarchical security of Capetown, were opposed to any expensive territorial adventures. Thus the Amsterdam stockholders had to watch the financial decline of a settlement that was becoming far too expensive just at the time the French and English were busily confiscating in their turn the lucrative trade of the Indies route.

Vicissitudes of the Cape Colony

The European population had turned its back on the sea, and now, in a spirit of headstrong independence, was going on toward the conquest of the great expanses of land in the north. The other part of the population, which depended on the contrary on international trade, was hostile to all adventure. It had an obscure premonition that made it mistrustful of the African reactions to incursions that were becoming bolder and bolder. In addition, the Cape colony was not really prosperous. In the world struggle between France and England, the Cape was just one more pawn. Without itself becoming an actual target of conquest, it had to welcome the noisy crews of the belligerents arriving and departing according to the vicissitudes of a struggle whose outcome would be quite uncertain for a long time. In fact the commercial and political decline of Holland in the course of the eighteenth century was translated into the growing isolation of Cape Colony. The thrusts toward the north, which went as far as Delagoa Bay and even Mauritius (reoccupied by the French in 1715), were mere fleeting episodes. Further northwards the Arabs, during the eighteenth century, had gradually reconquered their settlements on the east coast by pushing the Portuguese back to their starting points on Mozambique and to the few missions and commercial settlements that had been left over from the great attack on the Monomotapa.

In 1791 The Indies Company abandoned Cape Colony to its fate. Revolutionary ideas had made their way to this African outpost of European civilization. The Burghers of the Cape showed themselves to be Francophiles, by choice rather than necessity. In the end Great Britain, taking as its authority the treaties linking it to the House of Orange in exile, took possession in its name of the Dutch bases in Africa and in Asia. In September 1795 the Cape became British, and by August 1796 all resistance in the colony had come to an end.

The South African question had come into being.

South African village, from "Ancient and Modern Costumes-Africa" by Ferrario, published in Milan, 1827.

Left: "The Hottentot Woman", from "Voyages of Monsieur Le Vaillant into the interior of Africa (1781-1785). This French explorer charted the region between the Cape and the Orange River. His caravan included half-caste Hottentots from the Cape Colony. During the expedition these encountered other Hottentots, including women, who wanted to join the group. Monsieur Le Vaillant, however, noticed "a certain slackening in the standards of service" after the reunion, so refused to take them along. He made one exception: a woman who learnt to milk the goats of the expedition and do his laundry, while pursuing an idyll with one of the half-castes.

Another plate from Peter Kolb's "Description of the Cape of Good Hope". The early Dutch settlers of the Cape Colony met Hottentots and Bushmen roving in the interior and, further north, Bantus and Kaffas. The later were farmers who practiced a complex form of crop rotation and were very attached to the land.

Page 114
A plate from Peter Kolb's "Description of the Cape of Good Hope", 1719, showing how huts were assembled from woven panels in a primitive form of pre-fabrication. Peter Kolb was sent to South Africa by the Privy Councillor of the King of Prussia to study the native tribes, particularly the Hottentots. He remained in the Cape a decade.

British envoys received by the Ashanti king (Ghana) in 1817, from a book published two years later entitled « Mission from Cape Coast Castle to Ashanti » by T.E. Bowdich. Because of inter-tribal warfare the British trading post at Cape Coast Castle (Gold Coast) had been blocked. A British mission was therefore despatched, which conciliated the Ashanti king and drew up a commercial treaty.

The European Interregnum

Major events
and personalities in other parts of the world
1800 - 1914

1800	Fulton invents the steam boat
1804	Napoleon becomes Emperor
1805	Battles of Trafalgar and Austerlitz
1807	The Fifth Symphony of Beethoven is first performed
1812	Napoleon's retreat from Russia
1814	Stevenson invents the locomotive
1815	Waterloo. Treaty of Vienna
1821-1829	Greece liberated from the Turks
1829	Niepce and Daguerre invent photography
1770-1831	Hegel
1749-1832	Goethe
1837	Queen Victoria succeeds to the throne
1843	Morse invents the telegraph
1848	Revolutions in France Germany and Hungary Karl Marx publishes in London the "Manifesto of the Communist Party"
1850	Richard Wagner: "Lohengrin"
1852	Napoleon III becomes Emperor of the French
1854-1856	Crimean War
1859	Darwin publishes "The Origin of Species"
1861	Victor-Emmanuel, first king of unified Italy. Abraham Lincoln elected president of the U.S.A.
1861-1865	American Civil War
1869	Publication of "War and Peace", by Count Leon Tolstoï
1870-1871	Franco-Prussian War. German Unity
1876	Alexander Graham Bell invents the telephone
1877	Queen Victoria becomes Empress of India
1878-1881	Publication of "Crime and Punishment" by Feodor Dostoievsky
1879	Edison perfects the modern light bulb.
1883-1884	Nietzsche, one of the masters of modern philosophical thinking, publishes "Thus spake Zarathustra"
1802-1885	Victor Hugo
1887	First British Commonwealth Conference
1891	The papal encyclical "Rerum Novarum" defines the position of the Catholic Church in relation to workers and industrial society
1831-1892	Walt Whitman
1893	Foundation of the British Labour Party
1894-1895	Japanese war with China.
1896	Roentgen finds the X-rays
1897	In France, Clement Ader builds the machine which is generally considered as the first airplane
1895-1898	War in the West Indies. Cuba, Philipines and Porto-Rico defeat the Spaniards with the help of the United States
1898	The Lumiere Brothers show the first movies in Paris
1899-1901	The Boxer rebellion in China
1900-1903	First flights of the Wright brothers
1904-1905	Russo-Japanese War.
1909	First cross-Channel flight by Louis Blériot
1912	China becomes a republic
1912	Einstein publishes the Theory of Relativity
1913	Publication of "Swann's Way" by Marcel Proust

Chapter 13
The Neglected Continent

The three centuries following the great leap forward of the Portuguese explorers were a period of stagnation in the evolution of European and Asian influences on the African continent. North Africa and Egypt, in the very elastic framework of the Ottoman Empire and thanks to the diversionary offensives in Europe, gradually acquired a quasi-modern aspect. In this respect a glance at the maps of the epoch is revealing. From west to east, Morocco, Algeria, Tunisia, Tripoli and Cyrenaica (known as Barca) as well as Egypt had frontiers that were scarcely different from those of today.

In contrast, Africa south of the Sahara remained almost unknown. In going from north to south, beginning at Cape Verde, the principal European settlements in the eighteenth century were the following: at the mouth of the Senegal River Fort St-Louis was founded in 1700 by the French, who were also settled in the Isle of Gorée, which they had taken from the Portuguese in 1667. French traders had merchants settled in Rufisque, Joa and Arguin. The English controlled the mouth of the Gambia River and the sheltered harbour of Sierra Leone (where the city of Freetown was soon to be created). All along the coast of the Gulf of Guinea—the Coast of Grain (present-day Liberia), the Ivory Coast, the Gold Coast (present-day Ghana), the Slave Coast (present-day Togo and Dahomey), and Benin, which covers Nigeria west and east and the present-day Cameroons—there was a succession of fortified British, French, Dutch and Scandinavian settlements. The Spaniards were in occupation of the island of Fernando Po. The Portuguese had made the isles of Sao Tomé and Principé the principal relay point in their trade routes to Brazil.

European settlements

South of the mouth of the Congo River, the towns of St-Paul de Loanda and Benguala, founded in 1576 and 1617 respectively, were the only European settlements that looked like cities and not like mere fortresses. We already know that Capetown was the only European base at the southern tip of the continent.

The European powers were locked in implacable rivalry all along this coast. Substantial economic interests were at stake. The prosperity of the New World, that is, the two Americas, depended in large part on the slave trade. Bernardin de Saint-Pierre gave a cameo definition of this traffic, which reached its peak in the middle of the eighteenth century: "America was depopulated in order to provide a land to plant coffee and sugar on. Africa was depopulated in order to provide a nation to grow them."

In this era England seemed to be the chief beneficiary of the struggle for maritime and commercial supremacy in the Atlantic. In forty years the Royal African Company transported 100,000 slaves, carrying on a business estimated at more than a million and a half pounds sterling and allowing the British Treasury to strike a half-million "guineas" in gold. Questions concerning the trade between Africa and America were at the centre of its diplomatic preoccupations. In the various treaties it made with Portugal, Spain and France a point was always made of inserting the necessary arrangements for establishing a *de facto* monopoly on the African trade. France, which had been its chief rival, was practically eliminated.

Immense profits were amassed; certain historians find in them the origin of the capital that at the beginning of the nineteenth century was to permit the genesis and then the boom of industry in western Europe. Nevertheless far-sighted men understood that the status of this immense continent, which seemed reduced by an unhappy fate to playing the role of a country of slaves, was abnormal economically as well as morally.

An English geographer writing in 1779 (William Guthrie) made the point that "the situation of Africa for trade is extremely favourable, since it is located at the centre of the globe and thus has much closer communications with Asia and America than these two have with each other... Yet Africa, even though it represents a quarter of the inhabited planet, and seems to possess inexhaustible treasures and is capable, with some indispensable improvements, of producing in great abundance things that are delicious as well as useful, seems almost entirely neglected not only by the natives but also by the most civilized Europeans who have settled there, like the Portuguese."

A knowledge of the history of the states of North Africa, Egypt, and Ethiopia, which came to Europeans from classical authors as well as from the accounts of Leo Africanus, confirms the impression that the whole continent suffered a decline. One of the reasons for this might well be the debasing traffic of which Africa, in the west as well as in the east, was the principal victim.

The debate on the abolition of slavery that came into the open toward the middle of the eighteenth century is somewhat reminiscent of the great metaphysical discussion in the fourteenth and fifteenth centuries on the existence of branches of mankind at the Antipodes.

The philosophical and scientific thought of the West was preparing itself to pass through a new stage. In two centuries it crossed the immense distance between the anthropocentric idea of a mobile sun turning around a fixed planet, of which man was at once the centre and the ultimate purpose, and the idea of an eternal universe dominated only by an eternal God, in which the earth is only one planet among many. In Guthrie's fine phrase, the universe came to appear to be "thousands and thousands of suns, multiplied to infinity, scattered all around us, separated from each other by vast distances, surrounded by ten thousand times ten thousand other worlds all moving rapidly yet calmly, regularly, and harmoniously, and holding steadily to the ways laid down for them; and all these worlds were peopled by myriads of intelligent beings dedicated to an infinite progression toward perfection and happiness."

Progress of geographical science

This more accurate estimate of the place occupied by the earth in the universe was added to by a growing desire to increase our information about the earth itself. Thanks to the advances in mathematical studies, geographical science made some decisive progress in the eighteenth century. The errors in latitude and longitude made by the ancients and repeated on the basis of their writings in the atlases of the Middle Ages and the Renaissance were gradually rectified. With the aid of Cassini's and Picard's tables navigators on the high seas could take their astronomical bearings. The shortcomings in calculus that had given rise to inaccurate extrapolations on the shape of the continents were corrected. Maps were remade. In 1700 Delisle, the father of modern geography, published his map of the world, which improved Sanson's and Mercator's projections. His disciple d'Anville, geographer to the king, was awarded the highest honours; his map of Italy remained a model of the kind. At this same time Edmund Halley, a disciple of Newton's, combined to a degree rarely equalled the knowledge of the mathematician and hydrographer and the boldness of the navigator. Not only did he lay down the foundations of astronomical calculus (he was the first to predict the course of the planet Venus), but he invented the theory of magnetic variations. Thanks to him Captain Cook was able to embark on his first voyage. A little later, Arctic and Antarctic voyages were guided by his theories.

The cumulative effects of these scientific discoveries, of the technical progress made in navigation, and of the appearance of new sources of energy were to alter Europe's relations with the other continents.

Even before the independence movements in North America had raised the question in the political domain of the "colonial pact," enlightened European opinion was critically re-examining the doctrine of the unrestricted dominion of the great centers over their colonies, and the legitimacy of transporting human beings to ensure the prosperity of those colonies. If, in England, an individual could enjoy rights guaranteed by custom and the laws of the kingdom, it might well be wondered why an inhabitant of Africa should be subjected to such an indignity as slavery. A powerful movement of opinion supported the "abolitionist" movement, which, in the person of Fox, found an eloquent advocate in the British Parliament. Wilberforce, Granville Sharp, Macaulay and Clarkson placed themselves in the service of the new cause. In France, it was Montesquieu, Voltaire and the Abbé Reynal (in his celebrated history of the two Indias) who led the intellectuals' offensive against the institution to which so many interests were tied. The French Revolution, by carrying, at least on the level of theory, to its most extreme consequences the theory of the rights of man and of the fundamental nature of the principle of equality, had shattering effects in the Antilles and in Spanish America, which were great users of African manpower.

The "abolitionist" movement in England and France

Nevertheless the most direct consequence of the French Revolution was to be found in a new European civil war, into which the chief rivals in the race for African wealth poured all their ressources. The principle of the draft, initiated by revolutionary France, lent a new dimension to land warfare. At sea, England, in spite of the setback it had suffered in the course of the American war of Independence, remained the undisputed mistress of the Atlantic and Indian Oceans. In fact, its chief adversary, Napoleon, was well aware that trade with the East Indies, of which the English had a monopoly, was the key to British wealth and to Britain's inexhaustible capacity for resistance. Throughout the nineteenth century and the first half of the twentieth century the Indies route was to play for England the same obsessive role it had played for the Portuguese of the sixteenth century, the Dutch of the seventeenth, and the French of the eighteenth century. Since the American Colonies had been lost and Spain and Portugal still controlled South America, England, which lived by international trade, could not tolerate being excluded from the African way-stations to the east, whether it was a question of the northern gate to the Red Sea, that is, Egypt, or the southern gate to the Indian Ocean, that is, the Cape.

In other words, London's new geopolitical views harmonized with the moral preoccupations of the British people. No British possession of any consequence benefited directly any longer from the slave trade. Thus the attempts to explore the African land routes corresponded both to the great movement of curiosity about geography that marked the end of the eighteenth century and to the pressure of an enlightened public opinion, which wanted to destroy the slave trade to the Americas by controlling the maritime routes and the other trade, still more cruel, that depopulated central Africa in favour of eastern Africa and the Arabian Peninsula.

The "African Association," founded in 1788 under the chairmanship of Sir Joseph Banks, set itself commercial, scientific, and humanitarian goals. It was a question first of all of discovering the tributaries leading to the Niger River, which was still the object of confused ideas, a mixture of ancient accounts of the classical writers and of the Muslim travellers. The Europe of the Enlightenment had to wash itself clean of the reproach of having remained ignorant "of such an important portion of the globe." It was known or believed that the Niger River flowed from east to west. Yet it was not known whether it discharged on the Atlantic coast or lost itself in the marshlands of the Nile Valley. Nothing was known of the Congo River, the Zaire of the Portuguese, upriver from the great rapids. Nothing was known of the course of the Zambezi except what was said by some merchants from Mozambique. Only the sources of the Blue Nile had been explored, by Bruce in 1770, in a bold trip into the heart of Ethiopia starting from the coast of the Red Sea. For that matter Bruce had merely repeated the exploit of the seventeenth century Jesuits who for a brief moment thought they might lead the Coptic Church back to Rome. Nor was anything known of the Sahara routes that went from Morocco to the legendary city of Timbuktu and that went from Tripoli across the oases of Fezzan as far as the Kingdom of the Bornu and the Kanem and beyond as far as the Hausa Empire.

It was England, the great victor of the revolutionary wars instigated by France in 1789 and their Napoleonic aftermath, that was best prepared at first to cross this new frontier. To be sure, the first expeditions, including those of Mungo Park, preceded Waterloo by almost twenty years. But real means were to be given the pioneers only when Europe, abandoning civil war, accepted peaceful co-existence. After 1815 the energies and the capital released by eliminating the military burden could turn toward new worlds for constructive purposes. The Congress of Vienna had given the support in principle of the European general agreement to abolish the slave trade (though not to the suppression of the institution as such, which was to come later). France rallied to the new principles and so repaired the calamitous mistake made in Haiti where a French army had been sent to be defeated in its attempt to restore the slavery abolished by the revolution of the Friends of the Blacks. Portugal and Spain accepted the new policy, contributing substantial indemnities.

Like their Portuguese predecessors of the fifteenth century, though for different reasons, the new explorers could set out on the dangerous paths of the African bush, deserts and jungles with a good conscience.

Negre Anzikos armé en guerre.

Femme de la Suite du Roÿ de Loango.

Gentilhomme du Roÿaume d'Aardra

Esclave Favori du Roi de Congo.

The Ardra coast, Gulf of Guinea and its foreign trading posts (English, Dutch, French and Portuguese) from a watercolor by Desmarchais, 1725, illustrating his "Voyage to Guinea". European trading posts were established in Xavier, capital of the Juda kingdom. Shown here, according to the 18th century description, are the king's palace and residence of the European traders, 12 canons and a courtyard where natives and white men alike came to pay taxes to the king. Manuscript from the Bibliothèque Nationale, Paris.

Page 125
Anonymous portrait of the Scottish explorer James Bruce. His "Travels to Discover the Sources of the Nile in the Years 1768-1773" describes how he found the sources of the Blue Nile by leaving the Red Sea coast and crossing Ethiopia. At that time nothing was known of the course of the Zambezi, the Niger or the Congo rivers.

peint par P. J. Redouté.

In the minutes of a meeting of the Association for the "encouragement of the discovery of the interior portions of Africa," held in 1788, the following remarks may be read: "In spite of the progress made in the exploration of the coasts and the frontiers of this vast continent, the map of the interior regions is still a great white spot on which the geographer, basing himself on the authority of Leo Africanus and Idrissi the Nubian, has traced out with an uncertain hand a few names of unexplored rivers and doubtful nations." The Europe of the enlightened philosophers and of knowledgeable merchants wanted in fact to find the secret of the transcontinental African trade routes just as the Portuguese of the sixteenth century had hoped to rediscover a new route to the Indies. According to the reports of the consuls, "the shores of the Nile from Alexandria to Cairo, and the Kingdom of the Hausa enjoyed a moderate monarchic regime administered by written laws and recognizing property rights."

The Ancients had had a theory, taken up again by the Muslims, according to which the Niger River represented a horizontal stroke across Africa at the height of the fifteenth parallel: if this was accepted two access routes had to be taken by explorers. The first, leaving from Tripoli, went toward Fezzan as far as Agades and Timbuktu. It was this one that an attempt was made to take, under the aegis of the Association, by Lucas. He did not succeed in getting beyond Misurata (1789) because of an Arab revolt against the Pasha of Tripoli (put under the nominal allegiance of the Ottoman Empire). The second one left the European settlements of the western coast (Senegal and Gambia) and turned eastwards, following the commercial highways of the "Moors," that is the Muslims of various races who monopolized the exchanges between east and west.

Mungo Park has the deathless honour of having forced the western gate of a continent jealously garded by its rulers. This Scottish surgeon, who was already familiar with the orient, accepted the mission offered him by the Association after the failure of Major Houghton, a member of the British garrison of Gambia who had disappeared in 1790 in the Bambuk kingdom. The only team he had was a servant, a "boy," two donkeys and a horse. The country he wanted to explore was that of the Mandingos (an ethnic and linguistic group with various branches, including the Bambaras, who ruled the middle reaches of the Niger River, and the Malinkes, who had settled along its upper reaches). These were Africans who were often islamized and were themselves masters of servile castes whose condition was little better than that of the "Antilles slaves." The lucrative trade between the Europeans of the Coast and the Africans of the interior had not changed since the sixteenth century. Europe exported firearms and ammunition, alcohol, fabrics, and trinkets. Africa exported slaves, gold-dust, ivory, honey, and skins. In addition, the merchant castes were in control of the salt traffic that branched out either from the sea or from the rock-salt mines in the heart of the Sahara.

At the cost of a myriad of afflictions and a painful captivity in the hands of rapacious merchants who were fearful (quite rightly, for that matter) of possible competition, Mungo Park reached the Niger at Segu on 20 July 1796. This is how he describes

The African interior remained unknown

Page 126
The blue lotus of Egypt, *Nymphea coerulea*, by the famous painter of roses, P. J. Redouté (1759-1840). Redouté is best known for his plates reproducing the roses of Malmaison for Empress Josephine. His brother produced many plates for the Natural History section of the "Description of Egypt" published in France after Napoleon's expedition to Egypt. This vellum, in fact, closely resembles an engraving of the same plant done by the brother for "Description of Egypt." Muséum d'Histoire Naturelle, Paris.

his impressions: "I saw with infinite pleasure the great object of my mission—the long-sought-for majestic Niger, glittering to the morning sun." The Sudanese civilization was just as thriving as had been said: "The sight of this extended city, the numerous vessels strung out along the river, the dense crowds, the flourishing state of the country round about, all that gives an impression of civilization and of munificence that I had scarcely expected to find in the heart of Africa." (See map on page 331.)

Mungo Park came back from Segu following for most of his trip a caravan of slaves brought from the interior toward the coast by the Bushrens (islamized Mandingos). He was to try to resume the same route after a few years of impatient retreat in Scotland. The instructions given him in 1805 authorized him to draft 45 men from the British garrison in Gorée and set as his goal: to reconnoitre the course of the river to its furthest reaches, to establish relations with the diverse nations of the shores of the Niger, and finally to return either toward the Atlantic or as far as Cairo by taking the route leading to Tripoli. The budget of the expedition was fixed at £ 5,000. The expedition was a total fiasco. The soldiers all died of fever; Mungo Park, accompanied by the four surviving Europeans was attacked by the river-dwellers and killed in November 1805.

Investigating the North-South route

Eighteen years later the north-south route was traversed from the Mediterranean to Lake Chad. After Frederick Horneman, who enjoyed the protection of the Association as well as that of Bonaparte, at that time ruler of Egypt and got no further than Murzuk, Ritchie and Captain Lyon, Dr. Oulney, Lieutenant Clapperton and Major Dunham reached Bornu and finally Lake Chad on 4 February 1823. Echoing Mungo Park, Dunham expressed the emotion he felt at the vision that had inspired the ancients via the legendary accounts, and the moderns via the Muslim geographers. "The great Lake Chad, sparkling beneath the golden rays of the sun at its zenith, appeared a mile away from the place where we were encamped. I considered this lake the key to the principal goal of our exploration, and I could not restrain myself from silently imploring the unfailing protection of Heaven, which had allowed us to advance so far in full health and vigour until our mission was accomplished." Thus there was resolved a part of the enigma that had haunted Europe ever since it had begun casting its inquisitive gaze at Africa. The Niger does not flow into the central lake and the Nile did not seem to emerge from it at all. The region taken in by the Chad, the Chari and the Logone, was at this time the theatre of constant dissension between the "Arabs" and the Fulani, who probably arrived from the northeast, were on the move and vigorously expanding westwards. Dunham observed that "a war of extermination had been underway for years between the Bornu and the Baguirmi... The courts of enemy sultans are heavily loaded with eunuchs who were former prisoners of war."

His companion, Clapperton, braving the dangers of a war-torn region reached Kano, the capital of the Hausa Kingdom. He was disappointed by the mediocrity of the great commercial city, whose reputation had become as legendary as that of Timbuktu. Once again the accounts of the Muslim writers and travellers had proved to be exaggerated. The crowd was too busy to pay any attention at all to the explorer, who had put on the resplendent uniform of a naval officer. But the wares imported by the local merchants showed that Kano was well situated at the cross-roads of the trade routes coming from the north and those that went to the European way-stations of the Atlantic coast. Clapperton heard of the southward navigation shipping on the Niger River. The Sultan of Sokoto himself drew for him on the sand the course of the "Quarra River, which goes into the sea at Fundah." The preoccupation of the Fulani sultans was to keep control over the trade routes. They thought they had an undeniable right to the lands of the south, which then belonged to the Infidels. In fact, the Islamized sultanates of the north were in a perpetual state of war with each other and also with the pagan tribes that they were trying to thrust toward the south or to enslave.

Clapperton returned to England by land as far as Tripoli. Lord Bathurst sent him back at the head of a new expedition in December 1825; this time it left from the Atlantic coast. He started out from Badagri, near the city of Lagos, accompanied by Pearce, Dr. Morrison and Houston. A distinguished assistant followed him—Richard Lander. They crossed the Yoruba country and once again met Sultan Bello, still at war with the Sheikh of the Bornu. This trip did not settle the problem of the Niger's course. It was Richard Lander to whom the honour fell of the discovery that was completely to transform the fate of the people of the Gulf of Guinea. After the death of Clapperton in 1827 Lander was authorized to start out again for the south by the usual land route. He landed at Badagri, accompanied by his brother, on 31 March 1830, met the river at Bussa and in two little boats embarked on the descent of the Niger. The two men reached the coast at Brasstown in November 1830, not without having met with varying reactions on the part of the river-dwellers, who proved to be more and more avid and mercenary the nearer the explorers got to the zone of the lower river, which was already fully exploited by European merchants trade and their African intermediaries.

Richard Lander and the course of the Niger

In July 1831 Lander went back to England where the Royal Geographical Society bestowed its gold medal on him. The main mystery of African geography was now cleared up. The Niger flows toward the east, then turns squarely southwards, to come out on the coast behind the Gulf of Guinea. The great trading zone dominated by the islamized tribes on the rim of the great desert and the zone created by Europeans in the "rivers of the south" had a natural link in the regions that were not yet under any political organization of kingdoms recognized by Europeans. Almost half a century was to go by before European influences bound them in a common political structure.

The route from Tripoli to Kano via Fezzan was now well known, but Europeans still had to discover the other traditional caravan route, which, from the North African coast via the austere depths of the Sahara, led to Timbuktu, the mysterious. Major Laing was the first to reach the mythical city on 18 August 1826, to be assassinated a few weeks later on the way to Segu.

Here too the southern gate seemed easier to get through than the northern. René Caillé, with no official support and carrying nothing but some trading goods, yet animated by a real passion for discovery comparable to that of Clapperton and Lander, went north, leaving from the Gulf of Guinea in April 1827. Passing himself off as an Arab going back to Mecca after a long captivity in Egypt, he crossed the Fulani emirates of the Futa-Djallon, passed through Kankan, and then, after a lengthy stay in the Bambara country, reached the Niger at Djenné on 25 March 1828. He went up the river in one of the large fragile boats that transported the products whose transport had made the commerce of the Niger valley for many centuries—rice, millet, butter, honey, etc.

René Caillé and Timbuktu the mysterious 1847

On 20 April he crossed the short road that links Timbuktu and the river in the dry season. The mysterious city that had intrigued the imagination of European merchants since the Renaissance "at first sight showed nothing more than a mass of ill-looking houses built of earth. Nothing could be seen on the horizon in any direction but vast plains of yellowish sand. The deepest silence prevailed. Not even the cry of a bird could be heard. ...Yet there was something impressive in the look of this great city set up in the midst of the sands. The difficulties its builders must have endured cannot fail to excite the imagination." The city seemed scarcely to have changed in its social or racial composition or in its commerce since the description left of it by Leo Africanus. The influence of "Barbery," that is, of North Africa and more particularly of Morocco, was predominant in the religion, language, and customs. The "Moors" co-existed there with the Blacks, themselves Islamized. Goods could be found that had come from Europe by the Sahara routes just as the foodstuffs had come from the south by the Niger River. The slave trade aimed at North Africa was still thriving. The preoccupation of the Negro, Berber, and Arab ruling classes was exclusively business. Through either ignorance or mistrust, the merchants gave René Caillé nothing but misinformation on the course of the great river. The city continued to live in terror of an attack by the Tuaregs. Here too the situation did not seem to have changed since the sixteenth century. Caillé left Timbuktu on 4 May 1828, following the traditional caravan route, which passed by El-Arawan, Bir el-Telig, Mayara, Tafiket, Fez and Tangiers.

Europe was now familiar with the traditional route of Saharan trade. At the same time it was aware of the enormous material and political difficulties involved. Both nature and mankind united in scattering hardships of every kind from the Mediterranean to the Niger, as well as defenses in depth that were only to be really overcome with the aid of superior techniques in arms and transport.

Heinrich Barth:
from Tripoli to Timbuktu

The feat of René Caillé, who made his way through an enemy world with no arms other than his courage and determination to succeed was not repeated until twenty-two years later, by a German scholar Heinrich Barth, who left Tripoli to cross the various sultanates of present-day northern Nigeria and finally reached Timbuktu from Sokoto. He spent more than eight months in the mysterious city and returned to Tripoli: he had spent five years all told below the Sahara. In the account of his adventures (which had an enormous commercial success in a Europe that was now completely concentrated on expansion), he insisted that he had attained his goal practically without any means and at the mercy of the unpredictable reactions of the local chieftains, who were anxious to keep the secret of the trade routes. He expressed his satisfaction "at feeling that he had disclosed to the scientific public of Europe an extremely broad part of the closed world of Africa and had made it not only fairly well known but had also initiated regular communications between Europeans and these regions."

Thus the names of Mungo Park, Clapperton, Lander, Caillé and Barth are milestones on the path leading Europe and Nigerian Africa out of their nearly complete ignorance of each other at the end of the eighteenth century into the relative familiarity that encouraged them to enter into commercial and political relations in the second half of the nineteenth century. In addition, steamships were to allow for a more systematic exploration of the only river route toward the interior that emptied into the Gulf of Guinea. (See map on page 331.)

The replacement of "the degrading and immoral traffic" (in slaves) by legitimate trade (goods in exchange for goods) became a powerful incentive, with the advantage of combining business and ethics. When McGregor Laird organized the first trip up the Niger in steamships in 1832, he compared the river with the Rhine and the Danube, with the Mississippi and the Orinoco. The highway into the interior of Africa "offered merchants a boundless field for their enterprises, manufacturers a broad market for their products, and youth the irresistible charm of novelty, danger and adventure".

Yet Laird's effort was a failure, as had been the first expedition up the Niger which ended in a total fiasco, when Richard Lander and a number of his companions perished. It was not until 1854 that William Balfour Baikie, aboard the *Pleiade*, succeeded in going up the Niger to where it joined with the Benoue, just at the same time that Barth was taking the northern route toward Tripoli. This success cancelled out the failure of McGregor Laird and that of his unfortunate successors Trotter, Allen and Thompson, whose crew was to die of fever while trying to found a model farm along the banks of the river. Baikie (who for the first time used a boat with a propeller) distributed quinine to his companions and formulated a precept that should have been followed by his successors in Nigeria: "We must go into Africa as we would into other foreign countries, as visitors, as merchants, or as planters, while doing our best to improve the race by advice and by example, but avoiding any interference or any demonstration of physical force."

Pages 132-133

View of the Cabende mountain, and the funeral of a chieftain from "Voyage to the West African Coast Made in 1786 and 1787" by M. de Grandpré, French naval officer. Grandpré's book describes "customs, habits, governmental laws and the slave trade as it was practiced until the French Revolution". The Cabende mountain is near the mouth of the Congo river.

Right: a miniature of Mungo Park after Edrige and, below, an engraving from his book "Travels in the Interior Districts of Africa in the Years 1795, 1796 and 1797". This Scottish surgeon set off to investigate the course of the Niger river for the British "Africa Association" with only a servant, a "boy", two donkeys and a horse. After incredible adventures, he managed to reach the Niger at Segu; he died on a second expedition.

Chapter 15
The Secret of the Great Lakes

In Nigerian Africa it is men, more than nature, that constitute the obstacle. Persuasion is more important than conquest, and business goes on there even though it may deal with objects that are disapproved of.

But things are quite different in the Africa of the jungle, the savannahs, and the inaccessible highlands. No navigable route leaving the coast goes in there. Explorers had to move on foot. Even when they discovered navigable stretches in the waterways they had to carry their vessels either whole or disassembled in order to avoid the impassible rapids. With no means of communication with the outside world, they melted away into the brush or the jungle without anyone knowing whether they were alive or dead. Months or years later they would reappear, haggard visitors from another world. They came in contact with people who saw in a stranger primarily a potential enemy. They had to overcome a world of nature that was hostile to man in the difficulties of the terrain as well as because of the ferocious revolt of animal and vegetable life against its future conqueror. Unknown diseases might reduce them to total destruction through fever and madness. Extreme climatic conditions, from total drought to torrential rains, made whole regions physically impassable for months on end. The formidable defenses of this sealed off universe were added to by the exasperation of the subjugated peoples in the approach areas caused by the merciless cruelties of the slave-traders.

The sealed-off universe

If a lone man could cope with such challenges only with difficulty, any large expedition laboured under greater disadvantage. The necessity of portage, that is, the use of men as beasts of burden, represented a supplementary factor of enmity and impoverishment for central Africa. The ancient form of bondage, slavery, was soon succeeded by a new one. The more expeditions leaving the coast weighed themselves down with baggage and arms, the more manpower they had to pay for. To the Africans of the interior the European infiltration often appeared to be no more than an immense burden. The African auxiliaries of the great expeditions, whether volunteers or not, would turn up in territories often unknown and hostile. Men of the highlands, used to endless horizons, had to cross damp and sombre valleys: men of the plains or coastal regions had to clamber up difficult paths to completely unaccustomed altitudes. Their badly dressed bodies were exposed to variations in temperature that were often fatal. Though Africans, the other Africans they met were completely alien to them in language, race, and religion, and they defended themselves against them as they did against the white man.

In the magnificent adventure of the opening up of the eastern and southern gates of Africa men of all races were intimately associated in the same sacrifice, of whose fraternal secret the ancient soil of Africa, hitherto inviolate, was all too often the guardian.

David Livingstone belongs to the tradition initiated by Mungo Park and carried on by Caillé, Lander, Baikie and others. Born in 1813, that is, eight years after Park's death, Livingstone came to his end in the heart of Africa in 1873. Twelve years later the Conference of Berlin irrevocably marked the transition from the era of Africa's isolation to that of its entry into international life, with all its dangers but also with all its incalculable advantages.

A missionary, Livingstone devoted his life to the redemption of African humanity. His disinterestedness and his total courage as well as his talent and the simplicity with which he told of his extraordinary adventures, made him the spokesman of Africa and of the African man in the eyes of a Europe that was embarking on the era of industrial expansion.

In 1843 he was sent out to South Africa as a physician by the London Missionary Association, which instructed him to go up north of the Orange River. Indeed, the time seemed to have come for the Europeans settled in South Africa to strike out for the spiritual conquest of the peoples hitherto regarded by the Boer colonists as no more than beasts of prey to exterminate or serfs to be enslaved. At this point it was primarily a question of the Bushmen and Hottentots, who were progressively thrust back northwards from the Cape region by the European advance.

Scholars like William Burchell or Galton, missionaries like Campbell, (the first to get to Bechuanaland) or Moffat (Livingstone's father-in-law), merchants like Scoon, McLuckie and Young (who reached the site of Pretoria), sportsmen like Harris (who got to the Limpopo), were the pioneers of the opening up of southern Africa during the first half of the nineteenth century.

After crossing the Kalahari Desert and reaching Lake Ngami in the upper basin of the Oko-Vanggo River, Livingstone arrived at the middle reaches of the Zambezi River at Sesheke; then, in the course of a third voyage, he went up the valley of the Zambezi, crossed the region of the upper basin of the Kasai River and at the beginning of 1854 reached Kassanga, near the source of the Kwango River, the first outpost of the Portuguese settlements of Angola. He came back to Luanda on 31 May 1854. On his way back he followed the same route as far as Sesheke, went down the Zambezi southeastwards and "discovered" Victoria Falls. It is likely that other travellers of Portuguese origin had seen them before him, but he was the first to inform Europe, in the language of modern science, of the exact location of this natural wonder that all accounts coming to the coast made so much of. The "smoke does sound there" (Mosi oa tunya), as the Falls were known to the natives, was now explained as the result of "the prodigious fall of the Zambezi River into a fault of the hard basalt rock from the right to the left bank of the Zambezi, and prolonged, beginning with the left bank, for thirty or forty miles across the hills." Livingstone's description did away with the theories of the armchair geographers who thought the upper reaches of the river were a separate stream that lost itself in the sands of the Kalahari. Livingstone went on toward the east and came across the Portuguese outposts of Mozambique at Tete on 3 March 1856. He reached the coast of the Indian Ocean at Queliman on 22 May of the same year. (See map on page 331.)

Livingstone's accomplishments

In thirteen years Livingstone, with no arms other than his faith and his natural respect for the customs and outlook of the native peoples, had resolved the geographical puzzle of the land connections between southern and central Africa. On his geographical coordinates he located the route between the western coast of Africa and its eastern coast somewhere between the fifteenth and the twentieth southern parallels. He had reconnoitred almost the entire course of the Zambezi, and had crossed the southwest region of the basin of the Congo River, whose course was still unknown.

He did even more. He succeeded in convincing British public opinion that the only way to abolish slavery once and for all was to open up central Africa to "legitimate" trade. His missionary and humanitarian zeal, however, excited far more self-serving ambitions, in a paradox that was to become a commonplace in the history of the opening up of Africa.

The Portuguese claimed sovereignty over the Zambezi, a sovereignty based on the rights given by an undisputed historical priority. Yet England and all Europe were wondering about the "right of Africa to benefit by the influences of civilization and humanity." In the larger picture the Portuguese claims were mere obstacles on the path of an inexorable development.

Livingstone was designated "Her Majesty's Consul for Inner and Unexplored Africa;" before embarking on a new expedition, which this time was to enjoy official support. He announced that he was going "to open the African route to commerce and Christianity."

Four years after Baikie's trip by steamship up the Niger River, a flotilla commanded by Livingstone went up the Zambezi River to its junction with the Shire River. Lake Nyasa was reached in September 1859. It was clear that the Livingstone of this second expedition was playing a different role from that of the fresh-faced young missionary from the London Missionary Society. He was already a more or less conscious agent of a new stage in the European adventure in Africa—that of the deliberate conquest of the trade routes, and of the European and African conflicts that were bound to result.

Conquest of trade routes by steamship

The era of the solitary European explorer and of peaceful penetration was to be succeeded by that of armed expeditions and colonial wars.

Livingstone had made his start from the outposts of European penetration in southern Africa that were solidly backed up by Cape Colony, now expanding vigorously since its entry into the political system controlled by London. Mungo Park and his successors in western Africa had used the fragile springboard represented by the European trading-posts on the Gulf of Guinea coast. The mouth of the Zambezi River had been in the firm control of the Portuguese Empire during the two following centuries. The European travellers who had tried to venture into the region of the great lakes by starting out from the coast of the Indian Ocean had to keep in mind the existence of the Arab-African empire, which had re-established itself on the eastern coast following the dramatic defeat of the Portuguese by the Arab counter-offensive of the beginning of the eighteenth century. As a matter of fact, after the fall of the strong point of Mombasa (at the end of the seventeenth century) Arab merchants and navigators had gradually restored the trade underlying the prosperity of the coastal strip between the Island of Mozambique and Cape Guardafui. It was on the island of Zanzibar, an appendage of the Principality of Oman and Muscat, that the most dynamic Arab dynasty established itself; at the beginning of the nineteenth century it was to create an authentic empire of the sea, based on the control of the monsoon shipping between Asia and Africa.

In the hinterland the Bantu tribes, who normally were sedentary but for various reasons of population or terrain were shifting toward the south of the continent, and the Hamito-Negroid tribes that often ruled them, agreed to maintain mutually profitable trade relations with the rulers of the sea. The Arabs still mingled freely with the black population, as they had before the arrival of the Portuguese, creating a new people, the Swahilis, whose language served as a lingua franca for the highways into the interior. The influence of this Arab-African empire extended very deep into the continent. The trade in human beings was one of the elements of its prosperity, as was that in ivory and ostrich plumes. The entire region of the great lakes came into its economic orbit; Livingstone encountered Arab traders on the middle reaches of the Zambezi and along the approaches to Lake Nyasa.

Great Britain, which had occupied Aden in 1839 and had an interest in the Indies route—whether by way of the Red Sea or the Cape of Good Hope—soon took under its wing the fortunes of this empire, whose origin after all had been in Asia, at the gates of Mughal India, in the hope of taking it over. A British consul was able to write at that time that "if Zanzibar is ruled with prudence, it may play a very important part in the future of trade and civilization in East Africa. From Port Natal to Cape Guardafui the only state that any progress or any real stability can be expected of is Zanzibar." Thus the British Consul General at Zanzibar, from the middle of the nineteenth century on, in fact played the role of defender and coordinator of the scientific, religious and military penetration of the continent, which, with civilized goals, now followed the traditional routes of the detested slave-trade.

The existence of great lakes in the interior of the continent, in which the Nile was supposed to have its source, like that of mysterious mountains covered with eternal snows, had been suspected since antiquity and confirmed by the more or less distorted accounts of Arab merchants who had got as far as the eastern coast. Two German missionaries, Krapf and Rebman, probably deserve the honour of having first seen Victoria Lake, Mount Kenya, and the real Mountain of the Moon, that is, Kilimanjaro. Their accounts met with the skepticism of the same armchair geographers who had tried to discourage Livingstone, but they also stimulated the interest of missionary and business circles, who saw in the eastern route one more way of getting into Africa.

Richard Burton and John Speke

Richard Burton (the remarkable translator of the Arabian Nights and the intrepid explorer of Harar), accompanied by John Speke, his faithful lieutenant, crossed Somaliland, after leaving Zanzibar for the celebrated market town of Tabora (in the heart of present-day Tanganyika). They revealed to the world of European scholarship the exact coordinates of a hydrographic system that gave the key to the mystery of the origin and direction of the great African rivers other than the Niger. What was at issue, in fact, was to discover the line of demarcation of the waterways flowing north, west and south, and to disentangle the confusion rooted in the apparently contradictory European and Arab accounts.

Lake Tanganyika was discovered by the two explorers on 10 February 1858; it was Burton who described its magnificence, since Speke was half blinded.

Speke left by himself and made his way alone toward the north-east; he reached the southern tip of Lake Nyasa on 3 August. There was no doubt that it was a separate lake, which confirmed the accounts of the Arab travellers who also knew, for that matter, that a stream emerged from the northern part of the lake. Speke, accompanied this time by James Grant, left Zanzibar again two years later with the official support of the Royal Geographical Society. The two explorers, in going northwards from Tabora, crossed the Unyamwezi region which was where ancient traditions placed the "Mountains of the Moon." They came across kingdoms located at the southern point of the advance of the great tribes of Hamitic shepherds, who had probably come from the approaches to the Ethiopian plateau and who ruled over Bantu peoples. Speke reached Uganda in February 1862, where he was received by the Babaka Mutesa, chieftain of a well organized kingdom located at the cross-roads of the great highways that leave the coasts of the Indian Ocean or the Mediterranean coast via the Nile Valley. On 18 July 1862 Speke saw the chief source of the great river whose mystery had always been such a will-o'-the-wisp to Western imagination. The scene was presented "with the very perfection of an effect contrived in a well-kept park... I (Speke) told my men that they were to shave their heads and bathe themselves in the sacred river, the cradle of Moses." Speke had, in fact, discovered "old father Nile, which without any doubt had its source in the Victoria Nyanza, which, as I had predicted, was the origin of the holy river." It remained for him only to prove that this river was indeed the Nile.

Page 139
Victoria Falls, discovered in 1854 by David Livingstone, a missionary-physician sent to South Africa by the London Missionary Association. These prodigious falls of the Zambezi River were known to the natives as "smoke does sound there."

He made his way north-east, where to his great surprise he encountered two other European travellers near Gondokoro, Samuel White Baker and his wife, who, after leaving Khartoum, had gone up the White Nile with the same goal, that is, to discover the real sources of the Nile. The date of this meeting, 15 February 1863, may be considered the turning point of the great African explorations. This is Baker's comment: "Long

Left: photograph of Henry
Stanley, commissioned by
the New York *Herald* to
find Livingstone after no news
had come from the African
explorer for over five years.
Below: A contemporary engraving
depicting the historic Stanley-
Livingstone meeting at Vujiji on
November 9, 1871.

Page 141
Facsimile of front page stories
in the *Herald* announcing
that Stanley found Livingstone
(July 15, 1872 and July 26, 1872).

LIVINGSTONE.

Stanley's Letters to the Herald Describing the Finding of the Great Traveller.

The Battles with Mirambo, King of Uyowa.

Cowardly Conduct of the Arabs in Deserting Stanley while Stricken with Fever.

MIRAMBO'S VENGEANCE.

Tabora, an Arab Town, Nearly Destroyed, Five Hundred Arabs and Five Soldiers of the Herald Expedition Killed.

STANLEY TO THE RESCUE.

The Journey Continued Through Hundreds of Miles Rarely Traversed Even by Arabs.

Terrible Sufferings of the Herald Expedition Party on Its March.

UJIJI AT LENGTH REACHED.

The Expedition Enters the Town Triumphantly Flying the American Flag.

Livingstone and Stanley Face to Face at Last.

STANLEY'S STORY OF FIVE YEARS.

Livingstone's Own Account of His Explorations as Related to the Herald Explorer.

A STORY MORE ROMANTIC THAN ROMANCE.

Stanley's Special Corps at the Service of the Doctor and the Start of the Travellers in Company.

Personal Loneliness and Destitution of Livingstone When Relieved by the Herald Search Corps.

THE SOURCE OF THE NILE.

Livingstone's Refit for Further Surveying by the American.

Sanitary Condition of Livingstone When Last Seen by Stanley.

KWIHARA, UNYANYEMBE, }
September 20, 1871. }

The African expedition of the NEW YORK HERALD arrived at Unyanyembe on June 23, 1871. It had suffered considerably in its *personnel* and transport. One of the white men has died, he but lived to reach half-way here; two of the armed escort as well as eight pagazis died also from dysentery and smallpox. Two horses and twenty-seven asses have also perished. On arriving at Unyanyembe your correspondent wrote two letters and entrusted them to Said Ben Salim (Burton and Speke's former Ras-cafflan), now Governor of Unyanyembe. One gave an account of our journey from the coast here; the other of our battle with Mirambo.

THE SULTAN OF NZOGERA DEMANDS HEAVY TRIBUTE.
Here, after already dodging and paying four wars, which made the country of travellers, we were confronted and waged by Sultan Nzogera against another Sultan of Uvinza, which was an inconvenience to me—nay, it would... expedition. After passing heavily...

---

graceless retreat it became... was going to be a long affair... African. Livingstone's carava... to its first camp preparatory... been ordered back, and the g... lodged in my house.

The Arabs' cowardly retreat... follow them to their homes.

THE ARAB CAPITAL ENTER...
While I was debating what to... speed was a necessity with... Mirambo entered Tabora, the... tral Africa, with his ferocious... Tabora is one mile from Kwihar... date this telegram. The Kazeh... ton is not known here except... dence of an old Arab. Tabora... residences. The Arabs of Kwi... alarm and their thorough s... strongly. The Governor and ot... ning to the coast at once, decla... forever closed to travel and tra...

THE CAPITAL NEARLY DESTROY
DRED ARABS KI...
About one-fourth of Tabora w... nent Arabs were killed; cattle,... carried away. Expecting attac... erner's house into a little fort,... the property of the expedition a... stone from the Wat...fa.

STANLEY PREPARING TO RESIST
All fugitives from Tabora who... invited in, until I had 150 arme... tembe. Provisions and water w... five days. At the end of that... his allies retired with great boo...

THE AMERICAN FLAG
During the state of siege the... hoisted.

NOTHING MORE TO DO WIT...
After this event I informed th... not assist them any more, for if... they would run away again, and... tion to travel at once to Ujiji... They all advised me to wait unti... that I was going straight to deat... ing war time. But I was obstin...

LOOKED ON ME AS A...
I engaged thirty men of Zanzib... The effects of the expedition w... smallest scale consistent with... ties of the journey. As the... restlessness of the men incre... (Burton and Speke's handy man...

MY STUMBLING BL...
did his utmost to slacken the co... escort—the Englishman Shaw... smitten with fear that he cou... preparations. The Arab reports... our road were influencing the... tion.

The Journey to Ujiji—T...
Expedition—Over Four...
Through a Country R...
Even by Arabs—Stanle...
Pay Tribute to the Sult...
A Delay—Change o...
Reached and the...
Amid the Firing of G...
ican Flag in the Va...
Arabs—The Gray-Bearde...
Stanley and Livingston...
at Last.

UJIJI, LAKE...
Nov...

The HERALD expedition, upo... yembe, intended to make Ujiji in... stage, then to march to Manyen... stone had gone in 1869; then, th... the Congo, to go after and ove... was dead, as was often reporte... grave and satisfy myself of its t... the bones home in proper case... this telegram will prove, tho... such mournful task to perform... perform was far more meritoriou...

OVER FOUR HUNDRED MILES TH
SELDOM TRAVELL...
Instead of going west along a... the NEW YORK HERALD expe... regions very little known a... Arabs. For ten days it journe... bound for Western Urori, during... deserted and the Englishman had... perfectly useless. Crossing Unk... we travelled until we entered... tirely new country. After suppl... expedition with ten days' prov... into the wilderness and went nor... did not emerge until we had s... razi River.

NEW YORK HERALD

BROADWAY AND ANN STREET.

JAMES GORDON BENNETT,
PROPRIETOR.

Volume XXXVII........................No. 208

AMUSEMENTS THIS EVENING.

BOWERY THEATRE, Bowery—YACUP—THE RIVAL DUTCHMAN.

WOOD'S MUSEUM, Broadway, corner Thirtieth st.—CHRIS AND LENA. Afternoon and Evening.

OLYMPIC THEATRE, Broadway.—THE WITCHES OF NEW YORK—TRAPEZE PERFORMANCES.

UNION SQUARE THEATRE, 14th st and Broadway.—THE VOKES FAMILY—THE BELLES OF THE KITCHEN, &c.

WALLACK'S THEATRE, Broadway and Thirteenth street—ROBIN HOOD.

TONY PASTOR'S OPERA HOUSE, No. 201 Bowery.—STREETS OF NEW YORK.

PARK THEATRE, opposite City Hall, Brooklyn.—THE RAGPICKER OF PARIS.

CENTRAL PARK GARDEN.—GARDEN INSTRUMENTAL CONCERT.

TERRACE GARDEN, 58th st., between Third and Lexington ave.—SUMMER EVENING CONCERTS.

NEW YORK MUSEUM OF ANATOMY, 618 Broadway.—SCIENCE AND ART.

DR. KAHN'S MUSEUM, &c.

TRIPLE SHEET.

New York, Friday, July 26, 1872.

CONTENTS OF TO-DAY'S HERALD

Dr. Livingstone hints at the terrible instances of man's inhumanity that sickened his heart

---

DOCTOR LIVINGSTONE.

Grand Triumph for England and America.

The Flags of Both Countries United.

LIVINGSTONE SUCCESSFUL.

STANLEY SUCCESSFUL

Characteristic Letter from the Great Explorer to the Editor of the Herald.

Deeply Interesting Description of Five Hundred Miles Tramp.

"I Thought That I Was Dying on My Feet."

Deceived, Plundered, "a Mere Ruckle of Bones" and Almost Despairing at Ujiji.

The Inspiration of a Broken Photograph.

Plucking Courage from Superstition.

THE FIRST GLEAM OF HOPE.

Sighting the American Flag in the Distance.

SALUTATION TO THE GOOD SAMARITAN.

The Herald Commissioner's News.

THE NEW LIGHTS TO SCIENCE.

What Livingstone Has Discovered and His Description of the Great Watershed of the Nile.

How Africa May Become a Centre of Civilization.

"Suppression of Ujijian Slavery a Nobler Task Than the Discovery of All the Sources of the Nile."

Holding to the Last with "John Bullish" Tenacity.

TELEGRAM TO THE NEW YORK HERALD.
LONDON, July 25, 1872.

JAMES GORDON BENNETT, Esq.:—

SIR—I beg leave to transmit to you the following important and most highly interesting

live old England!... The mystery of the ancient ages has finally been settled..." Baker, at the cost of almost unbelievable suffering and hardship, explored the north-west region of present-day Uganda; he discovered Lake Albert on 14 March 1864. He then went up the White Nile and reached the great falls, which he named after the president of the Royal Geographical Society, Sir Roderick Murchison.

Livingstone was instructed by Murchison to settle the question of the river basins of southern Africa. Accompanied only by three Africans, he went up the Ruvuma River (the present-day boundary-line between Mozambique and Tanganyika) starting out from Mikindani, which he left on 4 April 1886. He rounded the southern point of Lake Nyasa and reached Bamboweolo Lake in July 1868. He reached Vujiji in March 1869. At that time the region of the great lakes was infested by slave-traders of Arab or Asian origin and by their African auxiliaries. Scenes like that of the massacre of Manyuema, where the slavers butchered hundreds of men, women and children, made a deep impression on Livingstone and through his writings on all Europe.

Stanley finds Livingstone
1871

For more than five years no news of the great explorer had come to the outside world. An American journalist of Welsh extraction was commissioned by the editor of the New York *Herald* to find him. Strinking straight out into the interior from Bagamoyo, Stanley inaugurated a new method of penetration, which was more like armed reconnoitring than exploration proper. He found Livingstone in Vujiji on 9 November 1871.—This was the site of the celebrated remark, "Dr. Livingstone, I presume."

Five years of a totally African life, in which all time and space seemed to have blurred, had not prepared Livingstone for the avalanche of news from an outside world bubbling with movement. Stanley told him that the Suez Canal was open, with regular trade going through it between Europe and India. The Pacific Railroad was finished. Grant had been elected President of the United States. Egypt had been invaded by scholars. The Cretan rebellion was over. A Spanish revolution had eliminated Isabella from the throne of Spain... Prussia had humiliated Denmark and annexed Schleswig-Holstein; its armies were encircling Paris. The French Emperor was imprisoned at Wilhelmshöhe... The Prussians Bismarck and Moltke had extinguished the Napoleonic dynasty. The proud empire of France had bitten the dust.

Page 142
The legendary "Mountain of the Moon," Kilimanjaro, Kenya. Giraffe heads peer out of the forest below.

A new Europe had, indeed, been born at the very moment that the old Africa was perishing.

In the first half of the nineteenth century Europe sent out its explorers, scholars, and missionaries in a quest for transcontinental routes that would fit the immense expanses of Africa into the vast and growing orbit of European exchange and European philosophical and religious ideas. After 1815 it attempted to catch its breath, to rest, and to knit together the threads of a civilization that was still frail, shaken to its very foundations by the revolutionary tempest.

In a sense, the often heroic search for the opening up of new routes in an unknown continent corresponded to the universal mission of a new world intent on finding in economic and commercial expansion an indispensable counterweight to nationalism and militarism, of which revolutionary Napoleonic France had been a brilliant model. Preoccupied by its internal dissension, Europe allowed England to consolidate the maritime routes under its own control, and did not make the slightest effort to dispute its sure-footed progress in the exploration of the great unknown spaces in Asia and Africa. Bonaparte had grasped the decisive geopolitical importance to the Indies route of the African way-station in the Nile delta. Yet the Ottoman Empire, which played a curiously obscure role in the first great episode of the European civil war, was quite vulnerable.

Except for Egypt, northern Africa played no role whatever during the Napoleonic wars. The French, for more than ten years in undisputed control of the Spanish, French and Italian coasts of the western Mediterranean, proved incapable of breaking through the efficient blockade established by the British fleet after its victories at Abukir
Decadence of the Ottomans and Trafalgar. For its part the Ottoman Empire did not take the slightest advantage of the deep division of western Europe to reopen to its own vessels the sea routes beyond the Straits of Messina. The truth is that the Ottomans, like their allies in the regency of Algiers, were decadent through and through. The military castes still commanding the redoubtable pirates who had made Charles V tremble and had thrust back the advances of the Spaniards, had lost their vigour beyond all hope of redemption. The three beylicates of Oran, Algiers, and Constantine (whose boundaries recalled Roman Africa) were mere administrative divisions, with no cohesiveness beyond a nominal allegiance to the Dey of Algiers and a rejection of any external domination, whether of Europe or of the neighbouring North African states. As long as Europe remained self-preoccupied, Algeria, still nebulous, could be neutral, and even play a fairly important economic role because of its abundant production of cereals ready for export. Its capital remained seemingly impregnable. In 1816 and in 1825 the British made an attempt to reduce this "nest of pirates," of which western Europe had any number of reasons to complain ever since the Barbarossa brothers. The major disaster at Navarin in 1827, where the Ottoman fleet was crushed despite all the efforts made by the Egyptians, raised a basic question—which European power was going to land in North Africa, and with what purpose?

It was Charles X, the reactionary philosopher-king and tardy disciple of an outlived eighteenth century, who was to give an army still quivering from the calamities and splendours of the Napoleonic era an occasion to find glory in an exotic country. A French army of 37,000 men, aboard 60 warships, six steamships, and 200 transport vessels run by 27,000 crew-members, left the French coast on 25 May 1830 and ranged itself in order of battle outside the city of Algiers on 13 June. The pretext of the intervention was rather flimsy. It had to do with an obscure disagreement on the settling of commercial debts, and with the ill-treatment the Dey was supposed to have inflicted on some French subjects. The means used were rather considerable, and in their abundance were reminiscent of those used in vain by Charles V three centuries before (170 vessels, 22,000 soldiers).

After a short engagement on 19 June at Staoueli, where the coalition of Berber, Arab, and Turkish soldiers failed to hold before the discipline of the French troops, Algiers the unconquerable fell at the end of June.

French expedition against Algiers 1830

Whatever was left of Islam as a political power was profoundly affected by this incontestable victory of the "infidels." The Mufti of Algiers, who witnessed the entry of the French troops, wrote at the time: "May God preserve every Muslim country from such a spectacle... The population, men and women, crowded round the threshold of my dwelling crying out pathetically, 'Since we must die, it is better to do so before the gate of the Halim.'"

It was soon apparent that Algiers was not Algeria. In order to ensure its security an advance had to be made east, west, and south. Without wishing it or being aware of it France was entering into the implacable logic of conquest on a national scale. The enemy had to be searched for in the refuges of which there were so many in the mountains very near the coast. The heavily encumbered military columns were harassed by the armed peasants who had turned guerilla. Marching in the footsteps of the Romans, the French encountered the same difficulties. It was not a mere question of protecting the access to the coastal plains suitable for colonization. It was also a question of opening up the routes leading beyond the high plateaux and across the Sahara into the heart of Black Africa.

While the Kabyle resistance in the east of the country was being organized (it did not end until 1871), the arabized tribes of western Algeria proclaimed a Holy War under the leadership of Abd-el-Qadir, a great tribal chieftain and subtle politician whom France for a short while regarded, in accordance with Bugeaud's view, as a "valid intermediary." (The Treaty of Tafna, ackowledging zones of influence, was signed in 1837).

Bugeaud, a member of the Périgord gentry and a brilliant soldier in the imperial armies, had learned how to fight guerillas in Spain. He had no illusions about the ultimate and inevitable goals of the French conquest. The failures of the various Spanish attempts on the African coast ever since the sixteenth century had taught him the lesson that "little Gibraltars" had no future in the face of "a nationality that was already so powerful... which would soon have a regular army and cannon provided by Morocco and Tunisia and by the Europeans themselves, and which would soon be capable of coming to besiege you in your towns."

Conquest of Algeria 1841-1847

In 1841 France decided to conquer Algeria totally. Bugeaud was given all authority and all available means. The Duke of Aumale, son of King Louis-Philippe, wiped out Abd-el-Qadir's camp (the Smala) in 1843. In 1844 the Algerian Moroccan armies were beaten at Isly. Abd-el-Qadir, after having taken refuge in Morocco, surrendered to General Lamoricière on 23 December 1847; he found a comfortable retreat in Syria.

Thus North Africa and Islam lost their first battle to the Westerners since the sixteenth century. The conquest of Algeria tended to confirm the impression in Europe that the race was now open for the domination of the whole of the African continent. During this same period the Anglo-Saxon peoples were plunging into the opening up and colonization of the vast expanses of North America and Australia. A gigantic movement of expansion seemed to have been launched that tended to integrate peacefully or forcibly all non-European populations into a vast network of exchange, colonization and investments whose center was solidly established in western Europe. In the middle of the nineteenth century, it was said, the "direction of history shows that the Bugeauds are right and the Abd-el-Qadirs are wrong."

Some said that France had assumed too heavy a burden, and that Muslim fanaticism was invincible. Others, arguing from the obvious decadence of the Algerian people, sparsely scattered over an immense area, and from the demographic pressure of a Europe overflowing with unused energy, proposed a policy of native "thrust-back" and "containment". In the capital many criticized the high cost of a military operation whose end was quite unforeseeable, since the interior had to be conquered for the coast to be defended. To open up to European colonization a gigantic, difficult country whose inhabitants were hostile seemed to them to be an inadmissible squandering of the national wealth at a moment when France ought to be modernizing itself and getting out of its peasant rut.

As a matter of fact, the French military victories, even though they allowed colonists from the mother country to settle on the relatively fertile coastal plains of Oran and Algiers, did not, of course, solve the problem of the co-existence of two peoples fundamentally alien to each other.

It was perhaps Emperor Napoleon III, most clearly of all his contemporaries, who realized that the success of European colonization was conditioned in the final analysis by an understanding with the "Arab" population that could be expressed in a mutually acceptable pact based on a common goal: to exploit the potential of the country and to open it up to the broad modern currents of trade and industry. This is how the problem was outlined in a report submitted to the Emperor in 1858: "We have to contain and civilize a martial people, attract a population of emigrants, secure a fusion of races, develop a superior civilization by the application of the great discoveries of modern science. We are confronted by an armed and vigorous nationality that must be eliminated through assimilation, and by a European population that is on the rise. All these opposing interests must be reconciled."

On 6 February 1863 the Emperor proclaimed Algeria an "Arab Kingdom". In his instructions to Governor General MacMahon, he emphasized the injustice and inhumanity of the policy of "containment" of the native population. He proposed that the Europeans restrict themselves to activities of a modern character, such as the exploitation of the forests and mines, the drying of the marshlands, the irrigation of the arid areas, the introduction of perfected crops and conversion industries. The native population was to conserve all its rights and to devote itself to traditional agricultural and pastoral pursuits.

This policy was never understood either by the European colonists—who needed land and manpower—by the Kabyle peasants of the mountains, by the Arabs of Oran, or by the army, which was supposed to put down the uprising of the population of these two regions in 1864. Taking advantage of the defeat of France by the Prussian army in 1870, and in spite of the new reforms of the civil administration, the Algiers and Constantine departments rebelled in 1871. In the eyes of the believers in force this proved that any policy of co-existence was a mere snare.

The lands of the rebel tribes were confiscated by the government. The French National Assembly allocated 100,000 hectares of native land to the inhabitants of Alsace-Lorraine who had opted for France after the annexation of their country by Germany.

From 1860 to 1880 the number of European colonists went from 200,000 to 375,000. The colonized zones were energetically exploited. The other parts of Algeria were for

Page 147
Watercolor from the Moroccan sketchbook of Eugène Delacroix, January-June 1823. The artist accompanied the Comte de Mornay, sent by King Louis-Philippe's government on a mission to the Sultan of Morocco, Mulay-er-Rahman. Delacroix returned through Oran and Algeria in June 1832. A visit to a harem made then was the point of departure for his celebrated painting "Women of Algiers", shown at the Paris Salon of 1834.

Pages 148-149
A 19th century Salon painting by Bellangé depicts a famous incident in the French conquest of North Africa: the capture of the Smala (encampment) of Abd-el-Qadir by the Duc d'Aumale in 1843. Abd-el-Qadir was an Algerian leader who led native forces against the French occupiers. Victorious at first in 1835, Abd-el-Qadir's bitter struggle continued until his surrender in 1847.

Watercolor from Eugène Delacroix's Moroccan sketchbook, 1823. The artist accompanied a French diplomatic mission to the Sultan of Morocco. He made minute, lively notations on everything he saw.

all practical purposes disregarded. The demographic expansion of the Europeans was soon countered by a downright demographic "revenge" on the part of the native population that had been thrust back into the least fertile zones, and that went from two and a half to four million in twenty years. Thus the destiny of modern Algeria had already been laid down by the end of the nineteenth century.

While North Africa was entering into the European orbit in the wake of the French conquest of Algeria, Egypt, guardian of the northern gates of Nilotic Africa and of the channel between the African and Asian continents, also found itself drawn into the powerful current of European expansion. It was in Egypt that France and England waged their battle at the end of the eighteenth century, and it was in Egyptian waters that Bonaparte lost his landing fleet and the control of the eastern Mediterranean passed into the hands of the British.

Bonaparte, by destroying the Mameluke army at the battle of the Pyramids in July 1798, freed Egypt of the oppression of a backward caste. He introduced modern ideas into a country that for a very long time had been cut off from any outside contacts, while at the same time showing the Egyptians their own glorious past.

Yet it was another foreign military caste, from Albania, that was to bring into the modern age the enfeebled descendants of the ancient empires of the Pharaohs and the Fatimids.

In 1801 Mehemet Ali and his Albanian troops beat the French. He was recognized as governor by the Porte; in 1806 and 1811, by a general massacre, he got rid of the last of the Mamelukes once and for all. In 1816, with the help of a French military mission, he organized an army of a modern type, based on the military service of the fellahs. He realized that the wealth of Egypt could only be based on abundant production and an active participation in international trade. Knowing that the power of Ancient Egypt was based on the disciplined, rational use of the Nile overflow, he embarked on a vast programme of cultivating and irrigating the land. The ancient canals were restored and new ones opened with the help of an abundant and almost free labour force. The production and export to European markets of food crops and textiles of good quality brought considerable sums of money into the state coffers.

The new ruler of Egypt was able to build a fleet and army whose existence seemed to threaten the strategic equilibrium of the eastern Mediterranean. The Egyptian armies, reverting to the millenial highways of Egyptian expansion to the north-east, penetrated Syria in 1831 and entered Turkey in 1832. The Bosphorus route was opened up to them by the victory over the demoralized Ottoman armies at Konya in December 1832. In 1839, after a calamitous Ottoman counter-offensive, Mehemet Ali seemed to have Istanbul at his mercy. The whole weight of British and Russian intervention was needed to make Egypt evacuate Syria, in spite of the help it received from the French (1840). Toward the south, the Egyptian army went up the Nile Valley as far as Nubia, that is, the heart of a region infested at the time by slave-traders who were pressing into the centre of Africa through the region of the Chad. Toward the east, it threw itself into a series of campaigns against the Bedouin rulers in control of the Arabian Peninsula at the time. But the Egyptians proved incapable of taming the Wahabi warriors; in spite of the forty years they had spent in campaigns there they evacuated Arabia in 1849.

The victories of Mehemet Ali

This remarkable military and political expansion was aided by the advance in hygiene and in the living conditions of the people. The bubonic plague, hitherto endemic, was practically eliminated with the help of European technicians. The population of Egypt rose from two and a half to more than four million in twenty years. Alexandria, which to Bonaparte's soldiers had presented a spectacle of poverty and desolation, rapidly became an active Mediterranean metropolis where merchants from all parts of the eastern Mediterranean settled just as they always had in the prosperous days of antiquity. A canal was built that linked it to Cairo and from there to the entire business network of the delta and Upper Nile.

A Frenchman, the Consul General and also a friend of Mehemet Ali's sons, Ferdinand de Lesseps, launched the idea of a canal across the Isthmus of Sinai; this was supposed to open to sea-going ships a direct passageway between the Mediterranean and the Red Sea. The British Foreign Office, fearful of a direct seizure by its Mediterranean rival of this new Indies route, did everything it could to oppose the enterprise. One of the sons of Mehemet Ali, Sa'id Pasha, who was very much under the influence of European ideas, decided to grant a concession to build the canal, for which a company constituted by De Lesseps had already studied the technical and economic background. Sa'id's successor, Ismail, confirmed this decision and, pressed by money needs, encouraged the systematic cultivation of cotton at the expense of the food crops. This placed Egypt squarely in the international circuits of trade and consumption, while at the same time dangerously weakening the country, with its rapidly increasing population, as a supplier of its own food.

The digging of the canal was finished in October 1869. In the course of a brilliant inauguration on 17 November of the same year, for which Verdi was commissioned to compose "Aida", Empress Eugénie and Ismail, who had become "Khedive", i.e., practically sovereign of the new Egypt as a result of a decision of the Imperial Court of Istanbul in 1867, saluted the advent of a new era in which Egypt was to resume its place as guardian of the maritime gates of the east.

The power of the Ottoman Empire over the northern coasts of Africa was practically broken. Only the Pashalik of Tripoli was still directly dependent on the Turkish government. A two-headed Europe, run by London and Paris, inherited the succession of the great Islamic power that a dozen centuries before had swept away the empire of the Greeks and Latins. And it prepared itself to surmount the countless physical and human obstacles in the way of its advance toward the domination of the African hinterland.

Page 153
Head dress in the form of an antelope, probably used for funerary ceremonials by the Kurumba tribe. Little is known about this tribe that lives between Mali and the Upper Volta beyond their elegant antelope sculpture. The Kurumba occupy the territory explored by Barth in 1850-1855 and later by Raffanel and Faidherbe. Private coll. Paris.

Left: Portuguese Guinea, a Papels king and his followers (Papels was a coastal town). Anonymous Italian engraving, 19th century. Below: "Camp of Douville when he crossed the Couango river in Sona Bakal territory" (Angola). A lithograph (by Engelmann) illustrating "Voyages in the Congo and the Equinoxial African interior made in the years 1828, 1829 and 1830". Douville explored the Portuguese possessions in the search for gold mines.

Page 155
"A Peulh marabout (chief)", lithograph from the Abbott Boilat's "Senegalese sketches", 1841. The western commercial outpost of the French advance into the Sudan centered around the city of St Louis. The peoples here were predominantly Muslim, there were also Peulh and Mandingo tribes. The Peulhs were fine-featured, as the Abbott recorded here. Behind the Marabout flies the French flag.

Chapter 17
The African Hinterland — A Prize for Europe

From the beginning of the nineteenth century on, the great movement aimed at exploring the depths of Africa, whose goals had at first been religious and humanitarian, was diliberately aimed at the direct or indirect conquest of the African hinterland.

Livingstone himself, in the course of his last expeditions, had already become an official agent of the British government in his capacity as "Consul General for Interior and Unexplored Africa." His quarrel with the Portuguese in Africa was explained by political considerations rather than by the exigencies of a missionary enterprise. French, British, German, Austrian, Italian, and Portuguese explorers, and still others, all placed themselves in the service of the European powers or of the Khedive of Egypt. These powers tried more or less successfully to cloak in a doubtful international legality their attempts at domination over native rulers whom nothing had prepared, politically, economically or culturally, for this brusque invasion from Europe.

The lure to further commercial and military penetration

The myths of the hidden African treasures, which in other ages had inspired Romans, Egyptians, North Africans and Portuguese to head toward Central Africa in the initial attempts at commercial and military penetration, were still the motive power of this new stage in the European advance. This new stage was to prove decisive.

Because he realized this fact, the far-sighted Burgeaud, in trying to reassure the French Government on the long-range prospects of an Algerian conquest that at first seemed protracted and expensive, demonstrated to it that the traditional highway leading toward the empires of Black Africa left from North Africa and passed through the Sahara.

In fact Barth had actually come across the Chad in leaving Tripoli via Ghadames and the oases of Fezzan and Bornu in order to reach the Niger. One of his admirers, the Frenchman Henri Duveyrier, encouraged by the French authorities in Algiers, specialized in the study of the Tuaregs, the direct descendants of the nomad Berbers who had been such a dangerous threat to Roman Byzantium. In November 1862, in a treaty signed at Ghadames, the chiefs of the big tribes undertook to "enter into friendly and neighbourly relations with Algeria and to make themselves the intermediaries of any commercial enterprises that France might wish to open up across their country on its way to the Sudanese regions." This was for the north-south route. For the east-west route, the heroic exploits of Mungo Park had shown that the commercial routes starting out from the Senegal and Gambia Rivers also led toward the Sudanese territories.

The French advance into the Sudan found a firm point of departure in the west as well as in the north. Indeed, the Treaty of Paris (1815) had returned the city of St.-Louis to France. This outpost of traditional commerce is situated on an island in the mouth of the Senegal River, at the cross-roads of the desert and riparian Africa. The restoration of the French rights after the Treaty of Paris was marked by the depressingly famous episode of the *Medusa* (when the frigate bringing the French administrators to Saint-Louis was shipwrecked on the shoals of the Arguin sand-bank (1818)).

The peoples around St. Louis were all Muslim. Some of them were descended from the nomadic Arab-Berber tribes that since the tenth century had been trying to impose

Page 156
"Peulh woman," another illustration from the French Abbott Boilat's "Senegalese Sketches."

157

their rule on the black kingdoms located along the Senegal River. Others were of Mandingo or Peulh origin. The little colony could survive only if legitimate traders (in gum arabic and gold) stopped paying tribute to the ruling castes. In 1843, Raffanel was commissioned by the Governor of the Senegal to study the prerequisites for opening a route that could link the gold country, situated south of the bend of the Niger, to the coastal points controlled by the Europeans. Then, in 1854, under the leadership of Faidherbe, the French launched a military campaign aimed at breaking the opposition of the Moors, the Wolofs, and the Tekrurs (still called Toucouleurs; they were related to the Peulhs or Fulhas). For the first time the advancing European army collided with organized African resistance. A talented chieftain, El-Hajj Omar, found the roots of his spiritual and political strength in a form of Islam that retained close connections with Arabia and with the great Muslim kingdoms of the middle Niger. In the face of a common enemy, he was able to federate groups divided by dynastic rivalries or ethnic differences. After his defeat at the fortress of Medina (1854), where the Senegalese Paul Holl and a handful of African and European defenders distinguished themselves, El-Hajj Omar took refuge in Macina.

On 22 February 1863 the Niger was reached by the Mage mission, which had come from Upper Senegal and had officially been instructed to "open up a new commercial route that would replace the traditional trade route between Morocco and the Sudan" (which had been travelled by René Caillé).

In North Africa, as in the Sudan, France was succeeding Islam as the effective master of the routes leading from the north and the west toward the interior of Africa.

In the heart of Central Africa the basin of the Congo (the largest river in Black Africa) had always been isolated from the great currents of trade and civilization, unlike the valleys of the Nile, the Zambezi, the Niger, and the Senegal.

After the decline and then the disappearance of the Christian Kingdom of São Salvador the Portuguese had renounced any attempt to make religious converts and to penetrate the interior. Only the southern part of the vast hydrographic network was crossed by Portuguese merchants and explorers, from the end of the eighteenth century on. The transverse route from Angola to Mozambique was reconnoitred by José de Lacerda, Pedro Jan Baptista and Amaro José. In 1852 Sylva Porto (Antonio Francisco da Sylvia) established a link between Belmonte, located on the highlands beyond Benguela, and Barotseland. In the course of this expedition he met Livingstone.

The basins of the Congo   Yet it was Major Cameron who had the honour of reconnoitring the three great basins of the Congo, the Zambezi and the Nile, and of understanding their separate character. He had gone off like Stanley to look for Livingstone, and he crossed Africa transversally from Zanzibar to Luanda (March 1873–March 1874). He described enthusiastically "the king of all the African rivers, the mighty Congo, whose discharge was exceeded only by the Amazon and perhaps by the Yang-Tsi-Kiang." He thought the basin of the Congo, that gigantic river "that extends across the two sides of the Equator but probably has its biggest section in the southern hemisphere," should be opened up to modern international trade. These routes of access were controlled by the Portuguese in the west and by the Arabs of Zanzibar in the east. The traffic in slaves, ivory, and rubber, and the portage necessary, imposed an unendurable burden on the local peoples.

Cameron's ideas on the basin of the Congo, just like those of Mungo Park's on the Niger, aroused the curiosity of the European world, where both scientists and capitalists, for different though converging reasons, wanted to open up these worlds that had remained so closed off.

Beginning in 1875, an international congress of geographical societies studied the Congo question. Leopold, King of the Belgians, proposed the creation of a "committee that would bring together geographers and philanthropists." On 12 September 1876, at the end of another conference, the first charter of European cooperation in Africa was approved. It acknowledged that Belgium, in its capacity as a "central and neutral State," was expected to receive a "certain international support" in its work of opening up the Congo basin to international, humanitarian, religious, and commercial undertakings. Every European country interested in opening up the continent created national committees in the framework of an "International Commission of Exploration and of the Civilization of Central Africa."

Creation of the Belgian and French Committees

It was as an agent of the Belgian Committee that Stanley had crossed Central Africa from East to West, and it was in the name of the French Committee that Brazza, coming from the northwest a year later, planted the French tricolour on the northern shore of the impressive natural lake constituted by the junction of the Congo River waters and the grand rapids.

The mystery of the Congo had been dissipated. The Congo question became the order of the day. The approaches to the highlands of southern Africa confronted the European advance with obstacles that were soon to prove formidable.

In rounding the vast desert of the Kalahari from the west and the north, Livingstone had encountered only the Hottentots and the Herreros, the somewhat debilitated descendants of the former rulers of southern Africa. By contrast, the Boers moving up at the east of the desert, the British starting out from their Natal settlements and trying to go westwards, and the Portuguese who for three centuries had been straining unsuccessfully to master the Zambezi River, all came up against the vigorous branches of the Bantu peoples who had been coming down from eastern Africa ever since the sixteenth century. This migratory movement grew more concentrated at the beginning of the nineteenth century; the eastern boundaries of the Transvaal plateau became the arena of a great movement of peoples that is somewhat reminiscent of the Time of Troubles of the great Teutonic invasions in Europe. This tragic period has been given the name *Mafecan*—the "crushing." Nothing, indeed, could resist the titanic pressure of armed groups that mobilized the most vigorous of the young men with no distinction of origin and imposed on them an absolute discipline. This was at the same time that the Boer groups were heading north, in quest of free virgin lands, and that British patrols were attempting to give Cape Colony a breathing space and to ensure the safety of the frontier region between the Great Fish River and the Kei River.

The "Nguni," a southeastern branch of the Bantu peoples (which includes the Xosas of the Fish River) had gradually been thrusting back the Hottentots toward the desert zones during the course of the eighteenth century. One of their tribes, known as the "Zulu Ka Malenda" (the kings of heaven) became the epicentre of a military and nationalist revolution whose effects were to be felt throughout South Africa. Their ruler, Chaka, had learned the art of war in the ranks of the army of Dingisweyo. Manoeuvring in serried ranks, which for so long had been the trump card of the European armies when coming up against their African, Asian and American Indian adversaries, was put into use by Chaka, the "Black Napoleon." From 1820 to 1828 the latter ruled the region between the Limpopo and the Savre. His wanton cruelties caused the terrified smaller peoples to stampede south as well as north. The conquered tribes fled toward the great spaces between the Vaal and the Orange Rivers just when the Boers were attempting to settle there. The Zulu armies led by Dingaan, Chaka's successor, collided with the advance patrols of the Great Trek under Piet Retief, and massacred his unit in 1838 at the "Hill of Slaughter."

Chaka the "Black Napoleon" 1820-1828

The "Voortrekkers," who were fleeing British domination, had to become warriors in order to withstand the bloodstained incursions of the Zulu armies. On 16 December 1838 a Boer "commando" under Pretorius crushed the army of Dingaan at the battle of Blood River. The Voortrekkers now sought to move northwards, beyond the Vaal River, and eastwards, across the country occupied by the Zulus. In the face of this conflict Great Britain took up an ambiguous position. It considered itself responsible for the protection of the native peoples and for the maintenance of their rights. But at the same time, through the support it accorded the British subjects in Natal, it favoured in fact an expansion of the European colonists' domination as far as the borders of the Portuguese settlement toward the north, and the boundaries of Cape Colony toward the south, across the native lands of Pondoland and of Kafireria (the land of the Xosas).

Thus the Trekkers, who in the eyes of the Cape government were rebels, were contained within the limits of the Transvaal Plateau and cut off from any access to the sea. Caught between the threat of British rule and the Zulu attack, the Boers rejected any compromise. Their churches, whose spiritual aid they had no desire to share with their African or European enemies, became the haven of their national life. They gave themselves a democratic regime on a racial and religious basis; its first head was Marthinus Pretorius, the son of a brilliant conqueror of the Zulus. The Boer National Assembly—*the Volksraad*— held its first session in the village of Pretoria in May 1856.

The advance of the Boers toward the north, beyond the frontiers of Cape Colony, that of the British starting out from the Natal colony, and the confused struggle of the various Bantu tribes against one another and against the Europeans, gave rise to a complex and dangerously unstable situation. The Governor of the Cape, Sir George Gray, laid it down in 1860 that the sole link that officially united the European states and the natives was the High Commissioner. "A single movement of ill temper, or an error of judgement on his part may provoke at any moment a local war, a general uprising of the natives or even a European rebellion. The country must always be at war on one side or another. It seems to lapse by stages into disorder and barbarism."

In addition, there were fundamental decisions to be taken that had to do with the future of the European settlers. Did the Africans have to be segregated in regions where they would enjoy total protection against European expansion? Or did that expansion have to be limited to the north or toward the east? (These were the same questions being asked at this same time at the other end of the continent, in Algeria.) In any case Great Britain was resolved to force the reunion of Europeans and Africans under common laws, within the framework of a coherent whole that would be capable of withstanding the tug of sterile rivalries.

Germany was also making an advance of its own, starting out from the settlements of the African southwest. This, as well as the arbitration of the President of the French Republic in acknowledging Portuguese sovereignty over the Bay of Delagoa (1876), showed in fact that it was high time to organize all local authorities with respect to the new factor of foreign intervention.

After the discovery in 1868 of gold and diamonds in Griqualand, at the edge of the Transvaal Plateau and on the "missionary route," the British government was more convinced than ever that a confederation of European states and the establishment of a protectorate over the African powers that were still independent was the indispensable prelude to any economic large-scale development. The rational exploitation of the mines that had just been discovered was expected to permit all races to be conducted into a joint prosperity within a joint political framework.

From a geographical point of view the three access routes that served the economic needs of the high plateau, starting out from the Cape, from Natal, and from the Bay of Delagoa, complemented rather than competed with each other.

Great Britain went into action. The British High Commissioner imposed himself on the Boers of the Orange Free State as arbiter in their conflict with Bechuanaland and Barotseland. The burghers of Bloemfontein seemed to be willing to accomodate them-

Page 161
Bateke mask. The Bateke are a large tribe, living around Brazzaville on the right bank of the Congo. Their art centers around their fetishism and the making of magic figures for defensive or aggressive purposes. Their masks treated the human face in a boldly stylized manner.

Left: the British occupation of
Pretoria, South Africa,
in 1881. The Boers had accepted
a British Protectorate which
assured them defense against
the warlike Zulus. This
menace once removed, the Boers
rose up against the colonial
constitution. A new threat from
native tribes led them to sign a
temporary compromise with the
British, the Convention of Pretoria.
Below: Savorgnan de Brazza
(1880), the French explorer
and administrator holding a
parley with Bateke chiefs
at the trading post which was later
to be named Brazzaville.
Brazza signed a treaty with the
Bateke chief (the Mokoko)
establishing a French protectorate.

Page 163

Bawongo dancers of the Congo.
This tribe lives between
the Kwango River and the Kasai.

selves to a situation of simple autonomy from which they derived certain commercial and financial advantages. London federated Natal and Cape Colony, annexed eastern and western Griqualand and finally the Transvaal in 1877. Thus the descendants of the Voortrekkers found themselves under British rule after all.

British defeat by the Zulus 1879

The warlike Zulus were a real problem. They had the advantage of a direct connection with war-mongers who sheltered in the Bay of Delagoa, and the existence of Zulu groups on the flanks of the zones where European control was undisputed could no longer be tolerated. The British Crown was now responsible for the protection of all its subjects. This protection extended to the Boers, who were militarily and financially quite incapable of withstanding alone the harassment of the Zulu warriors, whose chief, Cetshwayo, had an army of 60,000 men. He refused to respect the frontier line with the Transvaal and rejected the British High Commissioner's ultimatum. In January 1879 the British forces, made up of 5,600 Europeans and 9,000 African auxiliaries, crossed the boundaries of Zululand. The African army displayed remarkable powers of manoeuvre. It applied the "buffalo" tactic—the right and left vanguards of the main body making up the horns and the centre representing the chest. The British army was ill-prepared to face such an adversary, and a British detachment, surprised at Isandhlwana (January 1879) lost more than 1,500 men, including 800 Europeans.

The rumour of this defeat spread throughout South Africa. The latent ferment in the other African tribes was aroused. The Boers of the Transvaal, while preoccupied by thoughts of winning back their independence, were lying low for the moment. They had an interest in making common cause with the army of their European master in order to smash their African opponent. These initial disasters were wiped out by the triumphant campaign of Lord Chelmsford, who crushed Cetshwayo in July 1879. The Zulu menace was obliterated. The Boers took advantage of this to rise up against the colonial constitution imposed on them by Great Britain. They proclaimed the restoration of the Republic and opened hostilities at Pothefstroom in December 1880; a British column was shattered at Majuba Hill.

A temporary compromise between British and Boers 1881

Nevertheless the threat of a general uprising of the native tribes, a peril shared by both European peoples, weighed in favour of a new compromise—highly temporary—between the British and the Boers. The Convention of Pretoria, signed in August 1881, recognized the State of the Transvaal as having complete internal autonomy under British rule.

Under the leadership of the celebrated triumvirate of Kruger, Pretorius, and Joubert, a new nation projected itself into this first episode of the European civil war that was being played out on African soil. The Boer leaders had perfected a new tactic, inspired by the Bantu and Zulu armies they had had to come to grips with so often.

In a few decades a handful of farmers and stock-breeders had opened up a new route into the African hinterland. Thanks to them, other Europeans had finally discovered on the Transvaal plateau the mining treasures that had so long been wrapped in myth in the imaginations of Europeans and Arabs.

The Bantu peoples, who had been shifting southwards for some two centuries, were now stopped. In their resistance to the European advance they had displayed certain martial qualities, but had come to grief through the cruelty of their chiefs, who had terrorized Africans and Europeans alike, as well as through their lack of a comprehensive view of politics.

Nevertheless the intervention of Great Britain probably saved from annihilation the vanguard of the Boer people, which would have been unable to withstand the African thrust very long. At a time when Europe was becoming industrial at a feverish pace it could not allow any hands but its own to seize the gold and diamonds that guaranteed its paramount position.

Page 164
Stick of a Wabende chief. The Wabende (peoples of the East) live on the eastern shores of lake Tanganyika, Belgian Congo. Tervuren Museum, Belgium.

Europe had indeed entered the race for world dominion. Nothing seemed able to withstand its military, religious, and economic advance. Copious emigration had populated the virgin lands of America, Australia and New Zealand. In Asia the Queen of England was proclaimed Empress of India. The Chinese Empire was beating a retreat in the face of the military and diplomatic pressure of the French, British, and Russians. A small European army had come as far as Peking to sack the palaces and the age-old accumulation of treasure. Haughty Japan accepted the tutelage of the West. The Ottoman Empire could escape the Russian occupation and the partition of its holdings in Asia, Africa and Europe, only thanks to the intervention of Disraeli and Bismarck. Asia and Africa could no longer hope to save their independence except by a skillful exploitation of the rivalries that divided the powers of Europe, whose mutual jealousy was exceeded only by their determination to expand.

The European thrust

In the heart of Europe the concept of young nations and of decadent nations began to exercise its magnetism on the thought of the theoreticians of the new imperialism. The fundamental idea of the inherent superiority of the white race with respect to the coloured races was taken for granted. This relative inferiority of the coloured races or of certain European nations was not, to be sure, absolute: it could even be attributed to the play of physical and political factors. But it existed nevertheless.

To the mind of someone like Stanley, the conqueror of the Congo, the thrust forward of the Anglo-Saxon peoples was in the nature of things. It was inconceivable for him "that the basin of the Congo, with its 4,520 miles of navigable routes and its boundless resources, should fall to the Portuguese, who would do nothing but seal it up in the silence of the centuries to come. There can be no question (in Africa) of depriving millions of Englishmen as yet unborn of markets similar to those opened up by their ancestors in the Americas and India. The commands of nature must be obeyed. The English population of England is growing rapidly, its trade is expanding, its colonies are taking shape, wealth is overflowing every county in England while with every day that passes education is creating thousands of people ready to face up to the justification of life itself: increase and multiply."

It goes without saying that the French, German, Italian and Russian theoreticians presented identical arguments in favour of their own adventures. Five years after Stanley had said these words to young Harry Johnston, a French cabinet minister declared in the Chamber of Deputies (28 January 1885): "There is an irresistible movement carrying the great European nations to the conquest of new lands. It is like a gigantic steeple-chase on the track of the unknown... This steeple-chase is scarcely five years' old, and from one year to the next it is bounding forward as though thrust by the momentum it has acquired... In a phenomenon that is so general, so characteristic, should one see nothing but the caprices of ambition, the false ideas of men and of nations, or on the contrary, the peremptory manifestation and the inevitable law of an economic situation common to all Europe?"

Left: Gen. Charles George Gordon sketched in "Vanity Fair", 1881 by "Spy", was named governor of the Egyptian provinces by Nubar Pasha in 1872.
Below: English officers photographed in Cairo in 1882. The failure of Egypt's policy of expansion in Ethiopia and the Sudan placed this country in complete financial dependence on the European powers. Embittered by defeat, the Egyptian military under Colonel Arabi organized resistance and acts of terrorism. British intervention followed in 1882: Alexandria was bombed, English troops landed, Arabi and his army crushed.

THE ILLUSTRATED LONDON NEWS

REGISTERED AT THE GENERAL POST-OFFICE FOR TRANSMISSION ABROAD.

No. 2344.—VOL. LXXXIV.   SATURDAY, MARCH 22, 1884.   WITH SUPPLEMENT AND COLOURED PORTRAIT OF GENERAL GORDON   SIXPENCE. BY POST, 6½D.

SCENE ON THE BATTLE-FIELD OF EL TEB: BEHIND THE OLD BOILER OF THE SUGAR-MILL.

The end of Egypt's unsuccessful drive for expansion came with the Sudanese attack led by the Mahdi ("God- guided") in 1881. General Gordon, the hero of Chinese and Far Eastern campaigns, was called in 1884 by the British Protectorate to stem the revolt and save Khartoum. Khartoum fell in January 1886 and "Chinese" Gordon was dismembered by the fanatical Sudanese.

What did Europe do, during these five years that changed Africa as they did the rest of the world? First of all, it declared a truce to the internal quarrels caused by the turbulence of nations in the full flood of demographic, social and industrial development. France bandaged its wounds, paid its war debts, and pondered on the lessons of its defeat by Germany. The latter, ruled by a statesman of stature, was aware that blood and iron had to be followed by production and trade. Italy realized the exceptional character of the complex of circumstances out of which its unification had arisen: the romantic inspiration and audacity of a vibrant people, the patient calculations of a superior man, and the historic opportunities thrown up by the Franco-Prussian conflict. It was trying to take up without waiting any longer the threads of the great imperial Roman tradition, torn asunder for the past 1,500 years. Spain and Portugal were still staggering beneath the repeated blows inflicted on their prestige in South America, but the two Iberian nations still made much of the priority given them by their decisive and glorious role in the opening up of the new worlds. Muslim dominion in the Mediterranean and the independence of the countries of North Africa could no longer be guaranteed by an Ottoman Empire thrust back on the defensive after the European intervention in the Near East and even more so after the attack of the Russian armies in May 1877. Disraeli was quite clear in his mind that the keys to Asia were in Istanbul and Cairo, and if he saved the independence of Turkey it was only to keep them away from Russia, which was openly seeking to resume the legacy of Byzantium.

Hence the Congress of Berlin, in June 1878, marked a pause in the conflicts splitting Europe. It gave a free rein to Great Britain in Egypt and to France in Tunisia. It allowed Italy and Germany, which were indeed allies, to turn their eyes toward Africa, while Portugal feverishly sought to exploit history in order to influence reality.

Congress of Berlin
1878

The behaviour of the European powers during the five years following the Congress is explained by the improvisations due to circumstances, but it does not exclude the presence of long-range geopolitical views. When France and England, intervening in Tunisia and Egypt, gave the final blow to what had been left of the Ottoman order in the Mediterranean, they were taking advantage of a situation they had not attempted to create, but that entered into the framework of their grand geopolicital designs.

The Tunis Regency and the Khedivate, for different reasons but with the same result, had become completely dependent financially on the great European powers. Their rulers who, though theoretically still owing allegiance to the Turkish government, were trying, after the latter's enfeeblement, to keep up a tortuous political line between European demands that were becoming more and more impatient and the xenophobic reactions of their own people. The younger generation, as well as the traditionalist elements of Tunis and Cairo were learning nationalism in the hard school of humiliation.

Colonial expansion was not yet popular in Paris and London. It was only in the wake of lengthy debates in the two parliaments that credits were voted allowing a direct intervention in the affairs of Tunisia and Egypt. Nine years after the defeat of 1871, the idea that France might turn its military forces toward the conquest of African territories touched on what to some people seemed like treason. Clemenceau opposed Jules Ferry, who tried to demonstrate that French Algeria would never be safe as long as Tunisia remained a haven for plunderers and for unconquered tribes. The "Islamic specialists" emphasized the profound unity underlying the phenomena that were then agitating Mediterranean Africa: the persistent agitation in the region of Constantine, the flare-up of xenophobia among the Tuaregs (who massacred the mission led by Colonel Flatters in the region of In-Salah at the gates of the Sahara, in March 1881), the insecurity of Oran in the south, the agitation of the Senussis in the great Libyan desert, the veiled rebellion of the youthful Egyptian officers. The goal of all these movements was to fling the Europeans into the sea... if it was not already too late.

In practice the interests of businessmen had even more specific weight than the opinions of specialists. It was maintained that "under French protection all the natural resources of that region (Tunisia) could be developed with the energy and intensity of modern practises and methods." For still other reasons, Tunisia excited Italian cupidity, too. The politicians in Rome considered it a natural extension of a nation finally reunited. For them modern Italy was the natural heir of ancient Rome, whose security depended on the effective control of the rich plains of the Province of Africa and the maritime routes between the eastern and western Mediterranean.

The Treaty of Bardo, imposed on the Bey of Tunis in May 1881 by France, after a lightning intervention by Algerian troops, marked the beginning of a new era in Africa as well as in Europe. With no intention of retreat, France entered on its great North African adventure at the expense of a possible friendship with its Italian neighbour. It was Paris rather than Rome that took up the burden of imperial responsibilities on the soil of Africa, with everything it invoked in the way of fleeting triumphs, heavy sacrifices, and, as history had already shown, bitter disappointments and shattered dreams. The agreements of June 1883 and the administrative organization of the Protectorate on October 1884 did no more than formalize an accomplished fact.

Great Britain and Egypt

Similarly, by a chain of circumstances as inevitable as they were unforeseen, Great Britain became responsible for the fortunes of Egypt.

In spite of British opposition, the France of Napoleon III, by opening the Suez Canal, had brought Egypt back into the great currents of international trade and competition. At the same moment the Khedive, following the policy of Mehemet Ali, imposed on it the responsibilities of an African power with the mission of thrusting back toward the south the borders of civilization. The Sultan had assigned to him the responsibility for the rights of the Ottoman Empire, which since the sixteenth century had extended to the ports of Suwakkim and Massawa in the Red Sea and to part of the horn of Africa as far as the Somali coast. Sudanese Africa was regarded by Cairo as a natural zone of expansion for Egypt. In the name of the Khedive, Samuel Baker and his wife had already gone up the Nile as far as its source. Hence the abolition of the slave-trade, whose centre was located in this region, seemed to Ismail to devolve on Egypt.

In 1872, when Nubar Pasha offered Charles Gordon the opportunity to succeed to Baker as governor of the Egyptian provinces of the Equator, he was stitching together the tragic fate that was to seal the future on the Nile of the Sudan, of Egypt, and of Great Britain.

Gordon took a serious view of the idea that the Egyptian flag had to be the symbol of human freedom and dignity as well as of the liberation of Africa. But the realities of Egyptian power in the valley of the Upper Nile were quite different. Gordon himself noted "the absolute destitution of these countries." He imagined that "these black nations had to be bound up with our animal desires and our appetites." Thus paradox would have it that a Christian living according to the Scriptures was to be a knight in the service of the Muslim power being reborn in the valley of the Nile. Thanks to him the Egyptian flag was planted in the very heart of Central Africa. The rights of the Khedive were reaffirmed as far as the eastern coasts of Africa, where a futile expedition on the Somali coast was highly disturbing to the British Consul General in Zanzibar, who himself was backing the Sultan of Zanzibar's claims to Mogadiscio. Neither the slave-traders of Nubia and the Red Sea nor the Christian kingdom of Ethiopia approved this new outburst of vigour in Egyptian policy. Thus Great Britain found itself charged with the resolution of the still burning question of the fate of these countries of the Upper Nile. As early as 1867 a British army, under the orders of Sir Robert Napier, had crushed the Ethiopian armies that had started off rather imprudently on the conquest of Nubia; it forced Emperor Theodore to kill himself after a career distinguished by cruelty and xenophobia. The opening of the Suez Canal in 1868 was followed by a renewal of the policy of Egyptian expansion. The Egyptians annexed Harar in 1875, and became the successors of the Muslim kingdom whose existence on the flank of the Christian Amharas of the Ethiopian plateau had always been a thorn in their side. From 1875 to 1876, Egypt embarked on a series of attacks on Theodore's successor, Emperor John, but the defeat of its armies at Gura in 1877 tolled the knell of Cairo's pretensions in the Indian Ocean and the southern part of the Red Sea.

The failure of Gordon, who had been sent as plenipotentiary to Emperor John's court in 1879, wrote finis to the Egyptian episode. In spite of having made use of bold and brilliant Europeans like Samuel Baker, Munziger (who organized the luckless expeditions to Ethiopia) Emin Pasha and Gordon himself, Egypt had totally failed in its great African campaign. Mehemet Ali and his successors had set themselves goals that were far too ambitious for a nation that had scarcely recovered from the debilitating tyranny of the Mamluks. The price of this fiasco was a financial dependence on foreign countries that was now complete, and the embitterment of an officers' corps humiliated by a series of failures in adventures that were ill prepared and ill executed. *Egypt's failure*

In 1880 France and Great Britain were the great creditor nations of Europe and the world. They held at their finger-tips the deficit budgets of the Ottoman Empire and of its dependencies: Egypt and Tunisia. There was an immense temptation to make use of the control of "The Debt" to sway Istanbul, Cairo and Tunis, and to paralyse any desire on their part for resistance. Egypt alone reacted against the scarcely veiled threat of a European protectorate. Colonel Arabi, who had become Minister of War en 1881, organized a movement of resistance. On 11 June 1882, some fifty Europeans were massacred by a population activated in xenophobic fury.

The government of Paris was weakened by the violent political controversies due to its intervention in Tunisia and in Tonkin. France withdrew its squadron from the Alexandria harbour and left Great Britain the sole responsibility for the restoration of order. Alexandria was bombarded on 11 July 1882. The British army landed at Ismailia on 21 August. The Egyptian army commanded by Arabi was crushed on 13 September at Tell el-Kebir. It was a defeat that in the words of the German scholar Brockelmann "was to determine the history of Egypt for half a century."

Hence, at the moment when France had committed itself irrevocably in North Africa by its conquest of the Constantine region and by the protectorate it imposed on Tunisia, Great Britain became responsible for the fortunes of the Nile Valley.

The power of Cairo was threatened from the south. Taking advantage of the troubled times, and finding in Islamic Messianism the sources of a remarkably effective proselytizing movement, Muhammad Ahmad, son of a carpenter in the city of Dongola, successfully aroused the deepest instincts of the Sudanese people, who loathed both native corruption and alien intrusion. Proclaiming himself Mahdi (i.e., "the God-guided") Ahmad promised his people the total elimination of the Turks, the Egyptians and the Europeans. He considered himself the emissary of the Archangel Gabriel, charged with the restoration of the universal Muslim Empire at the point of the sword. *The Mahdi and his "mission"*

The Egyptian armies underwent a first setback at the hands of the Sudanese in August 1881; they were crushed completely in the summer of 1882. El-Obeid was occupied in 1883. It was a Holy War, led by a prophet and soldier of genius at the head of 100,000 fanatic warriors. The last rescue column, headed by the British General Hicks Pasha, was massacred in 1883. Egypt retained only a precarious control of its garrisons in Suwakkim, Khartoum, and Gondokoro, and Gordon had to be called back as Governor General of the Sudan Provinces to save the situation. He arrived on 18 February at Khartoum, now a fortress besieged by a fanatical and courageous army.

Did the Egyptian garrisons, isolated in the ocean of Sudanese fanaticism, have to be evacuated without dishonour, or were there still hopes of breaking the Mahdi's power?

This dispute raised a storm in the ruling circles of Cairo as well as at London; it wasted a great deal of precious time. A rescue column commanded by Colonel Wilson in the beginning of 1885 arrived too late. On 26 January Khartum fell to the assault of the Mahdi's followers. Gordon, who had seen death on its way, was dismembered by lances and swords. Great Britain had been able to master the first explosion of Egyptian nationalism on the coast, but in the Sudan it had collided with a phenomenon that was more elemental and vigorous. It withdrew temporarily from the valley of the Upper Nile, mourning with its queen the beloved hero of China and Africa.

While France and Great Britain were gradually assuming the responsibility for the routes of access to northern Africa, Leopold II, King of the Belgians, scion of a stalwart Teutonic dynasty, repeated, four centuries later, the miracle of Henry the Navigator. Like him, he had dreamed of a grand design. Like him, he had the same understanding of his own time, the same breadth of view, the same sureness of information and the same continuity in action. Like him, finally, he had a talent for attracting to his service exceptional men, animated by an irresistible drive, who were longing for means of action and were ready to give their sponsor the fruits of their enterprise.

Down to 1875 the Congo basin had not been the object of any systematic exploration. The Portuguese were busy looking for an east-west junction, and touched the basin only in its southern portion; the British and the Boers had not yet finished exploring the highlands of the Transvaal, while the British of the east coast, protectors of the Sultan of Zanzibar, were fully taken up with the abolition of slavery in his dominions.

The travels of Cameron, Stanley and Brazza approached this problem from a completely different point of view. It was obvious that each one of the committees of the International Commission of Exploration and of the Civilization of Central Africa, set up in 1878, was struggling to channelize all this exploration in its own interests. This international approach represented a coalition of contradictory and often competing efforts. England and Portugal, brought together by a common danger, were under no illusions. For these two countries, Savorgnan de Brazza — an Italian who had become French—and Stanley—a Welshman, and an American citizen in the service of Belgium —were equally dangerous. Portugal was running the risk of losing its historic rights in the mouths of the Congo. Great Britain risked being deprived of a profitable current of free trade. The Anglo-Portuguese Treaty of 1884 represented a purely tactical compromise between a rising imperialism (in Stanley's sense) and "the decadent imperialism of a nation drawing economic drafts on its political past."

Portugal wanted recognition for its traditional rights in the mouths of the Congo; this aroused the immediate opposition of France and Germany; they sided with the King of the Belgians, whose rights were no longer internationally recognized. Bismarck, in a note dated 7 June 1884, addressed to the British government, made a point of a "European" right to free trade in the territories of Central Africa.

Conflicting interests in the Congo

When the great European powers answered the joint convocation by France and Germany of a conference on Central Africa to be held at Berlin at the end of 1884, there was no question of disputing the status of South Africa or of North Africa, where Great Britain and France had assumed perfectly clear responsibilities. It was a question of deciding the status of areas that had not yet been appropriated, and of laying down certain rules of international law that would translate the ideas of internationalization and of protection. The diplomats who were to assemble in Berlin under the chairmanship of the wily Bismarck very often had only the vaguest idea of the areas and peoples over whom their governments were affirming their claims. They could have no idea that the Africans would later demand the most important right of all—the right that arose out of their very absence at the conference.

Chapter 19
European Diplomacy and the African Vacuum

In 1884, for the first time, Europe as a whole began to occupy itself with Africa for overtly political ends.

For more than a century the abolition of the slave-trade and of slavery had been a major problem, by which Great Britain skilfully profited. Thanks to its explorers and missionaries it took over the leadership of the abolitionist movement; willy-nilly it became responsible for the fortunes of Egypt, Nubia and the eastern coast under the sovereignty of the Sultan of Zanzibar, while on the western coast it controlled the mouths of the Niger. France, which had left from Senegal and Gabon later, advanced toward the Sudanese routes. The Arab and European slavers had to concentrate their business in the least accessible regions of Central Africa, from the valleys of the Zambezi and the Congo to the great lakes, upper Nile, and the country around Lake Chad. Hence central Africa became an object of international attention.

International attention drawn to Central Africa

In his instructions to Stanley, King Leopold of Belgium had been moved by the needs of the struggle against the Arab slave-trade, which was ravaging the area around the upper reaches of the Congo River, to set as his goal the creation of a "Free State", based on the installation of a series of stations (scientific, commercial and political) that were to cause "the principles of civilization to shine forth in the murkiness of Africa."

The King thought a State could be his personal property. He was inspired by such precedents as that of the Brook family, which had become owners and sovereign rulers of the State of Sarawak, in Borneo, and by the idea current in Europe at the time of the autocratic government of Gordon in the Sudan, where it was proved (very nearly) that will-power and imagination could transform a barbarous state by bringing it into the broad tide of civilization.

Unlike his illustrious Portuguese predecessor, King Leopold could not appeal to an undisputed political and spiritual authority—the Pope's—in order to validate claims that were, after all, founded on nothing more than the adventurous voyages of an explorer who had always been singularly indiscriminate in his choice of means. Nevertheless the flag of the International Association of the Congo was recognized as the symbol of a sovereign power by the United States in April 1884, by Germany in December of the same year and by France and Portugal in February 1885.

The Conference of Berlin had as its unavowed task, finally, the regularization and limitation of the extraordinary ambitions of a sovereign who had been singularly clairvoyant in organizing the efficient occupation of the African interior. The countries of Europe were ready to accept a sort of peaceful co-existence on the continent to be conquered.

Thus the Treaty of Berlin acknowledged a certain situation. It did not create it. It gave it a new status in international law that was, in fact, a projection of European law.

In 1885, the springboards from which the European powers were to launch a final onslaught on the last bastions of African resistance were the following:

* France occupied Algeria. It had been "protecting" the Regency of Tunis since 1881. In the Senegal it occupied Saint-Louis, and founded the city of Dakar opposite the Island of Gorée. It secured recognition of its rights in Guinea by the Franco-British Convention of 1882. On the coast of western Africa, it occupied a series of settlements (Grand Bassam, Assinié, Porto-Novo) that brought it into contact with the peoples of the interior. Further south it was in control of the coasts of Gabon, where it established the settlement of Libreville, originally a refuge for slaves (1849). Thanks to Brazza it secured recognition of its rights over the valley of the Ogwé and the right bank of the Congo and of the Ubangi (1878). On the other side of Africa it had its old colony, Réunion, a natural stop-over on the way to India. It asserted its claims, based on Révoil's explorations, to the African shores of the Indian Ocean, and was already thinking of putting Madagascar under a protectorate. Under Napoleon III it had occupied Obok on the coast of the former Sultanate of Adal, a coaling station on the new route to the Far East opened up by the Suez Canal.

* Great Britain occupied the mouth of the Gambia River, the settlements of Sierra Leone and of the Gold Coast, as well as the mouths of the Niger. It exercised total sovereignty over Cape Colony, and occupied all the approaches to the South African highlands. It was protecting Zanzibar, and through the Sultan exercised indirect rights over the whole of the East African coastline. Similarly, having become the protector of the Khedive, it was applying his theoretic rights over the Nile Valley.

* The Germans, newcomers to Africa, had established bases in the Togo, the Cameroons and in Southwest Africa, as well as in eastern Africa (as a result of the bold exploits of the Peters brothers).

* The Portuguese had kept only one point of support on the coast of the Gulf of Guinea. No one disputed the rights they had acquired over the coasts of Angola (Luanda, Benguela) and the islets of San Tomé and Principe. An international body of arbitration confirmed their possession of the coasts of Mozambique from the Bay of Delagoa to the southern limits—still poorly defined—of the zone protected by the Sultanate of Zanzibar.

* The Spaniards had been in occupation of the Canary Islands since the fifteenth century, and had established themselves in the island of Fernando Po.

* The Italians created a point of support on the Red Sea, at Assab.

It was only Morocco, Ethiopia, Liberia (created in 1825 by the American anti-slavery societies in order to facilitate the re-establishment in Africa of the emancipated slaves) and, paradoxically, the new Free State of the Congo that were in the eyes of Europe entities in international law. Such "recognition" was denied the other African states, though for centuries some of them had been in close touch with Europeans through the slave-trade.

Certain kingdoms in the interior, such as the Ashanti, had created a military force that was capable of withstanding the European invaders as well as of subjugating their African neighbours. The great states of Kanem, Bornu and Baguirmi had maintained an impressive political apparatus, even though they had been exhausting themselves in internal struggles in which, at the junction of the trade routes between central and western Africa and the Red Sea, the great Arab and Hamitic conquering races confronted the Negroes.

In the east of Africa, races from the north had established a few well-organized kingdoms, like those of the Uganda, the Ruanda and the Urundi, over a Bantu substratum. The tribes on the Red Sea coast, at the foot of the Ethiopian mountain range, had remained in tribal anarchy. Further south, Arab merchants had created something that seemed to some observers to be the beginning of a political system characteristic of eastern Africa, in control of the trade routes into the highlands of the interior. Along these routes, all the way south, beyond the Limpopo and the Zambezi, the Bantu peoples had broken up into a large number of groups slowly descending toward the highlands of southern Africa. The hazards of war and of various negotiations with the advanced elements of European power had thrown into relief as political entities the Bechuanas, the Swazis, the Basutos, and the Xosas, then the Zulus. Such "kingdoms" as those of the Congo and the Monomotapa, known to navigators and merchants ever since the end of the sixteenth century, no longer seemed to count. The loose formula of confederation they represented had proved unable to withstand the brutal impact of the new forces of foreign or domestic origin.

On the other hand, new centers of organization had emerged around political, military and religious leaders. The Mahdi in the Upper Nile, Ahmadu in the middle Niger, Samory in Upper Guinea, and Cetshwayo among the Zulus, in their spirit of resistance, their military and political skill, and their various systems of organization, represented so many highly significant reactions of African vitality to the intrusion of Europe. A desperate logic had led them to exercise their power primarily at the expense of their own African peoples, the great bulk of whom were ready to submit to the apparently invincible emissaries of the new order. Yet the initial weapons of African nationalism were forged in such undertakings, even if these seemed doomed to defeat.

The Europe of that day, to be sure, had only a very vague idea of these African political forms. The rights of local rulers were recognized only to the extent that they validated, through outright abandonment, the treaties alienating their territory through cession or the establishment of protectorates. Any one who resisted simply looked like a rebel. No one had the notion that the Africans would or could hamper for any length of time an advance that was simultaneously desirable morally and inevitable materially. *The European point of view*

Europe, in fact, thought it had rights and obligations in the African continent. It had the right to demand that it be opened up to trade and to the circulation of political and religious ideas based on the postulate of the dignity of the individual. It had the duty of eliminating the vestiges of slavery and of breaking down the isolation of immense territories that had been stagnating since the dawn of humanity. Missionaries, whether Protestant or Catholic, bore a formidable responsibility. They were the obvious mediators between the Negro peoples and the European invaders, both colonists and merchants, who had no interest in any law but that of their immediate profits. Such a burden weighing on the white nations, a burden in which economic motives and moral obligations were deep intertwined, called for a certain allocation of tasks.

France was already planning a junction via the Sahara between its Algerian settlements and those it was trying to protect and extend in the region of the Niger. It was also thinking of linking together, from east to west, along a single bold straight line, the Sudanese territories and the Ethiopian fortress with its natural outlet in Djibuti, by taking advantage of the good-will of the new emperor now reigning over the ancient Christian outpost.

By starting out from the points it held on the coasts of the Gulf of Guinea France could also go up the valley of the Niger, and thus make up an uninterrupted continental bloc from the Mediterranean to the Atlantic coast. By leaving from Gabon it could send its expeditions toward the closed basin of the Chad (which could also be reached from the west) and from there go up toward the Upper Nile and its Ethiopian sources as far as Obok and Djibuti (not forgetting that Djibuti was one of the indispensable way-stations on the maritime route that, passing through the Suez Canal, led across the Indian Ocean to the new French protectorates in Indochina).

Great Britain could also trace on the map analogous and competing axes of penetration. By making some exchanges (Dahomey for Gambia) it was possible, to be sure, to eliminate the French from their enclaves near the mouths of the Niger, and to regroup the British settlements into one entity. It was also tempting to try to bring together the coastal regions and the traditionally powerful kingdoms, north of the Niger and its principal tributary the Senoue, that were themselves in contact with the caravan route linking the Nile Valley with central and western Africa.

Moreover, it was now known, thanks to Speke, Grant and Baker, that the Nile Valley gave access to the kingdoms of central Africa. This piece of geographical information gave rise to a grandiose dream—of an artery of trade and civilization that would link the outposts of British rule (which under Cecil Rhodes's visionary drive had thrust northward even beyond Matabeleland), with the great lakes of the African interior and with the Upper Nile, where Britain was lending its protection to the Egyptian state. This dream was inspiring enough to channelize the energies of superior men like Rhodes himself, Johnston, Lugard, Gordon, Kitchener, and after them generations of officers, and civilian functionaries dedicated to the glory of Great Britain. The Germans too, as they contemplated the map, were thinking of a "Mittelafrika" stretching as far as Tanganyika from the Cameroons and German Southwest Africa. The Portuguese wanted to secure recognition for their rights to the traditional route followed by their trade between Angola and Mozambique. A little later the Italians were to think of starting out from Eritrea, conquering the Ethiopian mountains, and from there going up toward the Mediterranean across the western Sudan, Darfur, Fezzan and Tripoli.

A simple study of these broad outlines of the projected penetration, through spaces considered empty, will show that the axis imagined by the British, following at thirty degrees east, was bound to cut across the great east-west axis imagined by the French between the tenth and fifteenth degrees north latitude, the same horizontal axis dreamt of by the Germans at the height of the equator, and finally by the Portuguese at the level of the fifteenth degree south latitude. The points of conflict were quite clear: Bahr el-Ghazal for the French and the British, Victoria Lake for the British and the Germans, and the upper valley of the Zambezi for the Portuguese and the British. (Map p. 333.)

King Leopold and the Treaty of Berlin

The Treaty of Berlin did not make the slightest pretense at deciding between contradictory claims or aspirations. The signatory powers merely committed themselves to inform each other mutually of any seizure of "a territory on the coasts of the African continent located outside their present holdings." They also undertook to establish "an authority adequate for creating respect for acquired rights and if necessary the freedom of trade and of transit."

What it had primarily succeeded in doing was to "neutralize," under the personal authority of King Leopold, now the internationally accepted ruler of the Free State of the Congo, the basin of the great river of Central Africa, which hence was to be neither Portuguese, nor French, nor German, allegedly one of the great fears of the British Foreign Office.

The various treaties of territorial delimitation that the Free State of the Congo was to pass with its neighbours in the north, the north-east, the east, south-east and south-west during the following years were to do no more than affirm the great successes of skillful diplomacy, which had been able to place an enormous portion of Central Africa and its natural riches beyond the reach of the new and growing appetites of the European powers.

Page 177
Tuareg women in the Sahara. The nomadic Berber tribes controlled the trade routes through Black Africa that were opened up by the French after 1862. Sporadic flare-ups and the massacre of Colonel Flatters (1881) led to forming mobile French units to break Tuareg military power. It took twenty years of desert warfare to overcome Tuareg resistance.

Fernand Foureau, of the Foureau-Lamy mission, in his tent. In 1898-1900, this French Mission was one of three crossing to open up the Chad region, allotted to France through the Franco-British agreements of 1890.

Chapter 20
Europe's Influence Expands

After the Congress of Berlin, European international law grew richer through the addition of a new code concerning the conquest of Africa. The interests of the natives had to be protected, the freedom of international trade had to be respected, and the continent had to be opened up to the missionaries.

The explorers, both civilian and military, now saw their undertakings take on the mantle of a novel legality. The Chanceries of the powers reserved the right to disavow any enterprises that were too ambitious or clumsy, but they were well aware that a flag flying over some obscure outpost or a treaty concluded with some second-rate chieftain constituted remarkably powerful arguments at the negotiating table.

After the Treaty of Berlin was signed Europeans confronted Africans, either as allies or enemies, throughout the length and breadth of an entire continent. This confrontation produced exceptional personalities on both sides. It took place at a moment in world history that was revolutionary. The most remote regions, the most isolated peoples were gradually drawn into the orbit of a world that had begun fermenting more and more explosively.

Extensive confrontation of Europeans and Africans

The great desert and its Sudanese borders were, according to the terminology of the Berlin Congress, a hinterland to be occupied. Great Britain could claim to exercise certain rights toward the north, up-stream on the Niger River. Through the Franco-British agreements of 1890 it acknowledged France's right to extend its effective rule north of a line going from Say to Garoua, on the Benoué, near Lake Chad (a line that is now, except for a detail or two, the boundary of present-day Nigeria), with the addition of the region comprised between that and the "French possession of the Mediterranean", that is, Algeria. Lord Salisbury explained this decision, which seemed to many a sort of concession, by maintaining that "if you look at the map and are satisfied merely with measuring degrees, the impression may be given that France is laying claim to the possession of a great stretch of country. But a country must be judged not only by its extent but by its value... It is a question of the Sahara desert; hence the value of the region that France has asserted dominion over must be diminished by the entire extent of that desert."

Jules Cambon, who was at that time Governor General of Algeria, answered: "We shall scratch the sand that has been given to the Gallic rooster. We shall put rails on it. We shall plant the telegraph. We shall make artesian wells there and shall listen to the Gallic rooster crow out to us, from the tops of the casbahs and the oases, his most resounding and most joyous song."

The Arab and Berber trade routes were now well known, thanks to René Caillé, Barth, Nachtigal, and Duveyrier. The latter had signed the Franco-Tuareg treaty of Ghadames in 1862. As a matter of fact, in order to use these routes leading to Black Africa the Tuaregs either had to be befriended or their military power had to be broken. In addition, the route that leads to the Hoggar and passes by the oases located south of the Algerian highlands that govern the access to the great dunes, then crosses the Tademait plateau to reach the relay-station of In-Salah, was menaced by the threat of religious fanaticism. Abrupt flare-ups of this fanaticism would start from eastern Morocco, reach the south of Algeria, and give rise to the great armed uprisings that made the Algerian Sahara a danger zone.

From 1864 to 1869, the insurrection of the nomad Chambaas, led by Slimane had shown the French the de facto solidarity between the nomad groups roving about the region between the Wargla and the Tust, from the southern rim of the western sand-dunes as far as Wad Saoura. Ever since the Franco-Moroccan Treaty of 1845 France had been in control of the ksurs south of Ain Sefra, on the southern rim of the highlands; it could not remain indifferent to the agitation of the nomadic tribes on its borders. The effective control of the region of the great oases was an indispensable prerequisite for penetrating southwards. When Colonel Flatters was massacred by the Tuareg tribes around In-Salah in March 1881, the question was finally posed in an unmistakable manner. It was necessary to break the military power of the confederation of independent communities in control of the "avenue of palms" that extended 750 miles from the Atlas to the heart of the Sahara, as far as the Hoggar. The capital of the Gurara, Timimun, at the foot of the great western dune hill, and In-Salah in the south-east, were key positions to the region between the western Sahara and the Hoggar mountain range. In-Salah was occupied by French columns on 29 December 1899, following a bold expedition led by Captain Peine to the western rim of the great desert.

Desert dangers;
the Tuaregs defeated
1899

In 1901 Major Laperrine was instructed to organize the "Southern Territories." He founded the Sahara Companies, in which the nomadic Chambaas, now recruited as volunteers under the command of French officers, were grouped in mobile units that were largely autonomous. Laperrine had learned in the Sahara school of war that nomads could be subjugated only by a force that was as spare and mobile as their own, that knew the terrain and could spy out the enemy. In these inhospitable wastes, death by thirst or massacre by an armed band that would surge out of nothingness and quickly melt away back into it was the punishment lying in wait for any error of judgement. In October 1903 the Hoggar mountain range, a natural haven for the Saharan tribes, was occupied by French columns. It had taken twenty years of constant effort for the Tuareg resistance to be broken.

Further south, the frontier regions of the Sahara had been the stamping grounds for the migrating Peulhs from the east ever since the eighteenth century. The states bordering on Lake Chad and the middle range of the Niger (which Leo Africanus had described in the sixteenth century) had been subjugated or weakened ever since the beginning of the nineteenth century by Islamized Peulhs, who controlled the Emirate of Sokoto and had broken the rule of the Hausas. Ousman Dan Fodio became the "Commander of the Faithful" in 1804. The Peulhs extended their domination to the south-east as far as the mountain range of Adamawa and to the west as far as the approaches to the Senegal River. Their rule was given support by the numerous immigrants of the same race who were already settled in Macina and on the highlands of the Futa Djallon. Timbuktu was wrested from the Tuaregs. The Peulh conquest of the Sudanese great spaces was reminiscent of that of the Mongols in thirteenth-century Europe. It was the victory of a military caste with a highly mobile striking power. The Peulhs levied a land-tax on the conquered sedentary population, and turned themselves into an aristocracy of shepherds.

The Peulh Empire

The French collided with the Peulhs as well as with the Tuaregs. El-Haj Omar, the enemy of Faidherbe, was linked by race and marriage to the Peulh Emirate of Sokoto. A devout Muslim, he had made the pilgrimage to Mecca and was intimately familiar with the whole horizontal route linking the coasts of the Red Sea with those of the Atlantic, the whole length of which was in the grip of the Islamized sultanates. The

Behanzin and his family, photographed in 1894. The redoutable son succeeded a sanguinary father as King of Abomey in 1889. After two years of warfare against the fanatical enemy, the French under Colonel Dodds occupied Abomey in 1892, captured Behanzin two years later and deported him to Martinique.

Nubians and the Arabs went as far as the Chad, while the Hausas and the Peulhs controlled the middle stretches of the Niger as far as the approaches to the Senegal River, where the "Toucouleurs" (Tukrurs) and the Moors lived in harmony. The Tuaregs were thrust back to the north, the Bambaras to the southwest.

The region of the middle Niger soon lapsed into anarchy. The tribes that had been settled there longer, such as the Dogons and the Bobos, collided with the tribes whose military power gave them the upper hand. French columns, including a great many soldiers recruited in Senegal, were to finish off the Peulh empire.

Colonel Archinard occupied Segu in 1890, Nioro in 1891, Djenné and Mopti in 1893. Colonel Monteil demonstrated French talent by retracing, in the opposite direction, the itinerary followed more than thirty years before by Barth. He left Segu and came to Tripoli after crossing Say (located at the limit of the zone of influence recognized as French by the Franco-British agreement of 1890), Kano, Kuka in Bornu, and the Chad region as far as the Fezzan. Starting out from Bamako, Captain Binger reconnoitred the valley of the Volta and linked the axis of French penetration via the Sudan with the old settlements of the coast of the Gulf of Guinea, at Grand Bassam. Colonel Joffre crowned this transcontinental feat by occupying Timbuktu in 1894. The Tuaregs, like the Peulhs, were incapable of doing anything further against the French occupation. For that matter Timbuktu itself was no longer anything but the ghost of the once-thriving city that had been ruined by the Moroccan adventurers and the constant incursions of nomads from the north and east.

The opening up of the Niger route placed the French, coming in from Senegal, in contact with the Tuareg tribes of the south, who still ruled the Negro populations of the Saharan borders. Their natural fortress was Adrar of the Iforas, which Laperrine, coming from the north, did not reach until 1904.

Thus the marking off of what is now called the Algerian Sahara and the outposts of French rule based on the Senegal and the Niger Rivers is the result of the junction of the columns that had come from the north (commanded by Laperrine) and those from the south (commanded by Theveniau). It is the frontier of present-day Algeria and Mali. The great North-South route was now open, and its security was respected thanks to the very people that had blocked it for so long. All that had to be done was to carry on with the reconnoitring and occupation of the lands along the great horizontal line leading to the Chad across the sub-Saharan Sahel. Its geopolitical importance had always been recognized by Muslims as well as by Europeans.

Opening of the great North-South route

In the middle of the nineteenth century the picture of the kingdoms occupying the approaches to the Chad, as drawn by Leo Africanus, was modified by the Peulh revolt and by the efforts of the Emirate of Sokoto to conquer the ancient kingdoms of Katsina, Zaria and Kano. The Negro-Berber Kingdom of Bornu and the Kingdom of Kanem still maintained their resistance. Located at the junctions of the trade and pilgrimage routes, they had always been connected with the great currents that cut across the Muslim world community in Africa. They were thus linked to Mediterranean Africa and to the Near East as well. Thanks to the firearms that had been coming in from Turkey ever since the sixteenth century they were able to checkmate the Moroccan invasion that had swamped the Sonrhai Empire.

Thus the existence of these two states, Bornu and Kanem, both independent and both with military respect for each other, represented a factor of equilibrium for a long time. Nevertheless their constant rivalry with the Hausa kingdoms (their western neighbours) was weakening them, as was their resistance to the Peulhs' repeated attempts at invasion.

In the east, the kingdoms bordering on Baguirmi, Waddai and Darfur were themselves subjected to the pressure of armed slave-trading groups that had gradually been

Page 182
Left: King Glé Glé of Abomey (Gold Coast, Dahomey tribe) in the guise of a lion. This warrior king who massacred thousands of prisoners had as motto "I am like the young lion who spreads terror as soon as his teeth grow." He and his son Behanzin collided with the French after these established a protectorate in the neigboring kingdom of Porto Novo in 1882. Musée de l'Homme, Paris.

thrust back into the Chad orbit by the Egyptian and British advances in the Nile Valley. They too were threatened by the French columns that had started out from the Niger and the Congo and gone up toward Lake Chad, which at the beginning of the nineteenth century had become the "African turntable."

After the successive failures of the Cazamayou mission (massacred at Zinder on 5 May 1898), and Voulet-Chanoine (whose tragic mishaps were deeply disturbing to French opinion) three French columns reached Chad at the same time, at the opening of the twentieth century. The Foureau-Lamy mission crossed the territory still ruled by the Tuaregs and got as far as Agades and Zinder. Joalland and Meynier, coming from the west, reached Nguirmi on 23 October 1899. Gentil, who had started out from the settlements of central Africa and gone up the Chari and the northern tributaries of the Congo, reached the same point in February 1900. It remained for the French to break the rule of the slave-trader Rabah, who had come from the Nile Valley and established himself firmly in his Darfur base, and ever since 1893 had been in control of the section of the great horizontal line going from the Chad to the Red Sea. Rabah died 22 April 1900, when his camp was attacked by three French columns jointly. This French victory in the heart of Africa made the most audacious dreams of Faidherbe, Brazza and Laperrine come to life.

Rabah (an adopted son of Zobeir, whom Gordon had fought so often) has become a legendary personage, now that our historical perspective has changed. But in reality this brilliant general, who had broken the centuries-old power of the Bornu, had made himself unpopular through his demands, and his death was greeted by the populace as a veritable deliverance.

End of resistance in Algerian oases

In less than twenty years the centers of African resistance in the great Algerian oases, the mountain ranges of the Hoggar and the Iforas, the valley of the Niger River and the hollow of the Chad, had yielded to French political and military pressure, while at the same time the British and the Germans, starting out from the south, were outflanking Islam from the rear.

Islam proved to be the sole power that was capable of galvanizing African energies against the European intrusion. Brilliant military and religious chiefs managed to group together substantial forces and showed great strategical talent. Nevertheless they suffered from the passivity of peoples exhausted by constant exactions and ruined by the civil wars that had been tearing this part of Africa to pieces for three centuries. The sedentary populations regarded the abdication of the ruling military and political castes in the face of the Europeans as no more than a change of masters, and generally an advantageous one.

The vast areas located between the Islamic empires of the Niger Valley and the coastal kingdoms of the Gulf of Guinea were the victims of their geographic situation. They suffered from the military expeditions that came from the south as well as from the north, looking for slaves and gold.

The Europeans moved on into the interior by starting out from their coastal settlements by the river routes or by the traditional land routes. Wherever they could they negotiated treaties designed to encourage trade and set up protectorates. The only armed resistance they met with came from groups dismayed by the necessities of a trade based on violence, or those, further north, that were in contact with the Peulhs and could take advantage of their relatively advanced weapons.

Certain groups survived all efforts at conquest by a mixture of diplomacy and isolation. They kept their own character and their vigour. The study of their traditions is very complex; it is really part of ethnohistory rather than of history proper. The Koniaguis, the Kissis, the Tomas, Guerzes, Yacubas, Baoules, Senufos, Paragurmas, Dogons, Bobos, the pagans of the Jos plateau, the Bananas of the northern Cameroons, and many others have come down through history to our own day without seeming to have been affected by it at all. Other peoples, located nearer the great currents of war and of trade, defended their independence while yielding to the new situation created by the European ascendancy. In the Senegal the Wolofs and the Serreres accepted French rule from 1860 on, but they jealously preserved their own personalities just as they had with respect to the Peulhs and the Bambaras.

The Mossi Kingdom, founded along the upper Volta in the thirteenth century, successfully defended itself against the Peulh invasions from the east and north, which proliferated during the second half of the nineteenth century. The King was called the Moro Naba; his authority was religious as well as political.

The Mossi Kingdom; The Yoruba states

Further eastwards, the Yorubas, who in the north were subject to influences "emanating from the civilization of the steppes and of the Sahara" (Frobenius), in the south were threatened by the Dahomey slave-traders, who by 1851 had arrived at the gates of Abeokuta. At this time the Yoruba states were threatened with extinction because of the convergence of attacks by the powerful sultanates of the north and the raids from the south. They were saved by the British protectorate imposed on them in 1894.

The French in Senegal and the British on their way up the Gambia River collided with the Peulhs of the Futa-Djallon and the Malinkes from the Niger. Futa-Djallon was occupied by France in 1888. A Franco-German convention in 1885, a Franco-Portuguese one in 1886, and a Franco-British one in 1889 recognized the French right to a protectorate.

The Malinkes found a first-class leader in the person of Samory, who was something of an untutored genius. Samory took advantage of the violent disorder that was churning up the area between the Niger and the Upper Volta to organize the struggle against the European advance. He mercilessly applied the Muslim laws of war, that is, the conquered cities and tribes had the choice between submission accompanied by a conversion to the faith of the Prophet, and annihilation pure and simple. Modern firearms were supplied to him by European dealers settled along the coast of the Sierra Leone.

Colonel Archinard, after having reduced the power of El-Haj Omar's successor in the approaches to the bend of the Niger, launched a campaign against Samory's bands in 1889; he imposed French rule on the entire region of the gold-mines, traditionally located between Sigueri and Dinguiraye. Almost a decade was needed to cut the communications of the "Almany" with Futa-Djallon and the coastal regions. Samory was finally captured in 1898 by Captain Gouraud and exiled to the Congo, where he died a couple of years later.

Samory, military leader of the Malinkes 1898

His opponents have acknowledged his talents. According to Colonel Borges-Desbordes, "he has an undeniable knowledge of war. His rapid marches, his attacks and retreats indicate a real tactical skill worthy of European officers... His natural soldierly aptitudes make him an excellent leader... He is certainly cruel and a bandit, a repulsive barbarian; unfortunately he is also an intelligent being who exercises a quite understandable supremacy over all the Negroes." Like Chaka and Abd el-Qadir, Samory applied the policy of the scorched earth and sacrificed people to the demands of an implacable struggle. His defeat sealed not only the fate of the upper Guinea, but that of the Ivory Coast and the Upper Volta. In 1892 the French and the British came to an agreement on the demarcation line between their zones of sovereignty on the Ivory Coast and the Gold Coast. France and Liberia, in their turn accepted the Rio Cavally as the boundary of their respective zones of influence.

For their part the British had, since 1874, been intervening directly in the affairs of the Gold Coast settlements. They found themselves gradually becoming more and more involved in the ancient conflict between the coastal peoples and the confederation of the Ashanti tribes, which had been strongly militarized since the beginning of the eighteenth century. The Gold Coast colony itself was founded on 24 July 1874; it took in Lagos but was separated from Sierra Leone.

At this time the Fans, a people living near the coastal forts, were reduced to a near-desperate offensive by the victorious armies of the Asantehne, who had come down from Kumasi. The British officers in command of the local volunteers and of small contingents of troops recruited in the northern territories organized a counter-offensive under the orders of Major General Sir Garnet Wolseley. Almost 2,500 European soldiers were finally launched in a bold offensive against Kumasi, which was occupied for a short time in February 1874. The Asantehne signed a peace treaty at Fomena in March, and the power of the confederation seemed to have been broken.

It was very important for Great Britain to prevent both the French columns going through the hinterland of the Ivory Coast and the German columns going northwards from Togoland, from taking advantage of the disturbed situation of the territories under Ashanti control to effect a junction and thus cut off the Gold Coast from any possible expansion northwards. Yet despite appearances the Ashanti power was far from extinct; with the advent of Prempeh (1888) the Ashanti kingdom seemed to take on something of its former vigour once again.

The Ashanti Gold Stool
1896

Great Britain had a free hand after the Franco-British agreement, and could impose a definitive protectorate on Kumasi. It began a campaign of political erosion by signing a series of treaties with the local chiefs who owed an allegiance of principle to Prempeh, and at last despatched a new column of almost 3,000 men under the command of Sir Francis Scott. It sent out ahead some light reconnaissance units under Major Robert Baden-Powell, the future hero of the Anglo-Boer war and the founder of the Boy Scout movement. Kumasi was occupied for the second time, on 20 July 1896, and Prempeh, even though he surrendered, was deported, as were his family and his generals. The whole of the Ashanti people regarded his deportation and the violation of its sacred places as a betrayal. There were rumblings of discontent, and a revolt exploded when the British authorities demanded the handing over of the Gold Stool, the symbol of the ancient monarchy. The small British garrison was besieged in the Kumasi fort. A new expedition had to be sent out to break the desperate resistance of the Ashanti people in July 1900. Ashanti became a crown colony and an integral part of the Gold Coast in 1902, as did the northern territories that British columns had overrun at the time of the French campaign against Samory.

Like Great Britain, France found itself involved further to the east in the local wars that had ravaged the regions bordering on the coast ever since the initiation of the lucrative slave trade two centuries before. In 1882 it put the coastal kingdom of Porto-Novo under its protectorate. The principal danger at this time was represented by the neighbouring kingdom of Abomey, which like the Ashanti derived its origins and military power from its favourable geographical position on the slave route linking the coastal trading-posts with the markets of the interior. King Glé-Glé and his son Behanzin, who succeeded him in 1889, were rough-and-ready fighters who terrorized their neighbours and wallowed in blood-stained orgies where thousands of prisoners were massacred in order to satisfy religious and magical needs. Behanzin's armies were inspired by fanaticism. Their courage was constantly being renewed by predictions forecasting the imminent end of the Whites. Women fought in the front lines, and gave a new life to the legend of the Amazons, who had first been reported by the Portuguese soldiers fighting the armies of the Monomotapa in the sixteenth century. Colonel Dodds needed two years of very hard campaigning to occupy Abomey in September 1892; Behanzin was captured in 1894.

By contrast the Germans encountered no difficulties at all in making their way into the interior, starting out from Lomé and Alecho. They had made sure of the political

The capture of Samory, the brillant Malinke leader. When the French occupied Futa-Djallon, Senegal, in 1888 they collided with this resourceful Muslim warrior. After almost a decade of struggle, Samory was finally captured and exiled to the Congo, where he died. The upper Guinea region with its gold mines became part of the French protectorate.

support of the Ewe confederation, linked to the Dahomeyans by ancient tribal ties and steeped in western culture thanks to the active role it had played in the trade that for two hundred years had linked Brazil and the Greater Antilles with the Gulf of Guinea.

Since the beginning of the nineteenth century the mouth of the Niger had been a private preserve of British trade. We have already read of the great explorations that were launched from these coastal settlements. The Royal Niger Company received its official charter in 1886. In addition to its commercial monopoly the company assumed *de facto* all the rights of sovereignty, except for international relations proper, which were reserved by Her Majesty's Government. In opening up their commercial routes northwards, the agents of the Company collided at first with what was left of the sovereignty of the Yoruba Kingdom, the Benin Kingdom (which had reached its peak at the end of the fifteenth century), and then with the state of Mupe on the shores of the Niger. All these had been weakened by the pressure of the Peulh kingdoms, whose onslaught came from the north. The last ruler of the Benin, Overami, was deposed by the British in 1897 and banished to Calabar. The last ruler of the Mupe was beaten the same year, while the Peulhs reached the extreme tip of their southern advance, the city of Ilorin, which was wrested from the Yorubas. When the first Franco-British agreement on Nigeria was concluded the former coastal kingdoms were placed under British rule.

Beyond the now conquered forward outposts of the southward Peulh penetration, there were great African emirates that turned their back to the sea and found their spiritual, political and military inspiration in the Islamic world. For centuries Islam had been all-powerful from the coast of the Senegal to that of the Nile Sudan, and from the Niger to North Africa. We have seen France entering this region by starting out from Algeria and the Atlantic coasts of western Africa. Great Britain itself had neared the great transverse line by ascending the Nile Valley; this time it reached it from the south.

On 1 January 1900, the New High Commissioner of the Protectorate of Northern Nigeria, Sir Frederick Lugard, assumed all the sovereign powers of the United Kingdom, which replaced all the previous privileges of the Royal Niger Company. What had to be checkmated were the German attempts (starting from the Cameroons) and the French attempts (starting from Dahomey) that aimed at controlling the middle reaches of the Niger. Sir Frederick, who had only limited means at his disposal, announced his intention of making use of "native chiefs and taking advantage of their intelligence and governmental authority, and in particular, the chiefs of the Fulani caste, with all respect for the fundamental laws of humanity and of justice." Local resistance everywhere was crushed. The Emirate of Yola gave up in 1901. The plateau of Baushi and the Bornu were reached in 1902. Zaria requested a British protectorate the same year. It was the Emirate of Sokoto, the dynamic centre of the Peulh power allied to the ancient Hausa substratum, that offered the most tenacious resistance. Kano was not occupied until 3 February 1903 and Sokoto at the end of the same year. The region was to rise up once again in 1906, under the leadership of the Mahdi (the "rebellion" of the Satirou).

In less than twenty years the British had succeeded, through a combination of commerce, diplomacy and force, in grouping together under the same rule vast territories whose common axis was the great Niger River. For the first time the former coastal kingdoms were linked to the emirates of the north. The trade that plied the great caravan routes, which had always been linked with the trans-Saharan routes, now found itself channeled off toward the south. Pagan peoples came into peaceful contact with the Muslim castes that for centuries had considered them to be no more than possible subjects and slaves. A new civilizing factor had come into being.

The Germans, who had started out from their settlements in the Wouri, where their commerce had been established since 1868, were still marking time in their advance

The Royal Niger Company and the Benin Kingdom in collision 1886

189

northwards, to the rim of the Bamileke plateaux. In 1901 the Peulh kingdom of the Adamawa (which had only been recently conquered) was cut in two by the line of demarcation between the British and German zones of influence.

Thus, less than two decades after the Congress of Berlin, the partitioning of western Africa was practically an accomplished fact. Great Britain had consolidated the hinterland of the rich coastal trading-posts it had controlled since the eighteenth century. France had attained its geopolitical goals and had created an uninterrupted continental bloc under its rule. Germany was in occupation of two key positions in Togoland and the Cameroons. Portugal had survived in the Gulf of Guinea.

The military power of the African kingdoms had been broken. New nations were to emerge from a political partitioning between the zones of European influence that many thought entirely arbitrary. In reality, however, the great martial kingdoms were not divided up, except for the Peulhs, whose influence for that matter was, historically speaking, quite recent. It was the tribes of the intermediate regions that seemed to have been the most direct victims of the European partition.

In contrast a new factor had made its appearance in the history of western Africa— the free circulation of men and goods between the Muslim north and the pagan south, and the abolition of civil wars and slavery.

While French, British and German columns were trying to converge in central Africa and the basin of the Chad, the victory of Mahdism, symbolized by the murder of Gordon, seemed to have blocked off the Egyptians and Europeans from access to the route leading from the Nile to central Africa. After the British victory over the mutineers of the Egyptian army led by Arabi Pasha, Egypt remained theoretically under Turkish sovereignty. Its rights over the valley of the Upper Nile were still moot. The Egyptian advance southwards, through the interior as well as along the coast of the Red Sea, provoked the opposition of the British diplomats in the Indian Ocean who were in favour of an activist policy. Kirk, the British consul in Zanzibar, opposed the attempt at an Egyptian landing on the Somali coast in 1876, for instance, though this had been inspired by Gordon himself. Kirk's pretext was that it violated the quite theoretical rights of the Sultan of Zanzibar. In any case the defeats of 1885 had proved to Cairo as well as to London that there had been a serious underestimation of the organizational potential of the traditionally independent tribes that had forged their military unity in a common faith and in the shelter of a favourable geographical position.

Kitchener and the struggle for the Upper Nile routes
Major Kitchener, an engineering officer, who had seen his first campaigns in Cyprus and in Ottoman Palestine, devoted himself to a study of the tactical problem set by the Mahdist control of the routes of the Upper Nile. Did Khartoum have to be liberated by starting out from the north, that is, going down through Egypt, or, on the contrary, by starting out from Suwakkim, the chief Egyptian base on the Red Sea? Kitchener himself became governor of the "Eastern Sudan and the Red Sea Littoral" in 1886. His Residency at Suwakkim was practically encircled by the Mahdist tribes that had come down from the Black Hills and some of which had already settled on the coast. Through his heroism and audacity Kitchener proved that the Sudanese warriors could be faced as long as the initiative was taken and the idea rejected that encirclement was fatal. Suwakkim was indeed a key position. There was a very serious risk that the religious flame fanned by the Mahdi might spread toward Arabia in the east and as far as delta Egypt in the north.

At the same time, the Upper Nile was threatened by the plans of the French, who aimed at taking advantage of the still indeterminate international status of the region north and northwest of Lake Victoria in order to cut horizontally the north-south junction; for that matter, this was what the British who had reached the region of Lake Victoria were thinking of above all. It was also difficult to separate the fortunes of the Upper

Coastal landscape near Accra, Ghana, formerly the Benin Kingdom, part of the Gold Coast. The British were increasingly active in Gold Coast affairs as of 1874. They intervened when the coastal Fan people were nearly routed by the Ashanti confederation swooping down from Kumasi. A British counter-offensive under Sir Garnett Wolseley led to a temporary occupation of Kumasi and the confiscation of Ashanti treasure, but it took until 1902 to completely break the resistance of the Ashanti people.

Left: Menelik, Emperor of Ethiopia
from 1889 to 1913. He unified
the Ethiopian highlands,
conquering Harrar and beating
the Italians at Adowa in 1896.
Menelik signed agreements with
the French settling the limits
of French establishments on the
Somali coast.
Below: Lord Kitchener inspecting
the Egyptian army. From
Suwakkim, main Egyptian base
on the Red Sea, he crushed
the Mahdi movement that had
defeated General Gordon.
He was victorious at Dongola,
Berbera, and finally at
Omdurman across the Nile from
Khartoum, where a young
English cavalry officer
distinguished himself: Winston
Churchill (April 1898).

The Marchand Mission between Harrar and Djibouti, on their return
from the evacuation of Fashoda, 1896. The Mission's purpose was to
link the Congo to Abyssinia and Bahr-el-Gazal by French routes. The
five small boats of the expedition reached Fashoda on the Nile after
two perilous years. The British were to arrive under Kitchener however,
and force a diplomatic settlement by which France evacuated Fashoda
and the Nile Valley.

Nile from those of the Ethiopian fortress and from the whole horn of Africa, which took in the Ethiopian highlands as well as the littoral plains occupied by the Somali tribes, which were in frequent contact with the inhabitants of the Arabian Peninsula.

The sea gates of the Ethiopian mountain complex were held by the Italians, settled in Assab since 1870, and by the British, the successors of the Egyptian power at Zaila and Berbera. The legitimacy of the Italian occupation was acknowledged by the Emperor of Ethiopia in 1889 (for Massawa, Assab, and the rim of the Eritrean plateau). The Somali coast was divided between the French, who had settled in Obok, Tadjura and finally Djibuti (in 1885), the British, the heir of Egyptian ambitions, and the Italians, the direct concessionaires of the Ethiopian state. The Egyptian designs on Ethiopia proper were conclusively eliminated after the defeat at Gura in 1877.

The Mahdi menace to Ethiopia

As a matter of fact the danger represented by Mahdism was far more serious for Ethiopia than was the halfhearted effort at political and military dominion launched by the tottering power of Egypt, sunk in debt, whose base was located in the Nile Delta. The Mahdists seized Kassala in 1885. Harar, traditionally Muslim, proclaimed itself semi-independent as soon as the Egyptian garrisons had made a somewhat inglorious departure. It required the military genius of Menelik to conquer it in 1887. The rulers of the great plateau, Christian in tradition, could break this threatening encirclement only by taking advantage of the contradictory interests of Egypt and of the rival European powers. These latter were directly interested in the "sick man" that Ethiopia had become at least as much as in the destruction of the Mahdist peril.

This complex background was working itself out in a situation that was to give rise to a new geopolitical status for a region that for a long time had remained adamant in rejecting any foreign rule. Meanwhile the question of Nilotic Africa took its place in the spectrum of a world policy in which each of the European powers was caught up in the race for power.

Great Britain, while refraining from any precise military decision, was trying to block the French by signing an agreement with the Free State of the Congo in 1890. It completed it by leasing (in the name of Egypt) the region of Bahr el-Ghazal to the Free State in 1894. These local arrangements could not be extricated from the general context of the policies of the great powers, which at that time were busy dividing up Africa as well as the remnants of the great empires that had reached their zenith two centuries previously—the Ottoman and the Chinese Empires.

Russia, Great Britain and Germany were engaged in a more or less avowed conflict inspired by the Darwinian theory of the survival of the fittest. The Egyptian question and through this the African question entered into world politics dragging the Sudan and Ethiopia behind them.

Kitchener, who had become Adjutant General of the Egyptian Army in 1889, took the offensive at the southern border and in August 1889 carried off a clearcut victory over the Mahdist forces at Toski. He became Sirdar of the Egyptian army in April 1892, at the age of 41. His adjutant was the brilliant Sir Reginald Wingate. They were to lead the Egyptian army to the crushing of Mahdism and to the creation on its ruins of the modern Sudan.

Meanwhile the Italian armies were moving up the Nile. They defeated a Mahdist army and occupied Kassala in 1894. A decision was taken (which was to prove disastrous) to advance as far as the heart of the Ethiopian plateau by taking advantage of the quarrels between Emperor Menelik and some of his great feudal lords. Led by General Baratieri, badly equipped and badly prepared, and launched onto a difficult terrain under the pressure of public opinion, overexcited by the idea of the race for African dominion, the Italians were surprised and crushed by the Ethiopians at Adowa in 1886 (not far from ancient Axum). Adowa was reminiscent of the Battle of the Three Kings that

Page 194
Queen Ranavallo III of Madagascar, an engraving made in 1899 from a photograph. She became Queen of her island at the age of nineteen and signed a treaty making Madagascar a French Protectorate two years later. The French minister Gabriel Hanotaux convinced the French parliament to conquer the island outright. Ranavallo capitulated and was deported; she died in Algiers in 1917.

had been waged on Moroccan soil, for it was there that the Ethiopian nation forged its unity by crushing an invader. It was on the field of battle that Menelik crowned his patient work of unifying the Abyssinian highlands, after having already regrouped under his own authority the traditional cradles of Amhara power (the Tigre, Gojam Walla and the Choa) and the border zones of the Leke and Harar in order to take in Arusi, Yambo, and Kaffa.

The repeated failures of the Mahdist armies to take the Ethiopian fortress explain at least partly the decision taken by the Khalifa, the heir of the Mahdi, to set as his chief goal the liberation of Egypt and the restoration of the true Muslim faith, of which he claimed to be the envoy chosen by God. Thus the Italian defeat simply accelerated the evolution of the question of the Nile, which was now clearly outlined in all its essentials.

The British power could not, any more than its remote Roman and Arab predecessors, tolerate the existence on its southern frontier of a hive of political rebellion and religious fanaticism. While Italy had been militarily eliminated as a possible rival in the Upper Nile, it was still necessary to consider the French, whose policies were now founded on the conviction that a large-scale manoeuvre (such as the intercontinental junction attempted under heroic circumstances by the Marchand mission, which left the northern part of the Congo basin and tried to reach Bahr el-Ghazal) might alter the terms of a bargain in which France felt itself to have been frustrated.

At the same moment the French foreign office pushed forward its advantages in Ethiopia; it signed some conventions with Menelik that fixed the frontier of the French settlements on the Somali coast and confirmed the concession granted in 1894 for the building of the railway from Djibuti to the new Ethiopian capital, Addis Ababa.

The reconquest of the Sudan by the Anglo-Egyptian armies had become a necessity dictated by the very logic of the local situation and of international factors, and by the pressure of British public opinion, haunted by the tragic fate of Gordon.

Kitchener's final triumph over the Mahdi 1889

Kitchener, who was now supported without reservation by the Consul General in Cairo, Lord Cromer, methodically organized his advance southwards by building railways and improving the river transport. Dongola was occupied in September 1896 and Berbera in August 1897. The Mahdist armies led by General Mahmud attempted to reconquer this last city, planted at the junction of the communications with the north and the east, and were defeated at the battle of the Atbara in April 1898. On 14 April, Kitchener, mounted on a white horse, led a triumphal procession followed by the vanquished African general in chains. The final onslaught was launched by the Anglo-Egyptian army (numbering more than 25,000 men) against the armies of the Khalifa (numbering almost 60,000), from 1-3 September at Omdurman, on the right side of the river, opposite Khartoum, which had been abandoned for almost three years. Kitchener's army suffered infinitesimal losses (forty-eight killed) while 11,000 Mahdists perished on the field of battle. A cavalry officer distinguished himself—Winston Churchill. The Khalifa fled toward El-Obeid. Gordon's nephew presented Kitchener with the Mahdi's skull, after his tomb was razed to the ground and his ashes scattered in the Nile.

The very same day that Great Britain broke the Mahdist power, Marchand signed a treaty of friendship with a local chief of the Nile Valley, at Fashoda. Thus France was able to claim rights on the valley of the Upper Nile thanks to the extraordinary courage of a handful of men who had taken two years to cross the completely unknown region between the valley of the Congo and that of the Nile, at the price of incredible sufferings. On 19 September Kitchener, accompanied by Wingate, reached the small fort with the tricolour floating over it. The meeting of the two conquerors (with different claims) of old Africa marks the turning point in the contest that had been going on since 1880 between France and Great Britain for the conquest of a continent. In October the tension between Paris and London reached its peak. There was no question of opening up negotiations of a diplomatic nature, as the ebullient Hanotaux, the French Minister of Foreign Affairs, had hoped. Salisbury was set on a test of force pure and simple; it would have been embarrassing if the burning problem of the succession of the Ottoman Empire, the sick man of Europe, Asia, and Africa, was publicly discussed with respect to the fate of an obscure African territory where this Empire still, through the agency of Egypt, exercised some theoretical rights.

There was serious talk in London of a war with France, a war whose chief theatre of operations would actually be North Africa, which could serve as base for a French army thrusting toward Egypt via Tripolitania. To be sure, the consequences of this fratricidal conflict were by no means underestimated. Harry Johnston, at that time British Consul General in Tunis (and whom we shall encounter again in Central Africa) was well aware that a "British invasion of North Africa would upset for a certain time a goodly portion of the civilizing effort undertaken by France... But it would be the best way to strike France on land with any hope of a rapid and satisfactory result."

At the moment of this great international confrontation, France was plunged into the Dreyfus Affair, where its moral integrity was at stake. Delcassé, who succeeded Hanotaux, understood the force of the argument that the Sudan was "British by the right of conquest, which is the simplest and the most effective." He recalled Marchand in November. The question of the Upper Nile was provisionally settled by the Franco-British agreement of 21 March 1899. It provided a proof that the European powers, while ready to go to the brink of war in order to maintain their imperialist ambitions, would not go so far as to sacrifice the unstable equilibrium of a Europe in full economic upswing merely to seize possession of remote territories.

Hence France yielded to Great Britain, which could now dream of achieving total control of a new route from the Cape to Cairo, linking, via Central Africa, the newly conquered highlands of southern Africa with the oldest and most important of the routes of civilization and trade leading toward the heart of the continent. The sources of the Nile as well as its delta were now British. The Blue Nile itself, which rises in Ethiopia, was the object of an agreement in 1902 that allowed for the building of a trans-African railway (which, however, never saw the light of day).

In a letter to Kitchener, Salisbury defined in this way the goal of a policy that was now all-powerful: "The reconciliation of the races dwelling in the Nile Valley under the aegis of a government that will be essentially western in its principles and methods... the only way this reconciliation can be secured is to give the races you have conquered access to the literature and to the knowledge of Europe."

The competition between France and Great Britain was just as lively in eastern Africa as in western and Nilotic Africa. It was complicated, to be sure, by the intervention of Germany, but it remained governed nevertheless by a spirit of implacable rivalry.

Rivalry of France and England in Eastern Africa

Great Britain held a key position in eastern Africa and throughout the African coast of the Indian Ocean. Through its persevering and efficient action in the struggle against the slave trade (of which Zanzibar was one of the chief stations) it had acquired incontestable rights and responsibilities.

Under the *de facto* protectorate of the British crown Zanzibar had become for many a port of entry into eastern Africa. We have seen that all the expeditions into the interior started out from this island, in which the British Consul General was soon to play the role of coordinator *de facto* of the scientific, religious, and military penetration of the African continent. In 1876, under British pressure, the Sultan of Zanzibar, Seyyid Barghash, had signed a decree forbidding his subjects to engage in the slave-trade. In doing this he dealt a mortal blow to the prosperity of an empire that was wholly based on this commerce, as more than 20,000 people were transported annually from Africa to the sultanates of the Persian Gulf. In December Great Britain and Zanzibar concluded an alliance that had a strong resemblance to a protectorate and that in any case forbade the Sultan from concluding any international agreement without prior consultation with Great Britain. What had to be done, in fact, from the British point of view, was to block the Germans and the French from the route leading into the heart of eastern Africa.

In February 1885 the German Kaiser took legal cognizance of the treaties signed between 1883 and 1885 by the Peters brothers with the native chiefs in the Kilimanjaro region. Further south, the persevering policy of France in the great island of Madagascar that had been begun by Laborde was formalized by a treaty establishing a protectorate that was concluded with Queen Ranavallo on 10 September 1885. It was quickly followed by the establishment of the French protectorate on the Archipelago of the Comores, though theoretically this came under the sovereignty of the Arab empire on the coast of Africa.

Thus Great Britain saw the very basis of its policy undermined; this had been founded on the maintenance of the integrity of a political system that was dominated by the Arab dynasty of Zanzibar and whose sole reason for existence was the slave-trade that it itself was trying to abolish.

Germany intervenes

The German violations of Arab sovereignty (completely theoretical) over the African interior knocked over the whole house of cards that had been skillfully set by by Kirk. For that matter Bismarck's diplomatic agents had the use of information on the spot through the person of the Sultan of Zanzibar's own sister, who had been taken away eighteen years before by the German Consul, who married her, converted her, and made her into a highly respected consultant on eastern affairs.

A tripartite Anglo-Franco-German commission (whose British representative was Major Kitchener) was instructed to verify on the spot the existence of the bonds of allegiance that Sir James Kirk had made so much of in contesting the legality of the treaties signed by the German explorers in the hinterland of eastern Africa. The members of the commission concluded that the sovereignty of the Sultan of Zanzibar did not extend beyond a coastal strip that was three miles in depth but was very long, since it went from the boundary of the Portuguese settlements of Mozambique to the approaches of the Sultanates of the Somali coast, near Cape Guardafui (which the British, Italians and French were busy dividing up at that very moment).

The Anglo-German agreement of 29 October 1886 gave the Sultan complete sovereignty over the islands of Zanzibar, Pemba, Mafia, and Lamu, and recognized his theoretical rights for a depth of ten miles on the African coast going from Venta to Mogadiscio, including the former Arab settlements of Misimayu, Barawa, and Merka. The German zone of influence, starting from the coast toward the interior, was fixed above a line passing just north of the Kilimanjaro chain and cutting across Lake Victoria at the level of the first degree of southern latitude. This laid down the framework in which German Tanganyika and British East Africa were to develop.

In 1890, a Franco-British agreement took cognizance of this division and recognized the special interests of France and those of Great Britain in eastern Africa. In the course of the same year Germany recognized the British protectorate over Zanzibar. The coastal strip in the north of the German zone was leased by Great Britain to the sultan against payment of an annual rent.

The Swahili people was the only one that refused to accept this arbitrary division of the remains of the great Arab empire of the Indian Ocean. It took the British and the Germans more than a year to repress the uprising of the coastal tribes under the leadership of Busheri.

David & Goliath
Kruger   Buller

Above: The Boer War and Queen Victoria, as seen in a Dutch caricature from an album published in 1900 entitled "John Bull in Africa". This war aroused criticism among the liberal opposition in Great Britain itself and abroad.

A post card printed in France during the Boer War representing a small Kruger (President of the South African Republic) as David about to be bludgeoned by Buller as Goliath. It took over 400,000 British to beat the 60,000 Boer fighters.

Boer soldiers and a cannon near Ladysmith, where the British suffered
a defeat in December 1899, after a disastrous siege. The Boer War
was to last from October 1899 to May 1902.

Though Great Britain had to yield to the boldness of the Bismarckian policy and reluctantly accept the neutralization of the Congo Basin, which had been placed under the personal sovereignty of the King of the Belgians, it had no intention of yielding to the arguments made by Portugal, which was also trying to realize a transcontinental junction by joining together its settlements in Mozambique and those in Angola. The Protestant missions that were set up along the Shire River south of Lake Nyasa, and of which Livingstone as Consul General had emphasized the importance, were on the very route taken by the Portuguese expeditions into the interior.

And there was something still more serious. Cecil Rhodes, Prime Minister of Cape Colony, was the determined champion of an advance northwards. He secured recognition for the rights of Great Britain over Matabeleland and Barotseland.

The Portuguese lose out
1890

The Anglo-Portuguese conflict reached a climax in 1889, when Senhor Ser Pa Pinto, at the head of a Portuguese column, crushed a native force officially under the British protectorate. Lord Salisbury sent Portugal an ultimatum in January 1890. Lisbon faced the collapse of a whole policy. Under the leadership of Barros Gomes (like France eight years later under the leadership of Hanotaux) Portugal had embarked on an adventure for which it was unprepared to pay the inevitable price, that is, war with what was at the time the premier maritime power in the world.

By skilful diplomacy Gomes's successor, Ribero (as did Delcassé) tried to save what could still be saved. It took more than a year for Portuguese opinion to surrender to the evidence. The wager had been lost. A treaty finally concluded in June 1891 halted the expansion of the South Africa Company, which under the direction of Cecil Rhodes had designs on the whole plateau, leaving the Portuguese nothing but the marshlands of the coast. Manica and Tété remained Portuguese, while Great Britain was given recognition for its protectorate over Nyasaland.

In this way the fate was settled of the region lying between the Limpopo and the great lakes, the zones of influence of the former confederations of the Monomotapa and of the slave empire of Zanzibar. Imperialist and humanitarian motives were densely intermingled to justify the conduct of remarkable men like Lugard (whom we shall see a few years later in Nigeria), Sir Harry Johnston (the creator of Nyasaland), Cecil Rhodes (who was ultimately frustrated in his transcontinental ambitions by the German conquest of Tanganyika), and Senhor Pa Pinto, who was just as bold as Stanley or Cameron but was not so well supported politically. In the wake of Livingstone and Moffat, Christianity seemed solidly planted in the heart of Africa. For all practical purposes the outposts of the Arab empire of the coast dissolved into the population.

This is how Harry Johnston analysed the role to be played by the white man in these vast regions that were now opened to the outside world: "It is likely that between the Zambezi and the Upper Nile the Europeans will be counted not by hundreds of thousands nor by thousands, at least for the next two or three centuries... For the moment we must devote ourselves to the task that consists of emancipating Africa from the mindless order of nature by educating the black man and by bringing in the yellow man, and by settling in adequate numbers in the healthiest districts so that we can direct these operations on the spot... By opening up this vast region to enterprise and to the surplus population of the Indian Empire Africa, we will bring an important stream of wealth to the impoverished Indian peninsula and will give space to the excess population of southern Asia."

Thus France seemed excluded from any share in the division of the spheres of influence in eastern and central Africa. Still, it has been firmly rooted in the great island of Madagascar, opposite the coast of Mozambique, since the treaty of 17 December 1885 which established the protectorate. For that matter this treaty established the political success of the non-African races that ruled the highlands (the Merina) and put an end to the period of uncertainty during which the English-speaking Protestant missionaries tried to use the influence of the Hovas while the French merchants from the neighbouring island of Reunion or from France interested themselves in the peoples of the coast.

One of the best historians of this great island (Deschamps) emphasizes that the reigning dynasty "was slumbering politically on the comfortable mattress of the status quo ensuring the Merina preponderance... formal unity stopped with two-thirds of the island, effective unity scarcely went beyond the Merina." The French advance collided with a situation that might have come about in eastern Africa too if the Arabs from the coast had succeeded in fusing with the population, and creating a new people for which the region of the great lakes would have played the role of the Madagascar highlands: that of a center for the diffusion of techniques and culture, and of a common language that might ultimately have ended in the fusion of an African and an Asian civilization.

It was Gabriel Hanotaux (the activist cabinet minister who wanted to reopen the Nile question in favour of France), who had the French parliament vote the necessary credits for the complete conquest of the island. He used arguments that recalled those of Jules Ferry to justify French intervention in Tunisia. It was not permissible for France to be excluded from the division of eastern Africa.

The campaign to conquer the Madagascar highlands, waged by French troops in 1895, was characterized by a scandalous absence of preparation. More than half the expeditionary corps was laid low by fever. Nevertheless Queen Ranavallo capitulated on 18 January 1896, and the island was simply annexed outright. In September of the same year General Gallieni (future hero of the battle of the Marne), accompanied by Colonel Lyautey, embarked on a policy of pacification whose methods and results are still cited in our own day as an example of enlightened colonial policy. When Gallieni left Madagascar in 1905, French rule appeared to be the most powerful factor in the political unification of the island. Before defining itself with respect to the outside world Madagascar had had to reveal itself to itself—as other countries of Africa and Asia were doing at the same time.

Eastern and Central Africa thus took on an aspect that by now has become familiar. The Rhodesias gradually defined themselves with respect to the diverse European states in southern Africa. Mozambique protruded between the British and German possessions. Great Britain had still to organize Kenya and protect Uganda. As for the French, Madagascar was another France on the Indian Ocean.

If the spirit of competition that animated the European powers was based on a wholly problematical prospect of boundless wealth, it was not at all the same thing for South Africa.

From 1880 on it was well known in Europe that at the frontiers of Cape Colony and of the Orange Free State there were quite exceptional mining reserves. It was no longer a question of whether the Boers would be able to create a pastoral and quasi-Biblical economy on the vast lands of the South African plateau while keeping the Kaffirs at a respectful distance or using them as quasi-servile manpower. It was industrial Europe that was now plunging toward the new wealth. It was a question of nothing less than the control and the quasi-monopoly of the world diamond market.

In 1880 Cecil Rhodes, supported by Lord Rothschild, created the De Beers Company. Barnato, an astute Englishman who held the Kimberley concession, sold his share of it to De Beers in 1889. In this way the world diamond trust was created; it painlessly inherited the monopoly that had formerly been held by Brazil and that had underlain the wealth of the Portugal of Manuel. Cecil Rhodes also founded the company that controlled the gold-mines discovered further north, in the Rand, where the city of Johannesburg was established. Thus he had powerful financial means to sustain the expeditions toward the north, where he was persuaded of the existence of still greater mining resources.

The notion conceived by Rhodes and his associates, of the future of Africa, was founded on two remarkably simple ideas: the first was that the Anglo-Saxon race had the right and the duty to place under its protection the largest number of peoples and the greatest areas possible of the known world. The second was that the development of the mining reserves by itself could supply a basis for profitable investments on the African continent. It was obvious that the obstinate refusal of the Transvaal to enter, even in the form of a customs union, into the great empire imagined by Rhodes, whose industrial basis as well as language was anathema to the Boers and their leaders, constituted an obstacle to the realization of the imperialist dream just as did the German, Portuguese, and Belgian claims to central African.

The Boers had already crossed the Limpopo to the north. They could not expand westwards, where the Chuana country was now under British protection, nor eastwards, which was blocked by the Portuguese. Lobengula, chief of the Matabeles, also accepted British protection in July 1887. In 1888, he granted all his rights over the mining resources of his territory to Charles Dunnell Rudd, in exchange for an infinitesimal *Rifles for mining resources* recompense of a thousand rifles, a hundred thousand cartridges, and a rent of £ 1,200. This was how the British South African Company was founded in 1889; the greatest names of the United Kingdom participated in it, just as they had in similar projects in the eighteenth century, when distinguished individuals associated themselves with the prosperity of a business that in its nature, if not in its profits, was the most dubious on the coast of western Africa.

Thus the Transvaal was territorially outflanked toward the north, while the very sources of its future prosperity were in the hands of strangers. Immigrants made the law in new cities like Johannesburg, a few miles from the sacred spot where the Voortrekkers a few years earlier had founded their liberty. Although the Transvaal was linked by rail with the Cape in 1893, its government reacted with ever growing hostility to the invasion of British businessmen and engineers.

When Cecil Rhodes launched the raid led by Jameson on 29 December 1895, he was trying to overthrow the power of the Boer farmers by a subversive action in which the latent forces of discontent of the Uitlanders—foreigners—were to join such forces as *Cecil Rhodes and Kruger* could be financed by a company in control of the most lucrative mines in modern Africa. Diplomatically and militarily the expedition was badly prepared; it failed ingloriously. With it were interred the hopes "of a political federation for at least a generation" (Walker).

Kruger now had to look for some support abroad; he had nothing more to hope for from Great Britain. Cecil Rhodes's plans were unacceptable. The Boer people could not allow itself to be isolated within a solid bloc of British possessions and protectorates while on the very territory of the Orange Free State and of the South African Republic the diamond mines of Kimberley and the goldmines of the Rand were completely dominated by financial interests linked to the British crown. In addition, the British government, under the pressure of a public opinion that believed in Livingstone's ideals, had given all its sympathy to the sovereigns of the new protectorates: to Kaama, for instance, King of the Chuana country. Kruger and his government knew that the British were ready to use the Africans against them; in this way they justified their forebodings at the coalition, fatal for their people, of industrial interests, humanitarian yearnings, and imperialist ambitions.

Yet the British position was not so strong as it appeared. The bases established in Matabeleland and, furthermore, in Mashonaland remained rather fragile. Europeans had been massacred in the course of the 1896 uprising. Rhodes had to intervene in person and restore the situation by diplomacy rather than by force. The businessmen and technicians of Johannesburg depended, after all, for their production and trade on the goodwill of the Pretoria government. On the economic plane, the situation was scarcely satisfactory, since the costs of mining kept rising regularly. It was no better on the international plane, since Germany, which was now firmly rooted on the African south-west coast and on the east coast of Tanganyika, was going so far as to send warships to the Bay of Delagoa.

Thus, in 1898, when Kruger was re-elected President of the South African Republic, Great Britain found itself in a particularly isolated position. Its forces were scattered at the time throughout the world, from the frontiers of the Indian Empire to those of Canada, passing by the Nile Valley and the Niger Valley.

Yet before the year's end the Khalifa was defeated at Omdurman and the French thrown out of the Nile Valley after the Fashoda episode, while on the diplomatic plane an agreement with Spain indirectly reinforced the Anglo-Portuguese agreements concerning Africa.

The Boer war
1899-1902

The new High Commissioner, Sir Alfred Milner, was supported by a government under the control of Austen Chamberlain, a resolute champion of the idea of a British Empire based on free exchange, inside a system that while carefully closed off took in the maximum of territories and productive populations. Milner thought it intolerable for the Pretoria government to impose discriminatory legislation on the mining companies of the Rand, and in London public opinion was actively demanding outright intervention. The despatch of reinforcements to the Natal colony brought events to a head. On 9 October 1898, the supporters of the Republic in Pretoria, joined by the Burghers of Bloemfontein, flung an ultimatum at the British; the Anglo-Boer war began on 12 October 1899. It was to end on 31 May 1902 with a British victory. In order to undo the 60,000 Boer fighters London had to put into the field more than 400,000 men and spend more than £ 200 million in gold. Hundreds of farms were burnt or razed in reprisals. More than 100,000 Boer old men, women and children were shut up in regrouping centres (the first version of the later notorious concentration camps) where almost 20,000 died of illness and hardship.

The Liberal opposition in Great Britain was shattered by this war, which was of course a source of rejoicing to the rivals and enemies of the British. Once again British armies were losing battles but winning the war. Defeats like those at Maherfontein, Stromberg, the Tugela River and the disastrous siege of Ladysmith (December 1899) exposed the deep-rooted vices of a military system that cried out for the reforms soon to be undertaken by Lord Roberts and Lord Kitchener, the victor of Omdurman.

In the open country the Boers were unable to resist an army that was bigger than theirs and had a first-class artillery. After the liberation of the Mafeking garrison, which had been encircled by the Boers on 13 May 1900, the British army entered Johannesburg on 31 May and Pretoria on 5 June 1901. The last of the Boer organized forces, under the command of Martinus Princelo, was captured in August; Kruger fled to Europe.

Some thought the war over. But it was merely taking another form. Dewet, Botha, Smuts, Steyn, and still others harassed the lines of communication of the British armies with commandos using African tactics. The British military chiefs were angered by this constantly renewed resistance. Some of them envisaged the most radical steps, such as deporting the Boers *en masse* to the Pacific islands. In June 1901 Kitchener wrote prophetically: "I feel that it will be many generations before the Boers forget or forgive this war, that they will bide their time and that they will try once again to settle the question when we shall be least prepared."

The Boers won the respect of their opponents by their tenacious resistance, but they could not change the fortunes of the war they had lost. Johannesburg resumed its

The first armistice meeting of the Boer War at Middleburg in 1901. In the front row, from left to right: the Boer leaders Dewet and Botha, Lord Kitchener and Colonel Hamilton. The Boers continued to harass the British with commando tactics for another year. A treaty was finally signed at Pretoria in May 1902.

Kaiser Wilhelm II arriving with full military pomp at Tangiers in 1905.
Germany proclaimed itself the protector of Moroccan independence
against French ambitions. The Emperor demanded an international
conference to define a mandate. The Conference of Algeciras in 1906
gave satisfaction to France.

activity. The Uitlanders came back *en masse* and dominated the local administration. In May 1902 the Boers accepted peace with honour, and a treaty was signed at Pretoria. Now the question was one of rebuilding, on the foundations of a common prosperity and with the aid of credits generously granted by London.

Lord Milner, at the head of a brilliant team, tried to find a stable basis for the organization of a federation between the two races that had made modern South Africa. The South African Union was created during a convention that sat from October 1908 to February 1909. The leaders of the Cape province and of Natal, who were essentially pro-British, and those of the Orange and the Transvaal, the heirs of Boer nationalism, agreed on a compromise that had become indispensable. General Botha became Prime Minister of the Union, at the head of a cabinet that among others included General Smuts, who became Minister of the Interior, of Mines, and of Defence.

Formation of the South African Union 1909

This agreement between the two European peoples arose out of an economic development whose dynamism was partly founded on the use of abundant and cheap manpower of African and Asian origin. The South African Union has been at the crossroads of the great economic currents between Europe, Africa and Asia ever since the very creation of the Cape. Just as the Dutch had appealed to the servile or contractual manpower from Africa and from the Indian archipelago in order to ensure the cultivation of the farming zones near the Cape, so the British colonists in Natal had been importing labourers from India ever since 1860. Now the rapid development of mining created a demand for manpower that was still more important and of a different character. Since it was not known whether the Bantus would accept industrial labour, and in consideration of the needs of the Boer farmers who wanted rural manpower, serious thought was given to the import of Chinese.

A young Indian lawyer, Gandhi, landed in Natal in 1893, and at once threw himself into an all-out struggle against racial discrimination that aimed at refusing any political rights not only to Africans but also to the people of mixed blood at the Cape (the Cape Coloured) and to the new Indian immigrants. South Africa became the arena for the application of the new doctrine of non-violence, originally derived by Gandhi from the Russian novelist Leo Tolstoy, that some years later was to inspire the Indian nationalist movement and end in the liberation of the second largest nation of the globe.

Gandhi and the first application of non-violence 1893

Thus the creation of South Africa was marked by the emergence of two new tactics, both born of the response given by will-power and courage to the challenge flung down by superior force—the tactic of commandos and the tactic of non-violence.

But the import of Chinese was shelved; there could be no question of creating an "Asiatic cancer" on African soil. The Bantus had to be gradually led to accept work in the mines at the expense of the prosperity of the native protectorates and even of the European farms. Little by little the Bantus went down toward the Rand. In 1914 the African population on the highlands reached almost five million, while the Europeans numbered a million.

Industrial dynamism seemed sufficient not only to absorb African manpower, which was growing more and more numerous, but also to ensure a rising standard of living for the European population. London now dominated South Africa and controlled the gold and diamond markets. The Boer opposition was broken, yet without the Boer nationality or its language being eliminated. The martial African peoples seemed to be subjugated. For the most part they were put under a protectorate that seemed to guarantee their racial and cultural integrity.

Lord Milner and his associates seemed satisfied, and rightly so. It had been demonstrated that liberalism pays. Even on African soil it was possible to overcome the contradictions arising out of the conflicts between races and classes by introducing a new country, only just mastered, into the great stream of international exchanges.

At the dawn of the twentieth century the African question seemed settled. The geographical mysteries had been cleared up. The great rivers had been reconnoitred from their sources to their mouths. Africa, which had been covered from the north to the south and from the east to the west, had disclosed neither the wealth nor the monsters that had been expected. In fact, instead of the treasures that it had been thought would be found, the Europeans saw that natural conditions made any rapid and profitable exploitation difficult.

With rare exceptions the African political entities proved incapable of withstanding the shattering challenge of the military and economic advance of armies and merchants from the West, then at the height of its expansion. Ethiopia, Morocco and Liberia, still independent, saw their commerce, trade, communications, and military power kept within the narrow limits laid down by the play of outside influences. The only people of European origin, who had become Africanized after two centuries of relative isolation, had been reduced to the level of a satellite by a great European power.

European power predominates

After their glorious predecessors (Abd-el-Qadir, Chaka, el-Haj Omar) the chieftains and the peoples who were in the vanguard of the new wave of resistance (Arabi Pasha, Samory, Behanzin, the Khalifa, Rabah, the Ashantis, the Swahilis, the Herreros, the Tuaregs and still others) yielded to the superior arms and tactics of military forces in which, indeed, many Africans were serving under the command of European officers.

A large part of the population, especially in western and central Africa, welcomed with a certain relief the "European peace" that represented the positive aspect of the entry of the African interior into the system of world relations. Western and equatorial Africa was organized within frontiers that have broadly persisted down to our own day, and behind which French, British, and Germans embarked on colonial policies that were often very diverse. The Free State of the Congo, in a series of international conventions, laid down its frontiers with the French, German, Rhodesian and Portuguese zones of influence, and finally with the new British power in the valley of the Upper Nile. In southern Africa the Portuguese and the Germans had to repress local revolts in the frontier region of German Southwest Africa (the most bloodstained of which was that of the Herreros in 1913). In eastern Africa, the Germans also found themselves in difficulties, and went in for a brutal repression in the Tanganyika uplands. Further north the Somali peoples were in a state of open insurrection against the British and the Italians, who had been reduced to a rather shaky occupation of their coastal settlements. Yet these were the final convulsions of a resistance that could not seriously question the European division of Africa south of the Sahara.

In the north, on the other hand, it remained for Europe to go in for its third and final onslaught on Mediterranean Africa, the first one being the conquest of Algiers by France in 1830, and the second that of Tunisia by France and of Egypt by Great Britain.

At the end of the nineteenth century Morocco was undergoing great hardships. It had been trying to apply its traditional policy, aimed at thrusting back as far eastwards as possible its safety zone, in contact with an unstable Algeria, and extending its rule gradually from the plains to the mountains. Hasan, without succeeding in dominating completely the great Berber territories, had pushed the outposts of Moroccan rule back to the edges of the Sahara, at Tiznit and at Goulimine. His successor Abd-el-Aziz (who ruled from 1894 to 1907) had to confront a quasi-anarchic situation in which all the latent forces of dissociation in the Empire were encouraged by foreign influences that were more or less overt.

The territory of the Algerian-Moroccan borders, which extended from the coast to the zone of the oases via the steppes of the highlands, was for Algeria a large zone that was in a state of veiled rebellion and of constant insecurity. In the region of Ain Sefra and of Colomb-Bechar, west of Figig, the initial uprisings against the advance of the French forces had already taken place. In 1903 Colonel Lyautey was instructed to pacify it. He went about this energetically, and occupied Colomb-Bechar in November of the same year, Berguant in 1904, and Oudjda in 1907. In 1908 the whole of the upper Guir was pacified.

Advance in Morocco 1903-1908

France was not the only power involved in the destiny of Morocco. Commercially, Great Britain, which was firmly rooted in Tangiers, had maintained flourishing trade relations with Morocco since the eighteenth century. Because of geographical proximity and various related historical traditions linked with it, Spain was an open candidate for the succession of the "sick man" of North Africa. In 1902, indeed, the Spaniards signed a secret agreement with France projecting the possible division of Morocco.

Great Britain opposed the ambitions of Spain, but it was not up to claiming a protectorate on the costal zone around Tangiers, which would have put it in possession of the two keys to the Mediterranean—the Suez Canal and the Straits of Gibraltar. The Franco-British agreements of April 1904, which put an end to a long period of rivalry dating from the seventeenth century for the conquest of the American territories, included the recognition by France of the *fait-accompli* in Egypt that had placed it under the British protectorate. As a counterweight, the British "recognized that it was up to France to preserve order in Morocco and to give it any assistance for purposes of military, administrative and economic reform that may prove to be necessary." Spanish rights on the north coast were reserved, to be established several months later by a Franco-Spanish agreement.

The Germany of Kaiser Wilhelm II had made itself the protector of the integrity of the dying empires whose spoils were not supposed to benefit either its rivals or enemies. When the German emperor landed at Tangiers in 1905 with great military pomp, he declared that Morocco was to remain independent and that its ruler had a right to international protection. There could be no question of accepting a unilateral action on the part of France. Only an international conference was qualified to assign it a mandate that would be clearly defined and strictly controlled for the purposes of executing a programme of reforms.

Thus Morocco became a stake in the struggle between the European powers. The question was peculiarly delicate for the French foreign office, which had just completed its network of alliances (aimed at what Germany regarded as its encirclement) by the conclusion of the Entente Cordiale, based on the agreements of 1904, which was added to by the Franco-Russian alliance. In addition, it did not seem possible for it to allow Morocco to pass under the dominion of another great power. France obtained satisfaction at the Conference of Algeciras, held from January to April 1906, in which all the representatives of the European concert took part.

The European powers struggle for Morocco

Sheltered by a policy officially defined as a joint action of pacification by French and Moroccan forces, the French became more and more intimately involved in the domestic politics of the Moroccan government and in the difficulties it was undergoing, while at the same time its trade with France grew at the expense of British and German trade. The decisive crisis came about in April 1911, when a French column occupied Fez in order to come to the aid of the Sultan Moulay Hafid's encircled armies. The fiction of Moroccan integrity was now turned against Germany in favour of France. When the gunboat *Panther*, flying a German flag, arrived off Agadir on 1 July 1911, the question was formulated with the same clarity as it had been when Marchand arrived at the banks of the Upper Nile: Were two European countries going to fight for an African territory?

As in Egypt, a negative answer was given in spite of the excitement of French and German public opinion. An agreement of 4 November 1911 recognized Germany's right to extend its influence from the southern border of the Cameroons to a point on the Congo River (the Duck's Beak). In exchange, Germany gave France a free hand in Morocco. Great Britain was somewhat disturbed by the boldness of Wilhelm II's policy, which did not flinch at the risk of war to win a real diplomatic poker game. It was also disturbed by the Italian attack on Turkish Tripolitania, in 1911, at a time when the Senussi Confraternity was plunging the Libyan Sahara into an agitation of which the effects were to be felt as far as the western Sahara.

On 28 April 1912 General Lyautey was designated Resident General of France in Morocco. Hafid, Abd el-Aziz's brother, was replaced by Yusuf (great-grand-father of Hasan, the present ruler of Morocco). France had a free hand in the pacification of Morocco. Lyautey, inspired by the precedents of Bugeaud, Gallieni, and Kitchener, regarded the army as an instrument of organization rather than of conquest. ("Civil and military action proceed at the same pace, simultaneously alert and self-assured.") He opened up Morocco to entrepreneurs and transformed the Chaouia region into a zone of accelerated economic development. He freed the area around Marrakesh from the constant invasions coming from the extreme south. In 1914 a tenuous junction, was effected between eastern and western Morocco by the relief of the Tazza Gap. The only thing that still had to be reduced, consequently, was the great zone of Berber resistance in the Atlas and along the Moulaya River.

The fall of the Moroccan bastion and of the Tripolitanian way-station signalizes the passage of the whole of the African continent under the military, economic and political dominion of Europe. Liberia and Ethiopia survived as independent powers only by a complicated system of political guarantees in which the contradictory interests of the European powers were balanced against each other. The Ethiopia of Menelik had sought its assurances in agreements with France and Great Britain, which did not, however, prevent the latter from signing a secret convention with Italy in 1916 on the future of Ethiopia. In 1911, on the pretext of ensuring its financial guarantees, Liberia was placed under the virtual protection of France, Great Britain, Germany and the United States.

The weakest European colonial powers, such as Portugal, were not safe from the appetites of the great powers. In 1898 an Anglo-German agreement had forecast a division of the Portuguese territories south of the Equator, "in case it should prove impossible to maintain their integrity". In 1913, on the eve of First World War, London thought it could calm German imperialism by offering it the remains of Portuguese Africa. France took pains to secure a guarantee for its right of pre-emption to the territories of the Free State of the Congo, for which Belgium had assumed international responsibility in 1908, when the King of the Belgians ceded to the crown his personal rights.

All Africa lay at the mercy of Europe. In the world of the time there was no political or economic force that could modify this situation, which for the next few decades was to give the new colonial powers the conviction that they had just initiated a long period of political stability and of continuity in the conduct of the administrative, social, and economic life of Africa.

Right: Moulay Hafid, Sultan of
Morocco in June 1911. Increasing
German pressure on Morocco
led the French to occupy Fez as
a protective measure.
Tension mounted as a German
gunboat, the *Panther*,
arrived off Agadir to protest the
French intervention.
An agreement of November 1911
between Germany and
France avoided open conflict.
Below: Lyautey during the
Moroccan campaign. Marshal
Lyautey was put in charge
of the pacification of Morocco
in 1903. He was named
French Resident General in 1912
and used the army as a weapon
to organize the country and
accelerate economic development.

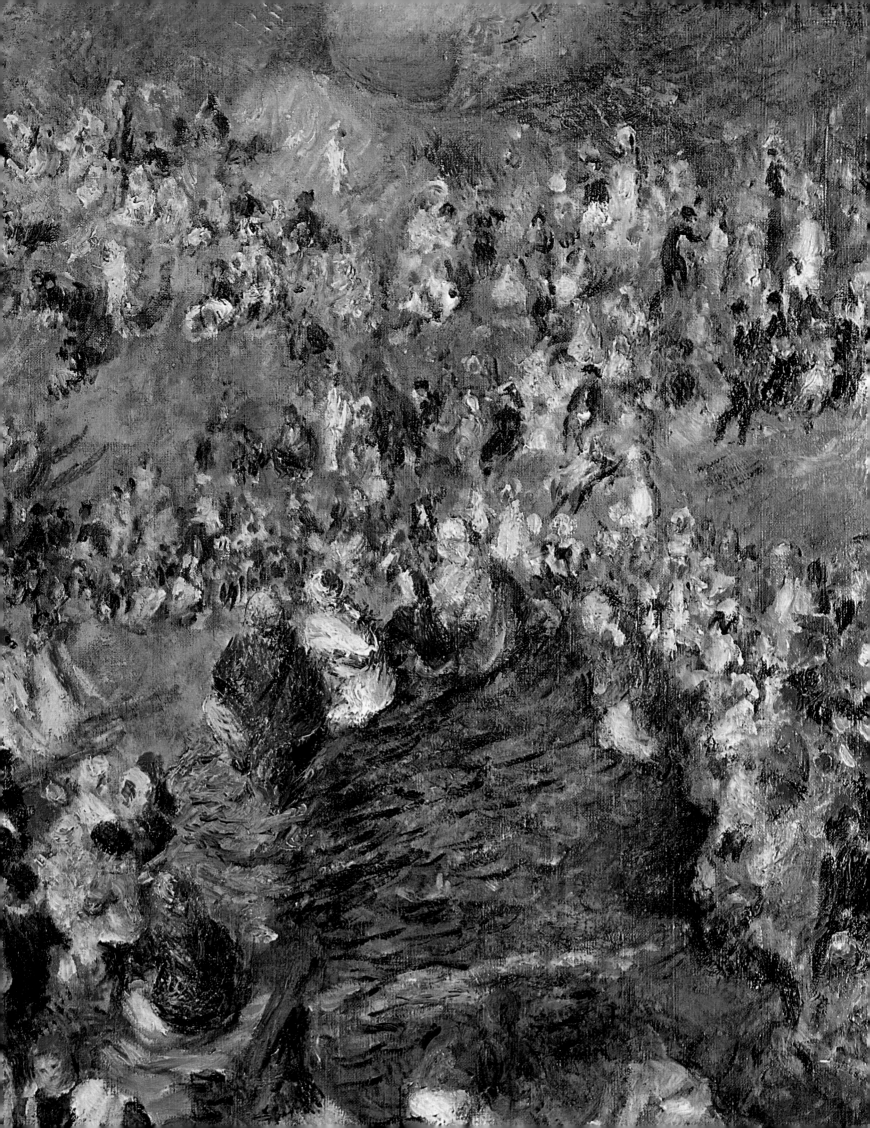

View of Constantine, Algeria, and the Rummel Gorges. The French
worked intensively at building installations and communications in
North Africa. Between 1885 and 1900 over 1,250 miles of railroad lines
were laid. At the center, the "Bridge of Falls"; above, left, the suspended
Sidi M'cid bridge built in 1912 (485 feet long) just left of the Casbah.

Chapter 22
A Continental Burden

Thus Africa came onto the threshold of the contemporary age exhausted by slavery and internal insecurity, the direct results of its initial emergence into world history in the sixteenth century. From that time on Africa had been stagnating and probably becoming regularly depopulated. As in other societies, and on other continents, the initial effect of the impact of a more dynamic outside world was disastrous, but this was less so than in America, in Australia, or in the Pacific, where whole peoples failed to resist the brutal shock of European conquest. Some African peoples vanished; others sank back in a passive rejection and took refuge in the mystical expectation of a better world.

Adverse factors affecting Africa

With the exception of the coastal fringes north and south of the continent, Africa's natural economy suffered, in addition, from its fundamentally precarious character. In the zone of the desert and semi-desert stepplands, pastoral peoples attempted to shift their flocks and herds toward the most favourable pasture zones. Sedentary people were often forced to look for new areas to cultivate under the pressure of foreign invasion or as a result of soil exhaustion. Frequent epidemics afflicted people or their domestic animals. Invasions of insects or of predatory birds ruined their crops. Whole populations and immense areas were often affected by these disasters.

Cyclical changes whose rhythm is still poorly understood transformed the pattern of rainfall. Settlements that had once been prosperous disappeared in the midst of a new desert. When attempts were made to combat adverse natural factors through a policy of irrigation, based on toil and ingenuity, that is, the investment of human energy, an invasion by scavenging nomadic warriors shattered the painfully won equilibrium and destroyed the meagre surplusses so patiently accumulated.

At the beginning of the European era a dangerous idea was added to this fragility of the natural economy. Even though slavery was no longer tolerated, the idea persisted that African manpower constituted an undifferentiated mass whose function was to serve the needs of the new enterprises of extraction, gathering, or export at the cost of its own productivity. Europe, which had become mistress of the land and sea routes of access, was living consciously or unconsciously on the momentum of the slavery policy. At the same time it upset the spontaneous play of natural forces by controlling disease and opening up communication routes.

Down to the contemporary era the potential of self-defense and of progress of the African peoples subject to the challenge of arduous natural conditions was in some way conditioned by the existence of great endemic diseases. In the most favourable regions such as North Africa, fevers such as malaria as well as venereal diseases affected the native population and the invaders equally. Ever since antiquity there have been countless instances of the historical role of disease, which has been at least as important as politics in determining the course of events.

Europe needed the advent of the industrial era, at the end of the eighteenth century, for sanitary conditions to improve. On the African continent, the relative dispersion of the populations and their philosophic ideas—which made disease seem to be a punishment visited upon man by some unearthly power—made this evolution more difficult to bring about, but also more decisive in its ultimate consequences.

Public health: first field of international collaboration

Leprosy, yellow fever, sleeping sickness and malaria, among others, affected the population very seriously. Thus the British administration of Uganda was barely set up when it had to face a sudden explosion of human trypanosomiasis that killed more than 250,000 people. On the coast of western Africa and in central Africa epidemics of yellow fever or of spinal meningitis decimated Africans as well as European missionaries and explorers. In Madagascar the massive losses sustained by the French expeditionary corps were due to "fevers." The Nile Valley, even though it no longer had to endure the ravages of the bubonic plague, thanks to Mehemet Ali's enlightened policy, still suffered from various kinds of trachoma and bilharzia, while further south black-water fever put potentially fertile valleys out of bounds at least as much as did the tsetse fly.

More than thirty years were needed by the medical services of the new European administrations to isolate the viruses and their carriers in the case of yellow fever, sleeping sickness, and malaria. Other diseases proved more difficult to control, though their incidence was gradually limited by measures of public health.

European administrations spent considerable sums to create minimal conditions of economic development. It was actually in the field of public hygiene that international collaboration found its first true field of action. The prophylactic campaigns led the European sanitary teams to penetrate into the most remote regions. The Africans who emigrated toward zones of modern activity had the advantage of satisfactory hospital treatment. In less than a generation the frontiers of disease were flung back. To be sure, the opening up of the communication routes facilitated the diffusion of certain germs while at the same time "social" diseases like tuberculosis spread far more easily. Nevertheless on balance there was a net gain. The systematic application of scientific methods demonstrated that in less than two decades it was possible to reduce disease to a point where it became a secondary factor in the exploitation of the continent.

The struggle against the great endemic diseases was not affected by the territorial divisions arising out of the European partition of Africa. This was not the case, however, with the various railways which, in combination with the rare navigable bays at the riverheads, were the only thing that could shatter African isolation. In thirty years and at very considerable cost the European powers launched the first links in a network of transport into the interior that solved the most immediate problems without taking into consideration for a moment the needs of the continent as a whole.

The building of railways

Kitchener prepared his advance into the Sudan by building a railway south of Aswan, which was ultimately to be extended as far as Khartoum, itself linked to Port Sudan. In Algeria, more than 2,000 kilometers of railroad were built all along the coastal plains from 1885 to 1900, with an initial spur southward as far as Tuggurt. It was a conflict of interest over the course of the great Moroccan strategic railways that gave rise to the Franco-German dispute of 1911 (in June 1921 Oudjda was linked to Casablanca and Marrakesh, and Fez to Tangiers).

In Tunisia the Franco-Italian dispute was settled by the establishment of the French Protectorate; Tunis was linked to the Algerian network. Even before the Sahara was pacified, the French in Algeria were thinking of a rail connection that would cross the Sahara as far as Nigerian Africa. Yet it was not until 1927 that a definitive report (Devallon) proposed the construction of the "Mediterranean-Niger" linking Oudjda and Gao via Colomb Bechar, the "palm route"—Adrar, Touat, Reggane, Tessalit, and In Tassit, or some 2,000 kilometers of railway of which 500 were in the Tanezrouft.

A branch route was to be built from Gao to Niamey and from In Tassit to Timbuktu and Segu.

Meanwhile General Laperrine tried to make the first connection by air, in the course of which he was killed; a little later Major Vuillemin proved that the Sahara could be crossed by air.

In 1924 the Citroen Caravan led by Haardt (The Black Cruise) linked the Mediterranean to the South Atlantic and to the Indian Ocean. The results of these trials by road and by air seemed to justify the hesitations felt by possible investors, public as well as private, with respect to a project as ambitious as the Mediterranean-Niger.

As far as Africa south of the Sahara and north of the Kalahari desert was concerned, economic needs and humanitarian demands were at one in requiring the rapid construction of railways that could eliminate portage, whose effects on the potential of production, already limited, were obvious. It was calculated that in the tropical and equatorial zones not less than 2,000 men were needed to transport a hundred tons of goods over a distance of 100 miles in the course of one month. The riverways were cut by rocky shelves and were inadequate for long-distance transportation.

In 1906 the Governor General of French West Africa declared: "The real cause of the prolonged stagnation of the vast region around the loop of the Niger is that it is separated from the rest of the world by the Sahara in the north, an inhospitable coast in the west, and in the south by a dense curtain of tropical forests that are so many obstacles to a civilizing mission ... Rivers encumbered by rapids allow only an irregular and inadequate traffic, and it has only been around the great navigable loop of the middle Niger that relatively important centres of civilization have been able to establish themselves. The resources of science and capital now permit us to open up these countries, hitherto hermetically closed off, by improving their outlets on the sea, by correcting the faults of their navigable routes wherever possible, and above all by creating artificial routes and railways."

At about this same time Sir Walter Eggerton said in reply to a request for a definition of his policy for southern Nigeria: "Open up means of communication, and if you want to know any more, I would say, open up others."

"Open up means of communication"

The linking up of the middle Niger and the coast, marked by the finishing of the Kayes-Niger, connecting the Senegal and the Niger basins, and by the connection between Dakar and Saint-Louis, was effected between 1904-1923. A contemporary has described the arrival of the railway in the region of the Middle Niger: "The region looks like the Senegal when it was crossed by the Saint-Louis railway thirty years before. Villages and towns sprang up as the railway advanced. Desert spaces were planted with peanuts. The railway fertilizes the desert."

The great region of civilization and trade that the caravans from the Tripolitanian Mediterranean or the Moroccan Atlantic reached after a long and dangerous voyage (as risky and difficult as a sea voyage) was gradually linked up with the world of international trade by an efficient combination of rail and water transport. The coast of the Gulf of Guinea was linked to it by the building of the Konakry-Niger railway, which went as far as the Sudanese steppe at Kankan over a dangerous and picturesque route. The navigable stretches of the Niger served the needs of local commerce from July to January, from Bamako to Kurussa, from Kulikoro to Ansongo; Mopti, Segu, Pamkuru and Timbuktu made up a network of commercial way-stations where steamships brought from Europe, aided by the traditional vessels, assured a stream of exchange linked to the coast by the new railways.

Starting from the Gulf of Guinea, other arteries were built into the interior. Freetown was linked to Pendembu (at the frontier of Liberia and Guinea) in 1908. On the Ivory Coast, Bouaké was reached in 1912, after ten years of work, Katiola in 1923,

Bobo-Dioulasso in 1934 and Wagadugu in 1954. The Ashanti was opened up by a permanent commercial route reaching Sekondi in 1903 and another at Accra twenty years later. The Lomé-Palimé line and the Lomé-Atakpamé were opened up to German Togoland in 1907 and 1913. In French Dahomey, the Cotonou-Parakou line was extended as far as Save between 1900-1936. In Nigeria it was a question of combining railways and river navigation: in 1898 the railway went as far as Kano, via Jebba, the northern limit of the river navigation traffic into the interior.

In the German Cameroons the Douala-Yaounde line, begun in 1914, was finished in 1927, while a branchline was built as far as the Bamileke plateau at Dschang.

Railway network of the Congo basin 1887-1897

The problems set by the access to the Congo basin were technically more difficult. The lower part of the river, which was not navigable, had to be paralleled, and a junction made with Stanley-Pool, from where more than 1,000 miles of the Congo River were navigable without interruption, as far as Stanleyville. The basic objective of the railway network of the Congo was to link up the navigable stretches. The 400 kilometers of the Matadi-Léopoldville line required a decade of labour (1887-1897). It was at the price of still greater efforts that the French built their own railway on the right bank of the river. They spent a thousand million francs, mobilizing 150,000 labourers from all parts of equatorial Africa.

The Portuguese, whose ports of Luanda and Lobito enabled them to control the service lines of their own possessions as well as of the region south of the Congo extended the line crossing Africa from east to west, with the aid of British capital: this was the physical embodiment of their great political ambitions. The Katanga was reached in 1913.

The Union of South Africa had the means to embark on the boldest policy. The Capetown-Kimberley line was opened in 1885. We know that one of the stakes of the Anglo-Boer conflict had been a service network for the Transvaal plateau. In 1916 the Union of South Africa had more than 9,400 miles of railway. The German lines in the Southwest Africa (from Luderitz to Windhoek) were finally linked to this network, which became one of the most important in the world, comparing favourably with those of Australia and Argentina.

Further north, the two Rhodesias were linked to the Portuguese and Anglo-Belgian line of the Katanga; by the Anglo-Portuguese treaties they obtained the right to build a line as far as the port of Beira on the Indian Ocean. They too were linked with the networks of South Africa. Nyasaland was served by a line going from Salima to Noutarara, at the junction of the Beira railway. In Tanganyika the Germans built the Dar-Es-Salaam-Kigoma line (on the banks of the Lake Tanganyika) between 1904-1914. A branch-line went from Tabora to Mwanza, on the banks of Lake Victoria (the route followed by Speke).

Thus, from 1920 on it was possible to cross the continent from east to west, from Lobito to Beira and from Dar-Es-Salaam to Leopoldville, crossing from Kigoma to Albertville, going up the river from Kindu to Leopoldville, and going on by rail as far as Matadi. In less than thirty years southern Africa was served by an efficient network of communications.

At the beginning of the twentieth century the Kenya highlands were reached by the railway coming from Mombasa and going to Kantala; Winston Churchill emphasized the importance of the economic prospects this opened in producing a country suitable for European settlements.

The Ethiopian mountain range was linked to the coast as a result of the construction of the Franco-Ethiopian railway, which had the advantage of a concession granted by Menelik in 1894. In 1902, Djibuti was linked to Diredawa and in 1917 to Addis Ababa, in spite of objections from the British.

The Citroën Caravan of 1924 marked the opening of the African continent to the automobile and "tourism". The expedition left Colomb-Béchar on the Algerian-Moroccan border, crossed the Sahara, reached Zinder and Chad, then descended towards the Congo, Lake Victoria and Uganda. It separated into two groups, one heading towards the Cape, the other reaching the Indian Ocean and Mombassa. Both groups met to cross Madagascar. The Mediterranean was linked to the South Atlantic and the Indian Ocean.

Above, the caravan in a village of the African equatorial forest, between Ubangi and the Congo.

The Citroën Caravan passed through the village of Maradi in the formerly French territory of Niger.

Page 221
Wrestlers of Kordofan. They are descended from the Nuba partisan fighters who, under the "Mahdi" Muhammad Ahmad, had fought General Gordon and were finally defeated by Kitchener in 1898.

In the Sudan, Wadi Halfa, at the Egyptian border, was joined to Berbera and to Atbara, shortening the distances between the second and the fifth cataract of a river with a very capricious course. The line was soon prolonged to Khartum and served the cotton zone of Jezira by being prolonged in the west toward El-Obeid and in the east toward Port Sudan, chosen as the Red Sea port in preference to Suwakkim. The Egyptian network followed the Nile Valley as far as Aswan.

Africa's isolation broken

In this way the isolation of Africa was broken. Man had been freed of the servitude of portage. The products of the regions of the interior could be taken to the coast under conditions that were economically satisfactory.

In the course of the same period Africa was endowed with a whole series of modern ports: Casablanca, Dakar, Conakry, Freetown, Monrovia, Abidjan, Takoradi, Lagos, Douala, Pointe-Noire, Matadi, Saint Paul of Luanda, Lobito, Benguela, Walvis Bay, Cape Town, Port Elizabeth, Durban, Lourenço-Marques, Beira, Dar Es-Salaam, Mombasa, Djibuti, Massawa, Port Sudan, and on the Mediterranean coast, Alexandria, Benghazi, Tripoli, Goulette, Bone, Bougie, Algiers, Oran, Nemours and Tangiers.

On the Indian Ocean Madagascar had three major ports: Majunga, Diego-Suarez, and Tamatave (which was linked to the highlands by the Tamatave-Tananarive railway, built at the beginning of the twentieth century under the command of Gallieni).

Page 222
Kordofan: traditional dancers. In remote parts of the country where the Nubas took refuge from slave traders, and where they remained even after Kitchener abolished the slave traffic, tribal traditions are still preserved. The Nubas with their exceptional eight—often seven—feet were in particular demand as slaves.

It has been estimated that more than $785 million were invested in the regions south of the Sahara for railway construction alone.

A Governor General of French Equatorial Africa, Antonetti, was able to declare, at the inauguration of the Congo-Ocean railway on which he had staked his career and his reputation: "Africa wishes and ought to pass directly from barbarism to electricity, by disregarding the lengthy stages that marked the same advance in old Europe."

The generation of explorers was followed by that of conquerors and administrators. Some thought it possible to direct the martial abilities of the conquered races into vaster designs going beyond Africa, by putting them in the service of a national imperialism on a world scale. Others, more farsighted, were fearful that such a change of policy might boomerang, and that one day Europe might repent of having armed Africa in order to serve its own ambitions. The "great men" of the new Africa wanted to do everything to achieve a rapid and spectacular transformation. With this in mind they showed more confidence in talent than in bureaucracy. Kitchener gave as a general watchword to his brilliant team of officers and university men: the "moral and industrial regeneration of the Sudan, which depends on the individual action of British agents working independently but accepting a common goal, and that of the natives whose confidence they have won." Gallieni and Lyautey echoed him by requesting "an elite personnel" for Madagascar and Morocco. Milner surrounded hismelf with the best brains of Oxford.

There was contact and confrontation on various levels. While the first governors considered themselves emissaries of a civilization that had more duties than rights with respect to Africa, the entry of the continent into world trade snowed it under with a great number of colonists and merchants who were looking for the massive and immediate profits that were seemingly guaranteed by the exploitation of cheap manpower. For these the administration was no more than a means of attaining their goal. Any policy that was directed to the moral redemption and material progress of millions of people seemed to them a piece of superfluous hypocrisy, and in any case an untimely

Concept
of the "fundamental
superiority" of Europe

brake. The relations of the European powers with the countries they had conquered and whose protection they had assumed, were conditioned, just as in the nineteenth century, by an unquestioned faith in the fundamental superiority of the civilization of Europe.

If we take this implicit or explicit premise into consideration, we can see that the various colonial policies were in the last analysis nothing but the more or less rationalized expression of the reactions evoked in the European powers by their new responsibilities. They varied according to natural conditions, the importance of the peoples under their dominion, the state of their traditional political structure and finally the "national" style that was projected onto a continent they wanted to think virgin and onto peoples whose political understanding they chose to deny.

At the very bottom of the ladder, that is, in the zones where the population appeared to be totally "primitive" and eked out a precarious existence in the midst of natural resources thought to be abundant, the "colonial" organization was as elementary as the situation seemed to call for. In the Free State of the Congo the lands decided on as empty were declared state property. Royal grants of exploitation were assigned to companies whose entire responsibility consisted of collecting for export massive quantities of products traditionally gathered, such as natural rubber. Roger Casement,

The Port of Algiers, 1925. At the beginning of the French occupation, Algiers was mainly a military outpost. Economic development progressed with the building of the Algiers-Constantine railroad in 1866, and the extension of the port to the south. A second port on the bay of Agha added tremendous useable surface for shipping. Algiers became an important financial and maritime center.

who at that time (1901) was British consul in the Free State, indignantly denounced the abuses perpetrated by European agents who were judged by the quantity of goods they supplied to the state monopoly. It needed the celebrated "red rubber" scandal, followed by an enquiry commission assembled in 1904 under the critical eye of Great Britain and France for the Free State to recognize the existence of rights of custom even on territories that were uninhabited or uncultivated. Semi-state, semi-private organizations, subject in principle to a strict control on the part of the public power, were granted concessions that included the exploitation of the mines, the outlying districts of urban growth, reserved for urban development or for special purposes, and finally zones suitable for industrial activities. This was what gave rise to the Special Committee of the Katanga, the National Committee of the Kivu and to enterprises like the Congo Palm Oil Company and the Congo Company.

There was a similar situation in the regions of central Africa of which France had taken possession following the peaceful advance of Brazza, known as the "conqueror of hearts." Between March and July 1899, 650,000 square kilometers were given as outright property to—if not into the outright sovereignty of—forty concessionary companies founded on the theory of the eminent domain of the state. The exploitation of this area was granted them with the right to consider the natives (actually not very numerous) as manpower to be worked at will. The intrinsic poverty of a country where man is crushed by nature led these companies, in a genuine vicious circle, to exercise their rights with a severity that was all the greater because the revenues were so small.

France as well as Belgium was upset by these abuses. In a curious inversion, Brazza, the pacifier, was instructed in 1905 to inspect the territories he had given to France and that were now over-run by terror. He came to his end in this final mission.

Africa was being asked for treasures it did not have or would not reveal until after stubborn and painstakingly prepared investigations. Twenty years later, André Gide, echoing Casement, was still able to observe in French Equatorial Africa the sequel to this short-sighted policy, a product of vulgar greed and even more of the profound European ignorance of the problems presented by the development of regions inhospitable to man. At the beginning of the twentieth century no one realized that only a rational development of natural and human resources could benefit Africans and Europeans equally. It was believed too lightly that the native races were the cause of an obvious underdevelopment that was due to their incapacity, whereas that incapacity was actually the effect of the phenomenon and not its cause. In addition, the civil administration installed on the spot by the European powers was given unbelievably feeble means of action. The rules of private capitalist profit-making were supposed to be applied to every business; budgets were established in accordance with local financial capacities, which were meagre. The European governments could not bring themselves to ask their people to make sacrifices on behalf of remote territories that though conquered remained largely unknown. Only altruistic missionaries, ambitious officers, adventurers, younger sons or hardheaded and enterprising merchants went to the "colonies" or talked of them.

The great men placed by Europe in the service of Africa were paralysed by the squalid penny-pinching imposed on them. Vast empires scarcely conquered had to be ruled with a handful of men. The colonies were supposed to produce without costing anything: indeed they had to bring back a profit. Thus everything was made use of, politically, militarily and administratively. Gallieni in Madagascar, Johnston in Nyasaland, Lugard in Uganda then in Nigeria, Lyautey in Morocco, expressed the same idea with greater or less felicity: after the autonomous power of states organized before the European conquest was broken, their political leaders had to be made use of in order to avoid direct administration and what it required in the way of money and men. The social

Inadequate facilities retard African development

Page 226

Henri Matisse: The Riffian. (Museum of Modern Western Art, Moscow.) The famous French artist painted this portrait of a Riffian when he was in Tangiers in 1913. The fierce Riffian warriors carried on resistance to the French for a long time. Strife continued in the Northern Rif region until the capture of Abd el-Krim in 1926.

and political structures of the African societies, themselves the result of a complex history, were to be respected, provided that they did not interfere with the free play of European trade and that the elementary rules of public order as conceived by the West were satisfied. There was no place for mutilation, arbitrary imprisonment and corruption, slavery and military requisitions.

The civilization that was militarily victorious and the peoples who were provisionally conquered managed to arrive at a compromise that was, for a time, satisfying to both sides. Lord Lugard, who was responsible for an expedition against Kano following the assassination of a British agent in 1903, wrote: "The advocates of conciliation at any price, who protest against military operations in Northern Nigeria, seem to forget that their nation has assumed before God and the civilized world the responsibility of maintaining peace and good order in the area declared as a British protectorate and that the cities of Kano and Sokoto are ruled by an alien race who buy and sell the people of the country in large public slave-markets, daily."

Some compromise between victors and conquered

General Lyautey organized the Moroccan protectorate in such a way that one of his contemporary admirers (Georges Hardy) could say: "Morocco is a country that is reviving. It is still the same social and political organism with its Muslim traditional law. It has simply been rejuvenated and regenerated by a blood transfusion that has done no harm to its personality. ... The agreement between French and Moroccans has brought into being the ideal type of protectorate, that is, the happiest form of colonization, the only kind that suits our age; this alliance between equals of two original civilizations and two stout-hearted peoples in an atmosphere of intense activity." This attitude on the part of these two great advocates of indirect rule should not make us forget that in Nigeria the troubles of 1903 were still being echoed in 1906, when the Emirate of Sokoto was the theatre of an anti-European uprising, in which the subject peoples, like the Hausas, reproached the Europeans with reinforcing the power of their Fulha masters. In Morocco whole regions remained untamed. Ten years after the pacification of the South Lyautey had to confront the Riff uprising, where he was to forfeit his reputation as a statesman.

Paris had the same goal as London—a regime that would be as efficient as it was thrifty. In Madagascar France found it difficult to keep to the formula of the protectorate, and after the troubles of 1895 it simply annexed the island outright, suppressing the Hova monarchy. In Ashanti the British troops had, as we have seen, a bone to pick with the Asantehne; the royal family was deported to the Seychelles.

Thus, acting in a quite empirical fashion with respect to the African rulers who had either to submit or to be undone by the triumphant power, the Europeans collided, especially in Muslim Africa, with complex systems where traditional law linked to local clans was intermingled with new laws of eminent domain created by the conquering powers for their own purposes. Colonization, in the strict sense of the word, was limited in impact to relatively restricted zones on the vast continent.

One idea remained vigorous—the notion that the highlands of eastern and southern Africa would help solve the population problems that were then afflicting Europe and India. The attraction and the illusion of insufficiently occupied spaces (like those of Madagascar and Kenya) were to play an obsessive role in the minds of the European nations that were ultimately to feel cheated in the great partition. What happened in fact was that the policy of getting Europeans to immigrate was executed rather slowly, while at the same time the growth of the native populations made the naive hope of a reconciliation between the European and the conquered Africans completely illusory.

The problems of exploiting African resources quickly came to seem tremendous. Substantial investments were indispensable for the creation of the minimal infrastructure. The European centers of civilization eked out a precarious existence on the brink of an enormous vacuum where for all practical purposes everything still remained to be done.

Converging Forces in Africa

Major events and personalities in other parts of the world

1914 - 1960

1914 Beginning of the First World War
1917 The Russian Revolution. The Bolshevik regime
1919 Treaty of Versailles
1920 First meeting of the League of Nations
1922 Founding of Soviet Socialist Republics
Gandhi is condemned to six years in prison, for preaching non-violent resistance to the British rule in India
1924 Death of Lenin
1928 Tchang-Kai-Chek becomes president of the Chinese Republic
1929 Wall Street crash. Beginning of the Depression
1931 Spain becomes a republic
1933 Hitler becomes Chancellor of Germany
1934 Independence of the Philippines
1937 The Moscow Trials. The Rome-Berlin Axis
1938 Germany annexes Austria
Munich Conference
1939 End of the Spanish Civil War. With the help of Hitler and Mussolini the rebel forces of general Franco defeat the republican army
Beginning of the Second World War
1945 Hitler commits suicide
United Nations Charter signed
The first atomic bomb launched on Hiroshima
1947 India, Ceylon, Pakistan win independence
1948 Berlin blockade
1952 Einsenhower elected president of the U.S.A.
1953 End of the Korean War
1953 Death of Stalin. Khrushchev becomes General Secretary of the Party
1956 Hungarian Revolution
1957 First space capsule, the Russian "Sputnik"
1959 Establishment of Castro regime in Cuba

The European crisis that had been looming ever since the first years of the twentieth century could not help but affect Africa too. Even the Franco-German crisis over Morocco—which underlay the compromise of 1911—was far more a European than a strictly African affair. The dynamism of the Kaiser's Germany was disturbing to France and Great Britain equally. Portugal felt threatened by the ever present danger of an Anglo-German compromise at the expense of its African territories. The same held for Belgium.

In the spring of 1914 the German Minister of Foreign Affairs said: "Only the great powers are in a position to colonize; the small nations will never be able in the future to take advantage of their previous state of independence, if consideration is given to the changes in Europe, which are in favour of the great states, themselves the product of economic forces and better means of communication." This idea of a hierarchy of European powers was soon augmented by the thesis that war fulfils an historic function by pitilessly destroying decadent cultures, exhausted systems of law and degenerated liberties. Certain German geopoliticians regarded a determined military action starting out from the German bases in Africa as a means of striking at the British Empire from the rear. In reality the military forces based in Tanganyika, the Cameroons, Togoland and Southwest Africa were scarcely enough to maintain public order. They were quite incapable of playing any role as an element of global strategy. This is why, at the last minute in 1914, the German Foreign Office tried to find in the Treaty of Berlin reasons to neutralize "the Conventional Basin" of the Congo. The other powers did not agree.

The Allies had no intention of regarding Africa as an important theatre of hostilities. Yet the temptation was very strong for them to take advantage of circumstances to eliminate an active rival whose commercial influence was beginning to make itself felt in the relatively restricted markets of Africa that had only just been conquered. Under these conditions their war aims were simple. Egypt had to be defended against a possible advance of the Turkish armies via the Sinai Peninsula, along the traditional route that had always been followed by invaders from the east. The German territories, covering more than two and a half million square kilometers, with twelve million inhabitants, had to be occupied.

Togoland and the Cameroons were relatively easy prey for the combined action of the British and French troops. Togoland was occupied in September 1914. The "Duck's Beak" was rapidly eliminated by French troops. In the Cameroons, the small German army displayed brilliant defensive qualities, but suffered from the hostility of the populace, especially in the region of the south, after the execution of the Douala chief Manga, who had been suspected of pro-Allied sympathies. The German forces capitulated in 1916.

In Tanganyika the Germans fought a splendid campaign, using native units that showed an astonishing loyalty with respect to their conquerors of the day before. In

*Mirror of the growing
European crisis*

*Allied Attack on German
Territories*

1918 the German detachments which had not been beaten took refuge in Mozambique, where they were disarmed.

Southwest Africa presented more complex problems. The brutal repression of the Herrero uprising had made the territory politically vulnerable to a determined action on the part of the Union of South Africa. From another point of view, however, the entry of the Union into the war against Germany, at the side of an England detested by a large portion of the Boer population, shook the fragile unity of the nation to its very foundations. It had not forgotten the sympathy shown President Kruger by the Kaiser.

The government of Botha and Smuts, which had been in power since 1910, was in favour of British policy, but the army was deeply divided. The troops of Boer origin (many of whom had fought in the Anglo-Boer war) were imbued with violent republican feelings. Circumstances seemed favourable for them to get rid of the British guardianship they detested. In October 1914 Major General Bayers called out the garrisons in the western Transvaal. The uprising was crushed by Botha with speed and firmness; more than 1,200 rebels were imprisoned. Botha was then able to carry out a lightning campaign against German Southwest Africa, at the head of an army of 6,000 men. The German forces surrendered in June 1915.

By and large the peoples of sub-Saharan Africa accepted passively the direct and indirect consequences of the fortunes of the war, such as labour requisitions, drafting, or change of rulers. But in the Saharan regions it was not the same.

Italy had established itself in a highly precarious way on the Libyan coast it had taken away from Turkey in 1911. The "Sanusiyah Brotherhood" based on religious orthodoxy and fanatic xenophobia extended its influence over the bulk of the Islamized peoples, the Berbers and Arab-Africans of the eastern and central Sahara. It made life very difficult for the Italian garrisons that were blocked up in their coastal outposts. In December 1914 the Italian troops occupying the oases of the Ghat were massacred. Senussi agents made their way as far as the Hoggar. The Great Senussi, Ahmad, made his headquarters at Salum, on the Egyptian border. The peace so recently established by the French in the western Sahara was itself being threatened. From his self-imposed exile in the heart of the Sahara Father de Foucauld watched with alarm the political evolution of the region he knew so well and had devoted his life to. At the beginning of 1916 he warned Lyautey that "things were not going well on the Algerian-Tripolitanian border, and that a Senussi-Turkish-German action was being carried on there that if not stopped would soon extend to the Algerian and Tunisian south, to the northeast of French West Africa and even the south of Morocco." After the fall of the Djanet outpost in March 1916, the Hoggar mountain range was squarely in the danger zone. Father de Foucauld was assassinated on 1 December of the same year.

Father de Foucauld

The situation was only restored in the French Sahara after the recall of General Laperrine, from the front, and in the Tripolitanian Sahara as the result of a joint political action between Great Britain and Italy, who had become allies in 1915, which led to the signing of a truce with the Great Senussi in Cyrenaica. The Italians were to need more than ten years of effort to reoccupy Ghadames and the oases of Fezzan, though the Senussi threat was never entirely eliminated until the final defeat of the Italians by the British in 1942.

In Egypt, on which the British protectorate was unilaterally imposed on 19 December 1914, the populace lent itself unenthusiastically to civil mobilization and to the military requisitions imposed on it for the requirements of the British campaign against the Turkish forces in Palestine. The war effort accelerated the movement of the political forces and paved the way for the demands that were to be expressed with growing energy from 1918 on.

North Africa remained astonishingly calm. In Morocco General Lyautey disobeyed orders from Paris to fall back, and sent to the French front not only the main body of the French occupation troops but a great many Moroccan volunteers. Similarly, Algeria made no difficulties about accepting the draft imposed on it in 1913. Tunisia also helped the French war effort.

North Africa and the outbreak of the war

The European war had caught Ethiopia at the peak of a domestic crisis following the death of Emperor Menelik in 1913. His successor, Lijj Liasu, declared himself a Muslim and an ally of the Turks. He made a rapprochement with the traditional enemies of his crown, the Somalis and the Gallas. In an act of remarkable political aberration he joined the Holy War proclaimed by the Sultan of Turkey in the role of Commander of the Faithful. Liasu was deposed in 1917 by a rival faction that put Ras Tafari (the future Emperor Haile Selassie) into power as regent of the Kingdom. Neither Italy nor Germany had been capable of taking advantage of Ethiopian weakness to achieve their own ends. The pressure of events did not spare the other African country that had remained independent: Liberia, threatened by a German squadron, declared war on the Kaiser in 1914.

Thus the role of Africa in the First World War was far from negligible. In varying degrees the European powers turned to their own ends the martial virtues of the peoples they had subjugated thirty years before. In 1914 German East Africa had almost 4,000 askaris, and the German Cameroons 3,000 native soldiers. At the same time the French had more than 20,000 men under arms in West Africa and almost 10,000 in Equatorial Africa. For the campaign waged by the Allies against Tanganyika, the British recruited almost 10,000 soldiers in Nigeria and the Gold Coast and 20,000 in Kenya. More than 200,000 men were mobilized to ensure portage and supplies for the troops. At the height of the Tanganyika campaign the Germans had an army of 16,000, of which only 2,000 were Europeans.

Yet it was France that imposed the heaviest burden on its African possessions for its desperate defense against the assault of the German armies. Nearly two million men were recruited in North Africa, Black Africa and Madagascar. Six hundred thousand were sent to the front lines. The French army, which in the first months of the war had suffered shattering losses, found powerful reinforcements in the African forces. The French people, which until then had heard of the African territories only in connection with heroic feats or sordid scandals, was aware of its debt to these remote peoples that gave it such loyal support in the most fateful hour. The idea took shape of a France of one hundred million people stretching from Dunkirk to Brazzaville and Tananarive.

The African soldiers who went off to fight in Europe returned with complex feelings; their admiration and feelings of brotherhood for their companions in arms were mingled with the conviction that they had now acquired a right to political dignity of their own.

This militarization of Africa did not occur without alarming far-sighted observers. General Smuts said: "My experience in eastern Africa has opened my eyes to the serious dangers that threaten the future not only of southern Africa but also of Europe. We have seen the excellent human material found in this great continent ... Until this war we had not been aware of the great military value of the natives."

Effects of African militarization

On the political plane the First World War let loose throughout the continent, from north to south, waves of unrest that did not, however, develop to any proportions. Islam itself proved to be divided. The spectacle given of Europeans fighting on African soil had no effect on the loyalty of the native peoples, except at the extreme north and the extreme south. It was not until later that the profound consequences of the great European turmoil were to make themselves felt.

Conquered Germany renounced all its overseas rights in Article 119 of the Versailles Peace Treaty, which it signed under compulsion. This renunciation affected Togoland, the Cameroons, Tanganyika and German Southwest Africa, as well as all the rights acquired by prior treaties in Equatorial Africa, in the basin of the Congo, and in Morocco, Liberia, and Egypt.

At this time international public opinion was under the influence of President Wilson's Fourteen Points, which for many people represented the charter of a new anti-imperialism. In other words, it was impossible for the victorious powers to go in for an outright partition of the German spoils in Africa. In addition, the division of European responsibilities in these newly acquired territories was an excellent occasion to formulate and apply new principles of international law; these laws were groping forward somewhat in the dark, but their clearly defined object was to codify the behaviour of "the advanced peoples with respect to the backward peoples." In February 1918 the Labour Party of Great Britain demanded that the future League of Nations organize the administrative and social control of all the colonies of the belligerents in Tropical Africa. This was echoed by the French Socialist Party.

*The League of Nations'
Mandate Commission*

After acrimonious debates the system of mandates was incorporated in the Pact created by the League of Nations in its Article 22. Togoland and the Cameroons, already divided up *de facto*, were assigned to the administration of France and Great Britain. Ruanda-Urundi, the former German protectorate attached to Tanganyika, was given to Belgium. Tanganyika itself passed under the authority of Great Britain. The distinctive personality of these territories was supposed to be maintained, not integrated into that of other colonies and protectorates of the mandatory power. An annual report was to be presented to a Mandate Commission made up of independent experts. Conscription was prohibited, as was any economic or religious discrimination. This held for mandates in Category B (Category A applying only to the Arabic-speaking states that succeeded the Ottoman Empire in Palestine and in Mesopotamia, which France and Great Britain had assumed the responsibility of leading to independence as rapidly as possible). On the other hand, German Southwest Africa was put in Category C, which amounted to making it an integral part of the Union of South Africa, it being understood that the rights of the native population were to be protected.

In practice and on the spot, the mantle of this new form of international legality scarcely concealed the classical traits of colonial occupation.

In Togoland, the French administration was organized in May 1915; the representative of France was placed under the authority of the Governor General of French West Africa in August 1917. The British authorities of the Gold Coast had adjusted their borders with the part of Togoland occupied by France, following the recommendations of a Franco-British military commission and without heeding the protests of certain coastal peoples like the Ewe, who found themselves separated from each other. Similarly, the German Cameroons were divided into a British and a French zone, following purely

Panorama of Cairo. A British protectorate was unilaterally imposed on Egypt in December, 1914. Civil mobilization and military requisitions for the British campaign against the Turkish forces in Palestine were unpopular. Political sentiment was crystallizing around the theme of independence.

strategic considerations of which the League of Nations was satisfied simply to take cognizance. Thirty years later this problem of reuniting both Togolands and both Cameroons was to spring forth once again.

Tanganyika aroused vaster ambitions. As long ago as 1890 Sir Harry Johnston had suggested that the highlands might constitute an excellent outlet for the Asian population surplus. Sir John Kirk, protector of the Arab state of Zanzibar, went even further by calling this region "the America of India." At the imperial conference held in 1917, the British Minister for India said: "The unrestricted opening up of all territories taken from the enemy in eastern Africa to the spirit of Indian enterprise would help lessen the bitterness aroused among Indian statesmen and journalists by this controversy (concerning discrimination against Indian immigrants in other parts of the Empire). It will give them the proof that the needs of the Indian peoples have not been neglected in the partition of the territories acquired by the Empire in the wake of the war."

Indian opinion was not asking for so much. All it wanted, for reasons of principle and of fact, was for the minority of merchants and plantation workers settled in the parts of Africa bordering the Indian Ocean not to suffer from unjust discrimination. It did not have the least faith in the risky prospects of massive colonization. For that matter this whole myth of the empty African highlands could not withstand the slightest examination. In order to install Indian colonists in Tanganyika either the natives had to be expropriated or the German plantations had to be divided up into small farms, with a loss of economic efficiency. In addition, the native agriculture, whose interests were now protected under the mandates system, was now providing an efficient competition to the agriculture of the Europeans.

The myth
of empty highlands

The two kingdoms of the Ruanda and the Urundi were themselves overpopulated. Stock-raising castes of Hamitic or Semitic origin, close kin to the ruling groups of Uganda, dominated Bantu peoples that had themselves thrust the Pigmies back toward less hospitable regions. Here there could only be a question of protecting and administering, not of colonizing.

German Southwest Africa, especially the regions of Namaqualand and Damaraland, offered vast areas favourable to a pastoral economy, in climatic conditions suitable for Europeans. These territories were reminiscent of certain regions of Australia and Argentina. According to some, the natives there would simply have to undergo the same treatment endured by Australian aborigines and the Patagonians. The Germans, forcing these peoples back toward the desert zones, had already reduced their number by almost two thirds. In 1914, 15,000 Europeans were settled there in conditions equalling those of the Transvaal.

The Boers felt an understandable sympathy for Europeans who like themselves were attempting to establish a white civilization on the flanks of Africa and to exploit the natural resources that the primitive inhabitants had completely neglected. Botha tried to annex the territory outright, but Smuts, who at Versailles had shown himself to be one of the most active negotiators within the British Imperial Delegation, saw to it that the Mandate C was accepted; this, while leaving to the Union of South Africa great administrative latitude, reserved to the Council of the League of Nations the right to intervene in any modification to be introduced into the status of the territory. This fragile international obligation was to give rise to a debate that is still in full swing. Smuts took advantage of it to outline a Monroe Doctrine for the southern portion of Africa as a shield against the intrusion of "European militarism".

The question of the German colonies was not the only one to come up at the peace conference. Italy was determined to press the rights it claimed to draw from Article 13 of the secret treaty it had concluded with France and Great Britain in April 1915. It intended to secure the important compensations it had been promised in case France and

Page 236
Young Lijj Liasu (mounted, left) was proclaimed Negus of Ethiopia in 1910 when Menelik became too ill to rule. Menelik's death in 1913 precipitated a domestic crisis: Lijj Liasu allied himself with Ethiopia's traditional enemies, the Somalis and the Gallas. He became a Muslim and joined the Holy War undertaken by the Turks. Lijj Liasu was deposed in 1917 by Ras Tafari, the future Emperor Haile Selassie.

Great Britain divided up the German territories in Africa. It wanted to enlarge Eritrea and Somaliland (which could only be done at the expense of Ethiopia and the Sudan), and to see its rights over Libya confirmed (which amounted to having its sovereignty internationally recognized over the Senussi empire of the eastern Sahara). The Italian demands pushed back the Libyan hinterland as far as Nigeria and Lake Chad; in the east they took in the traditionally Egyptian oases of the eastern Sahara. In the Sudan Italy demanded the annexation of Kassala as far as the Abtara River. In Somaliland it wished to go as far as the Juba River and annex the port of Chisimayo outright. The exchanges of notes between France and Italy in September 1919, and the Anglo-Italian agreement of May 1920, gave partial satisfaction to Italy with respect to Somaliland and the regions north of the Chad.

The Egyptian question   There also had to be a settlement of the question of Egypt, which had become a real tangle of international obligations and burdens ever since the decline and then the defeat of the Ottoman Empire. The unilateral protectorate of Great Britain, proclaimed at the beginning of the war, was legally worthless. Egypt still found itself yoked to the regime of capitulations inherited through the Ottoman Empire from the sixteenth and seventeenth centuries. It was subject to the authority of the Debt Commission, which had rights of intervention and supervision in its financial and economic life. In addition, unequal commercial treaties imposed on the Khedive restricted the liberty of action of the occupying power. Great Britain eliminated the mortgage of Ottoman sovereignty by the Treaty of Sèvres, in which Turkey waived payment of the symbolic tribute owed the Sublime Porte by the Khedive. It subsequently made an effort gradually to modify the regime of the capitulations until it finally disappeared completely.

Such are the broad outlines of an international settlement in which the questions set the European powers by the future of Africa and of Asia had taken on an unexpected importance. After 1919 the historic landscape was radically transformed. France and Great Britain were at the zenith of their power, yet the seeds of their imminent decadence were inherent in what in the minds of many people was ultimately, after all, merely the victory of one imperialism over another.

The idea of protecting the native peoples, and of the responsibility of European powers for them, was resuscitated by a new kind of propaganda as a mere humanized version of the old idea of a hierarchy of races and of civilizations. Many objective observers find Africa's future was a complementary and passive part of the economic and political system which reflected the priorities and demands of the western world.

Chapter 26

A Pyrrhic Victory

The Versailles settlement created a basic division in Europe among the satisfied powers, the dissatisfied ones, and the vanquished not to mention the absent (like Russia) which had to restore their energies before re-entering the arena of world competition.

African reactions differed in accordance with the function of the violence and depth of the shock produced on the traditional societies by European domination. In the north it was the military, the colonists, the merchants and the financiers that represented the components of the shock. In the south it was industry and the stock-exchange fever that smashed the traditional social structure, both of the white farmers and the Bantu labourers. Nowhere did Europe present itself as a unified force working toward unification. The Bantus had seen Boers and British fighting each other. The Egyptians and Tunisians were well aware that England, Italy and France, the Allies of the Great War, were rivals if not enemies on African soil. Ethiopia had long realized that European imperialism was as divided as it was cynical.

African reactions to the Versailles Treaty

On the diplomatic plane Great Britain had a free hand in Egypt. No one contested the international legitimacy of its position there. Thanks to its base in Cairo, and to the control it had exercised over the Suez Canal to the great advantage of the Allies during the four crucial years when the destiny of the British and French peoples was at stake, it had succeeded in popularizing the idea that the safety of its own imperial interests coincided with that of international liberties. The Egyptian nationalists saw the whole situation from a quite different point of view. The cause of freedom and of a parliamentary regime had been defended since the beginning of the century by westernized bourgeois like Mustapha Kamil, founder of the "Fatherland Party". The Egyptian poetry of the period celebrates the victories of the Japanese over the Russians as a model for all Asia to follow in its struggle against the European ascendancy.

The attempts at agrarian reform made by Lord Kitchener (who continued to be more interested in the Nile Valley than in Egypt proper) were incapable of lessening the agitation and the impatience that were linked far more to the abrupt modernization of the urbanized elements than to the deep but more or less unconscious desires of the fellahs. By and large the British administration was in agreement with the philosophy expressed by Kitchener himself in a letter to the Prime Minister, Sir Edward Grey (6 April 1912): "Whatever the value of the party system may be in Western political life, it is evident that its application to an intensely democratic community, the essential basis of whose social life is the brotherhood of man combined with respect for learning and the experience of age, is an unnatural proceeding fraught with inevitable division and weakness". True enough, the instrument of political democracy that was placed at the disposition of the politically conscious elements was not necessarily the most suitable to ensure the smooth evolution of a rejuvenated nation.

Two days after the signing of the armistice with Germany, the 13th of November 1918, Zaghlul Pasha, the son of an Egyptian peasant, who was administrator of the Khedive's property, appeared at the residency of the British Consul General in Cairo (Sir Reginald

Wingate, former conqueror of the Sudan) at the head of a delegation (Wafd), in order to ask for the right to plead the cause of Egyptian independence in London and Paris. He was deported to Malta in 1919. Egypt rose up as one, combining in one massive outburst the rage of the masses at the material requisitions and the huge financial costs imposed upon them by the policy of defence against Turkish-German imperialism.

Lord Milner, whose enlightened liberalism in South Africa had already given some grounds for thinking that the phenomena of European or African nationalism might be dealt with in a spirit of compromise, was given a mission with the object of "seeking the causes of the recent disorders in Egypt and reporting on the situation existing." It was soon demonstrated that the exercise of military force alone, even under the command of a chief as competent as General Sir Edmund Allenby, led to no solution. Milner recommended a settlement that would permit the "liberation of Egypt from the guardianship it was so violently opposed to without endangering the interests we must safeguard".

It took Great Britain more than two years to recognize the irrefutable fact of Egyptian nationalism. Zaghlul Pasha was deported a second time, returning in 1923. But the principle of Egyptian independence was recognized by London on 28 February 1922. Sultan Fuad Pasha was proclaimed King on 16 March 1923. The Egyptian nation, freed once and for all from rule by alien military castes, was able to work for its own interests. It remained for it only to eliminate the last traces of the control exercised by a foreign imperialism and whatever remained of the social and economic exploitation of the common citizen by ruling classes that were so often regarded as alien to the nation.

The resurgence of Egypt after the eclipse of the British Protectorate, necessarily brought up the question of the Sudan, on which Mehemet Ali and his successors had prematurely staked their military prestige and financial resources. Zaghlul, who became the undisputed leader of Egypt after the elections of January 1924, put forth the slogan of the unity of the Nile Valley. Yet the fact remained that the King of Egypt had not been proclaimed King of the Sudan. The assassination on 19 November 1924 of Sir Lee Stack, Sirdar of the Egyptian army and Governor General of the Sudan, was proof enough that if the politicians were able to inflame popular hatred they were incapable of controlling it. Great Britain's reaction was immediate. London had good grounds for thinking that the Egyptian government had proven "its incapacity or its refusal to protect foreigners' lives". It was at this time that the Sudanese and Egyptian armies and administration were separated from one another, and the Sudanese nation was brought under British protection against the wishes of Egypt.

To this awakening of the Egyptian nation there was a corresponding and steady growth of the spirit of independence in North Africa. France had emerged from the Great War with its prestige increased. In Morocco Lyautey had succeeded in creating "the spectacle of a grouping of humanity in which men of diverse origins, professions and races were, without abandoning their individual ideas, pursuing a common ideal and a common reason for living". (Leopold Senghor)

The unfortunate attempt of the Spanish armies to exercise occupation rights over the northern zone of Morocco (confirmed by the Franco-Spanish Convention of 27 November 1912) was the root of a war that Madrid did not like and was in any case badly prepared for. The Spanish columns entered Tafarsit in 1920, and collided with a Riff chief, Abd-el-Krim, a worthy descendant of the great Berber chiefs who had been the enemies of the Romans and Vandals. The Spaniards lost 15,000 men and all their arms. This was a new disaster for them; it recalled the defeats undergone in the sixteenth century by Cardinal Ximenes. The Berber chief, who had been brought up in Spain, knew its weaknesses. He wanted outright independence. Spain, already in

Right: King Farouk, at the time he came to the throne, addressing his people for the first time. Farouk was 16 when King Fuad died. Negotiations were already under way for the total independence of Egypt. England then recognized Egyptian sovereignty but kept the right to occupy Suez for 20 years (until 1956).
Below: Zaghlul Pasha, during a meeting which took place on his return from exile in 1923. He was first deported by the British in 1919 when he asked for the right to plead the cause of Egyptian independence in London and Paris. A second deportation followed which lasted until 1923. Britain reluctantly faced the inevitability of Egyptian nationalism. Zaghlul became the undisputed leader of his country after the elections of 1924.

the grip of social agitation and on the periphery of world history ever since its defeat by the Anglo-Saxon powers in the nineteenth century, once again had to drain an exhausted country to fling arms, men and money into the Moroccan furnace. The adroitness of the Riff chief gave some reason to think that international communism was using Morocco for its first test of strength in the anti-imperialist struggle.

France, the official Protector of Morocco, was alarmed. Fez and Tazza were directly threatened by the Riff warriors, who might reunite with the still untamed Berber tribes of the Middle Atlas. In 1924 the Painlevé government asked the Chamber of Deputies to understand that Fez must not be abandoned in the face of this "assault by Muslim fanaticism", because via Fez "it was the whole of Morocco, the whole of Algeria, the whole of North Africa" that was at stake. According to him, "it would be the end of our colonial empire, the end of our economic independence." Marshal Pétain, the victor of Verdun, was sent out at the head of French troops that soon numbered more than 200,000 men, against some 30,000 rebels. The Spaniards put 60,000 men in the front lines. It took a whole year to force Abd el-Krim to surrender (27 May 1926).

There were profound repercussions to this renewal of the conquest of Morocco, which had hitherto taken place on a plane that was essentially diplomatic. Lyautey, the pacifier, had to abandon Morocco, for which he had done so much. Spain sank still further into its domestic political crisis. The Communist International showed its hand in a telegram from the French Communist leader Jacques Doriot to Abd el-Krim. The effects of this telegram were as far-reaching as those of the Kaiser's to Kruger. France's position in Europe was much weakened. Some were suspicious of Britain's dark designs and looked for hints of discreet intervention on its part as a manifestation of Britain's natural hostility to any reinforcement of French positions. Though official diplomacy was successful in bringing about a settlement of the status of Tangiers in December 1923, it could not hide the abrupt deterioration of a situation in which great powers like France and Great Britain found themselves placed on the military defensive.

The pacification of Morocco was to go on for another ten years, ending in 1934 with the almost total unification of the country under the central government. France was to achieve what neither the Arabs nor the Vandals nor the Romans had been able to: the reunion under an undisputed authority of the interior and the coastal plains, the Riff and the Atlas mountains, and their Algerian and Saharan frontiers.

In a sense Abd el-Krim was a vigorous, though tardy witness to the first wave of African reaction against the European advance, like the Kabyle insurgents who had been such a thorn in the side of the French troops in 1871. He was the worthy son of a Morocco that had always jealously defended its rich and complex personality, with roots solidly planted in the Riff and the Atlas and at the gates of the great desert.

Tunisia, on the contrary, was the extreme point of the "intellectual" reaction against European imperialism in North Africa. Turned toward the eastern Mediterranean, it could not remain blind to the rapid evolution of the Egyptian situation. In Tunisia as in Egypt, an Islam rejuvenated under the influence of thinkers like El-Afghani and Muhammad Abduh attempted to reconcile European-style modernism with religious and social traditionalism and so to forge a weapon of effective defense against the cultural assimilation imposed by the west as an instrument of economic and political dominion. The programme of the Destour (Constitution) Party, published in March 1920, called for the convocation of an assembly made up of French and Tunisian deputies chosen by universal suffrage, maintaining that the government had to be responsible to it. The most current ideas of French democracy were applied to the local situation: separation of powers, the "unification" of the administrative offices, municipal liberties, liberty of the press and the right of association. All these demands were rejected by a French government supported by a majority that refused to compromise on what

Page 242
Police repression of strikes in Johannesburg, in 1922. The rapid industrialization of South Africa at the beginning of the century favored the creation of a Trade Union movement. Strikes broke out from Johannesburg in the Cape to Natal in 1917. In 1922, striking European workers were brutally assaulted by the police.

243

it considered the imperial mission of France, which itself was democratic and had moreover been victorious in a war for civilization and justice.

The reforms of July 1922, which created a "consultative council," represented a first step on the path of a timorous democratization that was bound to be halted short of any measure infringing on the principles of French sovereignty, which at that time were sacrosanct. Within the framework of European politics France's position was complicated by the persistent refusal of Great Britain to admit the legal consequences of the French protectorate with respect to individual status, and more particularly by the fact that almost 100.000 Italians who lived in Tunisia demanded a special statute. Mussolini's Italy saw in Tunisia an excellent terrain to test the possibilities of a revisionist movement aimed at changing all treaties that seemed unfavorable to the rulers of Fascist Italy. In Tunisia, the revisionist movement was actually rooted in the deep vexation of Italy with the unilateral action taken on behalf of France in 1881 by Jules Ferry. A series of Franco-Italian conventions (1896, 1914, 1919) had effectively preserved the rights of the Italian minorities. It was of course well-known that ever since antiquity Tunisia had been the crossroads in the struggle among western powers, eastern powers, and the resistance of North Africa. Thus the nationalism of Tunisia, like that of Egypt, was conditioned by its geographical situation.

In the west, French Algeria seemed to be reinforced by the application of the principles of a political and administrative integration based on the reforms of February 1918, which took into account the exceptional contribution made by Algeria to the French war effort. Further east, Fascist Italy, struggling against Mahdism, was attempting with difficulty to control the eastern Sahara.

While North Africa was gradually waking up to the possibilities of political life whose centres were in Paris and London more than in Cairo, Tunis, Algiers, or Rabat, the south of the continent was moving forward into an accelerated development of its economy. Gold and diamonds made the Union of South Africa one of the great industrial regions of the world. The trade-union movement had made its appearance there in 1917 as an autonomous force. The European workers protested against the increase in the cost of living. The Africans organized the African National Union, and took advantage of it to add some demands of a quite different nature. The police brutally repressed the African strikes that extended from Johannesburg to the Cape and to Natal. Following a prophecy of Wellington Butulezi, the rumour had spread that the Negroes of the United States were coming to free Africa aboard airplanes of the latest model. Biblical sects had been organized, like the "Israelites", which did not hesitate to instigate mass demonstrations against the armed police. Negro discontent was profound.

But it was the revolt of the European workers in March 1922, under the instigation of agitators who had come from Europe, that represented the most serious danger for the future of the Union. The police brutally repressed what seemed to be a premature workers' attempt to seize power on the slogan "Workers of the world, unite for a white South Africa!' After this double repression the Smuts government tried to create a coalition between the Boer elements of the country-side and those of the cities, who had a joint interest in pushing the Bantus back into a subordinate position in agriculture as well as in industry. A great opportunity had been missed, one that had been offered by economic progress based on the growing investments from abroad and the rapprochement between the workers of different races for whom the common struggle in the field of industrial demands might have brought about an easing of racial differences.

In the north as well as in the south of the continent, Europe seemed to pay no heed to the consequences of the revolution it had just imposed on Africa for its own immediate economic and political advantage.

Trade-Union agitation in South Africa

Chapter 27
Ethiopia conquered

Scarcely had the new African status quo been legitimized by the Versailles Treaty when it was imperiled by the contending, yet converging forces of European revisionists and African neo-nationalism.

With the unilateral settlement of the Sudanese question British rule in the Nile Valley became absolute. The Union Jack waved serenely over the Cape-to-Cairo road, with Tanganyika safely eliminated as an obstacle. The only problem left was the festering sore of Ethiopia, which, in spite of Ras Tafari's assumption of power, was in a highly unsatisfactory internal condition.

Internationally, Ethiopia was playing for high stakes. It had to create a diplomatic defense for its independence within a new framework, that of the League of Nations, of which it became a member in 1923 with the sponsorship of France and Italy. The powers of resistance of the thousand-year-old kingdom were rooted in the continuous existence of a military and religious caste that was the self-appointed guardian of the national tradition. This tradition may be summed up as the struggle against the Islamized peoples from the neighbouring deserts and against the Gallas, the pagan tribes living on the plateau itself.

The infamous episode of Lijj Liasu had, to be sure, damaged the prestige and unity of the ruling caste during the First World War, and, what was worse, the country felt isolated as it confronted all alone the unleashed ambitions of its Italian neighbour in Eritrea and Somaliland. Mussolini, after all, had said that Italy was suffering from "the undeserved defeat of Adowa, which has bled the Italian heart for forty years and must be healed once and for all."

Fascist Italy opposed modification in Europe, but backed it strongly in Africa. Italian public opinion was restive over the niggling compensations grudgingly accorded by France and Great Britain after the Versailles settlement. The Versailles Treaty had in fact given the lion's share of the settlement to the two greatest colonial powers in Africa, and when the League of Nations proclaimed that conquest could no longer be the source of political legitimacy it was doing no more, in effect, than functioning as a syndicate of the satisfied "haves."

The Italian Attack on Ethiopia 1935

An uncertain border between Italian Somaliland and Ethiopia heightened the general exacerbation. Nothing could have demonstrated more clearly to the Ethiopians the Italian determination to disregard their territorial integrity than the frontier incidents that constantly took place in the contested zone. For its part Italy, of course, regarded Ethiopia as a conquering empire with no genuine national unity.

After the Wal-Wal incident, and in the teeth of all attempts at arbitration by outsiders, the Italian armies launched an attack against Ethiopia on 5 December 1934, penetrating deep into Ethiopian territory. By a skilful use of propaganda Italy had succeeded in capitalizing on the traditional hatred of the Somali tribesmen for the Amhara oppressors, and thus consolidating its base of attack. All attempts at conciliation proved a dismal fiasco, and Ethiopia was obliged to mobilize.

Officially the Italo-Ethiopian war began on 3 October 1935, and ended 5 May 1936, when Marshal Badoglio entered Addis Ababa as a conqueror and Emperor Haile Selassie fled the country to go into exile in Jerusalem.

The campaign leading up to the Ethiopian defeat proved more difficult than anticipated. What had seemed to be the initially triumphant Italian advance, with Marshal De Bono entering Diredawa from Eritrea on 6 October and Axum on 15 October 1935, was substantially slowed down both by the difficult terrain and by the stubborn resistance of the Ethiopian warriors. De Bono was soon replaced by Badoglio, and a twin offensive was launched from Eritrea and Somaliland. By 4 April 1936 this had resulted in the defeat near Lake Achadji of the regular armies led by the Emperor and in the occupation of Gondar and Dessie. This put the heart of the plateau in the hands of the Italians, even though some scattered Ethiopian units could still go on fighting and thus maintain a reign of permanent insecurity. This lasted until 1941 when another European power, Great Britain, was able to attack the colonial Italian regime in its own African fortress, bringing about the total collapse of the Italian position.

As a result of its decisive military victory the Italian government was able to announce the outright annexation of the Ethiopian Empire. The King of Italy simply set on his own head the millennial crown of the Lions of Judah. The military victor, Badoglio, became Governor General of this new, and, as it turned out, last of the European colonies in Africa. Italian settlers were invited to colonize the fertile uplands of Abyssinia, thus opening up a boundless area for the surplus population of a rapidly expanding European people. For the first time in their lengthy history the Amharas seemed completely submerged.

How much had this enterprise cost the Italians?

What was the cost of this victory? The Italians threw into the battle more than a quarter of a million men, of whom 50,000 came from Italian possessions in Africa. They had a powerful force and the most modern armament at their disposal, which created the most staggering disproportion of forces, from the point of view of both manpower and firing power. The disproportion was even greater than that between the Anglo-Egyptian forces and the Mahdi's army at Omdurman. The Negus did not have more than 30,000 men at the most, in the regular army, and as for the hundreds of thousands of irregulars engaged in hit-and-run tactics, though they were remarkably courageous, they were practically without weapons. Whole populations were panicked by aerial bombardments and gas attacks. The Italo-Ethiopian war gave a bitter foretaste of the conflicts that were soon to engulf Spain and the rest of Europe.

The system of collective security established by France and Great Britain was fatally undermined by the Italian decision to disregard the resolutions of the League of Nations. In addition, the attack on Ethiopia seemed to everyone to be the first stage of forcible revision of the Versailles Treaty. From this point of view the crisis launched by Mussolini seemed to many to be a European rather than an African crisis, and European statesmen were faced by agonizing decisions.

A French Premier, Pierre Laval, said unequivocally that he attached far more importance to the maintenance of close ties with Italy, a pillar of a European order, including the independence of Austria, than to the safety of an obscure African kingdom that was not above practising slavery and human mutilation. He was supported by important segments of French public opinion, which had not forgotten Mr. Hanotaux, the Fashoda crisis, and Anglo-Saxon "insolence" in general.

Prime Minister Baldwin and Great Britain saw the conflict in a different light. It was obvious that British imperial interests were threatened by the emergence of an aggressive European power near the source of the Nile, and British opinion was infuriated by Mussolini's blatant contempt for international law and convention. London made

Page 247
Abyssinian warrior in full dress. The lion skin symbolizes the Ethiopian lion of Judah. After incessant border incidents between Ethiopia and Italian Somaliland, Italian troops attacked Ethiopia on December 5, 1934.

Italian troops spreading across the sands of Ethiopia. The campaign proved more difficult than anticipated. It took Marshal Badoglio until May, 1936 to conquer the country. Italy annexed the Ethiopian Empire. Haile Selassie fled to exile.

Italian artillery in Ethiopia. Mussolini considered the attack on Ethiopia a revenge for the "underserved defeat of Adowa". Italian feelings were resentful of the Versailles Treaty which gave the lion's share of Africa to France and Great Britain.

a serious study of the naval and military mobilization measures that might reinforce the economic sanctions the League of Nations had established with so many mental reservations.

From a more general point of view, it became clear that if collective security could not be made to function in the case of the Italian attack on Ethiopia, it would be even more futile if Germany ever became involved. In Geneva the Italian spokesman, Baron Aloisi, ardent champion of a proletarian Italy with a self-appointed civilizing mission and an inherent right to expansion, was answered by the representative of Haiti, General Nemours: "There cannot be two kinds of truth, one for Africa and the other for Europe. Agression must be defined in the same way on both sides of the Mediterranean. How can there be a difference between a colonial war and any other war?"

The "Hoare-Laval Plan" was contrived as a lastminute stop-gap. After the outbreak of hostilities it proposed a division of the Ethiopian sphere of influence among Italy, Great Britain and France, leaving the Emperor with a zone of restricted sovereignty around Addis Ababa.

It is quite conceivable that this kind of proposal might have been successful forty years before had the Italians been victorious at Adowa, but the savage reaction of the British and French press to this "betrayal" by the two powers who were supposed to be the bulwarks of collective security showed very clearly that the age of imperialism was long since past. Primitive as it was, the Ethiopian Empire had become the symbol of African freedom past and future. Muslim opinion, rapidly awakening in the Middle East and in North Africa, chose to see in the Christian Amharas' struggle against a European power a portent for the future. Ethiopia was supported by Egyptians, Sudanese, and North Africans, and in the far-off United States American Negroes hailed Emperor Haile Selassie as the heroic representative of the oppressed black masses. Relief organizations were created to support the Ethiopian armies, and the "Black Eagle," a flamboyant aviator from Harlem, joined the Ethiopian air force. Collections were organized by students on the Gold Coast, while Socialist militants in North and West Africa launched a vigorous anti-Fascist propaganda campaign.

The Union of South Africa, with Liberia, the only independent power on the continent, and one completely dominated by European settlers, took a curiously paradoxical stand by ardently supporting the Ethiopian cause at the League of Nations. Pretoria understood quite well that the Italian attack had practically destroyed the fragile balance of power established in Africa by Versailles, and had planted there once again the seed of unrest and mutiny. South Africa raised a lonely voice at the historic debate held in Geneva from 30 June to 4 July 1936, during which Haile Selassie in person vainly begged the League not to recognize the Italian conquest of his country as an accomplished fact.

But just because of its suddenness the Italian victory appeased many a troubled conscience. It became fashionable to say that the Ethiopians, after all, had to be forced into the 20th century in one way or another. And in any case the rapidly ensuing aggravation of the European crisis made nonsense of any idea of boycotting Mussolini's Italy any further.

On 18 July of that same year the Spanish Civil War began with the landing of Francisco Franco, a hitherto unknown general who had been meditating the destruction of the Spanish Republic on the mainland of Africa. Nearly a thousand years after the descent in Spain of the Almoravides, Moorish warriors were taking part in a new European Civil War, while Hitler's Germany denounced whatever was left of the military clauses of the Versailles Treaty.

The Europe born in Versailles had been killed on the Ethiopian plateau.

Haile Selassie's vain plea
1936

249

Chapter 28
A New Political Awareness

The defeat of Ethiopia had shown that France and Great Britain were declining. The politically conscious elements in Egypt and in North Africa were torn by contradictory feelings. To be sure, the weakening of the ruling powers encouraged the hope that they would make certain concessions in order to reconcile the local political forces. On the other hand, the strengthening of Italy and the sudden rise of Hitler Germany presented a new danger. The "proletarian" powers did not conceal their desire to seize African territories in order to reinforce their economic and military potential. As a matter of fact the "young" nations had remained bogged down in the geographical views cherished by the theoreticians of Mittelafrika and by Wilhelm II. The "old" nations had learned, in the course of thirty years of colonial administration, to have a correct appreciation of the active and passive powers of African resistance to all attempts at economic and cultural assimilation. Hence, up to the Second World War, the nationalist movements had only a narrow margin for manœuvring. They were to try to secure the maximum of concessions on the part of the occupying powers without, however, agreeing to be made the instrument of their enemies, who in fact were trying to do no less than substitute their own rule for that of the satisfied powers.

The Egyptian politicians were in the best position for taking advantage of the new situation created by the Italian conquest. Great Britain, as it had done during the World War, heedlessly made full use of its land and sea bases on Egyptian soil. The leaders of the major parties shelved their quarrels and made up a united front that insisted on opening up negotiations to bring about a new treaty recognizing Egyptian independence without qualification. These negotiations were begun in Cairo in March 1936, that is, just when Italian arms were dealing the final blows to the Negus's armies. Young Farouk had succeeded King Fuad, who had died in April 1936. Nahas Pasha, Zaghlul's successor as head of the Wafd, was sure of an absolute majority following the new elections, which gave him a clear mandate to free Egypt from the British military occupation.

Egyptian independence recognized

Egyptian independence was now solemnly and unreservedly recognized by Great Britain. Egypt became a member of the League of Nations and freely concluded with its former protector, as one power to another, a defensive treaty of alliance that gave the British armies the right to occupy the Suez Canal zone for twenty years. The ambiguity weighing on the status of the Sudan ever since the crisis of 1924 was dissipated. The High Commissioner at Khartoum was given full powers on behalf of both governments for the exercise of the Anglo-Egyptian condominium. Both parties were satisfied by the treaty. The dream of the Egyptian nationalists was realized, since for the first time in two thousand years Egypt was free of all foreign rule. Great Britain, while making all necessary concessions, had retained control of the Suez route, which since the Italian victory in Ethiopia had become still more vital for it. It was thanks to this treaty of 1936 that five years later Britain was to be able to cut the communications of the new Italian empire and to force the Italian armies of East Africa into a surrender.

North Africa could not remain indifferent to this reversal of the situation in the eastern Mediterranean. Agitation began in Tunisia, Algeria, and Morocco. Because this agitation was only episodic it was for this very reason noticed all the more by far-sighted observers, since they followed the period of imperial euphoria of the early '30s. After the collapse of the Riff movement of resistance and the pacification, by now almost total, of Morocco, there seemed to be nothing left but to celebrate the golden age of enlightened imperialism, which had been far better than the Romans able to reconcile Europeans and North Africans. The centenary of French Algeria in 1930, inspired sumptuous celebrations in which the Muslim leaders emphasized their faith in integration and assimilation into the French community as a solution to the problem of the co-existence of the two peoples. Marshal Lyautey crowned a magnificent career by organizing the Colonial Exposition of 1931, at which visitors could admire the tangible examples of the civilizing mission overseas carried out in less than a single generation by France, Great Britain, Holland and Portugal.

To be sure, the world economic crisis, which had struck Germany and the United States in 1929 and France in 1931, had begun to make its effects felt in the African territories. Their prosperity depended on foreign markets and they underwent increasing difficulties in ensuring the servicing of the loans, so essential to building up their economies, concluded during the euphoric postwar period. In fact the economic crisis contributed to sharpening the political struggle.

The three countries of North Africa were influenced by a dual political movement. The traditionalist elements were opposed to administrative and cultural assimilation. They found the best defense of their national identity in the Arabic language and the Muslim faith. A "modernist" faction, on the other hand, that was particularly active in Tunisia and Algeria, was hostile to any return to the past and to isolation. These neo-nationalists believed that independence would be achieved thanks to an active participation in the great labour movements and political currents of the western world

In Tunisia the old Destour Party was ready to yield and accept the authority of France as long as the latter lived up to the spirit and the letter of the Protectorate Treaty. On the other hand, it showed itself to be the most intransigeant of opponents when it came to any measure affecting the personal status of the members of the Muslim community. Inspired by the Egyptian example, a particularly eloquent and courageous young leader, Habib Bourguiba, organized the forward-looking and enlightened leaders in the" Neo-Destour" and embarked on an active opposition to the French administration. France immediately suspected the Tunisian nationalist movement of collusion with Fascist Italy, which at that time was carrying on a propaganda compaign in Libya designed to flatter a rejuvenated Islam (just as Wilhelm II had pretended to be defending Morocco and the Ottoman Empire against the aggression of France and Great Britain). In 1935 Peyrouton, the Resident General, had Bourguiba deported to the border of the Sahara. Meanwhile the populace became out-and-out nationalist; the very principle of colonization was attacked. Bourguiba had showed that "the (European) preponderance had been translated into a massive displacement of wealth to the disadvantage of the indigenous part of the population, and that the crisis had merely accelerated this and made it more odious." It seemed that the Anglo-Egyptian Treaty ought to serve as a model to be followed by the Neo-Destour, which claimed that France had an interest in having Tunisia prosperous and emancipated, and thus more deeply attached to France during a period of tension in which the balance of power in the Mediterranean was threatened.

The traditionalists in Algeria, led by the Ulema (specialists in Muslim law) had come together in 1931 and were preaching cultural and religious nationalism in the mosques. Two of their leaders, Ben Badis and Tayyib Oul Oukbi, instigated the first open

Habib Bourguiba
and the "Neo-Destour"

demonstrations against French policy, which they called anti-religious. On 2 August 1936 the Mufti of the great mosque of Algiers, Mahmud ben Ali, well known as a friend of France, was assassinated.

Messali Hadj and the "modernist" movement

The "modernist" movement was launched by Messali Hadj, who first organized the "North African Star", where a number of Ulema fought side by side with young militants who were influenced by extreme leftwing propaganda and by the slogans of the great French trade-unions. Ferhat Abbas, a pharmacist from Constantine, and a veteran of the 1914-1918 war, championed a more positive approach to the French regime. He helped found the Federation of the Muslim Deputies of Constantine. On 23 February 1936 he wrote in his newspaper *L'Entente*: "Nationalism—this is the feeling that moves a people to live within its territorial borders. If I had discovered the Algerian nation I would be a nationalist; I would not blush about it as though it were a crime ... I will not die for the Algerian fatherland because that fatherland does not exist. I did not discover it. I have interrogated history. I have interrogated the living and the dead. I have visited the cemeteries. No one has spoken to me about it. To be sure, I discovered the Arab Empire, the Muslim Empire that is the honour of Islam and of our race. But these empires are extinct ... For that matter no one believes seriously in our nationalism. What is struggling to emerge behind that word is our economic and political emancipation. This double emancipation is what we want with all the power of our will and of our social ideal ... We are the children of a new world, born of the spirit and the energy of France." It took Ferhat Abbas almost ten years to grasp the point that the emancipation he was speaking of could not, unfortunately, be secured as long as European colonizing interests and theories had paramount importance.

France itself was brutally awakened from the dream of cosmic grandeur its leaders had offered it as a reward for the horrifying losses suffered during the war. All possible questions suddenly emerged for a nation to whom no one had wanted, or perhaps had been able, to tell the truth. Triumphant European revisionism, plus the re-emergence of the German peril, were aggravated by claims to redress old social grievances that were falling due. The workers' dissatisfaction was profound. It was aggravated by the policies of Pierre Laval, who was trying to apply "orthodox" remedies to resolve a financial and economic crisis that was becoming more and more serious. The "Popular" Front government headed by the socialist Premier Léon Blum, brought to power in 1936, could not disregard the nationalist movements that were churning up North Africa. These were added to by generalized strike movements that extended the demands of the working class in France. The staggering successes of regimes based on an authoritarian and materialist philosophy threatened to encircle France, which attached all the more importance to the freedom of its communications with its African possessions and to the safety of its empire. The Spanish civil war, the Italian claims on Tunisia, the German demands for the return of the Reich's former colonies, put French policy in Africa on the defensive, just as they did Great Britain, more and more aware of the Italian danger.

Tied to the mother country by bonds of every kind, the three countries of North Africa could not help but share in its national crisis. They brought into it factors that were purely local, and that were at the root of a complex situation in which confused aspirations and contradictory slogans were inextricably intermingled.

A new style of anti-Semitism

The homogeneity of the political problems in the eastern and western Mediterranean was reinforced by a new style of anti-Semitism. The difficulties faced by Great Britain in Palestine, due to the Arab uprising of 1936, provided a rallying point for Arab nationalism in quest of self-definition in terms of a common theme. The Arabic language and Muslim religion seemed threatened, in the east by Zionism, in the west by the French policy of assimilation. The presence of Jewish communities along the North African coast, the enfeebled heirs of the Roman Diaspora augmented by the Jews expelled from

Spain by Isabella, provided sustenance for a hostile propaganda paid for by Berlin and relayed via Jerusalem.

These were the conditions in which Morocco (like Algeria and Tunisia) arrived at political awareness and grasped the possibilities offered by a developing situation, no longer encumbered by the intractability of the great Berber tribes, now completely neutralized by the military and political success of the Protectorate. A general economic slowdown due to the world crisis had succeeded the astonishing dynamism typical of the French administration under Lyautey. The Protectorate had grown more cumbersome. It tended toward direct control instead of limiting itself to the functions of supervision and advice implanted in it by the Marshal. Tribal nationalism had been tamed, to be sure, since the victory of the Franco-Spanish forces over Abd el-Krim and the brilliant pacification of the Atlas. But what was now emerging was a neo-nationalism comparable to that of Tunisia and Algeria, especially in Fez, the traditional capital of Morocco, whose islamic and academic traditions were reminiscent of those of Cairo.

A reform project was presented to the French administration by the Moroccan Committee of Action (MCA) in December 1934. But the French government (which tried to coordinate its North African policies in the framework of a Mediterranean High Committee), while divided, for reasons of general strategy could not show weakness in the face of a movement that tended to undermine its authority. The leaders of the MCA were arrested in July 1936. The MCA itself was dissolved a few months later, when the trade-union agitation led to a strike of a political character. The riots in Meknes in September 1937 were harshly repressed; Fez, encircled by French troops on 29 October, was threatened with aerial bombardments. El-Wazzani and other nationalist chiefs were arrested and deported.

Moroccan agitation suppressed

The North African malaise, which some people insisted on regarding as artificial, proved that North Africa could not remain sheltered against the variety of influences that had always made the Mediterranean region a zone of religious, racial, social and political conflicts. The outside influences that were accelerating the course of events in North Africa and Egypt were not their cause. The European order, by virtue of the very ease of its victory, had believed in its own permanence. Yet in reality it had been able to establish itself only because of the decadence of the Ottoman Empire and the feebleness of the political and military institutions in Algeria and Morocco. It had collided with a prolonged, though diffuse and unorganized resistance. By bringing in new administrative and political formulas backed by superior military force it had aroused and made conscious latent aspirations that were more nationalist than religious. By settling a million Europeans in North Africa and almost 200,000 Europeans and Levantines in Egypt, it seemed to be repeating the grandiose phenomenon of the Mediterranean unification that had been realized by the Roman Empire.

Nevertheless, like the Roman Empire, the seemingly undisputed dominion of London and Paris was itself being threatened by powerful opponents, for whom the fate of Africa was to be decided on the European fields of battle.

*Outbreak
of the European war*

When the European war broke out in September 1939, the bulk of the African continent ranged itself solidly on the side of the Franco-British allies.

Of the three independent powers that had survived all the various attempts at colonization, Egypt was tied to Great Britain by the Treaty of 1936, Liberia was favourable to the allies, and the Union of South Africa, though divided, had declared war on Nazi Germany. It seemed as though the theatre of African operations would remain secondary, as in 1914. In spite of his nationalist and anti-Semitic propaganda, which attracted many elements, Hitler was alarming. His vulgar racism was turning against him. Fascist Italy too was highly suspect after its Ethiopian conquest, even in Egypt where King Farouk made no effort to disguise his "Latin" sympathies. Nationalist chiefs like Nahas Pasha, Ferhat Abbas and Bourguiba were at one in recognizing that an Italo-German victory would mean a setback for the liberal policy that seemed at the point of birth in London and Paris.

The military collapse of France in June 1940, and the direct or indirect occupation of the country by the German armies gave rise to an ambiguous situation. The concept of "young" nations and the characteristic Nazi themes of the decadence of the western nations seemed to be justified by events. Yet Africa remained calm and gave no sign of wishing to take advantage of a situation that was, nevertheless, revolutionary.

The Anglo-French front having been broken in June 1940, and important military forces finding themselves neutralized in North Africa, the plans for a converging Franco-British offensive against Libya, starting out from bases in Tunisia and Egypt, were wiped out. Great Britain abruptly found itself isolated. Its position in Egypt and its communications in the Mediterranean were put under the mortal threat of an Italo-German exploitation of the French fleet. All North Africa seemed at the mercy of a bold Axis offensive.

In the three countries of North Africa, one of the determinants of a paradoxical situation lay in the fact that the North African units led by French, Algerian, Moroccan and Tunisian officers, had not lost hope at all and thought they could soon resume the struggle against the common enemy.

Egypt seemed to be the weak point in the Allied camp. Ali Maher, well known for his pro-Italian sympathies, had succeeded Nahas Pasha, who had become too pro-British for the liking of some people. In the very first days of 1940 Farouk started playing a dangerous game, which consisted of officially respecting Egypt's obligations to the allies (by virtue of the treaty of 1936) while at the same time taking discreet precautions in case they were defeated. In April 1940 the Wafd Party demanded that Great Britain promise that British troops would leave after the war once and for all.

At the time 50,000 British soldiers confronted 500,000 Italians in the Mediterranean and eastern Africa. In June 1940, after stabbing in the back a France submerged by the Nazi wave, Mussolini seemed ready to take the offensive in Libya with Marshal Balbo (who was to be succeeded by Graziani) and in Ethiopia with Badoglio. The

Page 255
Meharist machine gunners
of the Fezzan in December,
1942. Following the Allied
landing in North Africa, General
Leclerc's army left from Chad
and won Fezzan from Italy in
less than three weeks (end of
December to January 13, 1942).
The French troops then made
contact with the British forces
and entered Tripoli January 26.

Rommel with Field Marshal
Kesselring in Libya.
Rommel's offensive in the desert
was victorious until he reached
El Alamein (Egypt) where
Montgomery's counter-offensive
crushed the Italo-German forces.

Column of German prisoners in Libya, 1942.

Page 256
Landing of America troops near Oran, November 8, 1942. Other American landings were taking place at the same time near Algiers and Casablanca. These forces moved towards the East, while the 8th Army progressed from Tripoli towards the West, forming a vise in Tunisia which crushed the Italo-German troops. Their defeat was final at Cape Bon in May, 1943.

257

Ethiopian landscape. The country consists mostly of an inaccessible plateau which contributed for centuries to its isolation. During the last war English and Free French troops defeated Italian forces in Ethiopia and liberated Addis Ababa for the return of Emperor Haile Selassie.

Italian armies attacked Egypt on 3 September 1940. They penetrated a hundred kilometers into the interior, did not make the slightest use of their success and were finally surprised and crushed by the brilliant counter-offensive devised by General Wavell and carried out by General O'Connor at Sidi Barani on 9-11 December 1940. The British armies entered Cyrenaica, occupied Bardia on 7 January 1941 and Tobruk the 21st. They pierced through to Benghazi a few days later.

In eastern Africa the Italians found it easy to enter Berbera, capital of British Somaliland, on 19 August 1940. As in North Africa, these initial successes were to have no future. Another British offensive starting out from the Sudan reached Asmara and crushed the Italians at Agordat. The outpost of Kassala was reoccupied in January 1941. British forces from East Africa crossed the Juba River in February, occupied Mogadiscio on 25 February, Harar on 25 March, and Diredawa on the 29th. The Italian army lost 50,000 men, the British 500. On 6 April Addis Ababa was liberated. In Eritrea the key position of Keren was conquered on 27 March after the heroic assault of the Free French Forces and the Sudanese and British troops. Asmara was occupied on 1 April, Massawa on the 8th. On 11 April 1941 the theatre of operations in the Red Sea and the Gulf of Aden had ceased to be an official zone of hostilities. The Italian cancer on the flank of the British Empire had been eliminated. Ethiopia was free. Haile Selassie, who had come from the Sudan at the head of a small army commanded by Chindit Wingate, the nephew of Sir Reginald, made a triumphal entry into Addis Ababa on 5 May.

Ethiopia liberated
1941

Great Britain had wiped out the humiliation its diplomats had encountered one day in 1936 in Geneva when they had had to recognize, grinding their teeth, the accomplished fact of Italian aggression.

The Italian collapse in Ethiopia was the direct result of the strategic position of Great Britain in Egypt. Farouk and his entourage, like the politicians of the Wafd, were quite aware of the blackmailing power they enjoyed because of it. In spite of the Italian defeats, the intervention of Germany in North Africa, to say nothing of the ambiguous attitude of the Vichy regime, weighted the Egyptian life-and-death wager that was being made on the outcome of the war. An Italo-German victory was possible; therefore it was necessary to be sure that Rome and Berlin were ready to guarantee Egyptian independence. If Great Britain, which was being openly supported by the United States even before the latter's official entry into the war, was going to be victorious, the indispensable co-operation of Egypt ought to be made the object of very close negotiations. The military and logistical support accorded the forces of the British Empire, locked in the grip of a decisive conflict, had to be considered the trump card ultimately to be used in negotiations that might settle the fundamental question of the future of Egypt as a genuinely independent power. The court party, faced by this choice, leaned (just as did the French government of the unoccupied zone) toward an attitude of relative neutrality that in the last analysis was more favourable to the interests of the Axis than to those of the Allies. The varying fortunes of the encounters between British and Italo-German forces in the Libyan desert from 1941 to October 1942 account for this attitude without, of course, justifying it.

Marshal Rommel loosed an offensive that appeared decisive on 26 May 1942; after having routed the British Eighth Army, he overwhelmed the first Free French division at Bir-Hakeim, captured a South African division at Tobruk and reached Egyptian territory at El-Alamein on 1 July. The road to Alexandria and Cairo seemed open. At Cairo, the British Ambassador used tanks as his escort when he visited the Royal Palace and so imposed upon King Farouk Nahas Pasha. This new Prime Minister swiftly reacted in favor of the Allies: "I had to act in order to preserve the interests of the Egyptian people", he said, "protect its rights and inspire it with confidence...

Everyone is conscious of his duty to support our friend and our ally, Great Britain, in its hour of need."

In spite of its geopolitical ambitions and the brilliant improvizations of Marshal Rommel, the Italo-German alliance, champion of European-African revisionism, lacked the economic and military means to establish a new order in North Africa or in Black Africa. Montgomery, then Alexander, proved in action that the Anglo-Saxon world still had an effective superiority solidly supported by the American arsenal.

North Africa, which had briefly been neutralized by the French defeat of 1940, was the theatre of an allied landing operation in November 1942. At one blow this reintroduced French and North African forces into a struggle that had been inter-rupted since the humiliation of the 1940 armistice. Italy still thought it could seize the lion's share in a redistribution of the African territories. Mussolini had been dreaming of placing under his protection Tunisia, the Chad, the whole of the eastern Sahara, and the Nile valley. The Germans, sure of a pre-eminent role in a Nazi Europe, were to be satisfied with taking back their former colonies and with exercising a super-protectorate over the holders of the protectorates themselves. In the tropical areas the black races were to play the restricted role assigned them in the ethnic hierarchies defined by Hitler, Gœbbels and Rosenberg. As for the Spaniards, they hoped for the ultimate replacement of France by Spain as protector of Morocco and for the occupa-tion of Oran, doubtless as revenge for the defeats of Ximenes.

The Allied landing in North Africa

The North African political leaders, caught between the Scylla of French rule and the Charybdis of an Italo-German dictatorship, were in a still more difficult position than their Egyptian colleagues. Official France was represented on the spot by leaders who pretended to be wholly loyal to a regime that confused petty, short-range calculations with the abiding interests of a nation that was still at war with the Nazi aggressor. The nationalist chiefs who in 1939 had affirmed their unequivocal support of French policy were hesitant. It was again the problem of a military wager: Would the Axis win, or would the allies? Which side should the card of independence be played on? Echoes of this calculation can be found in the writings and statements of men like Bourguiba (interned at the time in Marseilles) who said quite clearly on 8 August 1942: "The role of all those who have a certain authority over the masses is to act in such a way that at the end of the war the Tunisian people does not find itself in the camp of the losers; that is, compromised with the Italians and Germans." In spite of the forced stay of the Tunisian leader in Rome, he did not change his convictions. His statements of May 1943 echoed those of Nahas Pasha, made at the worst moment of the war in Libya: "Our first duty at the present hour is to help the united nations to win the war. The best way to help them is to join hands with struggling France and to sacrifice everything to that end."

The sudden ebb of the Italo-German troops, after their rout in Tripolitania at the end of 1942, transformed Tunisia into an Italo-German base of operations just when Anglo-American troops landed in Morocco and Algeria. The Government party headed by Monsef Bey followed a political line with respect to the Vichy and the Axis representatives that was somewhat reminiscent of King Farouk's. On 2 August 1942 he had presented Admiral Estéva a demand for the revision of the terms of the protector-ate, a demand that was renewed in January 1943, this time with at least the tacit support of the forces of occupation. After these had surrendered in April 1943, Monsef Bey was deposed by General Giraud, Commander-in-Chief of the French Forces of North Africa. The new Resident General, Mast, tried to appease the nationalist claims with the customary device of reforms in non-political areas, but these left the Neo-Destour completely unsatisfied. In spite of its wholly different institutional structure, Algeria underwent a similar evolution. As an integral part of the mother country's territory it suffered directly from the repercussions of the policy of collaboration which came about as the result of the Nazi victory. On 8 October 1940, the Crémieux Decree was rescinded. Jews were excluded from the automatic enjoyment of full French citizenship. Some Vichy loyalist Europeans acted as transmitters of the propaganda of the new Italo-German order. Fascist agents approached Muslim extremists. Yet after the allied landing in November 1942 a striking event took place that is a milestone in the history of Algerian nationalism.

On 10 February 1943 a "manifesto" was handed to the government. It was signed by Ferhat Abbas and twenty-two elected representatives of the Algerian people. This document made much of the "race for power" provoked by the French in Algeria because of the colony's isolation from France that had been brought about by the allied landing. It took up the theme of "preponderance," so dear to the hearts of the Tunisian nationalists and advocated the juxtaposition of a French colony that was wholly European and of a Muslim Arab-Berber Algeria. In a striking summary Ferhat Abbas showed that the conquest, "that gigantic tragedy," had not overcome the obduracy of the conquered peoples. He compared the progress of France in Africa to a "swallow's wing touching a wave." He pointed out the failure of the successive attempts at reform that all had been clearly directed at facilitating the access of the Muslims to French citizenship (of which the Blum-Violette project, offering citizenship to more than 30,000 Algerians, had been the most recent example) and the stubborn opposition put up by the French mayors of Algeria, who had threatened to resign en masse. The Manifesto concluded with the formulation of a programme of five points that was inspired by the Atlantic Charter, and that demanded the political, linguistic, economic and constitutional recognition of the Algerian personality founded on the absolute freedom and equality "of all (Algeria's) inhabitants without distinction of race or religion."

The "swallow's wing touching a wave"

Despite a series of reforms (of 14 March 1943, promulgated by General de Gaulle, which put the Blum-Violette law to practical application, and of 7 March 1944, which abolished all discrimination between Muslims and non-Muslims) political impatience kept growing. On 15 March 1944 Ferhat Abbas founded the Party of the Friends of the Manifesto and of Liberty. Meanwhile the association of the Ulema pursued its religious, xenophobic propaganda in the traditionalist milieu and the Algerian Popular Party developed its own in the working-class milieu of the North African emigrants to France (themselves in close contact, through force of circumstance, with a highly active Communist and trade-union propaganda). The three parties organized in a united front that launched mass demonstrations in the streets. Kabylia rose in May 1945. Some particularly serious incidents took place in the cities of Setif and of Guelma, in the surrounding countryside and in the districts of Bougie and Bone. Hundreds of Europeans were killed. Thousands of Muslims died during the harsh reprisals ordered by the French authorities.

For the first time in several decades the deep-rooted conflict between the two communities came out into the open. The proletarian masses of the cities, as well as the Kabyle peasants impoverished by the war and by a series of bad harvests, took as their guide the slogans of equality and independence. The responsible authorities failed to disentangle the respective roles played by outside influences (such as pan-Islamic and pan-Arab propaganda or the themes of independence laid down in the Atlantic Charter) and that of the domestic factors, complex psychological reactions arising out of the contact of two societies that remained profoundly alien to each other.

Bitterness of the Algerian conflict

It was the same in Morocco. There could be no doubt that in scarcely thirty years France had achieved a prodigious accomplishment there. As we have seen it had grouped the whole empire under a central authority, with the exception of the Spanish zone and of Tangiers. It had renounced the policy outlined in 1930 that treated the Berbers as a separate entity and that seemed to aim at creating two nations based on different codes of law.

As the Sultan's protector, it had to give satisfaction to the most active elements in Arabized cities like Fez and Europeanized ones like Rabat and Casablanca, without at the same time losing the confidence of the great chiefs of the Atlas and of southern Morocco, who had not given up their political and military blackmail of the central government. From the zone it was occupying the Spanish Fascist regime embarked on a policy inspired by the German-Italian flirtation with the Egyptian nationalists. The High Commissioner, Beygbeder, encouraged the propaganda being carried on at Tetouan by Abd el-Khaliq al-Torres and directed against the French protectorate, with a degree of success that was, to be sure, rather limited. The Resident General Noguès who in 1936 had resumed Lyautey's policy, voluntarily yielded to the Throne, reinforcing its prestige in every way he could.

After 8 November 1942, and the hapless episode of the French resistance to the American landing, Morocco was subjected to a much more powerful outside influence, that of the United States, which was intrigued by the unexpected prospects of economic and political penetration. These proved dizzying to many of its representatives; there was something reminiscent here of the enthusiasm of the Wilsonian neophytes in the Near East when the Ottoman Empire was crumbling. President Roosevelt himself is supposed to have flashed in front of the Sultan the exciting vision of an "American-style" economic expansion taking in even the desert spaces, where water was soon supposed to be spurting into the air. For a brief moment Morocco became the arena of spectacular diplomatic activity. In the course of conversations held at Anfa in January 1943 Churchill and Roosevelt decided not only the future allied strategy in the Mediterranean, but also the fate of the High Command in North Africa, headed by General Giraud, and of the Committee for Free France, personified by General de Gaulle; both generals were invited with firmness to unite in the same provisional government.

In spite of these slightly different exterior factors, the growth of the nationalist movement in Morocco followed a path that parallelled that of Algeria and Tunisia. Balafrej (who like Bourguiba had been tempted by the Axis) formed the Istiqlal (Independence) Party that grouped together the nationalists who had been dispersed since the 1937 repression. He presented Puaux, the new French Resident General, with a manifesto that echoed the demands of Monsef Bey at the beginning of 1943: The Protectorate Treaty had been violated in letter and spirit; the European colony had been favoured at the expense of the Moroccan people; the part played by Morocco in the war gave it special rights; the Sultan ought to rule an independent and united empire, with a democratic regime comparable with that of certain countries of eastern Islam.

On 28 January 1944 the leaders of the Istiqlal were arrested. It was not difficult to suppress the demonstrations in their favour that were held in Rabat, Sale and Fez, but some lives were lost. A few months later, just as in Tunisia, the protectorate launched a series of socio-economic reforms; it promised an extension of education for young Muslims, and in June 1945 undertook an interesting experiment to modernize the rural sectors of the economy. Sultan Muhammad V gradually became the symbol of the nationalist aspirations that were aimed at a regrouping in a joint affirmation of ethnic, cultural, and religious dignity, of the highly diverse tendencies of the mountaineers and the plains people, the traditionalist milieu of cities like Fez and the dynamic and modern elements of cities like Casablanca. As it happened, and unlike Algeria with respect to "assimilation", the Moroccan masses did not feel the same bitterness and sense of disappointment about the protectorate that marked the reactions of the Algerian masses to the economic policy of the French authorities.

Thus North Africa suffered the direct shock of its active participation in the Second World War. All the nationalist movements benefited, in varying degrees, from the sudden enlargement of the framework that had encompassed their demands. Once again events

Page 263
Algiers, view of the Muslim quarters, with the Sahel hills in the background.

Left: the Algerian leader, Messali Hadj, who founded a nationalist "modernist" movement in 1936, "The North African Star", influenced by extreme leftwing propaganda. With Ferhat Abbas, another nationalist leader, and their followers, he contributed to persuading the French parliament to vote a compromise Algerian Statute in 1947. This was never put into effect. Messali Hadj was placed under surveillance in France from 1956 to 1959.
He was the only Algerian nationalist who never accepted the concessions of the negotiations with France.

Below: Ferhat Abbas, right, photographed in 1946, a pharmacist from Constantine who began his political career as a moderate Algerian nationalist. In 1943 he submitted a "Manifesto" to the French government demanding equality and recognition of the Algerian personality. Despite certain reforms, increasing political impatience led to the formation of new parties. By 1958 Ferhat Abbas was in Cairo founding the Provisional Government of the Algerian Republic. After Algerian independence, on July 3rd, 1962, he became the first President of the Republic. He was replaced by Ben Bella the following year.

had demonstrated the intimate historical link between the destinies of the north and south shores of the Mediterranean.

The Negro world south of the Sahara, relatively remote from the chief theaters of operation, was far from indifferent to the diverse fortunes of the world conflict, but it suffered only the attenuated effects of it.

Middle Africa seemed to accept passively the role of base of operations and zone of production of raw materials that was imposed on it by the geopolitics of the moment. An Africa that was so closely linked to a democratic Europe could not, of course, escape the indirect consequences of the temporary Nazi victory. The French Empire in Africa broke in two between the armistice and the creation of the National Committee of Algiers in 1943. Inspired by Governor General Eboué (a Negro from French Guiana), the authorities of Equatorial Africa rallied to General de Gaulle's Free France, as did Gabon and the Cameroons in spite of some incidents due to the obtuseness of certain local civilian and military elements. On the other hand, after the failure of a landing attempt directed by General de Gaulle at Dakar in July 1940, West Africa remained solidly on the side of the Vichy government until the allied landing on 8 November 1942. In 1942, some South African units landed at Madagascar, occupied the base of Diego-Suarez (to forestall a possible Japanese landing) and helped the Great Island to rally to Free France, after a difficult march from Diego-Suarez to Tananarive. The little enclave of Djibouti resisted all the offers of the victorious British forces in Ethiopia and yielded only to an implacable blockade in 1943.

General de Gaulle signalized the reunion of all the French territories in Africa under his authority by the Brazzaville Conference, which was held from 30 January to 8 February 1944. The presence of the head of the Government in the heart of Africa symbolized the displacement of the center of gravity of French policy to that continent. Here it found the base it needed to reaffirm its own independence and sovereignty now that the motherland itself was occupied. A whole series of administrative and social reforms was envisaged. These were largely inspired by lessons drawn from British policy, which was more decentralized and more indirect than traditional French colonial methods.

The Brazzaville Conference
1944

On the political plane, by promising an increase in representation within the consultative Assembly of Algiers, and later within the central French parliament in France, the Conference took into account the realities of a new situation, where troops from the heart of French Equatorial Africa once again had kindled a hope of victory by a bold attack on the Italian rear in the oases of Fezzan. Later, under the command of General Leclerc, the same troops rejoined the British Eighth Army, which allowed the forces of North Africa and of West Africa, helpless for two years, to re-enter the war.

For their part the British territories played an active role in the war effort. Units from west Africa fought as far afield as Burma, while regiments from Kenya helped liberate Somaliland and Ethiopia. In addition, the allied air fleets used the bases of Dakar, Liberia, and Nigeria, as well as of the Chad, to cross the desert and form an uninterrupted supply route for the Ethiopian, Sudanese and Mediterranean fronts.

The Belgian Congo, separated from its occupied mother country, ranged itself alongside Britain under the orders of the Belgian government-in-exile in London. For four years an unprecedented production effort (in agriculture and mining) helped supply the allied war machine and thus helped accumulate substantial monetary reserves that were to permit the rapid restoration of the economy of a motherland that was destitute and partially destroyed.

The Portuguese territories prudently awaited the outcome of the war.

The peoples of Africa, finally, were placed in a position to assess the profound changes introduced into a recently established order of things. This was a natural result of the intense traffic all along the great communication routes and because of the part played by their own soldiers in the battles waged on African soil. In international affairs Black Africa, like North Africa, was an integral part of a world order being born, in which it was to be called on to play an important role.

A broad movement of opinion emerged in the United States concerning the scope and the limits of the possible application to the African continent of the Atlantic Charter (proclaimed on 14 August 1941). Unlike President Wilson and his Fourteen Points (whose only practical application was the creation of a system of mandates that did not touch the principle of colonial domination), President Roosevelt insisted that the Four Freedoms (of speech, and religion, from want and from fear) had to be extended to Africa, which was to be developed in the interest of its own people. No territorial change could be effected without consulting the populations involved. The principle of self-determination had to be recognized and independence accepted as the essential goal of an enlightened colonial policy. Equal access to raw materials had to be understood as meaning for general freedom of trade between the different parts of the continent, with the full participation of African interests. The responsible powers had to agree to co-ordinate their policies in the fields of land tenure and land settlement, freedom of work, the improvement of native production and the protection of the people against exploitation. In a general way the colonial territories were to be put under a system of trusteeship that was to be an extension and improvement of the mandates system.

Such were the broad outlines of a new approach to the African problem, prepared by the Anglo-Saxon powers after having rid the world of the tyranny of the Axis Powers and Japan, within the framework of the new world order of which the United States was to be the main guarantor. This approach was far more the result of the application of universal principles to a specific problem than of a really clear understanding of the factors of the problem itself. The nationalist movement, with all its logic and its inherent power, had already been unloosed from Egypt to Morocco, while in Black Africa the seeds of impatience had been sown ever since the 'thirties.

In the Union of South Africa itself, internal forces of conflict and transformation were at work. Nazi propaganda had found a favourable soil among the extremist nationalists who had not given up hope of taking revenge on Great Britain, and who felt a natural sympathy for political propositions based on a hierarchy of races. The German elements, which had remained numerous in Southwest Africa, noisily reaffirmed their loyalty to the Third Reich and demanded the abolition of the mandate, which denied them any political rights.

The entry into the war on the side of the Allies had been secured with a very slim majority by General Smuts, who was simultaneously Premier, Minister of National Defence, and Commander-in-Chief of the armed forces of the Union. The clandestine activities of political leaders like Pirow, who were gambling on a German victory, were regarded as subversive. Numerous volunteers enlisted in the army and the air force. The participation of South African troops alongside the black troops from the Gold Coast in the battles against the Italian armies for the liberation of Ethiopia seemed to be the very symbol of the common struggle being waged by Africa, black and white, against totalitarian tyranny. In 1941 Smuts said: "When I speak of Great Britain I take off my hat. I have chosen the country that made us suffer forty years ago, but that, when we were at its mercy, treated us as a Christian nation should." South African battalions and squadrons also took a part in the struggle in the Mediterranean theatre. It was a South African division that was captured at Tobruk, after Rommel's first brilliant offensive.

The external safety of the country was fully assured, with the possible exception of the shore of the Indian Ocean. This was why the Union of South Africa, which

*Four Freedoms
for Africa*
1941

South Africa in the war

considered itself responsible for the strategic zone of the Indian Ocean, made the major share of the effort to invade Madagascar, which was suspected of sheltering Japanese submarines. In November 1943, General Smuts made a speech, since celebrated, to the Empire Parliamentary Association, pointing out how convinced he was that he had been right, as against Hertzog and Pirow, to gamble on a British victory: after Stalingrad and El Alamein, the total liberation of the Ukraine as well as of North Africa proved that the Allies were now well on their way upstream. Smuts assured his compatriots and the members of the Commonwealth that the future belonged to great political units like the British Empire, the United States and Russia. He declared that "in Europe three of the great powers will have disappeared by the end of the war (France, Italy and Germany)... France has departed, and even if it comes back it will be a long time before it emerges once again." He suggested the regrouping of the African continent into large regional units like West Africa, East Africa and Southern Africa, each one to be put under the authority of a Governor General; political entities that were not large enough should be absorbed into these. The Dominion that was on African soil could come closer to these vast federations for their greater benefit. London must decentralize its powers for the advantage of these new groupings, which for that matter would remain completely loyal, since Smuts considered the British system to be "the most effective missionary enterprise launched in the past thousand years."

At the same time, Malan, head of the modern faction of Boer nationalism, sent messages to the Prime Minister of Eire congratulating him on not having expelled the ambassadors of Germany and Italy in spite of Anglo-American pressure.

Under the very flimsy veil of Smuts's grand geopolitical ideas, the isolation and solitude of this tiny nation of the white race, deeply divided on the frontiers of Black Africa, became more and more clear. Black Africa itself, indeed, was now in its turn going to enter into the thoroughly familiar cycle of political demands, while at the same time, in the north of Indochina, the first cannon shots of a new war were being fired in which France was to confront Indochinese nationalism, reinforced by the international Communist movement.

The cultural, linguistic, and economic dominion imposed by the ruling powers of western Europe was parallelled by the massive extension of the theory of Europe's cultural and economic aggression against Black Africa. As far back as 1938 a young sociologist born in Kenya, Jomo Kenyatta, regarded by his teacher Bronislav Malinowski as "combining a knowledge of western manners and western modes of thought with an essentially African education and way of looking at things," gave a message that deserved some thought: "In expelling the Africans from their ancestral lands the Europeans have robbed them of the material foundations of their culture and have reduced them to a state of bondage incompatible with human happiness... The African realizes that he must battle unflaggingly for his complete emancipation, without which he is doomed to remain the prey of rival imperialisms that will sap his vitality and his energy more profoundly each year." Thus did a Kikuyu from the Kenya highlands protest in his own way; at the same time the North African leaders did in theirs, against the principle of the superiority of western culture.

The pre-conditions for an authentic pan-Africanism had not yet come into existence, and local leaders made use of simple political or insurrectionist means for purely tactical reasons, with no real adherence to a general principle. There was an historic revenge to be taken—the dignity of a continent to be restored. The end counted more than the means. Africa had become Machiavellian, and studied its European rulers of the moment with clear eyes. It was familiar with their political weaknesses, but it also knew they were the dispensers of modern technique and of capital (though not the only ones)

A battle
for emancipation

267

whose use alone could modify in depth the physical, economic and social factors militating against material progress.

Nascent Pan-Africanism, of which Kwame Nkrumah very soon became the outstanding representative, meant to encompass an entire continent, and combine in a new doctrine the aims of a nationalism that was territorial and even (some would say) tribal, with those that were necessarily broader, revolving around the promotion of an Africa that had become a partner equal in law to the other continents. The Fifth Pan-African Congress, held in Manchester in 1945 with Nkrumah as Secretary, gave rise to aspirations that were more "pan-Negro" than pan-African proper. It took place at a time when activities in America were tending to restore the dignity of the Negro race (and not that of the African continent as such). The much publicized Marcus Garvey had already had himself proclaimed "Provisional President of Africa" at the Second Pan-African Congress held in New York in 1920; a year before, the Senegalese Blaise Diagne (with the discreet encouragement of Clemenceau) had drawn the attention of the First Congress of "coloured" people to the fact that thanks to their active part in the European conflict the inhabitants of the four communes of Senegal had obtained the right to send deputies to the French Chamber of Deputies. Sierra Leone and Liberia, for more than a century the outposts of the struggle for the independence of the Negro race, also played an important role in the elaboration of an ideology born of the determination to wipe out even the last traces of slavery.

A movement that had so general a character, and was, after all, more American Negro than African, did not, according to Great Britain, deserve to be taken seriously. Great Britain refused to be forced by visionaries into airy generalizations. It intended to answer political demands only case by case, within a local framework. It refused to formulate any conclusions as to the probable rhythm of an evolution whose final goal, no one could deny, might be independence. France, on the contrary, made an effort to place all the parts of its empire, now become the French Union, under one single constitution. Whether it was a question of Algeria, the Moroccan and Tunisian protectorates, the Overseas territories, or finally the former mandates now under the guardianship of the United Nations, it intended to maintain a unitary façade of freely accepted unity.

Yet all this was no more than a terminological dispute. Some African deputies who were members of the French parliament had already participated in the Manchester Congress and expressed their sympathy for the objectives of the Pan-African movement. A year later, in 1946, the African Democratic Rally (*Rassemblement Démocratique Africain*) held its constituent meeting in Bamako. It grouped together political militants from every country in French West Africa. Some were members of assemblies in France, others of local assemblies. The R.D.A. called for the creation "of a union freely agreed to, based on the equality of rights and duties." It took less than ten years for this demand to culminate in the adoption of the Framework Law (*loi-cadre*) of 1956.

The mandated territory of Togoland was intended to be the object of new agreements between France and the United Nations so that it might become a trusteeship under the system outlined in the new charter. This time the local nationalists, who had not forgotten the lessons drawn from their failure at the Peace Conference a quarter of a century before, had decided to demand the unification of the Ewe people, and ultimately of the two separate parts of Togoland, under the separate administration of France and Great Britain, in the name of the right to national identity and to tribal solidarity.

The Cameroons were also placed under the new regime of trusteeship in December 1946. Though more complicated, the problem of the reunification of the Cameroons was expressed in a way similar to that of Togoland. This new regime laid it down that "the administering power must favour the progressive evolution of the peoples under trusteeship toward the capacity for self-administration and independence."

*Nkrumah
and the Pan-African idea*

*The African Democratic
Rally in Bamako
1946*

Page 269
Harvest in the Sudan, now the Mali republic. Agricultural resources consist of wheat, millet, rice, corn, tapioca and cotton.

Nigerian landscape.

It was only with difficulty that France and Great Britain could separate the institutions granted the territories under trusteeship and their own colonial territories proper. They were both gradually endowed with representative assemblies that by force of circumstance constituted a genuine financial and administrative autonomy, in which the seeds of independence were plainly evident. In the home countries some people engaged in combining awkward marriages between decentralization, federalism, confederation, internal autonomy and jointly exercised powers, but these were merely European attempts; they made no change in the evolution of events on the spot. The venom accumulated during the six years of war was expressing itself openly.

Because of circumstances the European administrative personnel was not adequately replaced. In Madagascar, for instance, the effort for "national" defence, in the eyes of the badly paid labour, was confused too often with the private interest of certain settlers. The presence of foreign troops had destroyed the myth of the invincibility of the home country. The discontent of certain peoples coincided here, as in North Africa, with the political interests of a class that had formerly been dominant, in which two generations of enemies of the colonial power came together. In March 1947 disturbances broke out simultaneously in the north, the south, and the east of Madagascar; hundreds of European settlers were massacred. As in Kabylia, the repression was harsh; it caused the deaths of thousands of innocent and guilty, directly or indirectly.

In a speech made to the Representative Assembly of Madagascar on 19 April 1945, the Governor General (De Coppet), a friend of André Gide, summed up the causes of the insurrection as follows: "During the past decade Madagascar came to know successively the world economic crisis, the Vichy regime, the British landing in 1942, the government of Fighting France, the difficult effort of adaptation that followed the liberation of France, and finally the profound reforms effected by the Fourth Republic. All these were so many shocks, changes in direction, and social upheavals inseparable from an epoch in which the whole world was seeking a path to follow, but they generated a profound and generalized malaise." It could not be better put.

The French thought the "Democratic Movement of Madagascar Revolution" (led by the Hovas) responsible for the uprising. The French parliament cancelled the immunity of the three deputies from Madagascar—Raseta, Ravaoahangy (who had fought the French during the First World War) and Jacques Rabemananjara (the hope of the neo-nationalist movement). The National Assembly, the bulk of which was made up of Frenchmen from France, was called on to make decisions concerning a remarkably complicated local situation that had no connection at all with political theories or with European and western principles. It was not the first or the last time. After a trial—of quite dubious legitimacy—the Madagascan deputies were condemned to death. The penalty was commuted to life imprisonment, then to exile under surveillance, to end up a few years later with a *de facto* political rehabilitation.

Retrospectively, the Madagascar uprising seems to have been premature, and even in some ways separated from the broad stream of African evolution. This should not be surprising, since the historic problems of Madagascar are quite specific. It was nonetheless of exceptional importance, since it put to the test the vaunted liberalism of the 1946 Constitution, which envisioned and encouraged evolution toward autonomy within the single framework of the "French Union."

An interesting parallel was provided by the Gold Coast, which in less than two years took to the path of "constitutional acceleration." At the very moment when Paris was paying tribute to the combined and cumulative virtues of administrative liberalism and financial openhandedness, the Gold Coast was granted by the Labour Government of London a new constitution that gave authority to local elected deputies and reduced the administrators to the rank of advisers. At the same time, and like the other colonies of the Crown, the Gold Coast benefited by the "Colonial Development and Welfare Act", which like the French Investment for Economic and Social Development Fund *(Fonds d'Investissement et de Développement Economique et Social)* supported acts of political boldness with some financial and economic foundation. Nevertheless, in Accra, on 28 February 1948 the former veterans of the war, who were complaining of the high cost of living, the difficulties of food problems, and the inadequacy of their pensions, marched at the head of a crowd of malcontents toward the former old Scandinavian fort that served as residence of the British governor. The police shot. The bloodshed provoked a demonstration in the course of which the shops of the city were plundered and burned. The agitation seemed about to spread to other cities. The British authorities, overwhelmed for a moment, arrested Dr. Danquah, head of the Gold Coast Convention. A commission of enquiry soon designated by the London Government ascribed the popular discontent to the following causes: "The fact that the educated elite considers the 1946 Constitution insufficient; the concentration of economic power in the hands of Syrians and Europeans; the high prices; the uneven distribution of consumer goods; the forced uprooting of the cocoa plants touched by a disease called 'swollen short'." In addition, while the chiefs were losing their power, the "Africanization" of the public services was going on far too slowly.

Creation of Nkrumah's Convention People's Party 1947

A year later, the Coussey Committee admitted that the problem was a political one, and that the Gold Coast needed a responsible government. Meanwhile Kwame Nkrumah, the brilliant secretary of the Pan-African Congress of Manchester, had become the secretary of the Gold Coast Convention in 1947, and had created his own party, the Convention People's Party (C.P.P.), in June 1949. He proclaimed a general strike in June 1950 with the slogan of immediate autonomy; he recommended the tactic of passive resistance and commercial boycott. The administration imprisoned him. After the elections of February 1951, in the course of which thirty-four members of the C.P.P. were elected (out of thirty-eight available seats), the Governor of the colony came to see him in gaol to make him the head of the Executive Council. It took another year before Nkrumah officially became Prime Minister and the Executive Council became a government.

Events just as important were unfolding in the neighbouring territory of the Ivory Coast. At the annual congress of the African Democratic Rally that met in Trechville on 5 January 1949 more than a hundred delegates carried on discussions under the chairmanship of Houphouet-Boigny (in the presence of a delegate of the French Communist Party, which at this time was sponsoring a tactical rapprochement with the R.D.A.). Representatives of Equatorial Africa, of the Cameroons (Um Nyobé, a militant nationalist) and of Western Africa were present. A few days later, some violent incidents took place at Dimbokro, leaving some ten victims. Nevertheless, in 1950, when the R.D.A. seemed to have lost a good deal of its prestige in favour of movements that were more clearly territorial, Houphouet-Boigny approached moderate groups in France and started to use the Ivory Coast section of the R.D.A. for his own political purposes.

Nigeria, braked by its regional diversity and by the existence of provinces in the north that had remained under the influence of the great Fulha and Hausa dynasties, nevertheless passed through the classic constitutional mutations. (The Richard constitution of 1946 was succeeded by the McPherson constitution in 1951). Dr. Azikiwe (an associate of Nkrumah's in the pan-African movement) led the fight in favour of an autonomous government, by getting the support of the peoples of eastern Nigeria, the Ibos, who displayed a surprising political vitality despite of their apparent anarchy. In spite of the rivalry of western Nigeria, little by little Dr. "Zik's" leadership, and the growing importance of the conservative forces of the north led by the Emir of Sokoto were becoming clearer and clearer.

General Smuts photographed near the Cape a few months before his death in 1950. He was the first Prime Minister of the Union of South Africa, in 1919. In 1940 he led his country into war on the side of the Allies in spite of extreme nationalist elements that were influenced by Nazi propaganda. He was defeated at the polls in 1948.

It is obvious that the political evolution of western Africa, both French and British, has been bound up, like that of North Africa, with the profound changes in the power relationships in western Europe, which was recovering with immense difficulty from the shock of the Second World War. It was impossible to disregard any longer the Russo-American competition for world dominion, or the emergence as independent entities of great Asian powers like China and India. Bourguiba, Ferhat Abbas, Balafrej, Nkrumah, Houphouet-Boigny, d'Arboussier (secretary general of the R.D.A.), Azikiwe, Sylvanus Olympio (Togo nationalist leader), Senghor, and others of the same generation, and, still more numerous, the new men educated in France, Great Britain, the United States and Eastern Europe, are completely modern in every respect. Without making any attempt to deny their ties with African tradition and with history, they are conscious of the intimate bond between their own political struggle, in relation to their own country, and the broad currents that determine world politics. They are attempting to insert themselves into the "direction of history." During the inevitable period of transition, some wish to ensure the protection and the help of the former motherland. Others, for theoretical or moral reasons, firmly believe in leaping immediately from a protected world into an open world, and in playing an active role in international competition.

Eastern and central Africa under British rule seemed for a short period to be sheltered from this "universalization" of African problems; yet a most eloquent warning had clearly been given by Kenyatta, a member of one of the most neglected tribes. In 1938 he had said aloud, for all ears to hear, that Italian agression against Ethiopia could not be a matter of indifference to African opinion. His teacher, Malinowski, had made the point that the inhabitants of even the remotest provinces might have their own opinion concerning the League of Nations, the dignity of labour and the brotherhood of man.

The proof of the incredible isolation that had been voluntarily chosen by the British administration in Kenya is to be found in the fact that Kenyatta was able to embark on an efficient policy of political education and agitation behind the shield of an apparently innocuous school policy. Missionaries of good will and thrifty-minded financiers congratulated this enlightened sociologist for having assumed the education of thousands of children neglected by a selfish administration. The key message of the Kenyan revolution spread like a wildfire from 1950 to 1952. Incidents proliferated throughout the territory. The "Mau-Mau" uprising made its appearance, a fearful mixture of primitivism, secret societies and of borrowings from the European arsenal of psychosexuality.

Great Britain, caught by surprise, wanted to send several thousand men to Kenya to establish a state of siege. A hundred Europeans were killed and almost 2,000 Africans were condemned to death by the administration, while tens of thousands were killed in a mopping-up campaign. Many observers regarded the Mau-Mau crisis as the first episode of a blind and generalized revolt against the white man's rule in eastern Africa.

Kenya
and the Mau-Mau crisis
1950-1952

Page 274
Kenya, trial of a Mau-Mau terrorist. Under Jomo Kenyatta, the Kenya uprising against the British started in 1950 and spread rapidly. The Mau-Mau revolt took the form of extreme violence; to stem it, the British condemned almost 2,000 Africans to death while many other thousands were killed in guerrilla campaigns.

The lightning development of Negro Africa in the direction of political autonomy could only hasten the march of North Africa toward independence. Reciprocally, the events that took place in North Africa were bound to weaken the principal imperial powers, such as France and Great Britain, who were obliged to face the forces of nationalism on several fronts at the same time.

In 1945 the Egyptian government made a formal demand for the opening of negotiations with a view to revising the Treaty of 1936. Egypt was led to accept and then execute the obligations of an alliance certain aspects of which infringed on its independence. The Egyptian note stated in particular that "it is not the letter of the agreements that determines their efficacy, but far more the good will of the people who accept them and the spirit which animates their implementation." The status of the Sudan was raised again, as well as that of the British military bases in the Canal Zone.

As in 1936, though this time in less favourable circumstances, Great Britain was unable to separate the question of the military control of the Suez Canal from an international context that was peculiarly worrisome. The Soviets at that time seemed, in fact, to be determined to maintain their occupation of the north of Persia and to alter the balance of power in the eastern Mediterranean by supporting an insurrection openly inspired by Communism in Greece. Egypt saw no reason for taking part in the disputes of the great powers. It concentrated on securing a recognition in principle of the unity of the Nile valley, which for a short while during the conversations between Bevin and Sidky Pasha it believed it could obtain. This was an illusion, since the British in the Sudan could not bypass the objections of Abd er-Rahman el-Mahdi, the descendant of the Great Mahdi, who at the head of a powerful party (the Umma) accused England of selling the Sudan to Egypt. For the first time since the Ethiopian affair an African question of major importance was brought before the Security Council of the United Nations, which from its very inception had shown a lively interest in questions connected with the peaceful liquidation of the old order. Nokrachy Pasha, Sidky Pasha's successor, was staking his political career on this complaint to the Council. For the first time, also, a question within the hitherto private field of the relations between countries associated more or less directly with the geopolitical ensemble of the Commonwealth was submitted to the study of an entity in which the United States and the Soviet Union played decisive roles. This was a decisive precedent that was going to affect all relations between the colonial powers and their former Empire. Nevertheless the Security Council did not arrive at a conclusion, and sent the question back to the two parties. All Egypt protested against what seemed to it to be a machination of the great powers. Political passions exploded: Nokrachi Pasha was assassinated on 28 December 1948 by a member of the secret society, the Muslim Brotherhood.

British fears concerning the Soviet attitude were vindicated by the Korean conflict, which broke out on 25 June 1950. Egypt was now conscious of the problem of its own national defence following Israel's victory over the combined forces of the Arab

An African question submitted to the Security Council

countries two years before. For Egypt, Sinai was a frontier to be defended. For Great Britain, the Canal was an indispensable line of communication with Asia.

Great Britain, whose "imperial" and oil interests were seriously threatened by the nationalization of the Abadan installations on the Persian Gulf, attempted to use the discussions with Egypt to secure recognition not only as the spokesman of the interests of the Commonwealth as a whole but also of a western alliance in which together with the United States it would be the "senior partner".

Nahas Pasha (who came back to power at the head of the Wafd in the 1950 elections), announced the unilateral abrogation of the treaty of 1936 five years before its legal expiration date. Egyptian opinion was by no means disposed to accept the Anglo-American proposals envisaging the setting up of a regional defence organization in which Egypt would be a full member and in which the Suez Canal would play an essential role.

Countless provocations were directed at the British troops in the Canal Zone. The British reacted with vigour. The tension reached its climax after an incident at Ismailia on 25 January 1952, in the course of which an encircled Egyptian police force heroically resisted a British attack. The next day serious incidents took place in Cairo, with some loss of life and substantial material damage in the European quarters. These disorders were attributed to the action of some well-organized groups like the Muslim Brotherhood. Communist influences were suspected. Order was restored by the Egyptian army, which occupied Cairo and Alexandria and thus found itself in a highly favourable position for some ulterior action aimed at a seizure of power. Nahas Pasha was dismissed by the King, who called in first Ali Maher then Sidky Pasha. It was obvious that King Farouk was no longer master of the situation. The young officers who had suffered the humiliation of a defeat by Israel in the course of a campaign that had demonstrated the total incapacity of the Egyptian state, decided to save their threatened homeland by assuming control of its destinies. General Naguib took power on 23 July 1952; a few days later the monarchy was abolished. Farouk left Egyptian soil for an inglorious exile. For the first time since the Roman conquest, Egypt was ruled by Egyptians.

This domestic revolution had immediate effects on the question of the unity of the Nile valley. As a matter of fact the Anglo-Egyptian discussions had touched on the official recognition of Farouk as King of Egypt and of the Sudan, thus regularizing a constitutional situation that had been ambiguous ever since the organization of the Anglo-Egyptian condominium over Khartoum.

The question had now disappeared. But Naguib himself had been born in the Sudan, of a Sudanese mother and a father who was an Egyptian functionary. Hence the way to a compromise seemed open. Great Britain, which had shown itself to be intractable with respect to King Farouk's claims (despite discreet American pressure) signed an agreement on 6 February 1953 that recognized *de facto* the identity of the Sudan. The right of the Sudanese people to self-determination was acknowledged. A Sudanese parliament was to be convoked on the basis of elections with a universal vote, under the supervision of an international commission made up of three Sudanese, one Briton, one Egyptian, one American, and one Indian. In addition the Governor General of the Sudan was to be helped in the exercise of his authority by a commission made up of three members under the chairmanship of a Pakistani.

Consequently Egypt now had to decide what role to play in the Sudanese elections. It made a point of doing so, and utilized the latent mistrust of the tribes in the south against the power of Khartoum in order to ensure itself a majority that was relatively favourable to a close Sudanese-Egyptian union.

The Egyptian military regime grew tougher after Naguib was retired. Colonel Nasser, who had become supreme leader, succeeded in obtaining, by means of the Anglo-

*End of the
Egyptian monarchy*
1952

Egyptian agreement of 1954, the outright evacuation of the Canal Zone. Britain's position was weakened by a clash of views with its American ally. From another point of view, the arrest of Naguib a little while after his triumphal trip through the Sudan inflicted a serious blow to Egyptian prestige in Khartoum.

Reaction to abandoning the Canal

Great Britain had yielded to the argument that it was impossible to maintain a viable military base on the territory of a country that considered it a threat to its own safety and independence. The treaty was hailed by optimists as the beginning of a new era in which Africa had arrived at a position to negotiate on a footing of equality with its former rulers in an international society based on collective security. In Western Europe pessimists wrote down the abandonment of the Suez Canal as one more item in a long list of successive setbacks that for ten years had marked the decline of the empires of Western Europe, including the Dutch departure from Indonesia, the independence of India, and the French defeats in Indochina. Everyone was, of course, right in his own way.

Confronted by the British "abandonment" in the eastern Mediterranean, what was France going to do in the western Mediterranean? Certain people in France, farsighted but few in number, were ready to recognize the inexorable character of a political evolution dominated by power relations that were no longer under the control of western Europe. Yet political thinking remained dominated by the opinions of the French who were settled in North Africa. For the French, as Bourguiba had noted, a "preponderance" guaranteed by institutions, and if necessary force, seemed to be the indispensable condition of any economic and social security. This, in their minds, in no way excluded the progress of the Muslims. Thus there were, by force of circumstances, two French policies. One was struggling for expression in Paris under the influence of liberal elements engaged in parliamentary debates that were often quite confused. Another was in fact applied in Algiers under the authority of high officials who were quickly convinced of the legitimacy of European resistance to the political claims put forward by the Muslims. The Muslim point of view was now openly supported by Nasser's Egypt and by the other countries of Near Eastern Islam, to say nothing of great powers such as Russia and the United States.

After a difficult debate, in which the Muslim deputies of the Democratic Union of the Algerian Manifesto (Ferhat Abbas's party) and the more extremist members of the Movement for the Victory of Democratic Liberties (made up of the followers of Messali Hadj) took part, the French parliament voted a new status for Algeria on 20 September 1947. It consisted of a compromise between the "autonomous" and "integrationist" tendencies. An Algerian Assembly elected by two Colleges was to be established. The first College was to comprise all the voters with a French civil status without any distinction of origin, as well as citizens with a Muslim civil status honored by certain

A new status for Algeria?

distinctions (diplomas, decorations, etc.). The second College was to represent, in fact, the majority of the Algerian population. . Financial autonomy was confirmed within the framework of a strictly Algerian structure. The domestic administration was completely made over. Arabic became an official language on the same footing as French. This decree, which fulfilled a large number of the conditions laid down by the Manifesto of 1943 was never, in fact, to be applied. The history of its defeat concerns France more than Algeria. The elections to the Algerian assembly in April 1948 seemed to reverse the currents that had after all been so evident since the end of the war. Almost everywhere conservative elements crushed the candidates of the nationalist parties. Many large-scale electoral swindles took place; they deceived no one and sharpened the conflict. The political leaders, even those favourable to Franco-Algerian co-operation, turned aside from what they regarded as a caricature of evolution. The champions of direct action found a great deal of support among the Algerian workers in

Habib Bourguiba rides back into Tunisia on horseback, in 1949. The nationalist Tunisian leader was returning from a "grand tour" to win sympathy for Tunisian independence. After 1943 he grouped anti-French, progressive elements in his Neo-Destour party. After banishment to the Sahara and internment in Marseilles, he finally won recognition of Tunisian autonomy. Bourguiba became Premier, then President in 1956.

Left: Nasser announcing the
nationalization of the Suez Canal,
July 6, 1956.
Israel felt its interests
menaced by Egyptian military
power aided by the Soviet Union.
Franco-British and Israeli
forces attacked Egypt in October
and were evacuated after
the cease-fire of December.

Below: the July 27, 1956,
editions of *The New York Times*
and the Parisian daily,
France-Soir, giving the news
of the nationalization of the
Suez Canal.

Page 281

Work on the Aswan Dam.
Nasser's plan to build a
tremendous dam on the Nile
became a political issue.
After first promising financing,
the World Bank and the
United States refused aid in 1956.
Work went ahead with loans
from the Soviet Union.
Waters backed up from this
project are what would engulf
the Abu Simbel temples
if these were not being raised.
The dam will be completed
by 1967.

The New York Times.

LATE CITY EDITION
Condensation of U. S. Weather Bureau forecast:
Fair and warm today. Hot, humid,
afternoon thunderstorms tomorrow.
Temperature range today: 86—71.
Temperature range yesterday: 86.7—78.5.
Full U. S. Weather Bureau Report, Page 48.

© 1956, by The New York Times Company.

VOL. CV..No. 35,979. Entered as Second-Class Matter, Post Office, New York, N. Y **NEW YORK, FRIDAY, JULY 27, 1956.** Times Square New York 36, N. Y. Telephone Lackawanna 4-1000 **FIVE CENTS**

DEATH OF A SHIP: The Italian liner Andrea Doria, after collision at sea, lists toward damaged side and . . . STARTING FINAL PLUNGE, turns over. Passengers and crew were taken off before the ship sank off Nantucket.

Egypt Nationalizes Suez Canal Company; Will Use Revenues to Build Aswan Dam

TIMES MAN KILLED

Cianfarra of Madrid and Two Daughters Among the Dead

At least seven persons were killed in the collision Wednesday night between the Andrea Doria and the Stockholm.

Among the dead were Camille M. Cianfarra, Madrid correspondent of The New York Times, his stepdaughter, Linda Morgan, and his daughter, Joan Cianfarra. Mr. Cianfarra's wife, Jane, was injured in the collision and res-

4 RESCUE SHIPS IN

Ile de France Brings 753 From Disaster—Other Craft Due

By MEYER BERGER

Four rescue ships stood in from the sea yesterday with 1,117 survivors of the collision between the Italian Line steamship Andrea Doria and the Swedish Line's Stockholm off the New England coast before midnight Wednesday.

The Ile de France brought 753 into this port, the freighter Cape Ann 129, the Military Sea Transportation Service transport Pvt.

Nasser Retaliates Against West's Denial of Aid —London Stunned

Special to The New York Times.
CAIRO, July 26—President Gamal Abdel Nasser's revolutionary regime seized full control of the Suez Canal today. The Egyptian leader announced that profits of the internationally controlled waterway would be used to build the High Dam at Aswan.

President Nasser proclaimed

Eisenhower's Four Years

Analysis of 'Partnership' on Resources And Democrats' 'Give-Away' Charges

This is the sixth of a series of articles analyzing the record of the Eisenhower Administration at the start of the Presidential election campaign.

BY ALLEN DRURY
Special to The New York Times.
WASHINGTON, July 26—When Dwight D. Eisenhower was elected President of a nation endowed

the expansion throughout the nation of upstream storage, with sound use of public lands, the

de 150 milliards pour l'Algérie

ESSENCE : hausse de 1 fr. par litre
ECONOMIES : 25 milliards

Si ces mesures ne couvrent pas les dépenses militaires, recours par décrets cette année à
4 IMPOTS SUCCESSIFS :

EMPLOYEURS :
Surtaxe de 10 à 16 0/0 sur les salaires distribués.

SOCIETES :
Majoration fiscale de 5 0/0 - Taxe de 5 0/0 sur les stocks
Supermajoration fiscale de 5 0/0

COMMERCANTS

LE DICTATEUR EGYPTIEN AYANT NATIONALISE LE CANAL DE SUEZ

Paris et Londres refusent d'accepter le coup de force de Nasser

« Andrea-Doria » : 8 morts ● Plus de 100 blessés ● Nombreux disparus

Réunion d'urgence des gouvernements français et anglais

CONSULTATION DES CHEFS D'ÉTAT-MAJOR

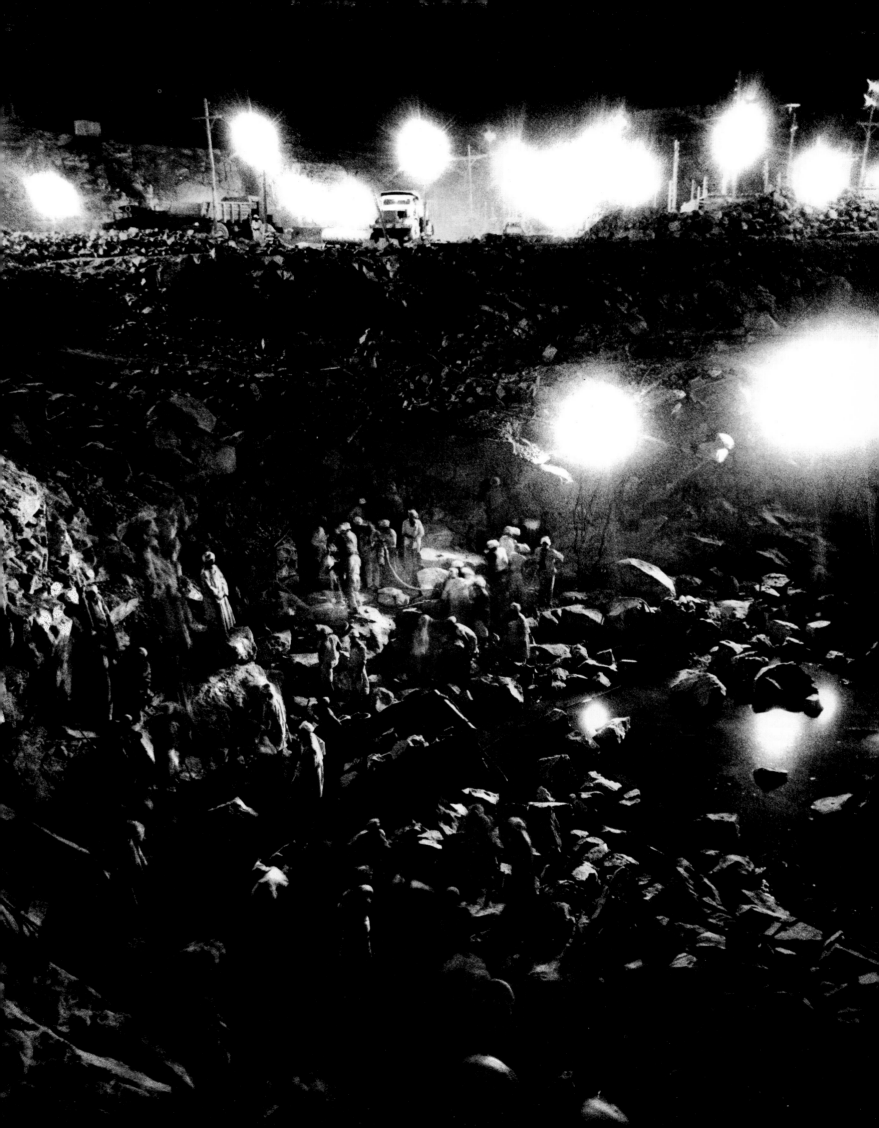

France who were in close touch with French political life, where the Communist Party's tactics and organization found admirers and imitators galore.

In addition, all North Africa was in ferment. The Algerian struggle seemed to be one more aspect of the common struggle being waged by Islam against the political domination of the West. Bourguiba came back to Tunis from Cairo on 8 January 1949, after a "grand tour" in which he had been able to win the sympathy of Indonesian, Indian, Pakistani, Egyptian, British and American leaders. He invoked this support in order to make a new appeal to France, in his press conference of 18 April 1950. The French government seemed to yield to this appeal. In designating the new Resident General it announced that "his mission would be to understand Tunisia and lead it toward the full flowering of its riches and toward the independence that is the ultimate goal for all the territories within the framework of the French Union". The master-word had finally been spoken. A little later, to be sure, all this was qualified by the claim that only "internal autonomy" was under discussion, to be attained by successive stages. Yet in fact a new page had been turned.

Bourguiba's appeal for Tunisia 1950

On 15 December 1951 the French government, which had very clearly gone into reverse, rejected the demands presented by the Tunisian Premier, Chenik, which were part of the Neo-Destour programme. The Chenik government decided to have the Tunisian question discussed by the Security Council. Chenik was arrested in March, together with Bourguiba and "removed" by the French authorities. The trade-unions and political organizations unleashed a general strike. Thirteen Arab-Asian nations had the Tunisian question entered on the agenda of the Council in April 1952. Though the Tunisian complaint came to nothing, it confirmed the novel fact of the existence of an international authority that was to become in the eyes of many a sort of supreme tribunal charged with ensuring the total emancipation of the only continent still waiting to be liberated from European rule.

France had already had to question the authority of the United Nations during the debates at the General Assembly in 1951, in the course of which the Arabic-speaking countries had wished to bring up the Moroccan question.

Nor was the French administration any more fortunate in its attempts to institute gradual reforms in Morocco than in the other parts of North Africa. In spite of the remarkable economic boom in Morocco, due to the massive investments of private and public capital from France and to the enlightened action of the Resident General Eirik Labonne, who championed a fruitful economic association, the slogan "politics first" seemed to have won. The unyielding temper of the French government, which had already been displayed in the organization of the election of a "satisfactory" Algerian assembly, motivated the precipitate reaction of Premier Ramadier to the Sultan's speech in Tangiers, which had failed to mention the part played by France in the progress of his empire. Marshal Juin succeeded Eirik Labonne. Sultan Ben Yusuf was soon to be confronted by the classic dilemma: submit or resign. The French government did not hesitate to imperil what was, nevertheless, its most serious claim to Moroccan gratitude, that is, national unity, in which plainsmen and mountaineers, Berbers and Arabs, were to be fused gradually into one people. The great chiefs of the south, under the leadership of El Glaoui, Pasha of Marrakesh, were encouraged to revolt against the authority of Rabat. After an initial false manœuvre, Sultan Muhammad ben Yusuf was deposed in August 1953 and deported to Madagascar. He was replaced by one of his relatives, Sidi Muhammad ben Moulay Arafa, who approved the reforms that Ben Yusuf had refused to sign. In Rabat, as in Algiers and Tunis, France seemed to be making a triumphant stand against the pressure of North African nationalism. But it took only a few months for this illusion to be destroyed.

Page 282 The Rand mines near Johannesburg, South Africa.

Great Britain had won a temporary respite from Egyptian nationalism by promptly evacuating its bases in the Suez Canal. It had yielded to Nkrumah's claims while hoping that his new responsibilities as Prime Minister would calm his militant pan-Africanism. It had crushed the Mau-Mau uprising and more or less reassured the British settlers in East Africa.

The bastion of the Commonwealth in Africa, on the economic and financial plane, remained the Union of South Africa, which seemed to be sheltered against the agitation of both Black and White Africa. This geographical isolation had its good sides, but it also had its dangerous ones. The situation of the Union after the Second World War was thus described: "Their country, isolated from all the great centers of western civilization, supported a restricted and highly mixed population of 2,600,000 Europeans, 1,100,000 "coloured", 360,000 Asians and 8,500,000 Bantus, and, in spite of the extravagant standard of living of the whites, it was an impoverished population" (Walker). The bulk of the Europeans lived in the urban centers, while the Bantus were still dependent on the rural zones, though the Rand mines employed more than 300,000 African workers of whom more than half came from territories outside the Union.

Malan's view of "white supremacy"

The Smuts-Hofmeyr team was disliked by the Boer nationalists because of its unconditional support for British policy. Dr. Malan had become the leader of the opposition, now backed by the European proletariat of Boer origin as well as by the Transvaal farmers. In the course of the electoral campaign of 1948 for the first time Dr. Malan presented a coherent body of doctrine—*apartheid*, which aimed "at the separate development, along parallel lines, of the diverse populations making up the Union". The nationalists won the elections, to be sure by a very narrow margin. Smuts was defeated in his own district; his role of "senior statesman", which had been so well played on the international scene, had not been of the slightest help. The European electorate turned its back on a policy that ultimately might have led to an increased representation of the African majority in the national parliament. It is curious to note that the French authorities in Algeria, at the same time and within a different framework, were making the same fateful choice. Beginning with 1948, the government of the Union committed itself, with no prospect of turning back, to a policy that found compelling reasons in the way the world was evolving to isolate and shield itself, and not to follow a liberal trend that might achieve the harmonious co-existence of different races within the same society.

The Malan government hardened the attitude of its predecessor. The interracial riots of Durban in January 1949, which brought Zulus and Indians to blows, reinforced Malan's view of the white race as an authoritative arbiter. The Union of South Africa regarded itself as the fortress of European civilization threatened by the rising tide of color and as the champion of western values against the Communist danger in Africa.

The Commonwealth of which it was a part was itself a victim of this pressure. For the Union the independence of the Gold Coast, which was very close at hand, marked the definitive turn of the Commonwealth toward an interracial formula the Union found abominable. The independence of India and of Pakistan in 1947 had already shown the Union that Smuts had deceived it as to the role it might play in a Commonwealth limited to the white nations. The High Commission territories (Bechuanaland, Swaziland, and Basutoland), which remained under the control of London, recalled the limited nature of the Union's own sovereignty on African soil. The Tseretse Khama affair was very disturbing to many people: a traditional chief had married a young European, and this was obviously the very negation of apartheid.

Britain's efforts for "partnership"

Great Britain, in fact, still maintained for reasons of principle that a "partnership" was still possible. Sir Geoffrey Higgins, Prime Minister of the autonomous colony of Southern Rhodesia, invoked Cecil Rhodes's authority to develop a policy of co-existence and growing prosperity, in which the Anglo-Saxon race would be able to display both its efficiency and its political liberalism. London was ready to brake the northward ascent of the Malan government's influence and to block the southward descent of nationalism of the Egyptian or of the tribal, "Mau-Mau" type. The problem was to federate the territories of British Central Africa which, for various historical circumstances, had been placed under the authority of different ministries. It was necessary to carry out fifty years later, what Sir Harry Johnston had proposed to Cecil Rhodes, that is, to reunite the autonomous colony of Southern Rhodesia, openly dominated by Europeans, Northern Rhodesia, a protectorate under the Colonial Office but dominated by the mining interests of the Copper Belt, and finally the protectorate of Nyasaland, overpopulated and with no natural resources. The Conference of Victoria Falls in September 1951 proposed the creation of a federal government with powers limited to national defense, economic planning, railways, civil aviation, customs and university education. A federal assembly was to include some representation of African interests. The Africans of Nyasaland and certain elements of Northern Rhodesia protested immediately against this project, which seemed to them a means of gradually imposing on them a policy inspired by the Union of South Africa for the purpose of perpetuating the inferior status of the Africans.

The Federation itself was not set up until after a hard-fought debate in the British Parliament in April 1953. It was a question now of opening up to European capital and immigration a vast area that combined substantial mining reserves (copper and coal) and inexhaustible hydroelectric energy (the Zambezi). The building of the Kariba dam was soon to symbolize, like the High Dam of Aswan in Egypt, a determination to increase the national output by gigantic works which would benefit the population as a whole. Sir Geoffrey Higgins, later Lord Malvern, was succeeded by Sir Roy Welensky, who by his ethnic and social origins symbolized the new world of Europeans who had become Africans and were sure of their rights to a country they had transformed by their labour and technology. Without denying the possibility of progressive evolution, the Rhodesians were bound to feel some sympathy for the attitude of the Union of South Africa, which seemed to have drawn realistic conclusions from the progress of Negro nationalism in tropical and equatorial Africa. In its turn this nationalist movement was encouraged by the abrupt change in the situation in French-controlled North Africa.

France's Fourth Republic and African nationalism

As a matter of fact the Fourth Republic, hard pressed in Indochina by Ho Chi-Minh's armies, was at the peak of an internal crisis. It seemed unable to face up simultaneously to the pressures of its allies (which wanted to force it into premature European integration) and to the nationalist movements in Indochina and Africa. On 2 March 1954 it initiated a new series of reforms with the support of a moderate Tunisian government, as a whole these reforms met the claims of 1951. After the defeat of Dien-Bien-Phu in Indochina and the Geneva settlement that barely saved Laos and Cambodia and a part of Viet-Nam from Communist rule, Pierre Mendès-France, who had become Premier, paid a visit to the Bey of Tunis on 31 July 1954. He was accompanied by Marshal Juin, who could hardly be suspected of indulgence toward North African nationalism after the cavalier treatment he had meted out to the Sultan of Morocco. Tunisia's internal autonomy was proclaimed. The Neo-Destour gave its support to a caretaker government under the presidency of Tahar ben Amar. In less than two years the autonomous regime gave way to a completely independent regime, recognized in principle by France on 20 March 1956 and confirmed by the Franco-Tunisian agreement of 15 June 1956. Habib Bourguiba became Premier of the Regency and shortly afterward its president, with full powers bestowed on him after the abolition of the monarchy.

In Morocco the strong-arm policy of 1953 came to nothing, as did the deportation or imprisonment of Bourguiba in Tunisia. Moroccan public opinion totally opposed the Ben Arafa regime. As in Tunisia, the nationalist parties (made up of bourgeois and intellectuals) like the Istiqlal, formed a united front with the trade-union movement (the General Union of Moroccan Workers) and demanded the return of Sidi Muhammad ben Yusuf. France, which had yielded in Tunisia, found it difficult to refuse concessions opposed to Morocco".

The attempts to make an accomodation with Moroccan nationalism, at the conference of Aix-les-Bains in the spring of 1955 collided with the preliminary question of the return of the Sultan. The Edgar Faure government decided, with some equivocation, to move ahead by limited but irreversible stages. Muhammad ben Yusuf the legitimate Sultan returned to France in November 1955. Events took a decisive turn when El Glaoui, the principal architect of the deposition of the legitimate sovereign, prostrated himself at the latter's feet in the chateau of La Celle-Saint-Cloud. He had finally understood that the French position of 1953 was an outdated relic of another historic period and that the new Morocco had been born through the sacrifice of the old. On 2 March 1956 France unreservedly recognized the independence of Morocco. Now the question of the status of the Spanish zone and of Tangiers was on the agenda.

Recognition
of Morocco's independence
1956

Meanwhile the Algerian war had broken out, on 1 November 1954. Bombs exploded, convoys were attacked, European and Muslim functionaries were assassinated. The Minister of the Interior, François Mitterrand, recognized that this was definitely a war and not merely a tribal uprising in the 1871 manner. Whether the cause or effect of an irremediably compromised situation, the Decree of 1947, in its very failure, seemed to be the turning point in Franco-Algerian relations. The "gradualists" and the "integrationists" on the Muslim side had lost. The helm had been seized by the Revolutionary Committee for Unity of Action, whose base was in Cairo and which tried to unite the veiled unruliness of the Aurès mountaineers, the discontent of the Algerians, the students and the bourgeoisie in France, and the military talents of Muslim officers and non-commissioned officers like Ben Bella, who had been trained in the splendid combat school of the Liberation during the Second World War.

From the vantage point of their own victories against European imperialism the Asians kept a close watch on all these events, which were now unfolding at an accelerated pace. Holland and France had been defeated in turn by a combination of military failures and diplomatic defeats. Great Britain had preferred to retire altogether from the vast Indian empire. Communist China, which regarded itself as having defeated the Americans after having confronted them as equals during the bloodstained Korean conflict, tried to channel the anti-European forces into the mainstream of its own expansion.

It was under these conditions that on 18 April 1955, President Soekarno opened the Bandung Conference, which was to give rise to the Afro-Asian Charter. He suggested the mobilization on the side of peace "of the entire political, spiritual, and moral force of Asia and Africa". "We, the peoples of Asia and Africa, number more than 1,400,000,000 human beings; we can mobilize what I have called the moral violence of the nations in favour of peace." This was, of course, no more than a figure of speech, since the Afro-Asian bloc was far from being either homogeneous or stable.

In fact, Africa was still playing no more than a modest role in the outline of this worldwide diplomacy. Egypt, Ethiopia, Liberia, Libya (independent since 1952), the Sudan (not yet independent) represented parts of the continent that in any case had centuries-old contacts with the outside world. Nevertheless the Conference made important recommendations on each nation's rights to a national culture, and criticized the artificial isolation imposed by the colonial powers. "This is particularly true in the case of Tunisia, Algeria, and Morocco, where the fundamental right of the people to study its own language and culture had been suppressed. An identical discrimination has been practised against the African and the coloured peoples in other parts of the African continent."

After the Bandung Conference, the moral weight of the nations still under the colonial yoke was thrown into the balance of the worldwide ideological struggle. Every country in Africa could persuade itself that its struggle was part of a vaster movement, simultaneously universal and irreversible.

Once more Egypt, in the person of Colonel Nasser, found itself in the vanguard of the movement for African independence. It had been the first country to struggle victoriously against an imperialism that at the time had been in the ascendant. Its chief was received as an equal by the outstanding leaders of Asian emancipation, who had managed to achieve not only their political but also their economic independence by demanding and practising an absolute freedom of choice between the West and the Soviet world in order to get, with no ideological consideration, the help that was indispensable. A third force was born, in which Egypt, the natural hinge between Asia and Africa, was able to occupy a pre-eminent position. Soviet Russia, invigorated by the elimination of the Stalinist straitjacket, proved that it could understand the ambitions of the evolving countries, which were concerned with concrete plans rather than with ideological preoccupations.

Egypt and the third force

Like Mehemet Ali, Nasser wanted to harness the Nile in the service of Egypt, now with a rapidly rising birthrate. In December 1955 he created a "High Dam Authority" that was instructed to co-ordinate the preparatory studies for the building of a gigantic dam on the Nile, at Aswan. One hundred and ten meters high, five kilometrs long, it would be able to store 130,000,000,000 cubic meters. The very dimensions of the dam raised a host of questions, simultaneouly technical and political. Was it appropriate to create such a reservoir in the middle of a particularly desert region that was subject to intense evaporation? Would it not have been better to study the Nile as a whole, and control it along its entire length in order to make use of the natural reservoirs located in the tropical and equatorial zones, like Lake Tana, Lake Victoria, and Lake Albert? The Sudan put forth arguments diametrically opposed to the Egyptian conception; it maintained that the base figures of the 1929 Agreement, which allowed for a certain allocation of the flood-waters, no longer corresponded to the relative distribution of populations. From another point of view, Egypt was well aware that the building of waterworks at the outlets of the great African lakes, like the Jinja dam recently completed at the outlet of Lake Victoria, put the keys to Egyptian survival in the hands of strangers, if not enemies. It needed the agreement of the Sudan, since the new artificial lake created upstream from Aswan would flood Sudanese territory for a distance of about 63 miles and force the evacuation of Wadi Halfa, a city of almost 70,000 people.

When asked for help, the West shilly-shallied. After envisaging a credit of $200 million, the World Bank refused to give its aid, referring to the terms of the recent Egyptian-Soviet agreements that granted a long-term mortgage on the revenues derived from the cotton crop in order to pay for the delivery of arms that could be directed only against Israel. On 19 July 1956 the United States refused to guarantee any international aid. This was an indirect thrust at the Soviet Union via Egypt, at a time when the East-West feud provided Cairo with a possibility of skillful diplomatic manoeuvering.

Playing his new role as leader of African and Near-Eastern nationalism, Nasser nationalized the Suez Canal. He applied its revenues to the financing of the dam. The fact that the Canal route was international did not seem to be an obstacle for Egypt, which gave its unilateral guarantee to the freedom of traffic, and considered that guarantee stronger and more legitimate than one derived from a treaty in which it had not been a completely free party. The efforts of the Western powers to elevate the indispensable guarantees to the level of undisputed international law wound up with the convocation of the London Conference of 16-23 August, and with the creation of an "Association of the Users of the Suez Canal" on 21 September.

Egypt, however, refused to participate in what it considered an illegal decision. It appealed to the Security Council on 24 September, a day after France and Great Britain themselves had presented a claim of violation of international law. The Soviet Union gave its full support to Egypt, which opposed any international administration of the Canal. France and Great Britain were trying to settle indirectly, by one decisive action, problems in which Egypt was merely an accessory party, viz., for Great Britain the control and the freedom of the India route, for France the destruction of militant Nasserism, a new version of a pan-Arabism in which North Africa was necessarily an ally of Egypt.

Israel, too, felt threatened by the massive modernization of the Egyptian forces now that they were being aided by the Soviet Union. Its interests and those of the two Western powers were one.

On 29 October 1956 Israeli armies penetrated Egyptian territory. The next day France and Great Britain addressed a joint ultimatum to Egypt and to Israel, demanding that they evacuate the Canal Zone, which for Egypt boiled down to its accepting the *fait accompli* of the Israeli occupation and for the Western powers to a denial of Cairo's sovereignty over its own territory.

In spite of their initial successes, the Franco-British forces swiftly revealed, through their hesitations, that they were insufficiently equipped to carry to ultimate victory an enterprise whose successful outcome depended after all, on swiftness and efficiency. British public opinion was deeply disturbed at seeing Great Britain isolated alongside France and Israel while the United States joined forces with the Soviet Union in the Security Council debates and condemned the unilateral action of the two Western European powers. The question of the Canal and the question of Israel found themselves indissolubly interconnected. The Arabic-speaking countries broke off all diplomatic relations with France and Great Britain, who finally yielded to a formidable coalition in which enemies of the day before, such as the U.S.A. and the Soviet Union, seemed to have become reconciled at their expense, after having been profoundly opposed in their reactions to the Hungarian insurrection of the same year.

After the cease-fire, the General Assembly of the United Nations ordered the immediate evacuation of British, French and Israeli forces from Egyptian territory (the despatch of an international force having been decided on fifteen days before). The last foreign troops left Egyptian territory during December 1956. The United States and the International Bank gave their assistance to the repair of the Canal, which had been blocked by the Egyptians during the first hours of the Franco-British intervention.

Failure
of the Franco-British and
Israeli campaign
1956

For all practical purposes the whole affair was finished in June 1957, when France and Great Britain authorized their ships to pay fees to the administration of the Canal, which was now entirely Egyptian.

This short and violent episode, by coinciding with Moroccan and Tunisian independence and with the deepening of the Algerian insurrection, marked a decisive turn in the power relationships between the countries of Western Europe and of North Africa. Ever since the Versailles Treaty, Egyptian policy had been able to establish a close link between nationalist ambitions and the international situation, and to evaluate all the broad trends correctly. This policy ultimately proved profitable.

For the first time the Soviet Union made a clear-cut appearance as a decisive factor in a debate in which the independence of an African nation was at stake. The United States, in the moment of decision, staked everything on Africa rather than on Europe. Great Britain was forced to abandon the myth of the absolute control of the India route. France lost all its levers of action, or very nearly, in the eastern countries where it had had so many traditional bonds, and with manifest regret was obliged to take cognizance of the fact that the solution to the Algiers problem was located in Algiers itself and not in Cairo.

Egypt, as an African, Middle Eastern, and Afro-Asian power, managed to transform into a national myth a victory that from all points of view was political far more than military. It was, after all, not the weight of arms that had won, but that of a new form of geopolitics in which the independence of Egypt proved to be guaranteed by a balance of power whose origin was to be found elsewhere than on the African continent, and even than in its Middle Eastern neighbours.

A political rather than military victory

The Bandung spirit had triumphed. In less than two years Africa had taken a decisive turn whose outcome, in the eyes of many observers, could be nothing less than the independence of the entire continent.

Chapter 32

The European Empires Liquidated

The diplomatic defeat inflicted by Egypt on France and Great Britain in 1956 was only one of the more spectacular expressions of a current that now seemed irresistible. The two great European powers were beating a more or less orderly retreat under the pressure of African nationalism. For obvious reasons of geographical proximity each stage of this retreat reacted on the next, and each was influenced by a well-informed public opinion, ready to help in the process.

From 1956 on the French and the British were competing with each other in West Africa, each nation in its own sphere, in order to secure the allegiance of the emerging political elites, on the theory that there was still time for this.

On 23 June 1956 the French parliament passed a "Framework Law" *(Loi cadre)* authorizing the government to promote the autonomy and the identity of the various territories in Africa that under the constitution of 1946 were still, after all, integral parts of the French republic, "one and indivisible." The powers of the representatives of the home country were limited to control, co-ordination, and arbitration. A skeleton government was set up for each territorial unit; for the first time local assemblies were granted semi-legislative powers. In this way France turned its back on a century-old policy whose fundamental principle was full political integration and centralized legislation. Though the responsible French cabinet ministers stoutly denied it, a decisive step had been taken on the road to independence for the African nations.

On 24 August 1956 Togoland, under French trusteeship, was given the constitution of an autonomous republic. It was a matter of course for the other territories of French West Africa, Equatorial Africa and Madagascar to make their claims for the same status. French policy managed to reconcile the growing autonomy of the French-speaking African territories with an ambitious project aiming at the integration of the newly united Western Europe with those African countries that sponsored a new "Eurafrican" dream.

In 1950 Robert Schuman, the French Minister of Foreign Affairs, had offered Africa to Europe as a sort of dowry, an inducement to the other European powers to set up the European Coal and Steel Community. First-rate minds saw in the European acceptance of the idea of an economic unit integrated on a broader base, including Africa, as a counterweight to the threat of an Africa divided up into countless very weak units, a process soon branded with the name of "Balkanization."

Ghana's independence 1957

While the French had accepted the accomplished fact of the break-up of the larger administrative federations of French West and French Equatorial Africa, Great Britain was giving up its own attempts to confederate British West Africa. On 6 March 1957, amidst magnificent celebrations, the Gold Coast was reborn as Ghana.

The celebration of Ghana's independence marked a turning point whose cardinal importance could not be obscured even by the last-minute hitches that marred the decisive day. The Ashanti deputies made an effort to obtain constitutional guarantees for freedom of the various regions, but they failed, as indeed they were bound to. From

The ancient fort of El Mina, in what is now Ghana, preserves its original character. This former capital of Portuguese Guinea, 5,000 inhabitants, has lost its importance today to Accra; the present Ghanaian capital.

Queen Elizabeth with President Kwame Nkrumah (seen from the back) in the car during the ceremonies marking the independence of Ghana, March, 1957.

a national as well as international point of view it was essential that the ruthlessly ambitious, yet highly competent leader of the new state should not be opposed. Kwame Nkrumah has since proclaimed his intention not only of administering his country as a closely-knit unitary republic, but also of making it the springboard for realizing the unity of Africa as a whole.

There were hundreds of delegates, official government guests, and personal guests of the Prime Minister; they all regarded the independence that a former European colony had managed to wrest from its rulers as a luminous goal to be attained by every single African territory without exception.

On 26 March 1957 the Nigerian House of Representatives instructed the Nigerian delegate to the Anglo-Nigerian constitutional conference in London to ask for independence. The complexity of this apparently simple demand for independence may be illustrated by the reserved attitude of the Prime Minister of the Nigerian Federation himself, El-Hajj Belawa, who said that the "Nigerian people are extremely diverse in their historical origins, their religious beliefs and their customs." At this stage, he thought, "Nigerian unity represents no more on this continent than a British intention.

But the Prime Minister's reluctance was swept aside by the pressure of the nationalist movement. From 14-22 April 1958 a conference of independent African states was held in Accra, at Nkrumah's invitation. Participants were Ethiopia, Liberia, Libya, Morocco, Tunisia, the United Arab Republic (i.e., Egypt as federated with Syria since 1957), and the Sudan (to be technically independent a few months later). The Conference issued a clear statement on the ideological ties of a militant pan-Africanism in the making: "We, the African states, gathered here in Accra in what is our first conference, conscious of our responsibilities to mankind and especially to the African people, desirous of affirming our African Personality on the side of peace, proclaim and solemnly reaffirm our unswerving loyalty to the charter of the United Nations, the universal declaration of Human Rights, and the declaration of the Afro-Asian conference held in Bandung."

Conference of independent African states 1958

The Conference entrusted the representatives of the members of the United Nations with the establishment of a permanent system of consultation on all subjects of common interest and the preparation of future meetings. Among these subjects the Conference mentioned the rights of the African people to independence and self-determination. The Algerian people in particular was to be assisted in reaching these goals. In addition the Conference asked the great powers to stop the production and testing of thermonuclear weapons.

Algeria had, indeed, become an international question. France itself helped bring about this state of affairs when French forces, alongside British and Israeli forces, had attacked the Egypt of Nasser with the objective of destroying the main center of militant Arab nationalism which was also a sponsor of the Algerian rebellion. The Arab countries were now openly organized to give growing assistance to a rebellious movement no longer limited to the terrorist actions of the badly-armed and scattered groups of the Army of National Liberation. The whole of Algeria was covered with an efficient network of guerillas and agents of internal subversion; by 1957 it had penetrated deeply into the capital, Algiers. The political situation in France itself had deteriorated when the most moderate elements of Muslim opinion abandoned their ties to France by boycotting the Algerian Assembly in December 1955, and by January 1957 the nationalists were in a position to instigate a general strike. On the military plane the tactic adopted by the rebels recalls that of Mao-Tse-Tung: they said "If the French army attacks, we scatter. If they occupy the towns, we shall build ambushes on the mountain roads. If they pursue us into the mountains, we shall take refuge in the cities. We will not squander our strength."

A meeting of the leading rebels at Summan (held 20 August 1956) was already able to set as its war aim either a cease-fire or an armistice leading to political negotiations. On the political plane, it was a question of gradually winning over the chief leaders of "official" nationalism, such as Ferhat Abbas (which was accomplished on 20 April 1956) and Messali Hadj, the aging leader living in France under surveillance, who was the only leader, in fact, who never complied, remaining deaf to this appeal. On 19 September 1958 the National Council of the Algerian Revolution, transformed into a Provisional Government of the Algerian Republic, was now the supreme organ of the rebellion. It set about at once to secure international recognition as the legitimate authority in Algeria. The National Liberation Front (the French initials are FLN) which controlled the army of national liberation from the outside, had already established *de facto* relations with Egypt, Tunisia (where Algerian troops were stationed in 1957), Morocco (where Egyptian-trained soldiers opened a second front on the western border of Algeria), and with other members of the Arab League such as Iraq, which granted the liberation movement a substantial financial subsidy.

The French reacted with great vigour. Almost 400,000 men were sent out to Algeria. The most isolated corners of this vast country were occupied in force. The rebel network was subjected to constant pressure, infiltration, and summary repression in what is perhaps best described as an uneasy combination of military and police action.

Ben Bella captured

On the 22 October 1956, when four prominent members of the Revolutionary Committee for Unity and Action were kidnapped from a Moroccan airliner that had been forced to land in Algiers, the repression seemed to have triumphed. Ben Bella and three of his companions, the hard core of the nationalist movement, were now securely in French hands. At the same time General Massu and his paratroopers had, by applying to the revolutionaries some of their own tactics, decimated the nationalist cells in Algiers itself.

But the repression was severely handicapped by a division in French public opinion which became more and more marked as passions rose higher. The objectives of a campaign whose final outcome was very much in doubt were sharply criticized.

The Muslims themselves, especially in western Algeria, suffered a great deal from the military operations, which forced immense areas to be evacuated and led to the setting up of a great many improvised camps.

The Algerian imbroglio imposed an almost unendurable strain on the entire French parliamentary system. It had seemed relatively simple to work out and implement a reasonable policy to end colonization in Black Africa, and to approve formal independence in Morocco and Tunisia, but the solution of the Algerian problem seemed fraught with all the deadly dangers of an authentic civil war. For that matter the Paris government was quite incapable of forcing its own officials and military men to obey it. The only outcome that could be imagined by the latter was the total crushing of the rebellion, and the deliberate implementation of an integrationist policy between the European and the Muslim populations. Some reforms were attempted on the plane of communal administration, social legislation, and the "Algerianization" of the civil service, but these half-hearted measures had no more political effect than similar measures had had in the neighbouring countries. The Resident Minister of the time, Lacoste, a socialist, was having a difficult time reconciling his democratic convictions with the exigencies of a military situation that in the nature of things was bound to become more and more severe and ruthless. At the same time, side by side with the military action, France was engaged in a massive, expensive campaign to help Algeria establish an industrial base that would be adequate to absorb a growing population.

A complication was added to the Algerian situation by the discovery of inexhaustible natural reserves of petroleum and natural gas in the northern fringe of the Sahara.

Paradoxically, socio-economic integration had become theoretically possible, through an equitable redistribution of the new resources, precisely at the moment that it had become politically unacceptable. In January 1957 a special organization was created (l'Organisation Commune des Régions Sahariennes) to exploit this enormous potential. This of course led to still another problem—the territorial division of a desert that hitherto had been totally unwanted, and had been disdainfully given the Gallic cock to scratch at by a British Prime Minister.

Natural treasure found in the desert

The brutal fact was that the whole future of North Africa was now bound up with the Algerian problem, which could not be disentangled from it. When the French forces, invoking the "right of pursuit", bombarded the Tunisian frontier village of Sakiet on 8 February 1958, leaving a hundred victims, there was an uproar of international public opinion. Tunisia submitted a complaint to the Security Council while Great Britain and the United States, in a hasty diplomatic manoeuvre, attempted to keep Bourguiba from imitating Nasser's precedent in seeking Soviet protection.

The French army chiefs maintained quite logically that it was impossible to restore peace in Algeria if the two neighbouring territories served as a haven for the rebel forces and protected their supply lines. For that matter it was in the name of this same logic that Tunisia had been put under a French protectorate in 1881 and Morocco in 1912. But times had changed. There was no longer a Franco-British Entente Cordiale for the division of Africa. There was an unstable balance between two powers, the Soviet Union and the United States, both equipped with the ultimate weapon, and both, for reasons contrary in their origin but convergent in their effects, in favor of the emancipation of the colonial peoples provided it was not accomplished for the benefit of one or the other.

Thus, having to face up in this way to an inherent impossibility (which though demonstrated by Suez had remained misunderstood) the army chiefs in Algiers, supported by an overheated local public opinion, took advantage of the dissentions of a parliament rent asunder by contradictory tendencies. A massive popular demonstration in Algiers on 13 May 1958 was used as an argument for demanding the formation of a "government of public salvation." General de Gaulle was called on to take power, and duly invested with authority by the last legislature of a moribund Fourth Republic. Just as in the decadent age of Imperial Rome, a tumult originating from the African soil had brought the mother country to its knees.

The new French Government born from these upheavals submitted a new constitution to the nation that made innovations on all levels, especially in relations between the home country and the Overseas Territories already granted autonomy by the Basic Law. No attempt was made to bring within a rigid framework diverse situations born of a development that was inevitable considering the trend of world events. The territories of Africa and Madagascar had a choice between accepting and refusing this new constitution. The referendum of 28 September 1958 allowed the home country and each of the territories involved to express itself freely and separately. The majority was overwhelmingly in favour, with only one exception—Sekou Touré's Guinea, which unanimously followed its leader, who promised immediate independence. General de Gaulle's France, with a certain reluctance, bowed to this unforeseen secession whose international consequences threatened the stability and the very *raison d'être* of a still fragile union whose representation and foreign defence continued to be ensured by France. For a short period the Republic of Guinea, which had become independent because of the leeway provided by a constitution that had certainly not been conceived with that aim, launched itself into the exciting world of international rivalry, like an acrobat on a tight-rope who disdains the net designed to check a fall that is, after all, always possible. The Soviet world sent its political and commercial

African tumult and French chaos

emissaries, as well as its technicians. To checkmate this, the United States, whose industrial interests directly involved association with French interests in the powerful FRIA organization, embarked on a political and technical counter-offensive that was to benefit by the blunders of its opponents, who probably overestimated their own influence anyway.

The political leaders of the autonomous units grouped in the Franco-African Community, who had accepted the discipline as well as the advantages offered by the constitution of the Fifth Republic, were disturbed by the rapprochement tentatively initiated by Sekou Touré and Kwame Nkrumah. It seemed to them unnatural. Yet they did not completely break off with Guinea any more than did France itself, which clung to a formal diplomatic recognition that severely limited technical and financial aid.

The independence of Guinea after Ghana's own independence seemed to be a harbinger of an accelerated development that was to affect the entire continent.

The countries that had been able to stand to one side of the movements of independence or of accelerated constitutional evolution, such as the Belgian Congo and the Portuguese territories of Angola and Mozambique, were also gradually drawn into the powerful undercurrents resulting from the entry of Africa, with such historical abruptness, into world affairs.

*Belgium moves towards
granting independence
to the Congo
1959*

In January 1959 a savage explosion of popular fury in Léopoldville, which followed the prohibition of political meetings, shattered the moral and intellectual tranquility of the Belgian leaders who had fancied themselves successful in producing an economic progress which obviated the need for political evolution. It was seen only too late that in spite of everything there were many symptoms of the growing impatience of the so-called "evolved" peoples with the discouraging prospects of a political progress that would be spaced out over decades, if not centuries. A mixture that was explosive in the literal sense of the word was created by the primitive nature of masses bogged down in primordial isolation and the exigencies of an elite that was too numerous and that envied the insolent luxury of its European masters. The Belgian Government, with a flash of intuition, understood this enormous danger; it made a right-about face away from a half-century of "apoliticalization", and decided not to speed up the removal of barriers to independence but quite simply to get rid of them entirely.

As 1960 opened, Portugal alone persisted in believing in the possibility that a small European power could maintain undisputed political dominion over countries in tropical Africa. Lisbon, without in the least denying the force of the nationalist tide, thought that history as made by the Portuguese pioneers would somehow shelter 20th century Portugal from history in the making.

Congolese tribes celebrating the independence of the Congo.

Page 298

A group of Ashanti dignitaries attending the celebration of Ghanaian independence. They hold traditional emblems of their authority: golden sticks carved with insignia.

Page 299

At the Accra Conference of 1958: maps showing the eight independent Africa states which participated at Nkrumah's invitation: Ethiopia, Liberia, Libya, Morocco, Tunisia, the United Arab Republic (Egypt federated with Syria) and the Sudan.

Intervention of troops in the Congo, 1960. Only a few weeks after celebrating its independence, the Congo was torn by tribal strife heightened
by the tensions of the Cold War, Tschombe declared Katanga had seceded
from the new republic and the Belgians sent troops to protect the European
population, Lumumba, the Congo Prime Minister, appealed to the U.N.
Many regarded the intervention of U.N. forces as a cloak for "neo-colonialism".

Africa Emergent

*Major events
and personalities in other parts of the world*
1960 - 1964

1960 Cyprus becomes independent.
1961 John F. Kennedy becomes
President of the U.S.A.
First Cosmic flight, by the
Russian Gagarin in the space
capsule "Vostok"
1962 First American space flight
(Glenn).
President Kennedy reveals
Soviet missile bases have been
installed in Cuba and announ-
ces partial blockade of the island.
The Œcumenical Council is
opened in Vatican by Pope
John XXIII
1963 John F. Kennedy assassinated
in Dallas, on November 22.
Succeeded by Lyndon B. John-
son, formerly vice-president
1964 Nikita Khrushchev
overthrown and succeeded by
Leonard Brezhnev and Aleksei
Kosygin.
Death of Nehru, Prime minister
of India since independence

Chapter 33
A Continent on Its Own

During the night of 31 December 1959, when the independence of Cameroon was proclaimed, the very presence in Yaunde of Dag Hammarskjöld, Secretary General of the United Nations, with his chief adviser, Hans Wieschoff, alongside the representatives of more than fifty nations, symbolized the identity of aims that inspired both the world organization and the trusteeship power: France. Colonization could at last give way to independence; principle and opportunity coincided. True enough, on the eve of this momentous day scattered bloody attacks directed at the airfields and means of communication, carried out by courageous though ineffective groups, made it clear to the far-sighted that if Black Africa had indeed entered on the road to independence the path would be marked by violence.

On 24 January 1960 the European population of Algiers rose up against General de Gaulle, in an attempt to checkmate a policy of self-determination whose logical consequence would have been independence controlled by a majority opposed to the Europeans' interests and hopes. The revolt and de Gaulle's resolution in repressing it had two results. It cast into high relief the critical importance of the choice that had been imposed on the French Army, torn between adventurism and loyalty. It also underlined the urgency of a political settlement that was long overdue.

The idea of Algerian independence as such was not, to be sure, either novel or revolutionary for the French leaders, who had examined and weighed its full significance. On the other hand, the Belgian statesmen and officials attending the round table conference called in Brussels a month later were far from prepared for the violence, the passions and the obscure complexity of an African political life whose very existence had been denied for half a century. Once again what was talked about were the intrigues and the ghosts that popped up out of the half-forgotten archives of the Congress of Berlin. The Belgian cabinet had to be reminded by France that one of its predecessors had given France a right of pre-emption over the Congo Free State in case Belgium were to waive its responsibilities there. Kasavubu, sought by the legal authorities of the Congo and defended by a French lawyer, and now a serious candidate for the presidency of the new state, embarked on more or less secret negotiations with Fulbert Youlou, President of the Congo Republic of Brazzaville, concerning the possible reconstruction of the ancient kingdom of Zaire, which had been ruled by their common ancestors.

Ghosts from the Congress of Berlin

Yet it was not with Fulbert Youlou that Kasavubu was to have his most important dialogue, but with Patrice Lumumba, upstart in modern politics. Like Nkrumah, whose advice he accepted, Lumumba believed that the liberty and independence of the African continent could be secured only at the price of abandoning without reservation all forms of tribalism and all other groupings rooted in relationships that might have been religiously and ethnically stimulating but were historically dubious and perhaps meaningless. The compromise that was to make Kasavubu the future President of the Congo Republic and Lumumba its Prime Minister was capable of deceiving no one but the politicians of Europe. It was unable to resolve the conflicts between two views of history.

The Union of South Africa also came to its moment of truth when mass demonstrations, inspired by the militant wing of the "Pan Africanist Congress," were organized against the strict application of the "Pass Laws." On 21 March 1960, at Sharpeville, the police fired on the crowd, killing seventy-two Africans and wounding more than a hundred and fifty, including women and children. With the support of the United States, the United Nations Security Council took up the matter. Hendrik Verwoerd, Prime Minister of the Union and a worthy successor of Strijdom and Malan, the author of the policy of separate development aimed at safeguarding the Boer people, announced his readiness to invite the Secretary General of the United Nations to a frank discussion, without, however, acknowledging that organization's competence in what he and his people considered a domestic affair. On 9 April Verwoerd barely escaped an attempt at assassination made by a South African of European origin, whose motives remain obscure but whose action illustrated the growing tension that dominated South Africa. A little later, on the 5th of October, 1960, the Union decided to withdraw from the British Commonwealth and to proclaim itself a republic. The dream of Kruger and of the Broederbond had now been realized. Once again the Boer people, as at the dawn of their history, were facing the African continent alone.

Nature
of the new relationships

West Africa, in spite of its close ties to its former French and British mother countries, perhaps, indeed, because of them, embarked on the inevitable transformation in a somewhat reserved mood. Certain hopes were mingled with a somewhat tardy regret for the familiar constitutional framework within which the most decisive events had taken place. Kwame Nkrumah, the spokesman for African independence, soon eliminated the last remnants of a British control that had become purely symbolic, by having himself elected President of a republic that now saw nothing more in the Queen of England than the head of a free association of nations and not a sovereign whose subjects owed her any allegiance.

The Franco-African Community, grounded in the generous principles of the September 1958 constitution, sought a formula of sovereignty that would not involve an irrevocable break, as with Guinea, and that would at the same time grant international sovereignty, an indispensable instrument of negotiations, defence and progress in an evolving Africa. From the beginning of April 1960, the new Mali Federation requested its independence, on the basis of a promise made by General de Gaulle during his trip to Dakar. In accordance with commitments undertaken with respect to the United Nations within the framework of trusteeship agreements, and in consideration of the Cameroon precedent, Togoland, under French administration, became independent on 27 April. Its president was Sylvanus Olympio, who for fifteen years had been carrying on a more or less open struggle against the French administration and who had won the 1958 elections held under the control of the United Nations.

In a few months all the African and Malagasay members of the Community were taking part in an international enterprise from which they had no intention of being excluded without at the same time breaking off ties they considered vital to their security and progress. Madagascar opened the way on 26 June; it was quickly followed, in August, by the republics of West and Equatorial Africa. At the same time the Senegal broke away from the Mali Federation.

This transformation, so abrupt historically, was sanctioned by the fifteenth session of the General Assembly of the United Nations, which, on 20 September 1960, admitted not only the Republic of Cameroon, Togoland, and Somalia (independent since 1 July 1960), all three of which had been territories under U.N. trusteeship, but also nine members of the Franco-African Community (Madagascar, Dahomey, the Ivory Coast, Niger, Upper Volta, the Central African Republic, the Chad, Gabon, and the Republic of the Congo (Brazzaville). Senegal and Mali were admitted separately on 28 September.

The Republic of Mauritania, independent since 28 November, was not to be admitted until the following year, over the objections of Morocco. Meanwhile the Federation of Nigeria, which had obtained its independence on 1 October, was admitted on 7 October.

On 20 September the Congo, that is, the former Belgian Congo, the old Congo Free State, also became a member of the United Nations. Under what conditions?

On 30 June the Belgian Congo had become officially independent. King Baudouin in person presided over the ceremonies of the transfer of power in Léopoldville. In accordance with the agreements made at the round table at Brussels, Kasavubu became President of the republic and Lumumba Prime Minister. For a brief moment of euphoria Belgian and foreign observers were still able to think that the unity and peace of the Congo would survive this abrupt change. To be sure, the haughty response made by Lumumba to the conciliatory speech of King Baudouin sent a shiver of political anxiety through the crowd of officials. Neo-nationalism and militant pan-Africanism could now be expressed freely and on the highest level. The Force Publique, made up of local recruits maintained in politically wholesome ignorance but well-officered and well-armed, represented the keystone of a policy that regarded independence as more a façade than a reality, a respite rather than an end in itself. On 5 July, at Thysville, this same Force Publique mutinied against its own officers, followed on 6 July by the Léopoldville garrison. In spite of the appeals of Lumumba, who was prepared to risk his life to pacify his discontented legions, the whole population was infected by fear. The Europeans were seized by panic and sought refuge en masse on the other side of the Congo. When Brussels decided to send out its own troops to protect threatened European lives, the intervention of its paratroopers had all the atmosphere of an attempt at reconquest. Secessionist forces vented their feelings freely. On 11 July Tshombe proclaimed the independence of Katanga. The following day Lumumba appealed to the United Nations to safeguard the integrity of the national territory and its independence.

On 14 July, the Security Council, by a vote of eight to zero, approved a Tunisian draft resolution authorizing the Secretary General to provide the Congo with "such military assistance as might be necessary" and calling upon Belgium to withdraw its troops from the Congo. The Soviet Union and the United States, for motives that were doubtless contradictory but that converged for the time being as they had in the Suez Affair of 1956, embarked on a policy that had all the advantages and shortcomings of opportunism, but that involved the very destiny and prestige of the world organization.

Many people regarded the Congo as a new arena of the Cold War. The political sympathies of certain members of the Prime Minister's entourage confirmed a number of observers, and not the least valid of them, in their opinion that Lumumba was a tool of a Soviet policy aimed at opening up on a continental scale a new front in Africa behind the West's positions. Pan-Africanism, still altogether novel, was undergoing its first test of arms as a factor in international politics. Representatives of Guinea and of Ghana were showing immense industry in Léopoldville, while more experienced and more secretive agents of better trained forces were preparing counter-offensives whose aim was to eliminate a man who seemed to them dangerous and irresponsible. Lumumba was thus thrown into the cauldron of a conflict on a world scale with no weapons but his personal magnetism and his own view of the goals to be attained, and severely handicapped by a certain ignorance concerning possible means, and by a lack of money, of civil servants, and of an army. The fact that the tribal situation rapidly deteriorated was no surprise to the specialists of an administration that had deliberately staked everything on economic progress while postponing for later all the problems of political integration.

The intervention of the United Nations, by its origin and its very nature, helped complicate this confused situation. The bulk of the United Nations forces came from independent African countries (Ethiopia, Ghana, Morocco, Tunisia, Guinea and Mali), which meant that the U.N. was represented essentially by Africans. On the other hand, the Secretary General of the United Nations, acting as instrument of a world organization, appealed to non-committed European powers like Sweden and Eire and to such Asian powers as India, Indonesia, and Malaysia, while modest but symbolic contributions were also received from Latin America. Finally, when the great African powers of Nigeria and Egypt joined this international enterprise there was no longer a doubt in anyone's mind that the Congo was a world problem as well as an African problem.

Via a tangle of Congolese factions that defy analysis the great powers were confronting each other. Without desiring it and without really quite understanding it, the U.N. was charged with the formidable task of avoiding a new "Korea" or a new "Spain." The Secretary General tried to achieve a sort of "neutralization" of the Congo; this seemed to satisfy the United States but it disappointed and disturbed the Soviet bloc and probably a great many Africans, who remained suspicious of any international cloak covering a "neo-colonialism" that dared not speak its name. The series of coups at Léopoldville, the gradual but efficient elimination of Lumumba, the seizure of power by one of the Congo army commanders, Joseph Mobutu, the *de facto* passivity of the U.N. representatives—interpreted by some as outright complicity in a gradual change that could lead only to hamstringing the forces of unification and nationalism in favour of traditionalist and tribal forces—all this helped turn an apparently constitutional affair into a fundamental question involving the destiny and the definition of the New Africa.

The Soviet Union made no secret of its support for Lumumba, and through him for a policy aimed at wiping out all vestiges of colonial domination and Western influence.

With the support of the majority of the African bloc at the General Assembly, Dag Hammarskjöld tried to bring together all the factions in the Congo. The resolution of 20 September 1960 gave him the mandate he was looking for, by combining the action of the Secretariat with that of the African bloc via a Commission of Conciliation charged with the arbitration of internal conflicts. Before this could intervene, Lumumba was arrested by Congolese troops on 1 December, in the course of his attempted flight to Stanleyville, where he intended to establish an independent government.

It was at this point that the crisis inherent in the somewhat sloppy compromises of Brussels became apparent to the whole world. In spite of the Soviet request the United Nations refused to help free Lumumba. The ex-Prime Minister's fate was sealed in January 1961, when he was transferred from Thysville to Elizabethville and handed over to his rival and enemy Tshombe. He was murdered the following month, in circumstances that have remained mysterious.

It might be said of Lumumba what was said in the sixteenth century by Henry III King of France before the corpse of the Duc de Guise: "He is even bigger dead than alive." The Soviet Union now denied its confidence to the Secretary General of the United Nations, and proposed a sweeping reorganization of his office at the very moment when the responsibility of the Secretariat, under the actual instructions of the Security Council, was becoming more and more direct. Indeed, the Commission of Conciliation, which visited the Congo at the beginning of 1961, recommended a reversion to the Fundamental Law, that is, in fact, the convocation of the Parliament, elected before independence, which took place on 22 July 1961. The portentous absence of Antoine Gizenga, the friend and disciple of Lumumba, and of the group of deputies from Southern Katanga, partisans of Tshombe, was noticeable. Cyril Adoula, proposed by President Kasavubu, was nominated Prime Minister. Gizenga, even though nominated Vice-Prime Minister, remained in Stanleyville. He was soon to be arrested, charged with secessionist intrigues with respect to the Eastern Province. As for Tshombe, after having accepted rather reluctantly the first contingent of U.N. troops on 12 August 1960, headed by Hammarskjöld in person, he openly organized himself if not for total independence at any rate for negotiations with the Leopoldville government as an equal. On 24 August 1961, when Adoula ordered the departure of all foreign military personnel (called "mercenaries" because they had been recruited directly by Elizabethville), he charged the U.N. itself with the execution of this order. The first operation now seemed to be a success. The second, which took place on 13 September, collided with the violent resistance of the Gendarmerie, headed by foreign officers. There was considerable bloodshed. The U.N. was accused of having failed in its mission, which was essentially pacific, and of having imposed its will by force. The British Government, disturbed by the sudden flare-up in the Katanga region, so close to Rhodesia, let it be understood that it could not give its support to any further military action. The Secretary General, then negotiating in Leopoldville, decided to visit the areas in person and agreed to meet Tshombe, who was seeking refuge in Northern Rhodesia. On 18 September the Secretary General's aeroplane crashed in the middle of the night a few miles away from the N'Dola airfield; all aboard were killed.

By their deaths in the course of duty Dag Hammarskjöld, Hans Wieschoff, and their companions placed an indelible stamp on the great hopes held out for an almost despairing enterprise, as well as on its frustration, at least in the short run. Was it possible to protect a large portion of Africa and its unprepared peoples from adventures and afflictions that were the normal consequences of an international rivalry over which at this stage they could have no control? Lumumba had never been given enough time to realize his ideal of national unity. Hammarskjöld was also denied the time to accomplish his mission, the construction of an international order respected by all.

Death of Hammarskjöld

After some new incidents with the U.N. troops, the Katanga authorities seemed to acknowledge the Leopoldville regime as a central government, with all the consequences entailed by Congo unity in the financial and military fields. The policy of national reconciliation permitted the draft of a federal constitution to be worked out. An amnesty was announced on 26 November 1962. This was, however, nothing but façade. Secession remained a reality, confirmed by the U.N. representatives themselves and by the U.N. troops, subjected to constant provocations of a local force that may have been emboldened by the hope of aid from outside. When the commander of the U.N. troops decided to take the offensive (on the basis of a Security Council resolution of 24 November 1961) the Tshombe government collapsed. Its Prime Minister fled to Portuguese territory. On 23 January 1963 the secession of Katanga was a thing of the past; it was this that had been the cause, even more than the mutiny of the Force Publique (of which it was, indeed, in a way no more than one aspect), of Lumumba's about-face with respect to the U.N. and all the tragic consequences that flowed from it. Katanga had profoundly divided Africa by making the spirit of conciliation a hallmark of suspicious weakness and not of patience. Katanga became the touchstone for the definition of mutually exclusive positions. It was Katanga, also, that led the U.N. to fling itself into a military action whose motivation, course and conclusion jeopardized to the point of rupture the moral and material mainsprings of this international organization. This trauma affected the world as well as Africa.

Significances of the Congo crisis

Passions were polarized around men who were all authentically African but whose political choices were suddenly loaded with universal significance. From this point of view, and in another context, the Congo affair is reminiscent of the Spanish Civil War, which for several decades served as a political touchstone for Europeans aware of the fundamental conflict they had been involved in by Spanish factions that were seeking a key to the modern world, either by rejecting or by accepting their traditional values. This time the conflict assumed epic proportions. An entire continent had entered into modern history, torn between its past, which linked it with a conception of man in which the living and the dead live on together in a mystical co-existence, and a still only dimly perceived future, in which nature, finally conquered, is to be put in the service of the African man, relieved of his age-old bondage.

The Congo tragedy almost seemed to overshadow events that were, nevertheless, highly significant.

In less than eighteen months the decisive step of Algerian independence was taken by both France and Algeria itself, in the wake of a complex imbroglio that mingled secret negotiations, savagely contested compromises, flare-ups of rage on the part of the Europeans in Algeria, the bitterness of a French army that was almost always victorious militarily but finally was politically defeated, and a force of resistance and of national insurrection that was reduced to guerrilla operations but was finally triumphant. It was an independence whose abruptness was equaled only by the remarkable patience and the great sacrifices that created it. The popular referendum of 6-8 January 1961 was followed by the negotiations at Evian-les-Bains on 20 May and the cease-fire unilaterally proclaimed by General de Gaulle on 27 June. The Lugrin negotiations of 20-28 July seemed to have been abortive.

It was at just this moment that President Bourguiba ordered an attack on the Bizerta base that provoked the immediate and violent reaction of the French garrison. Once again, this time indirectly, it was the question of the French position in North Africa and of the carefully planned retreat that the French Government was determined to carry out of its own free will that was brought up before the U.N. Security Council as a result of a Tunisian request. On this level, too, there seemed to be a total impasse. The allies of France wondered whether the whole of North Africa might not swing over to the Soviet side as a result of what they considered the blind stubbornness of Paris. In reality, however, events were simply following their natural trend. France informed the emissaries of the Provisional Government of the Algerian Republic that it was ready to accept Algerian sovereignty over the Sahara, which until then had been left undecided. In the course of his year's end message, General de Gaulle confirmed France's decision to recognize a sovereign and independent Algerian state. The cease-fire was signed between the French government and the Algerian Provisional Government on 18 March 1962. On 7 April a provisional executive of twelve members was established by France in Algiers under the chairmanship of Abderramane Fares. The next day metropolitan France ratified the Algerian settlement by an overwhelming vote (90%). The Algerians themselves also returned a plebiscite with almost 98% of the votes. On 3 July 1962 Algerian independence was proclaimed by General de Gaulle. Ferhat Abbas was President of the Republic for a short time, to be replaced on 15 September 1963 by Ben Bella.

If Algeria had to pay a heavy price for this war that might have been avoided (like many civil and foreign wars) France too had serious wounds to heal. A million of its citizens came back to the metropolitan soil, leaving behind them something that their toil and their sacrifices had, in their eyes, turned into an integral part of France. Republican liberties survived the grave menace of a disappointed army only because of the steadfastness of a government that had learned political realism in the hard school of the Resistance and the Liberation. It now remained for these three countries of North Africa to repair, if possible together, the ruins and the upheavals, resulting from ten years of agitation and of fighting aimed at an independence now wholly secured. They also needed to reconstruct their relations with France, Europe, the rest of the world, and with Africa itself, on new and positive foundations.

Thus France and Belgium yielded to the surging tides of African independence. Brussels had still to emancipate, in accordance with United Nations procedures, the

Recognition
of an independent
Algeria

308

The Katanga mine region. Since 1885, its mineral wealth had made the Congo the central element in European negotiation to divide up Africa. Similar interests intervened in the Katanga secession. After the offensive U.N. troops, the Tshombe secessionist government collapsed, but Katanga remained an issue that divided Africa and world opinion.

Insurrection of the French population of Algiers against de Gaulle: January 24, 1960. The Europeans hoped to overthrow the Paris government which was accepting Algerian independence. The French Army was split between those factions loyal to de Gaulle and others fighting for French colonial interests.

Page 310
De Gaulle in Algiers in 1958, addressing the French population at the Forum. Enthusiasm was at its height when the General appeared to share the aspirations of the French colonials to hold onto Algeria. Later they felt betrayed when they realized de Gaulle's policy inevitably led to Algerian independence.

two former German protectorates of Ruanda-Urundi, over which it accepted a mandate under the League of Nations and trusteeship responsibilities under the aegis of the U.N. The mixture of administrative methods leaning toward the forces of the aristocracy rather than toward those of the peasant masses (a ruling race and a subject race), of a missionary effort that was, to be sure, Catholic but that was represented locally by rival religious orders, of the influence of plebiscites supervised by international functionaries, and finally of resolutions adopted by a General Assembly that was itself obsessed by the Congo affair, were bound to have an explosive effect on the social and political structure of this African region that had long been thought isolated. At the end of July 1961 the Bahutu peoples of the Ruanda revolted against their ruling classes, represented by their Mwami (the King of Negro-Hamitic origin). The legislative elections held on 25 September 1961 under the aegis of the U.N. confirmed the popular desire to be rid of the centuries-old rule of the former invaders. In the neighbouring territory of the Burundi legislative elections were held on 18 September. The murder of the new Prime Minister cast a shadow over the first days of the new Kingdom. The trusteeship regime in the territories was ended on 1 January 1962; the two territories were admitted to the U.N. separately on 18 September of the same year.

Great Britain followed this movement after having led it. The only British territories that did not become independent were southern Rhodesia and the three territories of the High Commission (Bechuanaland, Basutoland, and Swaziland). Sierra Leone became independent on 27 April 1961. Two final plebiscites had disposed of the part of the Cameroon under British trusteeship in February 1961. Northern Cameroon voted in favour of joining the Federation of Nigeria. Southern Cameroon voted in favour of joining the Republic of Cameroon. Tanganyika, under trusteeship, was given an autonomous government under the presidence of Mr. Nyerere on 1 May 1960 and received its independence on 9 December 1961; it was admitted to the U.N. on 14 December of the same year. Uganda became independent on 9 October 1962. The Kabaka of the Buganda became its first president, thus reconciling the tradition of the old Mutesa monarchy and the requirements of a new situation in which the traditional authorities had to accept co-existence and collaboration with new forces. Ten years after the failure of the Mau-Mau rebellion, Kenyatta was called upon to preside over the new state of Kenya, which became independent on 12 December 1963, two days after the island of Zanzibar, key to the history of East Africa. In both cases London did not hesitate to bypass the objections it had made itself to giving unreserved power to Africans in a country (Kenya) where many Europeans were still settled on the best lands and to an Afro-Arab majority ruling an essentially African population (Zanzibar).

The Federation of Rhodesia and Nyasaland, which had been established in 1953, following a conference at Victoria Falls, against the explicit opposition of Nyasaland and the obvious reluctance of the African leaders in Northern and Southern Rhodesia, was incapable of withstanding the wind of independence coming from the north, a real tempest ever since the events in the Congo. Hastings Banda was authorized to return to Nyasaland in 1961. Kenneth Kaunda, an apostle of non-violence and of peaceful co-existence between Europeans and Africans, was soon irresistibly on the up-grade in Northern Rhodesia. N'Komo organized the opposition to the Southern Rhodesian government, whose political philosophy was founded on the continuous domination of a large European minority whose natural bent toward segregation was scarcely kept in check by liberal influences coming from the United Kingdom. The Prime Minister of the Federation, Sir Roy Welenski, aware of the paramount importance of the events in the Congo, desperately tried to give flesh and blood to a policy of "partnership" based on rapid economic development, without at the same time coming too close to the Union of South Africa. He also avoided giving too flagrant support to the

A wind of independence

Page 312
Algerian independence was finally declared on July 3, 1963. It came after a cease-fire signed in March, 1962 and a ratification of the Algerian settlement by the French electorate and the Algerians themselves. Ferhat Abbas was President of the Republic for a short time, followed by Ben Bella. Ben Bella was deposed in 1965.

Katanga secession movement, though in the short run this was a tempting course of action. The United Kingdom was guided by the Monckton Report, which, at the beginning of 1961, foreshadowed the dissolution of the Federation by preparing the departure and ultimate independence of Nyasaland. The General Assembly of the U.N. took up the question of Southern Rhodesia in February 1962; it regarded this colony, autonomous in the eyes of the British Constitution, as a "non-autonomous territory" according to the terms of the Charter. England's margin for manœuvring was lessened all the more by its refusal to acknowledge the legality of the U.N. intervention.

A shortlived Federation

The intervention of the General Assembly in the constitutional problems of Northern Rhodesia, which was prepared during the course of this same session, was obviated when the United Kingdom took the initiative and formed a coalition government instructed to prepare for independence. In March 1963 London took cognizance of the right to secession of the territories making up the Federation, which was already for all practical purposes defunct. The second conference at Victoria Falls undid the work of its predecessor, and recommended the formal dissolution of the Federation from the 31st of December 1963. A few months later Nyasaland became independent under the name of Malawi, and Northern Rhodesia under the name of Zambia, with Hastings Banda and Kenneth Kaunda respectively as Prime Ministers. Southern Rhodesia, which soon put into power a government that was hostile to any compromise with the African majority, now found itself quite alone facing the decisive choice: to join the Union of South Africa in a policy of apartheid, with all its inevitable consequences in the domain of foreign defence, or to accept the rule of "one man, one vote" that was already being applied by its northern neighbour, which meant, of course, African domination.

This interaction between phenomena of external pressure, expressed by the more and more active intervention of the U.N., and the strictly internal factors of a political evolution with a logic of its own, was still more striking in the case of the Union of South Africa. Ever since 1946 the General Assembly had been concerned with the question of the discriminatory treatment given to elements of the population originally from India. In 1952 it decided to study the racial question and the consequences of *apartheid*. After all attempts at conciliation and consultation were hamstrung, the General Assembly, during the course of its 17th session, requested the member states to take a series of diplomatic and economic steps aiming at a real boycott of the Union of South Africa. Exclusion from the U.N. itself was contemplated in case of failure. These recommendations were strengthened in 1963. The entire African bloc took the offensive, not only within the framework of the U.N. but throughout all its own organizations on a continental scale. Already the question of Southwest Africa had been raised, whose international character was undeniable even in the eyes of the Union of South Africa itself. The very prestige of the U.N. was at stake. The point at issue was whether the U.N. would have the material means to implement a resolution aiming at nothing less than the independence of the former German colony. Such an intervention on the other hand was unacceptable in the eyes of the Union government, since it would jeopardize its entire internal and external security. From the point of view of the Union of South

The Union of South Africa: a paradox

Africa, the situation was paradoxical. The country's economy was booming. Foreign investments had reached an unprecedented level. The immigration from Europe, vigorously encouraged, was of good quality. The practical effect of the sanctions decided on by the U.N. remained slight. To be sure, sea and air communications were affected by the boycott of the African and Asian countries. The cost of armaments kept growing each year. The moral isolation of the Union was a fact, since Great Britain and the United States themselves had joined with the majority of the U.N. in condemning *apartheid*. Verwoerd, and with him the majority of the European population, remained however convinced that there could be neither an external nor an internal compromise with any policy aiming at the physical elimination of three million Europeans who had considered Africa a homeland several centuries old. The only visible sign of any evolution, which for that matter also conformed with the logic of *apartheid*, was to be found in the application of the official policy of the "bantustans," that is, the internal autonomy granted the zones in which (since such zones were not favourable for European settlement) the rights of the natives had always been reserved, zones like Transkei, Zululand, and possibly the High Commission territories—Basutoland, Bechuanaland, and Swaziland—whose juridical status remained one of the oddities inherited from the great Anglo-South-African settlement treaty after the defeat of the Boers.

The historical and moral legitimacy of the one remaining European presence on African soil was vigorously contested by the new African nations in the case of Portugal, as well as in that of South Africa, with the exacerbating circumstance that Portugal was primarily a European and not an African power. As for Southern Rhodesia, the General Assembly refused to accept the claims of the Portuguese constitution, which had made the Portuguese territories in Africa overseas provinces of Portugal (resolution of 15 December 1960). Moreover, the abrupt independence of the Congo and the riots around Thysville and Matadi had imperiled the safety of the north-east frontier of Angola. Portugal had to confront simultaneously a vigorous and well-organized campaign in the heart of the General Assembly, aiming at the autonomy and ultimate independence of all its territories, and an offensive on the spot, which had begun at the very moment the Security Council was studying the question of Portuguese territories in Africa. Armed bands were crossing the border. Local uprisings were taking place, of which the European colonists were the victims. On 20 April 1961 the U.N., with the affirmative vote of the United States, gave its support if not to the rebellion itself at any rate to its targets. In the meantime Portugal sent its best troops to Angola, and embarked on severe repressive measures. Thousands of refugees crossed the Congo frontier, adding to the enormous difficulties the U.N. teams were facing. The attempts at conciliation, through an enquiry commission of five members designated by the Assembly, did not have the slightest result. The first military offensive of the rebels collapsed in the face of the Portuguese troops. It remained for Roberto Holden, one of the heads of the Angolese rebellion in exile, to reorganize his movement on a more solid political and military basis with the help of the new African nations, which were determined to play a militant role in the elimination of Portugal from Africa. Lisbon for its part set in train a series of internal political reforms, while coming closer on the international front to the Union of South Africa and preparing itself to confront a new assault, this time directed against the northern frontiers of Mozambique and launched from independent Tanganyika.

A small European country against the new African Nations

On the 14 December 1962 the General Assembly adopted the recommendations of the Committee of Twenty-four (called the Committee on Colonialism) and refused to acknowledge the validity of Portuguese policy, declaring it to be incompatible with the Charter. The members of the U.N. were asked to cease all support, direct or indirect, for the repressive policy embarked on by Lisbon. Security Council action was contemplated in case Portugal refused to yield.

In the face of all these threats the Lisbon government displayed a firmness that was no surprise on the part of a people whose sense of historical continuity has been exceptional. Recent events in Asia and Africa strengthened its leaders in their conviction that there could be no compromise with militant Pan-Africanism. On the other hand Portugal, in contrast with the Union, refused to see a racial conflict in this new stage of the struggle for supremacy between Africans and Europeans. Cultural, religious, and ultimately ethnic assimilation remains the goal that Portugal is striving for. According to this policy new Brazils may be expected to evolve one day, perhaps, on African soil.

Conclusion

Continental unity:
a difficult task

The prolonged resistance of these last bulwarks of European supremacy on the African continent—the Union of South Africa, Portuguese Guinea, Angola and Mozambique, and Southern Rhodesia—represent an important historic phenomenon. It is a decisive factor in the organization and strengthening of African unity.

The new African nations, which have to face an immense variety of political and economic tasks, have a natural tendency to concentrate on their internal problems while making alliances abroad in accordance with their immediate interests or for that matter with traditional habits of trade and culture. In addition, a number of countries situated on the mixed zones of co-existence between various peoples and religions (such as Nigeria, Cameroon, Chad, and the Sudan) must defend a unity that might prove to be precarious if it were to be exposed too quickly to the tensions of international rivalry. But these preoccupations have by no means damped down the profound aspirations toward continental unity. They have simply imposed a certain rhythm and a certain circumspection on the institutional developments aimed at expressing that unity and making its weight felt in the arena of world politics.

Hence the existence of a common enemy plays a catalytic role. The open challenge flung at Pan-Africanism by Portugal and by the Union of South Africa has forced the African nations to settle their disputes, and to come to a compromise on frontier problems that had their origin in the arbitrary division of Africa by Europe, but sometimes also in factors of historical rivalry that had long preceded that.

Like Europe, Africa is approaching the problems of its unity under the dual heading of economic integration and of the integration of defence and foreign policy. It is in this dual perspective that an analysis can be made of the results of the various conferences that have followed each other since the first conference of independent African states was held at Accra in April 1958. The question of the elimination of European colonialism occupied first place there, beginning with Algeria and finishing with Portugal and the Union of South Africa, passing over the territories under trusteeship and the Spanish enclaves. The themes of the neutralization of the continent, and especially that of the suppression of foreign military bases and the prohibition of atomic tests, were specially highlighted. The U.N. was considered the chief forum in which a united Africa represented by a growing number of delegations could play a decisive role as much by their number as by the intrinsic value of the moral and political nature of the positions Africa has been called upon to champion. Africa is struggling for its own rehabilitation and to support other countries and other continents that are also trying to free themselves from foreign domination.

The various means used and the actual spirit affecting the independence of the African states after the independence of Ghana have not failed to impose a severe test on the basic premises of Pan-Africanism. The first of the "Pan-Africanist" powers, such as Ghana, Guinea, and Egypt, aimed at immediate unity of action in order to achieve a number of fixed goals, many of which demand an unprecedented financial and military effort.

Many African countries of the West and East, however, which secured their sovereignty beginning with 1960 have wanted merely to gain time. By a declaration of union with Guinea in 1959, then with Mali in December 1960, Ghana tried to produce a West African nucleus as an initial base of action aiming at political unity in the shortest possible time and on the scale of the entire continent. In July 1959 Liberia, in the declaration of Sanniquellie, adhered to the proposal for the creation of a "community of independent African states." The African and Malagasy States that had emerged from the former Franco-African community (Cameroon, the Central African Republic, Congo (Brazzaville), the Ivory Coast, Dahomey, Gabon, Upper Volta, Madagascar, Mauritania, Niger, Senegal and Chad) came together at Brazzaville in December 1960 and passed resolutions whose moderation by no means excluded steadfastness with respect to Mauritanian independence, the Algerian problem, and the Congo problem. They decided to form an African and Malagasy united front and recommended the harmonization of economic policy in the French speaking states. The African and Malagasy Union was born.

A charter aiming at "the Union of African States" was proposed at Accra in April 1961 by Ghana, Guinea, and Mali; this outlined the creation of a supreme executive organ consisting of a conference of Chiefs of State, the harmonization of the foreign policy of these states, and the laying down of a policy of mutual defense. On all these points it made specific the recommendations that were more generally presented at the Casablanca conference of January 1961, which had brought together powers (Morocco, Ghana, Guinea, Mali, the United Arab Republic, Libya and the Provisional Government of the Algerian Republic) whose attitude toward immediate problems was clearly more militant than that of the participants at the Brazzaville conference. The attitude toward Mauritania and the Congo was the touchstone of their discussions.

On 5 May 1961, in Cairo, the members of the "Casablanca Group" signed the text of the "African Charter." A few days later the Monrovia Conference brought together the Chiefs of State of Liberia (presiding), members of the "Brazzaville Group," (including Mauritania) as well as of Togoland, Nigeria, Sierra Leone. Tunisia, the Central African Republic, Gabon, Ethiopia, and Libya were represented. Ghana, Guinea, Mali, Morocco, the United Arab Republic and the Sudan declined President Tubman's invitation chiefly because of the Mauritanian question. Congo (Léopoldville) was not invited at all.

Parallel with these meetings on the government level, the "Conference of the African Peoples," made up of militant members of the independence movements, had successive meetings in Accra in 1958, Tunis in 1960, and Cairo in 1961. It was these that echoed most directly the most advanced proposals concerning neo-colonialism, neutralism, the elimination of tribalism and the importance of a co-ordinated policy in the fields of trade-unions, youth and women's movements, etc.

When the powers of the Monrovia Group, in approving the Lagos Charter in December 1962, also declared their adherence in principle to "summit" organization, and the new countries of East Africa created the "Pan-African Freedom Movement for East and Central Africa" (enlarged later on to include the region of South Africa), the ground was completely prepared for an ultimate confrontation of the different groups and their merged joint organization. The Emperor of Ethiopia opened the Addis Ababa Conference on 22 May 1963. This time all the independent states were represented on the highest level, except for Morocco, which had meanwhile fallen into new difficulties with its Algerian neighbour and with the United Arab Republic. The Emperor emphasized that the looked-for union could come only gradually, and that it had to be based "on those areas of agreement in which action is possible." Joint action would in its turn reinforce the progressive building up of the union. Among these "areas of

The "African Charter"

agreement" Haile Selassie mentioned the organization of joint defence, the struggle against racial segregation and for the de-nuclearization of the African continent, and finally the establishment of joint economic organs such as the Inter-African Development Bank.

The Emperor's prudent approach was followed by the Conference. Kwame Nkrumah by no means abandoned his proposals for immediate organic unity, but provisionally accepted what he regarded as a compromise. The Conference provided for the periodic meeting of the Chiefs of State, the establishment of a Council of Ministers and of a *Conference results* permanent secretariat, the creation of a commission of mediation, conciliation, and arbitration, and finally a series of specialized committees in technical areas (which would, in fact, be continuations of the various organizations established under the aegis of the Commission for Technical Co-operation in Africa, the old 1950 CTCA). In the area of military action, with a view to the liberation of the territories still under European-dominated regimes, a committee of co-ordination was created. It was composed of Egypt, Algeria, Ethiopia, Senegal, Nigeria, Guinea, Uganda, the Congo (Leopoldville) and Tanganyika. It held its first meeting at Dar-Es-Salaam in July 1963. A sub-committee made up of Algeria, Egypt and Guinea was, in fact, charged with the preparation of plans for the training of future militants of emancipation in the territories of Portugal and ultimately of South Africa. What is noteworthy is the absence of Ghana, which in the Congo affair had already shown great independence with respect to the co-ordinated action sponsored by the other African countries that had supplied contingents to the U.N. troops.

The new Organization of African Unity immediately came to grips, quite successfully, with its task of conciliation in the border dispute between Algeria and Morocco and helped lessen the tension between Somalia and Ethiopia without, however, settling the problem at its roots.

Independent Africa now has at its disposal a tool of intervention on the continent whose activities correspond very closely with those of the African bloc within the framework of the General Assembly and the Security Council of the United Nations. Centuries of dispersion and passivity have now been followed by a new historic period.

In its violence, and its historically abrupt character, the intervention of the European colonial nations in Africa recalls the Napoleonic intervention in Europe, which at the beginning of the nineteenth century was in many respects still tribal and feudal. Yet in spite of this revolutionary intervention in the destinies of the African continent, a remarkable continuity can be observed in its history.

The question of Egyptian independence has always played a decisive role ever since the dawn of civilization. If the delta and the valley of the Nile pass under the dominion of a continental power from Asia or Europe, North Africa and the rest of Africa cannot maintain independence. The liberty of the African nations of the Mediterranean shorelands is the result of a balance of power between external forces. If the balance is disrupted their independence becomes nothing but a delusion.

Problems of The United Arab Republic, governed by Nasser, has had to face up to problems *the United Arab Republic* reminiscent of Egypt of the first millennium. The head of the Egyptian state has been supporting a policy that is essentially aimed at the welfare of the people. The technical improvement of the control of the water and the soil has enabled him, with immense difficulty, to face up to the dizzying increase in population of a people with confidence in a government it has produced itself. Egypt has continued to proclaim its African mission throughout the valley of the Nile and beyond. In this it has followed the path immutably outlined by geography and by its crucial position at the cross-roads of the great trade routes. It has added to this a religious mission that finds echoes in the regions crossed by the ancient caravans in the Sahara and the Sudan.

Libya of the Senussis, held over the baptismal font of independence by England and the United Nations, is the end result of the long struggle waged by the tribes of the desert against the foreign colonies that since the dawn of time have tried to settle along the coast and to constitute autonomous centers of power. Rome, Byzantium, the Ottoman Empire and Mussolini's Italy foundered one after the other in the face of the perpetual mutiny of the peoples of the interior, who since the seventh century of our era have been organized by Islam. The United Nations did the rest, by guaranteeing the unity of Libya against any further designs directed at the control of Cyrenaica and Fezzan.

Bourguiba's Tunisia is pursuing objectives similar to those fixed by the Haffisid monarchy of the thirteenth century, and before it, by the rulers of the ancient Province of Africa. It has been a question there of safeguarding the personality of one of the oldest centers of civilization of the western and central Mediterranean. Ties also had to be maintained with the European countries of the northern shore of the western Mediterranean, which Tunisia had always been associated with in one way or another.

Central North Africa, whose unity was finally forged under the name of Algeria after a century of French rule, established itself as a new nation, with deep historic roots in the tenacious self-assertion of a popular will. Its profound originality and spirit of independence have survived a thousand years of destiny in which wave after wave of Latin, Teutonic, Hispanic, Semitic, and French conquerors have succeeded one another.

Modern Morocco, an empire that has become a nation, has managed to find during the last half-century an antidote for the permanent divisions its successive invaders have benefited by. Since the fifteenth century, Portugal, England, Spain, and France have foundered in their attempts to turn it into an extension of a certain version of Europe. For the first time in its history its frontiers with Algeria are properly defined, except on the borders of the great desert. The isolation of the mountain peoples with respect to the peoples of the plains and the coastal zones no longer seems to play a decisive political role. The Moroccan government has deliberately carried on the work of the French protectorate by imposing on the country as a whole an accelerated rhythm of economic development and a modern system of education.

A modern nation: Morocco

These three countries of North Africa must still organize their co-existence and their collaboration around an area of common interest that in the course of history has always been more of a passageway than a dwelling-place subject to a clearly defined sovereignty. The historic routes leading beyond Mauritania to the frontiers of the Negro kingdoms have been added to by modern access routes aiming at the exploitation of such slumbering treasures as gas, petrol and iron. In the Africa of the twentieth century potential mineral wealth has played the same fascinating role as did the gold of the Monomotapa in the sixteenth.

Thus the countries of Mediterranean Africa have undergone a historical cycle comparable to that of the European nations with which they have always been associated. They are resuming their traditional policy while making use of the new means put at their disposal by the powers that were once dominant. (See map on page 334.)

The emergence of the African nations south of the Sahara, on the other hand, seems to have created new problems in spite of the phenomena of historic resurgence that are visible above all in the zones of contact between the Hamitic and Semitic civilizations (from the north and east) and the Negro civilizations. The maps drawn by the geographers of the eigtheenth century (on the basis of the accounts of Leo Africanus and the Muslim travellers) reveal the filigree of ancient Africa. The Wolof and Serrerre kingdoms can be seen regrouped now in the Senegal of Leopold Senghor; the Mandingo kingdoms between the Senegal and the Niger Rivers, with their paleonegritic protectorates, are found once again in the Mali of Modibo Keita. The Mossi kingdom and the Bobo districts are

319

included in the Upper Volta of Maurice Yameogo. The Djermas, the Sonrhais, and a section of their traditional rivals, the Hausa, are associated in the Niger Republic, with Hamani Diori at their head. (See map on page 334.)

Nigeria has brought together in one complex ensemble peoples that were both rulers and ruled, whose stratification is a result of the superposition of the Fulas on the Hausas, themselves the conquerors of peoples that had been settled there before them. The kingdoms of Sokoto, Kano and Bornu can be found there almost intact. In the Republic of Chad the more or less Arabized rulers of Kanem and Waddai co-exist with the Saras, who used to be dominated by their Northern neighbours. The Sudan represents the modern formula of the ancient federation of Nubian kingdoms; they have now extended their control over the Nilotic and Bantu populations of the tropical zones and over the arabized sultanates of Darfur.

The Empire of Ethiopia is at the peak of its diplomatic and military power. With the annexation of Eritrea, Haile Selassie attained the most ambitious goals of the Amhara people. Firmly based on age-old religious and linguistic traditions, a people of profound originality has reinforced its natural military virtues in a constant struggle waged on a difficult terrain against enemies from the north and east (emissaries of evolved civilizations like those of Egypt or Western Europe); or the vanguards of primitive peoples from the untamed solitudes of Arabia, like the Gallas; or else religious adversaries (like the Somalis or the Arabs). The Empire now has a maritime front along the Red Sea and an open door on the Indian Ocean. The approaches to the highlands are controlled in Harar as well as in Ogaden.

A new republic has succeeded the divided sultanates of the Adal that were once shared by Europe. The Somali peoples are still demanding lands regarded by Ethiopia as its own. The international and African community of 1963 is, indeed, an effective guarantor of the territorial status quo.

Modern Ethiopia has had to confront at home the impatience of the younger generation with all traditional forms; the first demonstration of this was the coup d'état of 14 December 1961, which was shattered by Haile Selassie's firmness.

The Negro-Hamitic kingdoms that came down the Nile valley in the course of the sixteenth and seventeenth centuries and imposed their rule on the Bantu peoples around Lake Victoria and the highlands of the Ruanda and the Urundi, have displayed uneven degrees of vigour. The Buganda kingdom and its allies or rivals in the neighbouring territories have been able to defend their characteristic way of life down to our own day. In 1953, Great Britain failed in its attempt to break the power of the young Kabaka by sending him to London to an exile that was as short-lived as it was comfortable. By passing protectorate treaties with the kingdoms of Uganda, the European conquerors had helped legalize on the international plane (just as in northern Nigeria) phenomena of conquest some of which were relatively recent. In an understandable paradox, the first "national" reactions against European domination came from the ruling castes and not from the dominated peoples, for whom in many cases European control represented a distinct improvement. The Bantu peoples, threatened by the Hamites and the Semites, could develop their institutions freely only in the relatively isolated areas of the continent. The historic center of gravity of their great kingdoms is located in the region that used to be known under the name of Monomotapa (on the territory of present-day Tanganyika and the Rhodesias). The fragmented tribes of the great basin of the Congo River and of the highlands of eastern Africa have always had episodic relations both in trade and in war, with this traditional center of power.

The eastern coasts of Africa, linked ever since antiquity with the great trade routes of the Indian Ocean, have always played—and still do—the role of frontiers of civilization. The Arab empire encountered by the Portuguese in their quest for the Indies route

Rowers in the port of Tema. This important port has recently been built
a few miles east of Accra, capital of Ghana. It was impossible to create
a modern port at Ghana itself.

showed a surprising renewal of vitality in the nineteenth century under the initiative of the Zanzibar sultans. Nevertheless geographic factors have prevented the coast from playing an active role of transformation and unification, while at the same time they have safeguarded the characteristic way of life of the African peoples of the interior. Following the slave raids of the Arab merchants, the European thrust was needed to establish permanent links between the coast and the highlands of Kenya, Tanganyika and the Rhodesias. In this way new units were forged, based on the logistics of trade and exchange, and not on the natural expansion of the African races.

Stanley had discovered, in the Congo basin, a cluster of peoples isolated by nearly invincible physical factors but grouped like a mosaic in a certain geographic unit. The Europeans who administered these peoples for more than a half-century were seeking their own economic and commercial as well as political and religious ends. Belgium brought them the initial principles of unification (including common European and African mediums of communication). Recent events have shown that there existed in an embryonic state a confused but definite aspiration toward the maintenance as well as the organization of a unit that would meet the needs of a new world from which the Congo cannot separate itself without risking a relapse into isolation and decadence.

The great beneficiaries of the European advance seem to be the kingdoms on the Gulf of Guinea, which have been trafficking with Europe since the sixteenth century and which, thanks to this traffic, have gradually extended their dominion over the peoples located between the coast and the great Sudanese kingdoms. To help their own advance the Europeans have broken the power of castes like the Malinkes and the Peulhs from the north which dominated the intermediate peoples, or which, like the Ashantis, tried to conquer the coastal tribes. Modern Guinea, the Ivory Coast, Ghana, Togoland, and Dahomey have emerged as nations from this mixture of influences and conflicts.

In Nigeria, European rule regrouped a whole series of diverse peoples from the north to the south. The Yorubas have been saved, by their British protector, from foreign rule coming from the north. The Ibos, in spite of their political diversity, have found a new vigour in a more auspicious framework. The movement of the Islamized peoples southwards, which seemed irresistible in the middle of the nineteenth century, has been replaced by a certain equilibrium.

Sierra Leone and the Republic of Liberia, created by the remorse of the white nations after the abolition of slavery, have seen their recent history dominated by the necessities of a gradual social and cultural integration at least as much as by political integration between the "homecomers" and the indigenous peoples of the hinterland. This mixed origin has not in the least diminished the African nature of these countries, which have distinguished themselves by maintaining intact, during the most difficult years, the flame of Pan-Negroism that was to kindle the torch of Pan-Africanism.

Between western and equatorial Africa the Cameroons represented, on a smaller scale than Nigeria but in conditions that may be still more difficult, an effort of unification which, while initially European, has been carried forward by the Africans themselves to build a nation out of peoples of diverse religions and origins, now linked together by common languages.

In former French Equatorial Africa, the new republics born out of purely administrative divisions are gradually expressing a personality that is still badly defined on an economic groundwork that is inadequate, with the possible exception of Gabon, whose problems are somewhat reminiscent of those of Liberia. It may well be that it is in this part of Africa (as well as in the Congo, so close by) that the threats and dangers of isolation are greatest.

Despite its regional diversities, Africa as a whole can have access to western culture through the medium of European languages such as French, English, and Portuguese, and to a lesser extent Spanish and Dutch. In addition there is the great vehicle of the Arab language, which in northern and Nilotic Africa has already assimilated in the course of the past centuries a great many peoples into a civilization with a sense of universal mission.

During the Colonial era, Western technique created a network of communications of all kinds that, while imperfect, was a powerful stimulus to African self-consciousness on a continental scale. The participation (even tentative or indirect) in collective life of many Africans charged with geopolitical responsibilities and subject to the challenge of international competition, has opened up to countless individuals prospects that are revolutionary in the literal sense of the word.

Yet this internationalization of African problems should not be overestimated.

Outside of an infrastructure that is still unfinished, immense zones of the African continent are still waiting to receive the benefits of technology and modern economy. Until the Second World War the only zones of accelerated economic development were in the neighbourhood of the great mining deposits of Katanga, the Copper Belt, and the Rand, along the coasts and at the cross-roads of the trade-routes. Everywhere else an agricultural economy was dominant, with no prospect but that of a slow improvement of the average income through the gradual introduction of a market-economy and the importation, in conditions that were sometimes highly dubious, of modern methods of cultivation and irrigation. It may be reasonable to maintain that the population explosion of peoples no longer victimized by endemic diseases and the progressive erosion of the soils has led to a genuine impoverishment of the agricultural potential not yet compensated for by a rational exploitation of the mining resources, which happily seem to be extremely promising.

Need to establish connections with the outside world

It is clear that Africa cannot live in isolation and that the argument for absolute independence, if carried to its extreme, would lead to an absurd situation, as indeed it would for other continents. For that matter this is well understood by the most enlightened African statesmen, who are by no means trying to cut themselves off from the outside world but, on the contrary, are seeking to establish more efficient and profitable connections.

Latecomers on the international scene, the Africans are equipped with ideological weapons forged in other continents and other circumstances, principally in Europe during the industrial age and secondarily in Asia during the quite recent period of active and passive resistance against European imperialism. Along the lines of western democracy, they have made use of free elections and majority rights. They believe they have found in Marxism a useful doctrine for understanding the state of dependence in which their economy existed for so long. In Soviet and Chinese patterns some of them see examples to follow in order to enable their peoples to merge in two generations from a state of underdevelopment. Trade-Unionism, as a method of organization, and the theory of the single party, have been pushed to their most extreme consequences.

The new Africa is also benefiting from its direct participation in the system of international solidarity being worked out under the aegis of the United Nations, and especially of its regional network, the Economic Commission for Africa, and in a general way from the balance of power between the two super-states. It is also trying not to lose the benefits drawn from its links with the former colonial powers, and is expressing an interest in the prospects offered by a Europe in the process of unification.

On the tactical level the African rulers may disagree as to those alliances that have the greatest immediate advantage. The tendency of Western nations is to think that the exercise of this choice is in and for itself the result of outside influences. Conversely, Soviet dialectic prides itself on perceiving in this one of the supplementary proofs of the gradual estrangement between the European and American societies on one hand and the former colonized continents on the other. It may be best to see in this an indispensable stage along the road leading to a political maturity which neither one side nor the other has as yet attained.

Africa, which is simultaneously Black and White, Semitic, Hamitic, Bantu, Hindu and Malay, is in any event demonstrating an unwavering resolution to go beyond the concept of race to achieve that of community. The tribal struggles seem to be, in the movement of history, no more than survivals of the past, incapable, despite their violence, of outweighing the forces leading toward unity.

On the political plane, indeed, Africa has made its entry into the great debates by means of which Europe itself achieved its own definition four centuries ago.

It is the victim of a technological backwardness, which has been thrown into striking relief in this age when the progress of contemporary science and technology seems to be tending toward the creation of a world society, with a center of gravity that seems to be solidly established in the northern hemisphere. Political factors, on the other hand, compensate to a certain degree for this unevenness of development by emphasizing the increased responsibility incumbent on the European, American, Soviet and Chinese nations, which possess all the gigantic means of a booming technology. A certain redistribution seems fated. In the harsh school of international give-and-take the African governments are acquiring the elements of realism and efficiency.

It is no longer Western Europe and its American ally alone that must display imagination in adapting to new circumstances and to political and economic relationships in which disappointments are often a match for initial hopes.

Soviet Russia established its position by the support it gave to the United Arab Republic at the time of the Suez affair, to Sekou Touré's Guinea when it found itself alone after the "no" of 1958, to Haile Selassie's Ethiopia, to Lumumba's Congo, and in a general way to all the countries, small and large, that have declared themselves ready to eliminate the last vestiges of European imperialism. However, the adoption of a Marxist interpretation of the present situation of the African continent, and the prospects of its gradual emancipation, as held by many African leaders (who have found intellectual havens in all the nuances of a socialist ideology that aims to define itself as African), should not deceive the doctrinaires of the Third International. Tactically, to be sure, certain positions seem favourable and applicable within the framework of the general struggle against the Western powers. Intellectually, however, there is no identity of views in the style, the methods, or the application. African originality has eluded Western analysis of the Marxist variety just as it eluded traditional socialist and liberal analysis.

The Soviet position

It is from this tactical point of view also, that Mao Tse-Tung's China, involved in the vast process of avenging the Chinese world for the humiliations imposed by the West ever since the 18th century, is grappling with the African problem. When Chou En-Lai, Prime Minister of China, visited Africa in 1963, he displayed remarkable political detachment, discretion, and originality. Wherever and whenever it was needed, he distributed promises of financial and economic agreements in order to unseat Chiang Kai-Shek's China, the continued representation of which at the U.N. depends to a large extent on African support. Algeria, the United Arab Republic, Somalia, Zanzibar (which in 1964 joined with Tanganyika in the new nation of Tanzania), and even the isolated kingdom of Burundi, were targets of special attention for a Chinese policy whose amplitude and ambitions are appropriately equal to the vastness of a people representing a fifth of the human race.

Chinese policy towards Africa

Along the lines proposed by the Bandung Conference, Communist China has adopted in its entirety resolutions proposed by the Pan-African conferences in the domains of neutralism, Pan-Africanism, and the denuclearization of the continent. Economic aid is to be based on the idea of equality and of mutual assistance, aiming at the strengthening of independent national units, by contrast with other policies of assistance that perpetuate ties of dependence and subordination. China also offers the model of its own development, accomplished with a minimum of foreign aid, in absolute independence of the Soviet bloc and in the face of the hostility of the United States. On the practical level, the tactical lessons of the revolutionary war carried to final victory by Mao Tse-Tung against a coalition of domestic and foreign enemies were proposed as a model and inspiration to the guerrillas of Angola, the eastern Congo, and to Mozambique, after having helped the military-political victory of the Algerians against the French army.

In inaugurating the second stage of the construction of the High Dam at Aswan, in May 1964, Khrushchev confirmed the ability of Soviet Russia to bring to the countries of Africa technical and financial assistance that is at least comparable with that of the United States, even though he could not substitute for the profound magnetism of the idea of permanent revolution that of an economic development of the classic type.

Militant Africans of the younger generation are now defending attitudes conditioned by the urgency and scope of the tasks still to be grappled with, of which the elimination from the African continent of the remnants of European domination, direct or indirect, is no more than the first stage. In this respect they take for granted as secured the extraordinary results obtained in the course of the decade of 1955-1965. They are naturally looking toward the vast area, China, whose reappearance in the forefront of world politics is the major fact of the second half of the twentieth century.

Still fragile, the edifice of continental African unity will be subjected to decisive tests, whose origin will have to be sought for just as much outside the continent as within· More than any other part of the globe Africa has now been confronted by decisive choices within the framework of a world order in which the centres of power seem to be shifting from West to East more than from North to South.

The concept of the African continent, as a geographical, political, and spiritual unit has at last been forged. The European interregnum, which lasted somewhat less than a century, has been succeeded by the Age of Africa.

Appendix

Maps

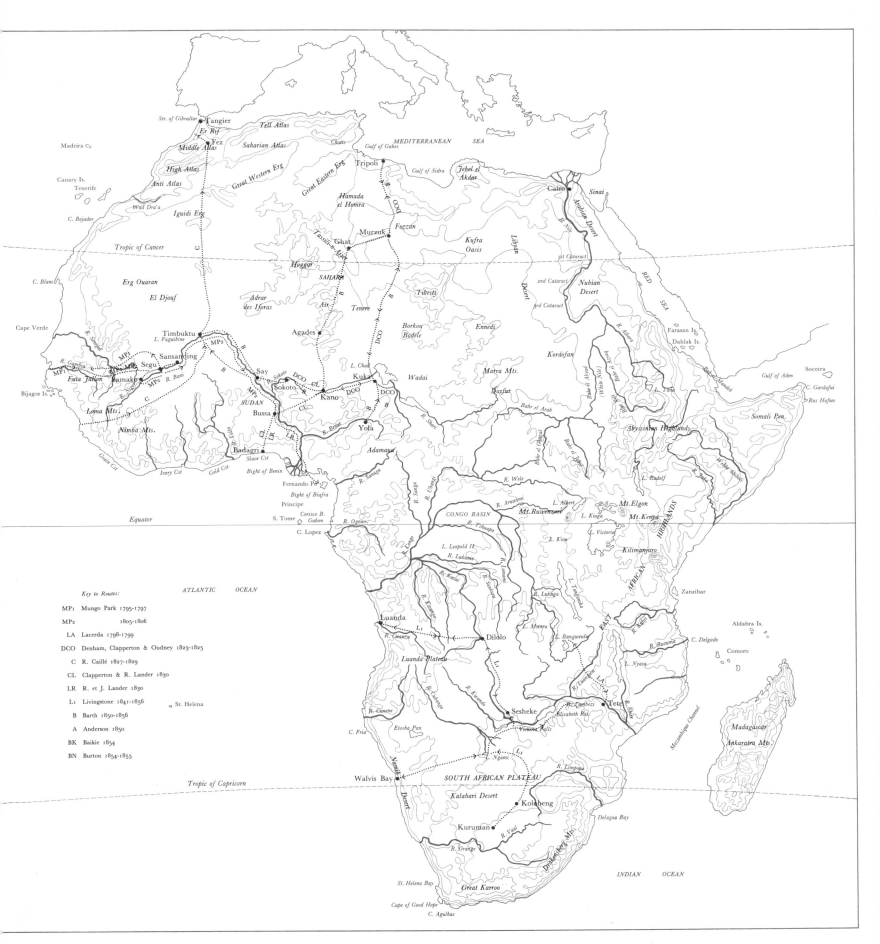

Str. of Gibraltar
Tangier
Er Rif
Fez
Tell Atlas
Middle Atlas
Saharian Atlas
Chotts
Gulf of Gabes
MEDITERRANEAN SEA
High Atlas
Anti Atlas
Great Western Erg
Tripoli
Gulf of Sidra
Jebel el Akdar
Cairo
Sinai
Madeira
Canary Is.
Tenerife
Wad Dra'a
C. Bojador
Iguidi Erg
Tropic of Cancer
Hamada el Homra
Murzuk
Fezzán
Kufra Oasis
Libyan Desert
Arabian Desert
R. Nile
1st Cataract
C. Blanc
Erg Ouaran
El Djouf
Adrar des Iforas
Hoggar
SAHARA
Aïr
Tenere
Tibesti
Borkou Bodele
Ennedi
2nd Cataract
3rd Cataract
Nubian Desert
RED SEA
Cape Verde
Timbuktu
L. Faguibine
Sansanding
Segu
Agades
L. Chad
Kuka
Wadai
Matra Mts.
Kordofan
R. Atbara
L. Tana
Farasan Is.
Dahlak Is.
Socotra
C. Gardafui
R. Gambia
R. Senegal
Bamako
Futa Jallon
Bijagos Is.
Say
Sokoto
Kano
Bussa
Darfur
Bahr el Arab
R. Shari
Abyssinian Highlands
Somali Pen.
Gulf of Aden
Ras Hafun
Loma Mts.
Nimba Mts.
SUDAN
R. Bani
R. Benue
Yola
Adamaua
Badagri
Slave Cst
Bight of Benin
Ivory Cst
Gold Cst
Fernando Po
Bight of Biafra
Principe
S. Tome
Corisco B.
Gabon
C. Lopez
R. Sanaga
R. Ogowe
CONGO BASIN
R. Tshuapa
R. Wele
R. Aruwimi
L. Albert
Mt. Ruwenzori
Mt. Elgon
Mt. Kenya
L. Kioga
L. Victoria
Equator
ATLANTIC OCEAN
R. Congo
R. Lulonga
L. Leopold II
R. Lukenie
R. Kasai
R. Sankuru
R. Lomami
L. Kivu
L. Tanganika
Kilimanjaro
AFRICAN HIGHLANDS
Zanzibar
Aldabra Is.
Key to Routes:
MP1   Mungo Park 1795-1797
MP2   1805-1806
LA   Lacerda 1798-1799
DCO   Denham, Clapperton & Oudney 1823-1825
C   R. Caillé 1827-1829
CL   Clapperton & R. Lander 1830
LR   R. et J. Lander 1830
L1   Livingstone 1841-1856
B   Barth 1850-1856
A   Anderson 1850
BK   Baikie 1854
BN   Burton 1854-1855
Luanda
Dilolo
L. Mweru
L. Bangweulu
R. Ruvuma
C. Delgado
Comoro
St. Helena
R. Cuanza
Luanda Plateau
R. Kwango
R. Kasando
R. Cubango
R. Cunene
Etosha Pan
C. Fria
Sesheke
Victoria Falls
L. Ngami
R. Zambezi
Elisabeth Rd.
Tete
R. Shire
L. Nyasa
Mozambique Channel
Madagascar
Ankaratra Mts.
Tropic of Capricorn
Walvis Bay
Namib Desert
SOUTH AFRICAN PLATEAU
Kalahari Desert
Kolobeng
R. Limpopo
Delagoa Bay
Kuruman
R. Vaal
Drakensberg Mts.
St. Helena Bay
R. Orange
Great Karroo
Cape of Good Hope
C. Agulhas
INDIAN OCEAN

Physical Africa, with the routes of European exploration until 1856 (the first voyage of Livingstone)

331

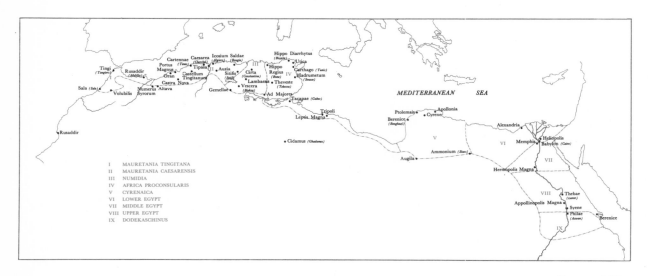

Roman Africa

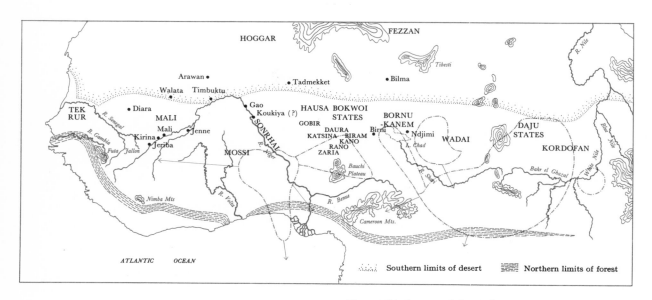

Zones of influence of the 14th century Sudanese Empires

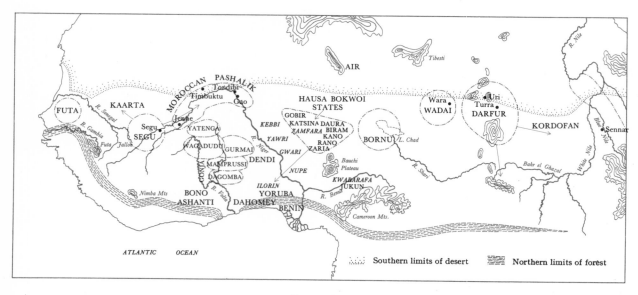

Zones of influence of the 17th and 18th century Sudanese Empires

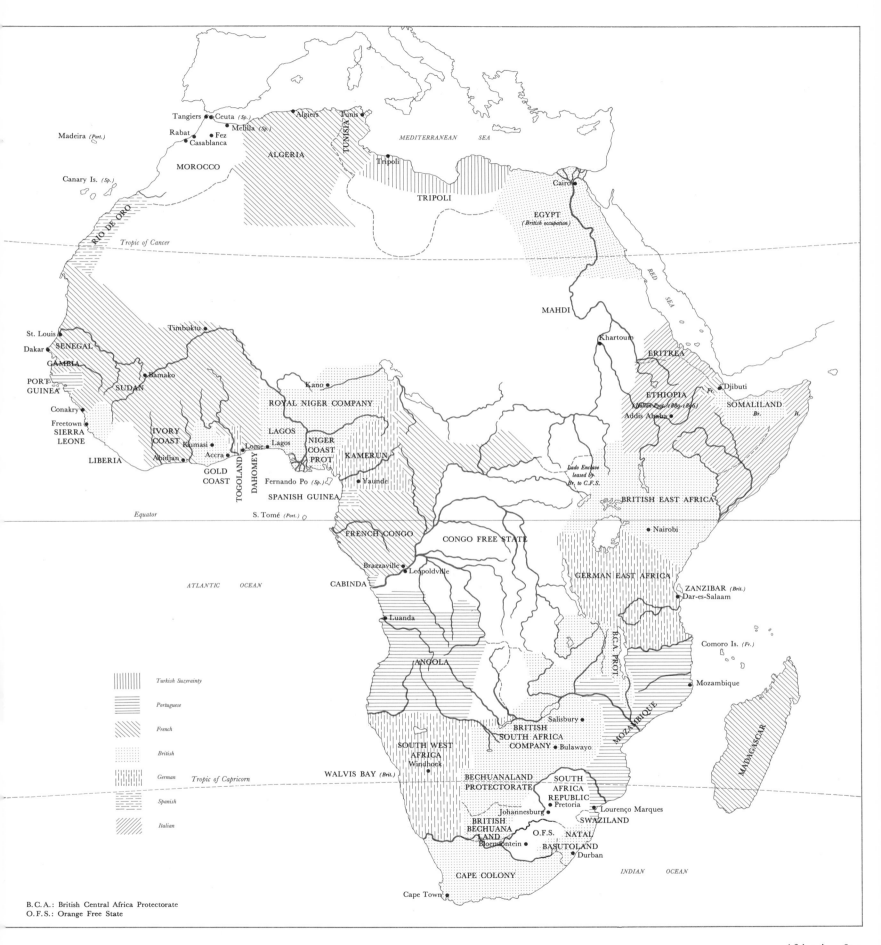

Tangiers ● ●Ceuta (Sp.)
Madeira (Port.) Rabat ●Melilla (Sp.) Algiers ● Tunis ●
● ●Fez
Casablanca TUNISIA MEDITERRANEAN SEA
MOROCCO ALGERIA
Canary Is. (Sp.) Tripoli ●
TRIPOLI Cairo●
RÍO DE ORO EGYPT
(British occupation)
Tropic of Cancer
RED SEA
MAHDI
St. Louis● Timbuktu● Khartoum●
Dakar● SENEGAL ERITREA
GAMBIA Kano● ETHIOPIA Djibuti
PORT. Bamako● (Italian Prot. 1889-1896) Fr. SOMALILAND
GUINEA● SUDAN ROYAL NIGER COMPANY Addis Ababa● Br. It.
Conakry● IVORY LAGOS
Freetown● COAST Kumasi● Lome● Lagos NIGER
SIERRA Accra● COAST KAMERUN Lado Enclave
LEONE Abidjan● PROT leased by BRITISH EAST AFRICA
LIBERIA GOLD Fernando Po (Sp.) Yaunde● Br. to C.F.S.
COAST SPANISH GUINEA Nairobi●
Equator S. Tomé (Port.)
FRENCH CONGO CONGO FREE STATE
Brazzaville● GERMAN EAST AFRICA
CABINDA Leopoldville● ZANZIBAR (Brit.)
ATLANTIC OCEAN Dar-es-Salaam●
Luanda● Comoro Is. (Fr.)

ANGOLA B.C.A. PROT. Mozambique●

Salisbury●
BRITISH MADAGASCAR
SOUTH WEST SOUTH AFRICA
AFRICA COMPANY Bulawayo●
WALVIS BAY (Brit.) Windhoek●
Tropic of Capricorn BECHUANALAND SOUTH
PROTECTORATE AFRICA
REPUBLIC
Johannesburg● Pretoria● ●Lourenço Marques
BRITISH SWAZILAND
BECHUANA NATAL
LAND O.F.S.
Bloemfontein● BASUTOLAND
●Durban
CAPE COLONY INDIAN OCEAN

Cape Town●

||||| Turkish Suzerainty

═══ Portuguese

//// French

···· British

|||| German

─ ─ Spanish

//// Italian

B.C.A.: British Central Africa Protectorate
O.F.S.: Orange Free State

Africa in 1895

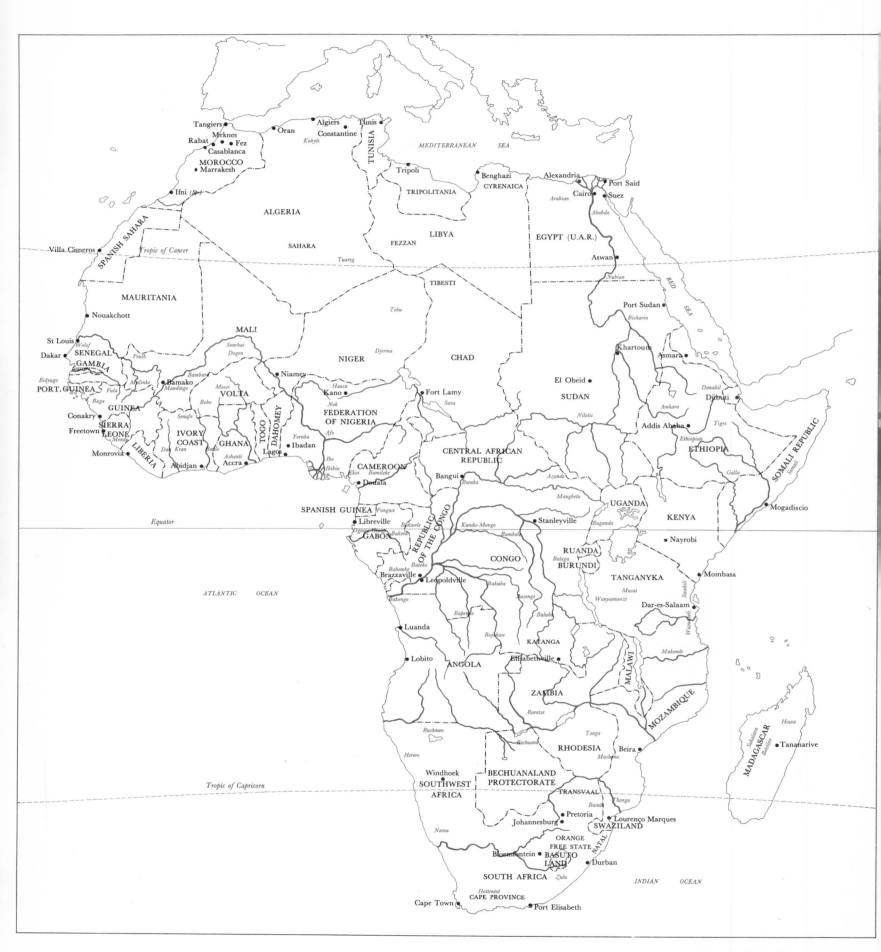

Africa in 1964. Political map with the zones occupied by the ancient tribes (in red)

Index

A

Abadan, Iran: 277
Abbasiyyah, Tunisia: 57
Abbassids: *54*, 97
Abd al-Aziz (8th cent.): 56
Abd el-Aziz: 209, 210
Abd el-Khaliq al-Torres: 262
Abd el-Krim: *227*, 240, 243, 253
Abd el-Mathi: *105*
Abd el-Qadir: 145, *146*, 185, 208
Abd er-Rahman el-Mahdi: 276
Abderramane Fares: 308
Abeokuta, Nigeria: 185
Abid: 107
Abidjan, Ivory Coast: 223
Abomey, Dahomey: *181, 183*, 186
Abou-Simbel, Egypt: *27, 280*
Abukir, Egypt: 144
Abydos, Asia Minor: 24
Abyssinia: 64, 107, 193
Accra, Ghana: *191*, 218, *291*, 293, 297, 316, 317, *324*
Achadji, l., Eritrea: 246
Acheans: 24, 29
Achaemenian Empire: 31
Actium, Greece: 41
Adal Sultanates: 68, 174, 320
Adamawa, mt., West Africa: 180, 190
Addis-Ababa, Ethiopia: 196, 218, 246, 249, *258*, 259
  Conference of (1963): 317
Aden: 137, 259
Adoula, Cyril: 306, 307
Adowa, Ethiopia: *192*, 195, 245, 246, *248*, 249
Adrar, Algeria: 183, 216
Aegeans: 24, 29
Africa: See Black Africa, North Africa, South Africa (regions, no political units)
African Association: 121, 127, *134*
African Charter: 317
African Democratic Rally: see R.D.A.
Agades, Niger Republic: 127, 184
Agadir, Morocco: 210, *211*
Agathocles: 34
Aghlabids, Aghlabid Kingdom: 58, *59*
Agordat, Eritrea: 259
Ahmad (Ahmad ech-Cherif, the Great Senussi): 232
Ahmadu: 175
Ain Sefra, Algeria: 180, 209
Aix-les-Bains, France: 286
Akhenaton: 29
Alawite Dynasty: 107, 108
Albania: 151
Albanians: 89
Albert, l.: 143, 287
Albertville, Congo: 218
Albuquerque, Alfonso d': 82
Alexander the Great: 32, 33, 36, 41
Alexander (4th cent. A.D.): 44
Alexander, Marshal: 260
Alexandria, Egypt: 31, 41, 43, *54*, 55, 56, *59*, 127, 152, 167, 171, 223, 259, 277
Alfonso V, King of Portugal: 83, *84*
Algeciras, Spain: *206*, 209
Algeria: 41, 58, 62, 97, 119, 144, 145, 146, 151, 157, 159, 160, 174, 179, 180, 183, 189,
209, *214*, 216, 233, 243, 244, 250, 251, 253, 261, 262, 268, 278, 283, 284, 287, 293, 294, 295, 303, 308, *311*, 316, 318, 319, 327
Algerian Republic: *264*, 294, 317
Algiers: 58, 92, 98, *101*, 107, 108, 144, 145, *146*, 157, *195*, 208, *210*, 223, *225*, 244, 257, *262*, 265, 278, 289, 293, 294, 295, 303, 308, *311*
Ali, son-in-law of Mahomet: 57
Ali Maher: 277
Allah al-Ohmari: 72
Allen, William: 130
Allenby, Sir Edmund: 240
Almeida, Francisco d': 82
Almohads: 58, 62
Almoravids: 58, 71, 72, 249
Aloisi, Baron: 249
Alotia, Nubian Kingdom: 64
Alsace-Lorraine: 146
Amazon, r., Brazil: 158
Amenophis IV: 29
Amerdoul, Morocco: *103*
America: 19, 90, *106*, 112, 119, 120, 121, 146, 166, 169, 170, 215. See also U.S.A.
Amharas: 97, 171, 245, 246, 249, 320
Amon: 41
Amr Ibn al-As: 55
Amsterdam, Netherlands: *106*, 110
Anatolia, Anatolian Plateau: 24, 29, 92
Andes, mts., South America: 83
Anecho, Togo: 186
Anfa, Morocco: 262
Angola: 83, 84, 89, 90, 136, *154*, 158, 174, 176, 201, 296, 315, 316, 328
Ansongo, Mali: 217
Antarctic Ocean: 121
Antilles, is.: 90, 121, 127
Antonetti: 223
Antony: 41
Anville, Jean-Baptiste d': 120
Anzikos: *122*
Arab Empire: 56. 67
Arab League: 294
Arabi Pasha, Colonel: *167*, 171, 190, 208
Arabia, Arabian Peninsula: 42, 55, 58, 64, 67, 90, 97, 121, 151, 158, 195, 320
Arabia Felix: 24, 43, 64
Arabs: 50, *54*, 55, 56, 57, 62, 71, 73, 77, 78, 82, 89, 91, 109, 112, 130, 137, 145, 146, 158, 165, 183, 202, 243, 293, 320
Arab League: 294
Aragon, Spain: 79
Arboussier, Gabriel d': 273
Archinard, Colonel: 183, 185
Arctic Océan: 120
Ardra, Dahomey: *122, 124*
Argentina: 218, 237
Arguin, Mauritania: 119, 158
Arianism, Arians: 24, 29, 49
Aristotle: 33
Armenia: 82
Aruj: 98. See also Barbarossa Brothers
Aryans: 33, 45
Arzila, Morocco: *84*
Ashantis, Ashanti Kingdom: 77, 78, 116, 174, 186, *191*, 208, 218, 228, 290, *297*

338

X

Y

Z

This book was made with the collaboration
of Monique Schneider-Maunoury
and Marie-Geneviève de La Coste-Messelière
Lay-out and supervision by Pierre Faucheux

Color photographs

Ian Berry-Magnum: p. 282 – Bibliothèque Nationale, Paris: p. 1-2
Jean-P. Bonnin: p. 235 – Cercle d'Art: p. 226 – F. Dubus: p. 164 – Elliot Erwitt-Magnum: p. 12, 25
R.B. Fleming & Cº: p. 69, 76, 187 – Giraudon: p. 28, 93, 148-149, 213-214 – Ernst Haas-Magnum: p. 312
Marc Lavrillier: p. 126 – Claude Michaelides: p. 60, 65, 100, 105, 113, 116, 153, 156, 161, 182
Mario Novaïs: p. 88 – Marc Riboud-Magnum: p. 263, 270, 291, 309
Emil Schulthess: p. 11, 139, 142 – Roger Wood: p. 38-39

Black-and-white photographs

Arquivo Historico Ultramarino, Lisbon: p. 154
Ian Berry-Magnum: p. 292, 297, 298, 300, 321, 322-323 – Edouard Boubat: p. 269
René Burri-Magnum: p. 280, 281 – Compagnie Aérienne de Photographie: p. 40
Dalmas: p. 311 – René Dazy: p. 162, 178, 188, 192, 193, 194, 205, 206, 211, 214, 225, 241, 248
R.B. Fleming & Cº: p. 140, 167, 199 – Giraudon: p. 48 – Ernst Haas-Magnum: p. 15
Keystone: p. 257, 264, 273, 279 – Erich Lessing-Magnum: p. 310
Marc Lavrillier: p. 70, 75, 95, 96, 99, 102, 114, 115, 134, 162
Libraires Associés-Club des Libraires: p. 141 – J. D. Lorieux: p. 219, 220, 241, 255, 256, 280
D. Jacques-Meunié: p. 103 – Françoise Masson: p. 155, 168, 242
Claude Michaelides: p. 53, 85, 94, 101, 106, 124, 131, 132-133, 140 – Musée du Bardo, Tunis: p. 37
Musée de l'Homme, Paris, Archives: p. 181, Cl. Félix: p. 17, Cl. Griaule: p. 66
National Portrait Gallery, Londres: p. 125, 134, 167 – Mario Novaïs: p. 86-87
Office Marocain du Tourisme: p. 104 – Agence Rapho-R. Michaud: p. 247, 258
Marc Riboud-Magnum: p. 191, 324 – George Rodgers-Magnum: p. 163, 177, 221, 222, 274
Roger-Viollet: p. 54 – Emil Schulthess: p. 16, 18 – Kryn Taconis-Magnum: p. 299
Unesco-P. Almasy: p. 26 – Unesco-Laurenza: p. 27 – Roger Wood: p. 47, 59
Maps drawn by Robert Lhoist.
The maps on pages 331, 332 and 333 are based on J. D. Fage's "An Atlas
of African History" (Edward Arnold Ltd, Londres, 1961)

Printed October 15th, 1965 on the presses of the Imprimeries Réunies S.A., at Lausanne, Switzerland